THE CHURCH AND CULTURES

The William Carey Library Series on Applied Cultural Anthropology

William A. Smalley, Editor

Becoming Bilingual: A Guide to Language Learning by Donald N. Larson and William A. Smalley, 425 pages

The Church and Cultures: An Applied Anthropology for the Religious Worker by Louis J. Luzbetak, 448 pages

Culture and Human Values: Christian Intervention in Anthropological Perspective by Jacob A. Loewen, 464 pages

Customs and Cultures: Anthropology for Christian Missions by Eugene A. Nida, 320 pages

Manual of Articulatory Phonetics by William A. Smalley, 522 pages

Message and Mission: The Communication of the Christian Faith by Eugene A. Nida, 253 pages

Readings in Missionary Anthropology edited by William A. Smalley, 384 pages

Understanding Latin Americans with Special Reference to Religious Values and Movements by Eugene A. Nida, 164 pages

THE Church AND Cultures

AN APPLIED ANTHROPOLOGY
FOR THE RELIGIOUS WORKER

LOUIS J. LUZBETAK, S.V.D., PH.D.

William Carey Library

533 HERMOSA STREET • SOUTH PASADENA, CALIF. 91030

Library of Congress Catalog Card Number 75-108055
International Standard Book Number 0-87808-725-7

Reprinted in 1975 by arrangement with Divine Word Publications

Published by the William Carey Library
533 Hermosa Street
South Pasadena, Calif. 91030
Telephone 213-799-4559

PRINTED IN THE UNITED STATES OF AMERICA

FOREWORD

During the 1950's and 1960's in the United States there was the flowering of a movement which might be called an "applied cultural anthropology in Christian mission." Early in this period (1954) came Eugene A. Nida's *Customs and Cultures,* which stated in a semi-popular way the need for anthropological insights in the missionary task and alerted large numbers of Protestant missionaries to the cultural implications of what they were doing. At the peak of the period (1963) came Louis J. Luzbetak's *The Church and Cultures,* which provided a textbook for Roman Catholic missionaries in training, to give them a grounding in some concepts of cultural anthropology and their implications for mission work.

The present volume, which we now welcome to the William Carey Library Series on Applied Cultural Anthropology, is the second (1970) edition of Luzbetak's work. It joins seven other books, all of which belong to this same period, and brings back into print a much-needed textbook for which there is still no substitute.

There are several points of view which underlie the application of cultural anthropology to the Christian proclamation of the Good News. One is that although this Good News comes to modern peoples in the cultural behavior and idea systems of the Jews of the Middle East c. 2,000 BC to 100 AD, it has meaning which is pan-human and which should be shared with all people. But corrolary to this is the fact that all peoples have their ways of living and their idea systems in myriad varieties, and that for any people it is through these that the hearing of the Good News takes place. Because of this, for some there is no hearing at all; the message never gets through. For some it becomes bad news, because the distortions and dislocations which follow the hearing do not improve people's relation to God, but they do make the human situation worse. For some it is genuine understanding which leads to a new life. It is at this interface of communication of the Good News across cultures that the focus of applied missionary anthropology lies.

Together with his knowledge of theology and anthropology, Father Luzbetak brings to his examination of this interface his

v

experience in New Guinea, experience in supervising missionary training, and directorship of the Center for Applied Research in the Apostolate. He is now President of Divine Word College.

The Church and Cultures was written for Catholics, but has been widely used by Protestants as well. If there had been opportunity for updating the book for this publication, it would have been done with the fact of its publication and use across denominational boundaries in mind. Inevitably there are differences of wording and emphasis, occasionally of concept, from what might have been written in one branch or another of Protestant Christianity, but Luzbetak's solid, well-documented sensible over-all approach is valuable to all.

The organization of *The Church and Cultures* is by anthropological categories; the applications are missionary ones. The viewpoint is that of anthropological understanding of the patterning of behavior; the object in view is the multiplicity of cultural processes in which the Good News is spoken and the church grows. These questions have become commonplace in missiology over the past twenty years, much more so today than when this book was written. But whether commonplace or not, they are things that have to be learned by each new generation of missionaries, whether they be among the diminishing number who move across the boundaries from western to third world countries, the growing number who work in other third world countries than their own, or the many who live and work among people of other cultural classes, generations, languages or national backgrounds in their own countries.

William A. Smalley

PREFACE

The present book is called THE CHURCH AND CULTURES because it attempts to throw some light on the problem concerning the proper relationship between the ways of the Church on the one hand and the earth's cultures on the other. The Church is indeed *one*, for unity is an essential mark of the Kingdom founded by Christ. The Church, however, is also diversified, as diversified as mankind itself. This diversity is sacred and must be preserved no less than the unity; and it is here that Anthropology, the Science of Man, can, in the light of Theology, make a major contribution. Anthropology is indeed "a mirror for man," as Kluckhohn (1949a: 11) so aptly put it, but Anthropology is also "a mirror for the Church," enabling the Church to see herself as *she* really is, in *her* infinite variety.

The subtitle chosen for THE CHURCH AND CULTURES is: *An Applied Anthropology for the Religious Worker*, for the book was written not for the professional anthropologist but for the non-professional who is daily confronted with the problem of "Church and Cultures." It introduces the religious worker, engaged in the direct or indirect apostolate, to the wealth of scientific knowledge now available and useful for effective action across cultures and sub-cultures. Apostolic effectiveness will always presuppose due regard for local ways and values. The present *Applied Anthropology for the Religious Worker* discusses, in a theoretical as well as practical way, the meaning of this "due regard." The basic assumption of the book is that, no matter what art or science, sacred or profane, the Church may wish to apply in carrying out her social and religious mission, she will have to apply that knowledge and skill in full cultural perspective, with the ways and values of the particular society in view.

This book does not aim to describe any particular culture as such; it is rather a collection of basic culturological concepts and principles that hold for all cultures, including that of the religious worker himself. "Know thyself!" is a maxim particularly applicable to anyone engaged in activities outside his own cultural environment. Older churches must know themselves before they can adjust properly to newer churches. It was this consideration that made the author choose the majority of his examples (400 of some 700) from the way of life of the religious worker himself. The remaining illustrations were selected from all over the world: 30 from American minority groups, especially the Negro; 40 from Latin America; 45 from Africa; 95 from Asia; 90 from Oceania. The Oceanic customs include some 50 from New Guinea, not because this island is considered specially important in the missionworld today but because the author is personally acquainted with that part of the world more than with any other and because the island represents a primitive situation ideally lending itself to the illustration of certain cross-cultural concepts. References to concrete cultures, therefore, do not aim to describe the cultures as such but to illustrate *universally valid* concepts and principles. The theory discussed is useful for the understanding of *any* culture, primitive or sophisticated, and it is basic for effective work, whether one is dealing with simple, illiterate food-gatherers or with highly-cultured individuals. The theory is valid at home no less than in distant lands — among U. S. Negroes, for instance, or the Puerto Ricans, Cubans, Mexicans, or any other migrant group in the United States — and it is valid even in such subcultural situations as found in slums and gangs.

THE CHURCH AND CULTURES does not attempt to cover the entire field of anthropological knowledge and skill that might prove useful for apostolic action: an inventory of culture, field techniques, and a systematic application of anthropological theory to problems of Catechetics, Education, Medicine, Social Work, *etc.* would likewise be necessary for an ideal and complete general course in missiological Anthropology. The present text paves the way for meaningful area studies and for on-the-spot inquiries into the truly-local and actual cultural situations. It should be noted that many of the topics not expressly or not fully treated in the text are sufficiently taken care of by means of suggested readings and topics for discussion.

An introduction to the ways of man is an essential and indispensable part of apostolic formation: it teaches the modern apostle how to adjust his professional knowledge and skill to the "strange" cultural or subcultural situation in which he must labor, and it teaches him how to interact effectively with people he calls "strange." The principles discussed in the present book may throw some useful light also on the many basic problems facing Superiors of mission-sending organizations, especially problems relating to training, selection of personnel, and practical mission policies. Finally, it is hoped that this book will prove of some interest also to those who perhaps themselves may never be able to serve the Church outside their own cultural boundaries but who are, nevertheless, keenly interested in the problem of "Church and Cultures." The following pages will leave no doubt in their minds about the importance and complexity of the problem and will indicate to them how the modern, well-trained religious worker might approach the problem in a way consistent with the scientific age in which he lives.

A word of thanks is due especially to the American Anthropological Association for permission to reprint Figure 4; to the Institute of Mission Studies of Fordham University for the selections taken from the *Four Great Encyclicals;* to Rev. John Boberg, S.V.D. and Rev. R. Wiltgen, S.V.D. of the Divine Word News Service (Rome) for most of the illustrations used; to the author's many missionary friends and fellow-anthropologists for their useful suggestions. The author feels particularly indebted to Very Rev. Leo Hotze, S.V.D., Provincial of the Eastern Province, and Rev. Vincent McMahon, S.V.D., Director of the Divine Word Publications, without whose encouragement and cooperation THE CHURCH AND CULTURES would have been impossible.

LOUIS J. LUZBETAK, S.V.D.
Washington, D. C.

PREFACE
To the Second Printing

A thoroughly revised edition of THE CHURCH AND CULTURES, as in the case of any other book, would no doubt be more desirable than a mere second printing. The latter, nevertheless, seems justified, considering the many requests for this book, now out of print for more than a year, and the fact that the concepts and principles treated, despite the rapidly changing times, have not only remained unchanged but now require even less convincing than they did when the book was first published. "Unity in diversity"—the central theme of the book—has become generally accepted throughout the Christian world. However, we still need treatises such as this which present ABC's of Anthropology that must be understood if the principle of "unity in diversity" is to progress from mere theoretical acceptance to reality.

A complete revision would call for additions and omissions and for slightly different emphases here and there, more in accord with our present-day challenges and opportunities and more consonant with the growing ecumenical spirit, the existential needs of the younger churches, and the various theological developments of recent years. In lieu of such revisions, the author has prepared an updated annotated bibliography of almost a hundred entries.

It is the author's sincere hope that this new printing of his work will prove useful at least in some small way to those striving to bring to our times a world-Christianity that would indeed be *of* the people and *of* the land, of the time and place—a Christianity that recognizes, as does God Himself, that the particular culture here and now is the "language" best understood by and dearest to both creature and Creator.

To the
Dedicated and Generous Men and Women Called
"Missionaries"
Whatever Their Task and Wherever They May Be

CONTENTS

V. EPILOGUE

I.

INTRODUCTORY

CHAPTER ONE

THE MISSIONARY APOSTOLATE
IN ITS CULTURAL CONTEXT[1]

EVEN centuries before the Science of Culture was born, the most effective missionaries were those blessed with a deep appreciation of the diversity of cultures and of the important role which cultures play in human behavior. The most successful apostolic approaches have always been the ones geared most closely to the character and needs of the particular life-way. Missionary effectiveness has always gone hand in hand with immersion in local cultures. St. Paul, Ricci, de Nobili, and other great apostles of the past had, of course, no choice but to rely on their own *innate* anthropological sense; today, however, to rely on anything less than a *Science* of Culture would be as foolish as to rely on anything less than a *Science* of Medicine.

Although there is still very much that anthropologists do not know about culture, and although their various concepts, principles, and techniques are only now being organized into a systematic body of practical knowledge called "Applied Anthropology," modern culturological theory is being employed today with considerable profit by educators, social workers, lawyers, doctors, military experts, technicians, government administrators, and other specialists engaged in activities outside their own cultural environment.[2] There is,

---

[1] Much of the present chapter has previously appeared in the author's "An Applied Anthropology for Catholic Missions," *Studia Instituti Missiologici Societatis Verbi Divini*, No. 1, pp. 63–83.

[2] See, for instance, the many articles in *Human Organization* (Cornell University, Ithaca, N. Y.) and *Economic Development and Cultural Change* (University of Chicago). Surveys of recent developments in Applied Anthropology will be found in A. L. Kroeber, ed., *Anthropology Today: An Encyclopedic Inventory* (Chicago, 1953), pp. 740–895 and *Some Uses of Anthropology: Theoretical and Applied* (Anthropological Society of Washington, Washington, D. C., 1956). Clyde Kluckhohn's *Mirror for Man* (New York, 1949) is a well-written, popular account of (as the subtitle puts it) "The Relation of Anthropology to Modern Life." The literature on specialized applications of anthropological principles to modern problems is growing very rapidly. The student would find it profitable at this point to glance through the following studies: S. Polgar, "Health and Human Behavior: Areas of Interest Common to the Social and

however, no profession that could profit so much from Cultural Anthropology as the missionary apostolate.[3]

Cultural Anthropology is indeed a "missionary science" par excellence. There is no other art or science that can help the missioner divest himself of his cultural prejudices more surely than this science. Moreover, the cultural context (the subject-matter of this science) is one of the most basic tools of the missionary. No matter what his particular task may be, he is a professional "builder of a better world," and like all builders he too must constantly have recourse to his basic tools — his plumbline and his level — lest the building which he is constructing get out of line, or even collapse. The missioner's pumbline is Truth (theology, philosophy, science, prudence, and the aims of the apostolate); his level is the local cultural context.

It should be noted that until "culture" is defined more exactly it will be sufficient to understand it to mean "the total life-way and mentality of a people." "Cultural Anthropology" may be tentatively understood as "the science which provides the concepts and methods for analyzing and understanding a people's mind and customary ways." "Applied Anthropology" might for the time being be under-

Medical Sciences," Current Anthropology, III (1962), 159–205, see especially the bibliography; B. D. Paul, ed., Health, Culture, and Community (New York, 1955); L. Saunders, Cultural Difference and Medical Care (New York, 1954); L. W. Simmons and H. G. Wolff, Social Science in Medicine (New York, 1954); H. G. Barnett, Anthropology in Administration (New York, 1956); E. H. Spicer, ed., Human Problems in Technological Change (New York, 1952); A. H. Leighton, The Governing of Men (Princeton, 1945); M. Mead, ed., Cultural Patterns and Technical Change (UNESCO, 1953); G. M. Foster, Traditional Cultures and the Impact of Technological Change (New York, 1962).

[3] See, for instance, L. J. Luzbetak, S.V.D., "Toward an Applied Missionary Anthropology," Anthropological Quarterly, XXXIV (1961), 165–176; M. Gusinde, S.V.D., Die völkerkundliche Ausrüstung des Missionars (Steyl, Holland, 1958); J. Amyot, S.J., "The Mission Apostolate in Its Cultural Context," Mission Bulletin, Hongkong (November, December, 1955, and January, 1956); J. Franklin Ewing, S.J., "Anthropology and the Training of Missionaries," The Catholic Educational Review, LV (1957), 305–311; J. Franklin Ewing, S.J., "Applied Anthropology for the Missionary," Worldmission, II (February, 1951); T. Burke, S.J., Four Great Encyclicals (Fordham, New York, 1957); E. A. Nida, Customs and Cultures: Anthropology for Christian Missions (New York, 1954); E. A. Nida, Message and Mission (New York, 1960). See also the many articles in Practical Anthropology (a non-technical periodical for Protestant missionaries). Catholic missiological journals, e.g., Christ to the World, contain numerous articles of anthropological interest. For the views of active American missionaries, see J. A. McCoy, S.M., Advice from the Field: Towards a New Missiology (Baltimore, Dublin, 1962).

stood as "that discipline which shows one how anthropological knowledge might be employed to promote a given cause." It should also be noted from the outset that although Applied Missionary Anthropology is deeply involved in the theoretical notion of "culture" it treats the subject not in a purely theoretical or unrealistic manner. After all, an adequate theory regarding human behavior, such as is required for apostolic work, must be concerned not only with culture as such but with the interplay of culture, society, and personality. A practical missionary does not deal with culture in the abstract but with *individuals* (psychological aspects) who live in a given *society* (sociological aspects) and share a common *way of life* (culturological aspects) — hence, the justification for the integrated approach to culture in Applied Missionary Anthropology.

CULTURAL CONTEXT AND CULTURE CHANGE

The missionary apostolate and Cultural Anthropology share an important common interest, culture change. They are both interested in knowing how the mind and ways of a people change; how such change might be predicted; how such change might be directed and how best maintained; and how change might be introduced with as little disorganization as possible. Anthropology can, therefore, be of considerable usefulness to the missionary.

Some missionaries become quite annoyed and very defensive when accused of tampering with the age-old, albeit "pagan" traditions. There is a considerable amount of truth to this accusation; nevertheless, the missionary need not become apologetic about it. The fact is that the greatest cultural transformation in the history of mankind was brought about by a single Missionary, the Divine Legate Himself, Who declared Himself to be nothing less than "the Light of man" (John 1:4) and "the Way, the Truth, and the Life" (John 14:6), Whose mission it was "to cast fire" upon the earth until every tribe and nation, even those in the remotest corners of the earth, would be consumed by that "fire" (Luke 12:49). "Go ye, therefore, and make disciples of all nations" (Matt. 28:19) was the command given to His Church, and every "iota" (Matt. 5:13–19) of His Gospel was to be preached just as He preached it, without compromise. If all this is not tantamount to changing the world and its cultures, what, one might ask, is? Religion and morality, the prime concern of missionaries, are essential elements of culture (see pp. 317–320). Moreover, on account of the close "organic" interconnection between the various aspects of culture, it is impossible to bring about a religious or moral transformation without at the same time affecting the entire "organism" (see p. 135). Sometimes, in order to bring about a necessary change in belief and moral behavior (necessary because sound principles of morality and Revelation demand it), the missioner will actually have to strive to bring about economic and social changes as well. It is indeed foolish for any missionary to deny the multi-faceted consequences of his seemingly purely-spiritual activity. Whether missionaries are inclined to admit it or not, they are professional agents of culture change, for there is no other way of establishing, consolidating, and perpetuating the Church in a society than through its culture. Since missionaries are by their very vocation uncompromising agents of culture change, the study of missionary techniques cannot be divorced from the study of culture.

Inquiries into the local culture cannot be superficial, for culture change is a complex process, and the changes sought, whether in matters spiritual or temporal, are intended to be deep and lasting. Especially in spiritual matters the transformation sought is meant to be more than the mere adoption of externals that might be accepted one day and discarded the next. The transformation sought is meant to be more than the recitation of a creed and a theoretical acknowledgment of certain articles of faith or the mere adoption of a ritual. "Conversion" means a "turning" away from old ways toward new ways, a basic reorientation in premises and goals, a wholehearted acceptance of a new set of values affecting the "convert" as well as his social group, day in and day out, twenty-four hours of the day and in practically every sphere of activity — economic, social, and religious. The changes effected must become living parts of the cultural "organism" (see pp. 180–190). In fact, Christianity, it is hoped, will eventually become the very heart and nerve center of the culture. This is the tremendous task and ideal of the missionary apostolate, the immensity of which cannot be properly appreciated unless the nature, organization, and dynamics of culture are properly understood and taken fully into account.

Anyone accepting the role of an uncompromising agent of culture change assumes a grave responsibility — the responsibility of introducing necessary changes in such a way as to avoid as much social and cultural disorganization as possible. Personal conflicts generally associated with culture change must likewise be reduced to a minimum. The prudent, well-trained, and responsible missioner will, therefore, introduce and direct change not in a haphazard manner but in a way most in accord with the existing life-way. But to do so will require a thorough acquaintance with culture in general as well as with the particular way of life in which the missioner must labor.

"Accommodation," "adaptation," "the principle of cultural relevancy," or "the indigenous principle," as this missionary approach is sometimes called, is the official policy of the Church (see pp. 342–344). As Pius XII expressed it:

> The Church from her very beginning down to our own day has followed this wise policy. When the gospel is accepted by diverse races, it does not crush or repress anything good and honorable and beautiful which they have achieved by their native genius and natural endowments. When the Church summons and guides a race to higher refinement and a more cultured way of life, under the inspiration of Christian religion, she does not act like a woodsman who cuts, fells and dismembers a luxuriant forest indiscriminately. Rather she acts like an orchardist who engrafts a cultivated shoot on a wild tree so that later on fruits of a more tasty and richer quality may issue forth and mature (*Evangelii Praecones*: 89).

Accommodation is the official policy of the Church, but, unfortunately, it is only too often a policy that is talked about in missionary circles rather than understood and carried out. Nevertheless, the missioner has no choice in the matter; it is a policy which the Church requires him to follow, and it is a policy implied in the very mandate given the Church to go and "make disciples of all nations," for the command comes from One Who believed in adapting Himself to His people.

> Who being in the form of God thought it not robbery to be equal with God: but emptied himself, taking the form of a servant, being made in the likeness of men, and in habit found as a man (Phil. 2:6–7).

No missionary could ever "empty himself" of the ways and values most natural to him and become like his adopted people to so high a degree as did the Divine Word, when He, the Son of God, became the Son of Man, not only in name but in very deed, "tempted in all things as we are . . ." (Heb. 4:15). St. Paul was but imitating His Master and Ideal, the Word made Flesh, when he chose as his missionary policy the motto "All things to all men!" (1 Cor. 9:22.) St. Paul was a Jew to the Jews, a Gentile to the Gentiles. Only a thorough understanding of the meaning of "culture" will unveil for the missionary the true meaning of "all things to all men" and what is involved in "emptying" oneself. An essential part of every missionary's knowledge and skill, therefore, must be exactly how he is to proceed in becoming "all things to all men," how he is to remove the barrier created by his cultural background (see pp. 73–78), how he can best remove the colored glasses through which he views all cultures other than his own and finds them "strange," "odd," "definitely inferior," and, at times, "positively disgusting." Before the missioner sets out to change the world he should first study it with detachment.

Such an understanding of matters cultural is, of course, not sufficient by itself to achieve actual detachment from one's own ways and values. Missionary adaptation will call for deep spirituality, especially genuine humility, living faith, and limitless generosity (Illich, 1958). Nevertheless, even a perfect saint having only sanctity at his disposal will not know in what he is to accommodate. Only an understanding of the full meaning of "culture" (see pp. 345–347) will enable him to understand the full meaning of the object of accommodation.

CULTURAL CONTEXT AND SPIRITUAL GUIDANCE

It would be difficult indeed to find a missionary who would in his right mind claim that he could give adequate spiritual guidance in the confessional, pulpit, classroom, or elsewhere without a proper grasp of the ways and mentality of his flock. What advice can the confessor give to his penitent whose problem he does not even understand? What motivation can the preacher suggest to his congregation if he is unfamiliar with the existing value-system? Unless the missioner is acquainted with the fine details of the native life-way and with the usage, function, and value attached to these details he should not expect to be able to provide the necessary guidance which his struggling and often confused converts seek. He will not succeed in making Christianity palatable and a twenty-four-hour-a-day affair. Without a knowledge of the local ways and values the missioner may succeed merely in producing a hodgepodge of Christianity and paganism (see pp. 239–248). His sermons and catechetical instructions will almost invariably give the impression of being illogical and without much sense; his advice and admonitions will be considered unrealistic and therefore not to be taken too seriously. Prospective Christians are very easily taught to recite the Ten Commandments by heart, but only a missionary who really understands their ways and values will be able to present the Ten Commandments to them in terms of their daily lives.

Spiritual guidance in a "strange" cultural milieu presupposes among other things the ability to recognize what is "in accord with human nature" and what is not, what really is "morally right" and what is not. Dogmatic and Moral Theology, Philosophy (especially Ethics), and common-sense will always be necessary; however, broad and basic principles and even common-sense may become quite insufficient when applied in a concrete socio-cultural situation. There is need for precise ethnographic data to provide the necessary light for the application of principles and common-sense. If such data fail to remove the doubts and obscurities, they will at least be a salutary warning to the overzealous reformer to proceed with caution before beginning any campaign against behavior which he does not fully grasp but on account of his cultural conditioning tends to condemn as "against human nature" and "morally wrong." It is not easy to say whether a particular custom, a certain form of corporal punishment, or the existing laws regarding property rights, for instance, are really contrary to "the rightful position of women." The moralist with only common-sense and a knowledge of Theology and Philosophy to rely on, but with little or no knowledge of culture and the particular cultural context, is indeed a dangerous "expert" in the Missions.

In a word, whether the missionaries are trying to change or to preserve native ways — and their spiritual activities require them to do both, change and preserve traditional ways — they must be "experts" regarding culture in general and "specialists" regarding the ways and values of their flock.

CULTURAL CONTEXT AND SOCIAL ACTION

The Role of Social Action in the Missions

1. CHRISTIANITY A RELIGION OF CHARITY

A glance through the various social and missionary encyclicals will be sufficient to convince anyone of the immensity of the task facing the modern apostolate. The Missions must, of course, be primarily occupied with the souls of men, with the preaching of the Gospel, and with establishing and consolidating the Church (Schuette, 1960:47–58; *Princeps Pastorum*:18). The Missions, however, cannot claim to be truly interested in souls, in the Gospel, or in the Church unless at the same time the preachers of the Gospel remain true to the basic law of the Kingdom which they preach — charity. Christianity is, after all, a religion of charity, charity toward God and man. The missionary has no choice but to be deeply concerned about such "mundane" matters as law, medicine, agriculture, secular education, and almost every type of social action.

The Acts of the Apostles tells us that Christ, the Ideal Missionary, did not limit His ministry to preaching but that He "went about *doing good*" (Acts 10:38). The Gospels describe numerous incidents showing His deep concern for the temporal welfare of His people. He instructed the ignorant, consoled the bereaved, gave sight to the blind and hearing to the deaf. The mute spoke and the lame walked. He objected to the injustices done to helpless widows. He fed the hungry multitudes that followed Him into the desert, lest they faint along the way (Mark 8:2–3). In fact, as St. John put it:

> . . . there are also many other things which Jesus did: which, if they were written every one, the world itself, I think, would not be able to contain the books that should be written (21:25).

From the earliest times followers of Christ carried out most faithfully the twofold command "to preach the kingdom of God, and to heal the sick" (Luke 9:2; Canova, 1958:72–80).

To disregard the temporal welfare of mission countries would be to neglect a major part of the missionary task — or as both Pius XII and John XXIII call it, a serious neglect of "duty." Pius XII speaks of

> . . . the *duty* of lessening, soothing and relieving the distress, the miseries, the anguish of our fellow man . . . is incumbent on each of us according to his ability (*Evangelii Praecones*:70; my italics).

Or in the unmistakable words of Pope John XXIII:

> We have today an *undeniable duty* toward men, in *justice and charity*, to do everything possible to ensure the subsistence of undernourished peoples, to develop everywhere a more reasonable exploitation of the riches of the soil and underground for the benefit of a rapidly-growing world population and to safeguard at the same time the social equili-

brium of the regions affected by this economic development (*Semaine Sociale*, Angers, July, 1959; my italics).

There can be no doubt that these words were seriously meant. John XXIII calls it a duty "in justice and charity," while his predecessor emphasized the gravity of the obligation in words hardly less forceful:

To disregard this plea, to pass it over in silence would not be without guilt in the sight of the Eternal God (*Evangelii Praecones*: 73).

2. THE THREAT OF COMMUNISM

Social action in the Missions is more urgent today than ever before. In fact, it has become a matter of life and death. The most formidable enemy of the Missions today is God-hating Communism, which threatens to destroy all that heroic apostles throughout the centuries have achieved at the cost of untold blood, sweat, and tears. To disregard the temporal needs of mission countries is to disregard the threat of Communism. A missionary policy that does not insist on intensifying the role of the modern apostle in community development projects and the general socio-economic advancement of peoples in the developing nations of the world is actually blind to the only-too-real threat of complete destruction. Communism is not an enemy that can be defeated by such negative means as condemnation and name-calling, no matter how true the labels "persecutors of the Church," "atheists," and "anti-Christs" may be. Communism is an enemy that must be defeated on the battlefield which *it* has chosen — social action. Communism will be defeated not by name-calling but by actual demonstration that, in imitation of the First Missionary, the Church of today has genuine "compassion on the multitude" (Mark 8:2), a compassion that moves the Church to teach mankind *meaningful* action, not only to offer alms but to help provide socio-economic opportunities. Communism will not be defeated by closing our eyes to the fact that the followers of Lenin and Marx are sincere, dedicated idealists genuinely interested in creating what they consider to be a "better" world for the down-trodden and starving millions throughout the world. Even such detestable practices as brainwashing, concentration camps, ruthless dictatorship, and mass executions usually do not proceed from malice as such but from a fanatical hatred of a real evil — social injustice. According to the teaching and conviction of Communists, such measures are definitely undesirable in themselves but unavoidable if poverty and injustice are to be eradicated and if the Communistic Utopia is ever to be realized. Douglas Hyde, once a leading Communist and now an ardent convert to Catholicism, considers his entry into the Communist Party as "the most unselfish act of my life." In a word, not by attacking the sincerity and intentions of the Communists or by closing one's eyes to misery and social injustice will godless Communism be crushed but by outdoing the Communists, by demonstrating to the world that Christian social teaching is a better answer to the problem than the theories of Lenin and Marx. To borrow Douglas Hyde's own words:

> It happens that the colonial countries are also the mission countries. There, the missionary and the Communist confront each other. It is the job of each to wrestle for minds and hearts in those great, rapidly changing areas of the world. Hearts and minds are, generally speaking, more open to be won there. . . . New ways mean new thinking, new beliefs. The Communist and the missionary are both there to steer its course. The missionary and the active Asian layman are front-line fighters in the battle of our time just as much as are the trained cadres of Communism. Upon the outcome of their activities an enormous amount depends (Hyde, 1956:5).

Douglas Hyde then goes on to suggest that the Missions become a "shop window" for the application of Christian social teaching and prove to the world by actual demonstration that "there is an alternative to Communism." In some areas, like Flores (Indonesia) and China, the Missions have done what Hyde suggests, and his observation is very much to the point: "The pre-occupation of the Chinese Communists with their tiny Catholic minority is one of the most eloquent tributes ever paid to the Church" (op. cit. 87, 263–264).

3. Interwebbing of Socio-Economic and Religious Patterns

A final, but no less important reason for missionary social action, as has already been intimated (see p. 6), is the fact that the elements constituting a culture are interwebbed into a *system* or a kind of "organism" (see pp. 135–190). Consequently, to bring about a change in beliefs and moral behavior the missionary may have to bring about economic and social changes first, or at least work toward such changes. The beautiful flowers of religion and morality cannot thrive where the weeds of starvation, unemployment, ignorance, and injustice flourish.

The Necessity of a Culturally Relevant Social Action

In carrying out the important "duty" of social action which binds the Missions "in justice and charity" (John XXIII) and which cannot be neglected "without guilt in the sight of the Eternal God" (Pius XII) and in meeting the challenge of the Communists in modern revolutionary times the missionary cannot be satisfied with out-of-date and inefficient approaches. In so serious an obligation and threat he cannot be satisfied with old, unreliable methods, the so-called "common-sense" and often "hit-or-miss" techniques. Effective social action in a "strange" cultural environment presupposes not only technical or professional knowledge and skill but (1) a thorough understanding of the cultural context in which the social action is to take place and (2) an adjustment to that cultural context.

1. PROPER UNDERSTANDING OF THE SOCIO-CULTURAL CONTEXT AS THE FIRST STEP TOWARD EFFECTIVE SOCIAL ACTION

To understand a "strange" way of life one must know (1) *what* the particular society does and (2) *why* it does it. The best, although perhaps not complete, answer to both questions will be found in Cultural Anthropology, "The Science of the Ways of Man." The *why* is, of course, much more difficult to arrive at than the *what*. Very often the society concerned is itself unable to give the reasons for its behavior (latent functions). Very often, too, the attributed functions of a custom are not objective. Thus, the reason for wearing a charm may be "to bring good luck to the wearer" or, more specifically, "to deflect a bolt of lightning coming at you" or "to keep you from drowning." Objectively, of course, the charm does not bring good luck; it cannot do anything about a bolt of lightning heading for you; nor will it succeed in keeping you afloat. Nevertheless, the charm does serve an objective purpose in the given culture: it generates initiative and self-confidence and serves as a source of security. To understand a particular cultural context in which the missioner must labor, all *why*'s have to be investigated, the manifest as well as the latent, the objective as well as the merely supposed and attributed (cf. Nadel, 1955–56:157–

173). It is quite true that at times even the most skillful anthropologist will have to admit defeat or be satisfied with a reasonable, culturologically founded conjecture. Despite the difficulties involved, the why of behavior must be investigated if the cultural context is to be properly understood (see pp. 135–154).

In recent years a rash of novels, newspaper columns, magazine articles, and printed protests of all sorts have appeared, mercilessly denouncing the mistakes being made by Americans in their dealings with other countries (Hart, 1962:60–84). The best known of these exposures was The Ugly American (New York, 1958) by W. Lederer and E. Burdick, who wrote the novel not to entertain the reader but to jolt him, "to dramatize what we have seen of the Americans who represent us in the struggle [in Southeast Asia]." Such writings (and they are many) triggered a number of serious investigations, which aimed to sift fact from fiction, only to discover that there was more fact than fiction. The Overseas Americans (New York, 1960) by Cleveland, Mangone, and Adams was one such report representing four years of serious research. Costly mistakes are being made by diplomats, technicians, military specialists, businessmen, and missionaries because the culturally defined behavior of the people to be assisted is not sufficiently understood and taken into account. In spite of the good will, honest intentions, and, not seldom, dedication, the United States seems to be failing in many of its dealings with other nations, not, as is sometimes supposed, exclusively on account of Communistic propaganda and the ingratitude of human beings but because the overseas Americans only too frequently do not understand the "what" and the "why" of the culture in which they must work.

2. ADJUSTING ONE'S APPROACH TO LOCAL WAYS AND VALUES AS A SECOND STEP TOWARD EFFECTIVE SOCIAL ACTION

It is not sufficient merely to understand the cultural context. The educator, social worker, economist, technician, doctor, and any other mission specialist, no less than the missionary engaged in the direct apostolate, must as far as possible gear his interpersonal relations (see pp. 229–239) as well as his professional knowledge and skill (see pp. 3–19) to the new human surroundings. Social action must be relevant to what the local people actually believe in, value, and do. Their milieu, their needs, their values, and their assumptions (not the missionary's) should as much as possible determine the missioner's interpersonal and professional approach in working toward the socio-economic betterment of a people. The only effective way to sell a socio-economic idea on the foreign market is to present the "wares" as necessary in terms of *local* needs and values.

To adjust one's general behavior and specialized skill to local ways will call for a recognition, appreciation, and even actual adoption of numberless shocking attitudes and practices. Not the sacrifice of the luxuries of an American home or the consolations of relatives and friends but the sacrifice of one's own ways and values will be the missionary's greatest sacrifice; in fact, it may even become a slow martyrdom. The missionary who claims that he has never felt the weight of this sacrifice has most likely never made it. Some examples illustrating the truth of this statement might be worth mentioning here. It will take violence to self to recognize, for instance, the value of an "insignificant" dialect and to go through all the painful hours required to master it. It will take violence to self to feel about the "grotesque" local art and "savage" music as the local people feel about such matters. To bear up with the local ignorance of hygiene and to feel about the "filth and smell" the way the local people feel about "filth and smell" may at times call for heroism. Then there are the numberless little things, insignificant in themselves but constant, that irritate the outsider: the "out-of-place" smiles, the "uncomfortable" postures, the "wrong" gestures, the "sheepish" gait, the "deafening" tone of voice, the "indistinct" enunciation, the "complete lack of appreciation for certain virtues, such as exactness and punctuality," the infinite variety of "foolish" taboos, and, of course, the many "nonsensical" rules of etiquette which even foreigners are forced to observe. During World War II many Americans in Japanese prison camps suffered unnecessarily simply because they refused to make the sacrifice of their attitude toward bowing. To the Americans bowing was a kind of adoration or the ugliest form of human degradation, while to the Japanese bowing was only the ordinary, everyday sign of respect (E. T. Hall, 1959:103–104).

Even unscientific prejudices and superstitions must be reckoned with and respected. An agronomist who does not agree with the teaching of Islam but must work among Mohammedans would not stop a farmer along the road to inquire about the expected yield. To do so would not be a sign of friendliness as it might be in Iowa but rather an insult, the equivalent of calling one a blasphemer, for only Allah knows the future (E. T. Hall, 1959:16).

Another important but difficult adjustment is that regarding the roles in a given society. The roles played by old men, women, priests, doctors, and maternal uncles in America are not necessarily those of old men, women, priests, doctors, and maternal uncles in Ghana. Where a young man may be needed for effective work in an economic or social project in one culture, an old man may be required in another; where a man may be necessary in one society, a woman may be required in another; what only a father might do in one society, a mother or maternal uncle may do in another. To disregard and confuse roles is a common but serious mistake and stumbling block in missionary social action. Especially important in this regard is the necessary adjustment to the local conception of leadership, vital for success in any socio-economic program. Important personages in America are not necessarily important in Africa. Age, on the other hand, may be highly respected, as it is in Japan for instance. Age may be a sign of genuine wisdom and ability, and may be considered far more vital in a leader than technical skill, even when the program concerned happens to be highly technical in nature. To win the co-operation of the local people the missionary engaged in a socio-economic project should seek out true native leadership whenever possible and whenever prudence will allow, the type of leadership that is meaningful not so much in the missioner's home-country but in the particular socio-cultural situation in which he finds himself.

THE CULTURAL CONTEXT AND COMMUNICATION

Communists and other would-be reformers may use politics, violence, trickery, suppression, and other ethical and unethical means to achieve their ideological and practical ends. The Church, on the other hand, has only one means at her disposal — communication. The missionary cannot bring about a change, whether it be in spiritual or temporal matters, unless his people themselves desire the change. Effective communication is vital for successful apostolic work; the Church must *communicate* her social and religious doctrine. However, if communication is to be effective it must be transmitted on the proper "wavelength," the socio-cultural context of the receiving society. Whenever a message is sent from an "outside" culture, the message is necessarily clothed in the terms of that culture unless a positive effort is made to the contrary. Although in intercultural communication it may happen that at times the receiving society will try to interpret the message in terms of the sending society's way of life, such is generally not the case in regard to the missionary's message, which is interpreted (and misinterpreted) almost exclusively in terms of the receiving society's cultural experience. The communication that takes the receptor's cultural background into account has the best chance of remaining substantially unaltered and of being properly understood (see pp. 215–220).

But besides successful information apostolic work calls for conviction and persuasion. Conviction and persuasion, in turn, call for effective argumentation and motivation, aims that are utterly impossible unless the missioner employs culturally meaningful premises, values, and motives. Each element of a culture has a "price-tag" attached, a culturally defined value. In intercultural communication, such as is involved in apostolic work, arguments to be effective must be clothed in terms of the values of the receptor society. The missionary, therefore, wishing to communicate the Gospel or a socio-economic idea must proceed not only from the known to the unknown but also from the felt to the still unfelt, from the wanted to the still unwanted, and then from there he progresses again, further and further, but always from the known to the unknown, from the felt to the still unfelt, from the wanted to the still unwanted. Above all, conviction and persuasion call for the use of effective, culturally pertinent "starting-points" of reasoning, feeling, and motivating, the so-called basic assumptions, emotionally charged attitudes, and goals that underlie all conviction and persuasion (see pp. 157–169). Human beings, no matter how simple or how sophisticated, may indeed reason, react emotionally, and be moved to action according to the same psychological laws, but the underlying assumptions and drives will differ from culture to culture. A successful argument must be in harmony with such underlying assumptions and premises (for example, face-saving in the Orient) otherwise the best oratory and logic will fail. Persuasion is successful only if the motives be real, that is, real to the receiver of the message. This is the only effective procedure in intercultural communication, a procedure that presupposes a thorough acquaintance with the culture content and the particular value-system of the receiving society.

SUMMARY AND PRACTICAL APPLICATION

Cultural relevancy is indeed an important apostolic principle. The cultural context constitutes a basic missionary tool, necessary for the missioner in his role of agent of culture change, necessary for spiritual guidance, necessary for effective social action, and indispensable for successful communication. Anthropology is a "missionary science" par excellence because it teaches the missionary how to apply this all-important tool.

All missionaries seem to admit the necessity of understanding their people; nevertheless, there is a deplorable lack of appreciation in some missionary organizations of the very science that teaches them how to understand a people. Unfortunately, such organizations seem to look upon Anthropology as some sort of curious study of apes, dry bones, and museum curios, and upon anthropologists as individuals who are not quite normal. Such misconceptions and prejudices have made these otherwise practical missionary groups brush the science aside as something purely speculative and unrealistic, "something without which we have gotten along so far, and, no doubt, will get along quite well in the future." It is difficult indeed to understand how any missionary society can call itself "modern" and at the same time refuse to consider a tested and genuinely scientific approach to the understanding of human ways. Professor Kluckhohn of Harvard University has aptly entitled his prize-winning book on the relation of Anthropology to modern life as the Mirror for Man. "Anthropology," he writes, "holds up a great mirror to man and lets him look at himself in his infinite variety" (Kluckhohn, 1949a:11).

Anyone having a correct notion of Anthropology and at least some idea of the many implications of a cross-cultural endeavor like the missionary apostolate would never claim that "our seminary curriculum is already so crowded with essentials that there just is no time for such side-branches as Anthropology." Such individuals fail to grasp the most basic human problem in missionary work — the socio-cultural context. They also fail to understand what the aims of Anthropology are. Cultural Anthropology is an essential aspect of missionary formation — not a "side-branch" — and time must be found for it. In our modern times we would be unnecessarily handicapping the missionary if we failed to provide him with basic anthropological knowledge and skill. The missionary, whether priest, Brother, Sister, or lay-missionary, needs at least a basic training in missiological Anthropology, even if he already possesses a degree in Education, Agronomy, Medicine, or some other field. The missionary may know all the Philosophy, Theology, and Canon Law that there is to be known; he may know all the latest methods of teaching Christian Doctrine; he may be acclaimed as a great orator; he may be an outstanding Bible scholar; he may be a degreed educator, technician, agronomist, or a fully-qualified physician — as long as he has not learned how to apply his professional knowledge and skill to the particular needs of his people and has not learned how he is to interact with them he is anything but a well-trained missionary. In fact, as emphasized before, an expert on the mission field without a knowledge of the local cultural context may turn out to be a rather dangerous "expert" indeed.

SELECTED READINGS

1. The Apostolic Principle of Cultural Relevancy

    1) L. J. Luzbetak, S.V.D., "Toward an Applied Missionary Anthropology," *Anthropological Quarterly*, XXXIV (1961), 165–176.

  * 2) J. Amyot, S.J., "The Mission Apostolate in Its Cultural Context," *Mission Bulletin* (Hong Kong), VII (1955) 736–739 and VIII (1956) 8–13.

    3) J. J. Considine, M.M., *Fundamental Catholic Teaching on the Human Race*, pp. 59–75.

    4) J. Franklin Ewing, S.J., "Anthropology and the Training of Missionaries," *The Catholic Educational Review*, LV (1957), 300–311.

    5) J. Franklin Ewing, S.J., "Applied Anthropology for the Missionary," *Worldmission*, II (February, 1951), 105–107.

  * 6) E. A. Nida, *Customs and Cultures*, pp. 1–53.

    7) W. A. Smalley, "Anthropological Study and Missionary Scholarship," *Practical Anthropology*, VII (1960), 113–123.

    8) G. H. Smith, *The Missionary and Anthropology*, pp. 15–27.

  * 9) J. A. McCoy, S.M., *Advice from the Field: Towards a New Missiology*, pp. 32–100.

---

* The asterisk before an entry indicates required rather than merely suggested reading.

2. Mission Encyclicals
   * 1) Benedict XV, *Maximum Illud.*
   * 2) Pius XI, *Rerum Ecclesiae.*
   * 3) Pius XII, *Evangelii Praecones.*
   * 4) Pius XII, *Fidei Donum.*
   * 5) John XXIII, *Princeps Pastorum.*

3. The Missionary and Culture Change
   1) D. W. Kietzman and W. A. Smalley, "The Missionary's Role in Culture Change," *Practical Anthropology*, (1960), Supplement, 85–90.
   2) A. Rosenstiel, "Social Change and the Missionary," *Practical Anthropology*, VIII (1961), 15–24.
   3) J. Franklin Ewing, S.J., "Local Social Custom and Christian Social Action," in J. Franklin Ewing, S.J., ed., *Social Action in Mission Lands*, pp. 25–42.

4. The Missionary and Social Action
   1) J. J. Considine, M.M., *The Missionary's Role in Socio-Economic Betterment*, pp. 56–75.
   * 2) J. Franklin Ewing, S.J., ed., *Social Action in Mission Lands*, pp. 25–49.
   3) J. Rosner, S.A.C., "Missionary Adaptation in Theory and Practice," in D. J. Hatton, ed., *Missiology in Africa Today*, pp. 96–107.

5. The Missionary and Communication
   1) E. A. Walsh, "Communications and the Missionary," in J. F. Ewing, ed., *Communication Arts in Mission Work*, pp. 5–24.
   * 2) E. A. Nida, *Message and Mission: The Communication of the Christian Faith*, pp. 171–188.
   3) L. W. Doob, *Communication in Africa: A Search for Boundaries.*

6. Overseas Americans and Their Problems
   * 1) D. V. Hart, "Overseas Americans in Southeast Asia: Fact in Fiction," *Practical Anthropology*, IX (1962), 60–84.
   2) E. A. Nida, "The Ugly Missionary," *Practical Anthropology*, VII (1960), 74–78.
   3) W. Lederer and E. Burdick, *The Ugly American.*
   4) P. Spector and H. O. Preston, *Working Effectively Overseas*, pp. 1–179.
   N.B. For further bibliography see D. V. Hart's article cited above.

REVIEW QUESTIONS

1. Why do we call Cultural Anthropology a "missionary science" par excellence? (p. 4)

2. Why do we say that a missionary is "an agent of culture change"? (pp. 5–6)
3. Why should an agent of culture change be interested in the local cultural context? (pp. 5–8)
4. Why is the knowledge of the local culture necessary for spiritual guidance? (pp. 8–9)
5. Is the socio-economic betterment of peoples a concern of the Missions? (pp. 9–13)
6. Show that missionary social action to be effective must be culturally relevant. (pp. 13–16)
7. Why is the knowledge of the local culture necessary for communication? (pp. 16–18)

TOPICS FOR CLASSROOM DISCUSSION AND PAPERS

1. ". . . long before Cultural Anthropology, 'The Science of Culture,' was born the most effective missionaries were those who were blessed with a deep appreciation of the diversity of cultures and the important role which a culture plays in human behavior" (see p. 3). Prove this statement from the lives of such great missionaries as St. Paul, Father Ricci, Cardinal Lavigerie, Father Joseph Freinademetz, Bishop De Bresillac, Father Charles de Foucauld, Father Lebbe, Father Bartolomé de las Casas, etc.
2. A fellow-missionary complains to you that only women and small children come to Mass and religious instruction. From what has been said in Chapter One what might you suspect as being possibly responsible for this situation?
3. Debate: A missionary is (is not) primarily an agent of culture change.
4. Debate: A missionary need be but deeply spiritual, humble, and self-sacrificing and he will of necessity have the required empathy and detachment from his own culture.
5. Discuss the necessity of knowing the cultural context to be an effective preacher, good confessor, and successful educator.
6. You are working as missionary in southern Mexico. What would you say to your fellow-missionary who would tell you, "Punctuality is a virtue, and it is about time our people learn to be punctual. From now on I'm going to insist on beginning services and instructions promptly"?
7. Read Clyde Kluckhohn's Mirror for Man and draw up a list of "Practical Lessons for Missionaries."
8. Read The Ugly American or one of the many available novels on the same subject and draw up a list of "Do's and Don'ts for Missionaries."
9. Read E. T. Hall's The Silent Language. Compare "the silent language" of your own American subculture and that of the American Negro, Puerto Rican, Mexican, or some immigrant group from Europe.

10. Summarize and evaluate Annette Rosenstiel's article, "Social Change and the Missionary," *Practical Anthropology*, VIII (1961), 15–24.
11. Write a critical book review of one of the books mentioned above in the Selected Readings, "6. Overseas Americans and Their Problems." In your evaluation make sure that you are arguing from an *anthropological* point of view, not political, religious, *etc.*
12. Summarize and draw a practical application from Willis E. Sibley, "Social Structure and Planned Change: A Case Study from the Philippines," *Human Organization*, XIX (Winter, 1960–61), 209–211.

CHAPTER TWO

NATURE AND SCOPE OF APPLIED
MISSIONARY ANTHROPOLOGY

A DISCIPLINE is most conveniently defined by pointing out its aims, subject-matter, premises, and methods. But before any attempt is made to describe the nature and scope of Applied Missionary Anthropology it will be helpful first to indicate the nature and scope of Anthropology as such and to show its position in relation to other associated fields.

WHAT IS ANTHROPOLOGY?

The word "anthropology" derives from the Greek *anthropos,* "man," and *logos,* "word, discourse." Anthropology, therefore, is a "man-study" or a "science of man." But is this not a misnomer? After all, other sciences have man as their object too, for instance Political Science, History, Psychology, and Biology. What right does Anthropology have to claim a monopoly on man?

An etymological definition usually only hints at the real meaning of a word. Thus, "baptism" literally means "a washing," although Baptism is definitely more than a mere washing. We must, therefore, qualify "man-study," "the study of man," and "the science of man" by adding a few more words to the definition: "Anthropology is the study of man and his works and behavior" (Kroeber, 1948:1). Kroeber rightly maintains that we cannot be satisfied with this definition until we define the word "man" somewhat more accurately. Unlike Psychology and Physiology, Anthropology is interested in "man" not as an individual but as a member of a group of men; unlike History, Biology, Medicine, and Psychology, Anthropology, moreover, does not focus on any particular point of man but takes a *holistic* or total viewpoint of him — the entire man, over the entire earth, and throughout the entire history of mankind, from the beginning to the present. When we speak of Anthropology as a study of "man" we mean "the study of races and peoples and mankind in general."

Philosophers define the "entire man" as an *animal rationale*. Anthropology, being the study of the *entire* man, treats him as he is in nature — composed of body and soul. The various fields of Anthropology never lose sight of this wholeness of man, of the biological and the "social," the inherited and the acquired, the biologically transmitted and the learned behavior, the organic and the superorganic, the purely animal and the essentially human.

Quite logically, Anthropology branches off into two specializations: the one centers its attention on what the philosophers call *animal*, while the other concerns itself with the *rationale*; the one focuses on man as a physical organism, while the other concerns itself with what is distinctly a manifestation of the human soul — his culture. Unlike even the most manlike animals, man alone makes tools in the strict sense of the term; he has a unique economic, social, and political organization; he alone has religious beliefs and practices; he alone can boast of a language. "Physical" and "Cultural Anthropology," as these two branches are called, are separate fields of study, but, as is generally done by American scholars, they should be treated as closely interdependent subdivisions of one and the same "Study of the Total Man." Scholars in Continental Europe generally claim that the two fields are so vastly different that they can never justifiably be brought under the same general science or name. The one is a *Naturwissenschaft* while the other is a *Geisteswissenschaft*. As a concession to these scholars the international meetings of anthropologists are officially referred to as "The International Congress of Anthropological and Ethnological Sciences." One should note the conjunction "and" in this title as well as the plural "sciences."

Physical Anthropology

Physical Anthropology is interested primarily in the biological aspects of man. It seeks out all possible causes (including environmental and social) for the particular state of the human body as it occurred in the past ages and as it appears among the numberless living ethnic groups scattered throughout the world today. Physical Anthropology may have a distinctly historical orientation, or it may be "scientific" (Hoebel, 1958:12). By "scientific" we mean that the primary interest of the field consists in the formulation of laws or generalizations. Historical studies, on the other hand, are primarily interested in discovering and documenting the uniqueness of facts. When Physical Anthropology focuses on the origin and evolution of the human body, it is an historical discipline and is known as Human Paleontology (Gr.: *palaios*, "old" + *onta*, "existing things" + *logos*, "word, discourse, study") or Paleoanthropology (Gr.: *palaios* + *anthropos* + *logos*) or simply as "The Study of Fossil Man." When Physical Anthropology has a scientific orientation with focus on structure and function of contemporary human forms, it is referred to as "The Study of Race" or, as it is sometimes called, Somatology (Gr.: *soma*, "body" + *logos*). To achieve its aims Physical Anthropology has recourse to highly specialized auxiliary fields, such as Anthropometry (Gr.: *anthropos* + *metron*, "measure"), Biometrics (Gr.: *bios*, "life"+*metron*), and Human Genetics. The Study of Race branches off into such subfields as Human Morphology (Gr.: *morphē*, "form"+*logos*) and Comparative Human Physiology (Gr.: *physis*, "nature"+*logos*).

Physical Anthropology is defined as "the comparative science of man as a physical organism in relation to his total environment, social as well as physical" (Montagu, 1951:ix). By very minute measurements and comparisons of fossilized and unfossilized bony structures of human and prehuman forms the paleoanthropologist tries to discover the origin of the human body, its genetic relationship to lower forms, its evolution through the half million years or so since the first appearance of man on earth. When studying prehistoric man the anthropologist must rely on minute comparisons of bony structure alone. When he begins to study living races, however, he has more than bones to compare; he has the whole living man, with skin, hair, eyes, internal organs, blood, secretions, etc. A good physical anthropologist will be an expert anatomist and physiologist, perhaps even more so than a physician generally is. Since the anthropologist is interested in *groups* of men, he studies the bodily characteristics of individuals not as individuals but as members of a group. It is for this reason that he is so preoccupied with indices and averages.

As one can readily see, Physical Anthropology is too specialized a field, well beyond the grasp of the ordinary missionary, and therefore not directly practical for apostolic work. However, it is not to be supposed that Physical Anthropology can do nothing to advance peoples in mission countries. Physical Anthropology, for example, provides some of the scientific arguments against claims to racial superiority (see pp. 325–327) and it is making considerable contributions to the general health of mankind (Caudill, 1953:771–806; Krogman, 1951:211–218; Kluckhohn, 1949a:86–90). Physical Anthropology provides a useful background for Cultural Anthropology, the missionary's chief field of interest.

Cultural Anthropology

Cultural Anthropology analyzes and compares the way of life of living as well as of extinct peoples; it interprets their ways in historical perspective; it establishes "laws" of human behavior. The particular orientation (historical vs. scientific) will depend to a large extent on the particular subdiscipline and sometimes on the "school" to which the cultural anthropologist happens to belong (Lowie, 1938; Tax, 1955b:445–481; Beals, Hoijer, 1953:600–627). Today Cultural Anthropology is being broken down more and more into highly specialized studies, such as Ethnomusicology, Mythology, Primitive Art, Folk-medicine, Dialect Geography, Primitive Law, and other specialized interests, and it includes three major divisions, Prehistoric Archaeology, Linguistics, and Ethnology (Hoebel, 1958: 7–13; Keesing, 1958:4–6). Not everything treated in these three subfields of Cultural Anthropology will be found equally useful for missionary work. The present course will have little to say about Archaeology, the main concern being Ethnology. Although Linguistics is important for practical apostolic methods, relatively little space can be devoted to the subject only because Linguistics is too highly specialized a field requiring several volumes to present its techniques satisfactorily.

The following outline may throw some light on the various divisions of Anthropology, Ethnology in particular.

I. *Physical Anthropology*
    A. Paleoanthropology (Fossil Man)
    B. Race (Somatology)

II. *Cultural Anthropology*
    A. Archaeology
    B. Linguistics
    C. Ethnology (understood in a broad sense)
       1. Ethnography

2. Ethnology (understood in a restricted sense)
3. Social Anthropology

Applied Missionary Anthropology is interested primarily in Ethnology taken in the more generic sense.

Like Physical Anthropology, Cultural Anthropology may be oriented historically or scientifically; that is, some of the branches of Cultural Anthropology may focus on origins and historical developments, while others may limit their interests to structure and function; some may be interested in the uniqueness of cultural development in time and space (i.e., in history), while others may be concerned with "laws" governing cultures in general or with generalizations about particular cultures. The following chart aims to throw light on the rather confused ensemble of disciplines all calling themselves "Anthropology." As intimated above, there are finer specializations than those actually indicated in the chart; it should also be noted that some of the anthropological approaches of some "schools" cut across the boundaries or orientations given in the chart. Strange as it may seem, anthropologists have still not agreed upon the names to be given to the various subdivisions of their field: as noted above, the Continental scholars insist, sometimes with considerable emotion, on calling Physical Anthropology by the name of "Anthropology," while Cultural Anthropology to them becomes "Ethnology." To add to the confusion, some anthropologists call Ethnology in its generic sense "Social Anthropology." The chart

FIGURE 1
ANTHROPOLOGICAL ORIENTATIONS

The Study of Man	Orientation	
	Historical or Descriptive	Scientific
as a *biological* animal **Physical Anthropology**	Paleoanthropology	Race
as *rational* animal **Cultural Anthropology**	Archaeology Linguistics Ethnology	Social Anthropology

represents a recent trend among American anthropologists in classifying the various anthropological disciplines.

1. ARCHAEOLOGY

Archaeology (Gr.: *archaios*, "ancient" + *logos*, "word, discourse") is sometimes spoken of as the "Ethnology of Extinct Cultures." It is also known as "Prehistory" or "Prehistoric Archaeology" to distinguish it from such fields as Classical and Biblical Archaeology. Archaeology recovers, analyzes, compares, and interprets cultural products and subsistence remains with view to discovering as much as possible about the life-way of prehistoric times.

2. LINGUISTICS

Linguistics (L.: *lingua*, "tongue, speech, language") is a highly specialized form of Cultural Anthropology. Just as some anthropologists concentrate on such interests as music (Ethnomusicology) or myths (Mythology), so the linguist, a highly specialized cultural anthropologist, concentrates on the aspect of culture known as "language." Some linguists are interested primarily in analysis and description; others are interested primarily in the history of languages; others are interested primarily in the influence of language on thought and behavior, and vice versa (Hoijer, 1954).

3. ETHNOLOGY

Ethnology in the broader sense of the term is subdivided into Ethnography, Ethnology in a more restricted sense, and Social Anthropology. (1) Ethnography (Gr.: *ethnos*, "race" + *graphein*, "to write") is the factual, non-interpretative description of particular modern or recent cultures. (2) Ethnology in the restricted sense of the term is the analysis and comparison of raw ethnographic materials in historical perspective. (3) Social Anthropology differs from the preceding field in the fact that it limits its interest to the discovery and formulation of "laws," especially regarding social structure and social behavior. Ethnology in the restricted sense of the term is historically oriented, while Social Anthropology is scientifically oriented; Ethnology is equally interested in the whole of culture, while Social Anthropology is almost exclusively occupied with the social aspects of culture. Social Anthropology is sometimes confused with Sociology. The two disciplines coincide in their general object of research, group behavior; they differ, however, in methodology and point of emphasis, Social Anthropology being almost entirely taken up with less complex societies and Sociology being almost exclusively concerned with highly complex Western societies.

Although not limiting his interests exclusively to so-called "primitive" peoples the cultural anthropologist has a definite predilection for the more simple cultures. This procedure in no way reduces the validity of his generalizations; nor does it affect the validity of the applications of anthropological principles to missionary problems among more advanced peoples such as the Indonesians, Indians, Japanese, or for that matter the American Negroes, Mexicans, and Puerto Ricans. In fact, there is a great advantage to studying simple societies rather than the complex. In the first place, the anthropologist is less inclined to be prejudiced when investigating simpler ways of life than his own (Linton, ed., 1945:11–12). Moreover, as anthropologists have frequently pointed out (Kluckhohn, 1949a: 12–13; Herskovits, 1950:79–93; Benedict, 1946a:15–18), the closest approximation to a laboratory for a social scientist is a "primitive" situation. By reducing the number of unknowns to a minimum the physical scientist can without much difficulty set up for himself in his laboratory ideal conditions to test his hypotheses. The social scientist cannot follow this procedure. Instead, the homogeneous societies having simple cultures become the anthropologist's laboratory: the group of human beings under study is generally small and not too unwieldy; the members of the group are usually isolated and relatively free from outside influences; practically all members of the group have the same limited education and experience; they all live in the same physical environment; they have a rather constant way of life; the individuals of the group being studied also have more or less the same biological inheritance due to the relatively high degree of inbreeding among them. In this human laboratory the anthropologist is able to reduce his study to a limited number of variables and thus is in a much better position to discover the relation between them (Kluckhohn, 1949a:11–12). Generalizations about "culture" therefore hold also in regard to our complex Western civilization, for "civilization" is only a variety of "culture." Consequently, a missioner can make good use of culturological concepts and principles in a highly sophisticated society no less than in "primitive" surroundings. The problems will be fundamentally the same whether one is dealing with the culture of the African Pygmies, the American Negroes, or the Pennsylvania Dutch.

THE RELATION OF ANTHROPOLOGY TO ASSOCIATED FIELDS

There are various types of sciences: there are the natural sciences and the historical or descriptive; there are the biological sciences, social sciences, and the humanities; there are pure sciences, to offer still another category, and the applied sciences; and, finally, there are the so-called "exact" sciences. Where does Anthropology fit into this picture of Science?

Anthropology is an integrating type of study. If an organized body of facts is demonstrable under controlled observation and as a consequence consists of predictable laws it is a natural science. If, on the other hand, it consists in an organized body of documented events that are unique in time and space it is a historical or descriptive science. We have already seen how Anthropology can have either a "scientific" or historical orientation. When the anthropologist studies the living races he is in the field of biological sciences; when he makes generalizations regarding human behavior he is in the field of social sciences; when he describes the more noble aspects of a culture, such as music, art, philosophy, and religion, or when he traces the culture history of a people he is in the field of humanities. Sciences are "exact" when the generalizations and predictions are infallible laws. Exceptions would be true miracles. Cultural Anthropology is definitely not an exact science, for infallible predictions regarding human behavior are impossible. Man possesses a free will and therefore is not bound to any given way of acting. Moreover, in any attempt to predict human behavior there are too many variables even for a genius to cope with — the numberless cultural, personal, social, and physical unknowns. Nevertheless, Cultural Anthropology can and does, to some extent at least, enable one to make valid predictions. The fact is that human beings do act according to definite psychological, cultural, and social patterns. Anthropology, although still in its infancy, has discovered many of these patterns or regularities.

Anthropology has always been closely associated with other fields of research. The physical anthropologist and the prehistorian lean heavily on Geology and Chemistry for determining the age of their data. The ethnologist has frequent recourse to such auxiliary disciplines as Human Geography, Psychology, and Sociology. Anthropology, of course, reciprocates through its contributions to such fields as Medicine and Sociology.

A science can be "pure" or "applied," and Anthropology is developing in both directions. When anthropological concepts, principles, techniques, and controls are employed to promote a given cause we speak of Applied Anthropology. Thus, especially in recent years, anthropological theory has been widely applied in industry, government and international affairs, medicine, education, and missionary work. The present course is a form of *Applied* Anthropology, specifically tailored for the needs of the apostolic worker engaged in activities outside his own cultural milieu.

Applied Missionary Anthropology, however, is not to be identified with Missiology or Mission Science. Actually it is only one of the many disciplines that might fall under the general term of "Missiology." Missiology includes aspects of History, Dogmatic Theology, Canon Law, Sacred Scriptures, Catechetics, and other fields, including Anthropology — all studied from the missionary's point of view.

In Missiology, therefore, one might draw valid arguments from Sacred Scripture and tradition, from papal encyclicals and various decrees, from established practices and policies of the Sacred Congregation for the Propagation of the Faith, from the Codex of Canon Law, and from other purely ecclesiastical sources, for Missiology is essentially a theological field (Jetté, 1950; Clarkson, 1952; Hoffman, 1962a). However, the present course is intended to be a study in *Anthropology*, not in a specialized field of Theology. Nevertheless, although not resorting to the Sacred Scriptures, papal decrees, Mission History, and other similar sources as anthropological evidence, we shall make frequent and quite legitimate and necessary references to ecclesiastical sources. Our situation is very much like that of the applied anthropologist dealing with medical problems. Although not using Medicine as evidence, he nevertheless must frequently refer to medical concepts, principles, and authorities. In Applied Missionary Anthropology we are obliged to refer repeatedly to non-anthropological and purely ecclesiastical sources: (1) in order to introduce a particular mission problem that happens to be founded on such sources; (2) in order to illustrate such a problem; (3) in order to indicate the framework or limits within which the problem must be studied and solved, limits dictated by ecclesiastical (not anthropological) sources; (4) in order to indicate the deeper meaning and latent consequences of a particular missiological text from the Bible, or an ecclesiastical document, or of an historical event as seen in the light of anthropological theory; (5) in order to indicate the usefulness and importance of an anthropological concept or principle for practical apostolic work, the importance of which happens to be derived not from Anthropology but from purely ecclesiastical sources; (6) in order to show the anthropological wisdom of a doctrine or policy of the Church as reflected in the particular encyclical, Church legislation, tradition, or passage from the Bible. We are, therefore, not confusing Missiology with Anthropology and the Missions: *we are examining nonculturological aspects of Missiology in the light of culturological theory.*

The relationship between Missiology and Applied Missionary Anthropology might perhaps be best viewed as a kind of syllogism: the major premise is set up by Mission Theology, Mission History, Mission Law, and other non-culturological subfields of Missiology; the minor premise consists of pertinent cultural anthropological theory. It is the task of Applied Missionary Anthropology to bring together the pertinent culturological theory and to draw the logical conclusion from the premises.

THE AIMS OF AN APPLIED ANTHROPOLOGY FOR MISSIONARIES

Applied Missionary Anthropology has two distinct aims. (1) It aims to clarify more fully (i.e., in culturological terms) the meaning of mission theory as proposed in the Theology of the Missions, Mission History, and other subfields of Missiology, e.g., the culturological consequences flowing from the theological fact that the Church is by its very nature supranational, the culturological consequences of the impossibility to compromise doctrine, the culturological reasons for historically established missionary success, etc. (2) The second aim is to foresee and to predict, as far as possible, the results of missionary action as well as to suggest what appears to be the most effective, most efficient, and least disorganizing line of action in the given cultural context.

THE PREMISES OF AN APPLIED ANTHROPOLOGY FOR MISSIONARIES

An applied science always presupposes a set of values; it is, after all, being applied for some purpose or "cause." Applied Anthropology in any form is, as already intimated, a kind of "interventionism," and interventionism demands justification. There must be a "cause," a "good" cause, to justify "Action Anthropology" or "Social Engineering," as Applied Anthropology is sometimes called. Anthropology is, so to speak, hired to work for the "good" of others: for the technological *advancement* of a people, for *better* social conditions, for *improvement* in health and hygiene in a *backward*, *underdeveloped*, or *developing* area, or for the spiritual *welfare* of men. Such values, however, must be previously established by a non-anthropological source. Even Sol Tax's "self-determination" and Holmberg's "human dignity" as goals of Applied Anthropology are basically a problem of Philosophy rather than Anthropology. In the case of Applied Missionary Anthropology one must go to Missiology (Philosophy, Theology, History, etc.) to justify the activities of an anthropologist in the Missions. The relatively few anthropologists who condemn missionary activities and the application of "so noble a science to so foolish and unjust an enterprise as mission work" are entirely out of their field and indeed talking nonsense. Until they carefully inquire into the missiological premises in question, may we suggest that they save their breath, eloquence, and prejudice for other purposes. The justification of any "cause" which applied anthropologists serve, Democracy or Communism for that matter, must be sought, as we have said, outside of Anthropology. In questioning the justification for such activities as those of the UNESCO, the World Health Organization, the Food and Agricultural Organization, or the Catholic Missions, the anthropologist qua anthropologist must realize that he is outside his field and may be talking nonsense.

It is quite conceivable that an applied anthropologist hired by a government or the U.N.O. might not believe in the cause or set of values for which he is working. He can sit back, as it were, and watch the drama of "interventionism" (whether economic, social, or religious) unfold itself, and as an indifferent observer predict what is going to happen next on the cultural stage. It is also conceivable that an applied anthropologist might act as a neutral advisor. Without necessarily espousing the particular cause, he may offer positive advice regarding the restoration of social or cultural equilibrium, the most effective way to promote the cause in question, or the surest way to avoid harmful disorganization. Because the missionary-anthropologist is a practitioner and not a mere observer and advisor he is anything but neutral in regard to the premises that underlie Applied Missionary Anthropology. He is convinced of the righteousness of the cause to which he is dedicated and which he serves. This conviction is based primarily on Faith. Faith, however, is not contrary to reason: it is a *sacrificium intellectus* but at the same time a *rationabile obsequium*. In fact, a major portion of his long seminary training was devoted to nothing else than what might be called a very careful and detailed scrutiny of the premises of Applied Missionary Anthropology, the justification of the cause we call "Catholic Missions," a justification found in Philosophy, Sacred Scriptures, Fundamental Theology, etc., summed up for him in Missiology.

THE SUBJECT-MATTER OF A COURSE IN APPLIED MISSIONARY ANTHROPOLOGY

A missionary training program sacrifices half its potential value if it fails to provide basic anthropological knowledge and does not show the future missioner how this knowledge might be applied to his work. The use of examples and problems taken from mission conditions to illustrate a point in a class of Moral Theology, Catechetics, or Canon Law, as commendable as such a practice may be, is not the full solution. Nor are so-called "area-studies" acceptable substitutes for a generalized study of culture. In one sense area studies are too localized; in another sense they are not specific enough. An essential part of a missionary's knowledge of culture includes a knowledge of his own way of life and of mankind in general — a knowledge area studies cannot provide. Moreover, valuable and necessary as area studies (the ready-made descriptions of a given area) may be, such descriptions are not satisfactory substitutes for a knowledge that is tailored to the actual socio-cultural situation in which the missioner will have to live and according to which he will have to solve his problems. A

generalized course, such as is given in Applied Missionary Anthropology, enables the missionary to study and analyze the truly-
local cultural context rather than merely to have a general idea
about the customs of a broad area like Japan, Latin America, or
India. It enables him to see the particular socio-cultural context
as it really is, not only right here but also right now, a context that
is constantly changing and that varies from one subgroup to another
within any given area. Without belittling area studies as such (they
will always remain valuable and necessary) we wish merely to emphasize the indispensability of a cross-cultural, universally valid and
highly adaptable understanding of cultures, an understanding that
alone will enable the missioner to know (1) human behavior as
such, (2) the behavior of his adopted people, and (3) his own
socially acquired habits. Only such a generalized course in cultures
will make area studies meaningful and practical, enabling the missioner to stand on his own feet, whenever necessary, and to make
wise decisions regarding the many unforeseen and even unheard-
of problems awaiting him on the mission field. And are not all
problems in the last analysis unheard of and unique?

A missionary course in Applied Anthropology would consist of
three parts, the present text being only the first.

Part One: Basic Anthropological Concepts and Principles

Part One presents basic anthropological concepts and principles
pertinent to mission theory as well as mission practice and includes
modern anthropological thought especially regarding the nature,
organization, and dynamics of culture.

However, Part One must do more than impart useful knowledge
and train the missioner in a skill. It must help him acquire the
attitude of an unbiased scientific field worker by ridding him of the
attitude of a know-it-all reformer. It must teach him to view all
strange ways as the people concerned view them. Strange behavioral
patterns (even worship of fetishes, sorcery, and polygamy) must
make sense to him; and they will, if he has learned to look upon
all behavior in its full native context rather than as the behavior
would look in a thoroughly Christianized and Western culture. A
proper understanding of Part One should enable the missionary to
appreciate "strange" customs, which must cease to be "ridiculous"
and "barbarous" even when objectively unscientific, unethical, and
untenable. Even the term "pagan" must lose much of its traditional

and derogatory connotation. Cultural detachment does not mean compromise or approval and acceptance of the untenable; rather, it means *understanding* why the local people are as they are no matter what they are.

However, this sympathetic understanding of a local life-way is only the first step. A missionary must be prepared to go even further than a scientific observer of custom; he must become "all things to all men." Part One of the proposed course would indicate to what extent the missioner can and should be identified with his adopted people (see pp. 347–351).

A proper grasp of the first part of the course would, moreover, enable the missionary to see his vocation in an entirely new light, in a positive rather than exclusively negative light, in the same light in which Christ viewed His vocation: "I come not to destroy but to fulfill" (Matt. 5:17). In other words, "I come to perfect the ideals of My adopted people because I know that they have ideals worth perfecting." Without denying that a nation that does not know God and that has not yet accepted Christ really lives "in darkness and in the shadow of death" (Ps. 106:10), the missionary nevertheless must see *more than* "the darkness of sin and the night of heathenism." The first part of the course should help him realize that his vocation is to make the beautiful in the so-called "pagan" heart even more beautiful, to seek out the naturally good in order to make it supernaturally perfect, to present Christianity not as an enemy of the existing way of life but as a friend possessing the secret that will enable the culture that is already beautiful in many respects reach its God-intended perfection. In short, the lessons of the present book (Part One of the proposed course) should go a long way toward putting an end to missionary negativism, which, unfortunately, is only too prevalent among otherwise zealous and capable apostles of today. To borrow the well-chosen words of Pius XII:

> . . . When the gospel is accepted by diverse races, it does not crush or repress anything good and honorable and beautiful which they have achieved by their native genius and natural endowments . . .

> Although human nature by Adam's unhappy sin has been tainted with an hereditary blemish, it still retains a naturally Christian propensity. If this is illumined by divine light and nurtured by divine grace, it can in time be raised to genuine virtue and supernatural activity (*Evangelii Praecones*:87–88).

Part Two: Ethnographic Techniques for Missionaries

The ethnography sought here is not merely a general description of the culture in question but a kind of "Action Ethnography." Applied Anthropology is interested especially in ethnography that will help bring together the type of information that "Action Anthropology" requires. While general ethnography is equally interested in all aspects of a life-way, "Action Ethnography" is primarily interested in *action* — in our case, *missionary action*. Without neglecting any detail directly or indirectly pertinent to the proper understanding of the local cultural context, "Action Ethnography" would lay *special* stress on such questions as: What qualifications must a native leader possess? What behavior is expected of a spiritual guide? What type of personality in the given society is most influential in bringing about culture change? Who decides the policies of the community? What characteristics make one "likable," "respected," "influential," *etc.?* Through which roles and social rank does the strongest current of communication flow? (Cf. Goodenough, 1962:174–176; Gilbert, 1962–63).

This second portion of the course would consist of two sections, an inventory of culture and field techniques. By "an inventory of culture" is meant a survey of *what* should be looked into. After all, before one can begin an investigation one must know *what* he is to investigate. Since at the present time there is no such "inventory" available, the missionary might in the meantime have recourse to the well-known field guide *Notes and Queries on Anthropology* of the Royal Anthropological Institute of Great Britain and Ireland or the *Outline of Cultural Materials* published by the Human Relations Area Files, Inc., of New Haven, Connecticut. Besides these field guides one should make a careful study of a modern textbook on General Anthropology, such as Honigmann's *The World of Man* or Keesing's *Cultural Anthropology*. These manuals will not only cover the inventory of culture and make the field guides understandable but will also suggest useful selected readings on more specialized topics. Quite in keeping with the nature of culture as an "organism" and with what has been said in the first part of the course, one might very appropriately speak of an "anatomy of culture" (Ewing, 1951) rather than of an "inventory." It is here that the various aspects of culture (economic, social and ideational) are closely scrutinized, dissected, and described.

After the missionary has been thoroughly briefed as to what he should investigate in the way of life of the people with whom he must deal, he can be shown how to go about such an investigation and where he is to look for the necessary data. In the section on "field techniques" he learns the "tricks of the trade" of a missionary-action-ethnographer. Again, until a practical manual on missionary field techniques is available, one might very profitably make use of the following: R. Piddington, An Introduction to Social Anthropology, II, 525–563; R. F. Spencer, ed., Method and Perspective in Anthropology; B. H. Junker, Field Work: An Introduction to the Social Sciences; R.. N. Adams and J. J. Preiss, eds., Human Organization Research.[1]

Part Three: Missionary Anthropology in Action

The third part of the course aims to illustrate concretely and in an orderly manner how the various missionary techniques are to be adjusted in accord with the theory expounded in the first two parts. The following outline might best illustrate what is meant:

I. Anthropology in Intercultural Communication
  A. Homiletic and Catechetical Theory in Cultural Context
  B. Translation in Cultural Context
  C. Mass Communication in Cultural Context
II. Cultural Aspects in Moral and Ascetical Theology
III. Cultural Context and Canon Law
IV. Liturgy and the Cultural Context
  V. Anthropology in Social Action
  A. Education Theory in Cultural Context
  B. Social Work
  C. Medicine
  D. Agricultural and Technological Development
  E. Other Socio-Economic Action and Problems, e.g., Communism, urbanization, industrialization, migrations, etc.
VI The Cultural Context and Training for Leadership.

---

[1] For facts of publication see General Bibliography.

METHOD EMPLOYED IN APPLIED
MISSIONARY ANTHROPOLOGY

Basic Procedures

As already indicated, Applied Missionary Anthropology follows three basic procedures: (1) it goes to the missiologist and the active missionary to learn from them what the theoretical nature, aims, means, and limits of apostolic action are and what the actual needs, problems, goals, and means happen to be; (2) it brings together existing culturological concepts, principles, and techniques pertinent to mission theory and practice; (3) it integrates the two foregoing procedures with view to a better theoretical understanding of the apostolate and with view to arriving at the most efficient, most effective, and at the same time least disorganizing practical approach to missionary work.

Soundness of Procedures

1. THEORETICAL SOUNDNESS

The available culturological concepts, principles, and methods of analysis, experimentation, control, and prediction provide the initial body of theory. We speak of an "initial body of theory" because we have just begun to gather the modern anthropological knowledge and techniques pertinent to missionary work. The present available set of theories, concepts, principles, and techniques must, of course, expand and grow to full maturity; the experimentation, controls, and predictions must become ever more and more refined. The available body of theory must constantly grow in its ability to indicate to the active missionary, with ever greater clarity and certainty, the most effective and least disorganizing policies and approaches truly representative of the scientific age in which we live. There is need for further collation and elaboration of existing theory and there is need for further hypotheses relating to missionary conditions and requirements. Only in this way will the initial body of theory now available grow to maturity and deserve to be numbered among the different subfields of Applied Anthropology (Luzbetak, 1961:165–166).

Although relying heavily on the anthropological developments in Medicine, Industry, Agronomy, Education, and other applied fields, the missionary-anthropologists cannot be mere wholesale borrowers; they must develop their own body of theory because the needs, problems, goals, and means with which they deal differ, at times essentially, from those of such agencies as the U.N.O., the A.I.D., and the Peace Corps. Such agencies, for instance, believe in a policy of non-intervention in local religious and moral beliefs and practices, while the missionary specialist, say an educator or doctor, would not, as a rule, hesitate to help his fellow-missionary engaged in the direct apostolate modify, substitute, or remove a missiologically undesirable religious and moral belief or practice. Then there is also the fact that while government and industry may be interested in medical or technological changes as ends in themselves independent of any other consideration, the missionary specialist must always consider such changes only as subgoals and, therefore, his techniques and policies must never conflict with the main goal, Christianization. Thus a government anthropologist or doctor might very easily suggest birth control devices as the "best" solution to a problem, a solution that is unthinkable as far as the missionary specialist is concerned. Since the limits within which the government and mission anthropologist work are often vastly different, their recommendations as well as theoretical procedures must also differ. The missionary-anthropologist will always have high regard for the authority of the Church which he serves, while other applied anthropologists qua anthropologists need not. The latter have their authorities and policies to obey. The missionary-anthropologist must at all times be guided (as well as limited) by Christian Philosophy, Theology, Canon Law, the statutes of his Prefecture, Vicariate, or Diocese, and even the Rule or Constitutions of his religious order or Congregation, within which limits he must operate both as missionary and as applied anthropologist (Luzbetak, 1961:170–171).

A good missionary-anthropologist will never be so naïve as to suppose that anthropological theory by itself has all the answers. A good applied anthropologist is fully aware that there are many other fields and sources of practical knowledge besides Anthropology: Economics, Sociology, Agronomy, Psychology, Medicine, and other pure and applied sciences — not to mention the various aspects of Missiology, especially Mission History and the Theology of the Missions. The applied anthropologist in the service of the Missions respects and appreciates all these fields, although he realizes that it is humanly impossible for him to master them all. He not only admits their rightful position in missionary work and their validity, but by giving them a culturological perspective he renders these other sources of knowledge and skill truly practical. Thus, for instance, modern Catechetics with its special emphasis on *kerygma* (the essential core of the Christian Good News) has a definite place in modern missionary methods. It is the task of Catechetics to provide the proper content of instruction in Christian Doctrine and to establish the relative theological importance of the various doctrines to be taught. Modern Catechetics emphasizes the importance of keeping Christ constantly in focus when preaching the Good News, for *He* is the heart of the *kerygma* and the "inner core" of the core of essential Christian doctrines. The more closely related a doctrine is to this focal point, the more important it is for true Christian living. As Father Domenico Grasso, S.J., of the Roman Gregorian University puts it:

> . . . grace will have more importance than sin, sanctifying grace more than actual grace, the Holy Spirit more than Our Lady, the Resurrection of Christ more than His childhood, the mystical aspect of the Church more than its juridical, the Church's liturgy more than private devotions; baptism more than penance, the Eucharist more than the Last Anointing; the Bible more than any other book (Grasso, 1961:54).

Not Applied Anthropology but Catechetics tells one in *what* the message of the Good News should consist and what the *relative importance* of each item of that message should be. On the other hand, not Catechetics but Applied Anthropology will tell the missioner *how* this content and its relative importance can be communicated effectively across cultures (see pp. 16–18). Moreover, the aim of preaching the Good News is not knowledge *about* religion but rather a *life* of religion. Here, too, Catechetics tells the missioner what a life of religion is, but it is the task of Applied Anthropology to spell out *in detail and concretely* what a life of religion implies in the given cultural context. In a word, a good missionary-anthropologist clearly understands the complementary role which his field must play in the modern apostolate, at the same time fully appreciating the important roles played by other fields in apostolic action.

2. Practical Soundness

Although a missionary may and should, to some degree at least, be interested in purely theoretical Anthropology, he cannot afford to be a mere theoretician. His must be a practical course in Anthropology because he happens to be a "practitioner." Applied Missionary Anthropology without entering into useless speculations will nevertheless have to deal with a considerable amount of theory. Paradoxically enough, at times nothing could be more practical than "theory."

To be practical the missionary-anthropologist must be, above all, a true realist. True realism does not make it impossible for him to have grand ideas, ideas which he is entitled to defend and promote. He may and even at times should urge Church authorities to alter the purely human limits within which he must operate as missionary and anthropologist, for instance Latin liturgy. Realism merely excludes foolish and blind insistence on impossible solutions.

True realism will also recognize priorities and degrees of urgency. If one cannot cope with all problems, one will cope with those that are most urgent and those with which one is able to cope. If what may be considered to be the best happens to be impossible, the true realist will be satisfied with the second-best. In other words, when applying Anthropology to missionary needs and conditions one must take into full account all obstacles to the theoretically ideal solution. The obstacles may be political, ecclesiastical, or perhaps just the prosaic but only-too-true shortage of men and means. What these obstacles are matters little; as long as they are genuine obstacles one must take them into account. Not a few anthropologists who happen to be visiting or doing field work in a mission country or perhaps are merely reclining in their armchairs and peacefully smoking their pipes thousands of miles from the scene make themselves obnoxious by the many "simple" solutions which they endlessly offer territorial governments and the Missions. This is also true of some armchair missiologists. Such "simple" solutions can come only from pure idealists who do not know the world as it is. Some, of course, are so blind that they do not even try to understand the many important factors that make their "solutions" no solutions at all. The apathy toward Anthropology which certain otherwise practical and experienced government administrators, businessmen, UNESCO and other specialists, as well as not a few mission superiors and bishops feel is not entirely due to ignorance of matters anthropological but often the result of an unfortunate experience with such blind anthropologists. Anthropologists would, therefore, do well to examine their own consciences to see how much they themselves have contributed to the lack of interest in and the prejudice against the application of their science to human problems on the Missions and elsewhere. Blindness especially to non-strictly-anthropological matters has led some anthropologists to do a disservice to their profession by their foolish insistence on the unreal and impossible. Some anthropologists, whose number is fortunately small, become so enamored of what they call "primitive simplicity" that they consciously or unconsciously oppose all change even in a necessarily changing environment. A good missionary-anthropologist, professional or otherwise, will not be an anti-acculturationist no matter how much he personally would prefer to see his people remain in their "primitive simplicity." The policy of missionary accommodation calls for an adjustment to an actual, living, and therefore changing culture, not to a static way of life or to some sort of "golden" past (see p. 347).

The best applied anthropologist is the one who has both the spirit of a good practitioner as well as the spirit of a good theoretician, an idea that goes back to Plato. As a trained anthropologist he will tend toward the theoretically ideal; as one having the down-to-earth views of a practical administrator or active missionary he will have a proper appreciation of the real; and a blending of these two ingredients, the ideal and the real, will give us the type of applied anthropologist that the missionary apostolate needs.

3. THEOLOGICAL SOUNDNESS

The culturological approach to missionary work as developed in the present course may perhaps give one the impression that we are overemphasizing the human element in apostolic action and disregarding the divine. Nothing could be farther from our intentions and from the truth than just such an assumption. Missionary work is essentially a spiritual activity, and true success cannot be measured except in terms of the supernatural. Before taking the present course, or perhaps simultaneously with it, the student should carefully review the tract on Grace in Dogmatic Theology, reflecting seriously on what each doctrine should mean to him personally as missionary; he would do well to read prayerfully the spiritual classic by Dom J. B. Chautard, *Soul of the Apostolate* (Techny, Ill., 1943); and he should meditate fervently on the encyclical *Mystici Corporis* by Pius XII. Nor do we deny the necessity of personal holiness in the missionary. To borrow the eloquent words of Benedict XV:

> But for the man who enters upon the apostolic life there is one attribute that is indispensable. It is of the most critical importance, as We have mentioned before, that he have sanctity of life. For the man who preaches God must himself be a man of God. The man who urges others to despise sin must despise it himself. Preaching by example is a far more effective procedure than vocal preaching. . . . Give the missionary, if you will, every imaginable talent of mind and intellect, endow him with the most extensive learning and the most brilliant culture. Unless these qualities are accompanied by moral integrity they will be of little or no value in the apostolate . . . especially let him be a devout man, dedicated to prayer and constant union with God, a man who goes before the Divine Majesty and fervently pleads the cause of souls. For as he binds himself more and more closely to God, he will receive the grace and assistance of God to a greater and greater degree (*Maximum Illud*, 26–27).

Missionary work is essentially a spiritual activity, and success is primarily the work of Grace and the Holy Spirit. Behind every human effort there must be the Power and Gift of God, otherwise the missioner would indeed be but "as sounding brass and a tinkling cymbal" (1 Cor. 13:1).[2] Scientific planning is no substitute for the Holy Spirit; nor will scientific planning ever force the Holy Spirit to act in any particular way (Amyot, 1955). In fact, sometimes God deliberately chooses "the foolish things of the world" so that He might "confound the wise; and the weak things of the world hath God chosen, that he may confound the strong" (1 Cor. 1:27). These are all basic assumptions or preambles of Applied Missionary Anthropology, established in Theology, not Anthropology. As applied anthropologists we are not denying these basic truths: in a course such as this we must limit ourselves to the *human* side and the *natural* approach and aspects of apostolic problems, for *that* and not the supernatural is the burden of missiological Anthropology.

---

[2] For more on the spirituality of the Missions, see: "Efficiency in the Apostolate," *Christ to the World*, IV (1959), 533–546; "Holiness and Technique: Natural and Supernatural Means of Apostolate," *Christ to the World*, I (1956), No. 4, 132–141; "Christ the Soul of Our Apostolate," *Christ to the World*, IV (1959), 124–132; Andre Seumois, O.M.I., *L'Anima dell' Apostolato Missionario*, Parma, 1961; J. A. McCoy, S.M., *Advice from the Field*, Chapter 6.

By no means can we as missionary-anthropologists be accused of "the heresy of action."

Applied Missionary Anthropology does not deny the free and all-important role of the Holy Spirit in apostolic activities. As far as it is Anthropology it prescinds (but does not deny) the supernatural. It should be noted, however, that Applied Anthropology can be an aid rather than a hindrance to the missioner's supernatural attitude toward his work: first of all, Anthropology presents mission problems to him in their natural but true and overwhelming immensity, thus forcefully convincing him of his own inadequacy and urging him to seek the supernatural assistance which he needs; secondly, it is especially in Anthropology that the missionary learns to know the Nature which Grace presupposes in apostolic work and builds upon.

There is no necessary connection between Grace and Nature, but de facto according to God's usual way of doing things, there is a very close correspondence between the two (Amyot, 1955:739). Although "faith moves mountains," it would definitely be very unsound theology to adopt some sort of "miraculous approach" in mission work rather than the "natural-plus-supernatural" policy. St. Paul advocated this approach when he wrote to the Romans:

> For whosoever shall call upon the name of the Lord, shall be saved. How then shall they call on him, whom they have not believed? Or how shall they believe him, of whom they have not heard? And how shall they hear, without a preacher? And how shall they preach unless they be sent, as it is written: How beautiful are the feet of them that preach the gospel of peace, of them that bring glad tidings of good things! (Rom. 10:13-15.)

Missiological Anthropology maintains, as did St. Paul, that missionary work presupposes a "preacher." This preacher must be "heard," that is, be understood, for to preach in any other way would be the same as not to preach at all. Unless the preacher is "heard," the people would still be without the necessary preacher, the natural instrument of Grace. Applied Missionary Anthropology aims to train the preacher to understand his people so that his people could understand him, so that he might really be "heard," so that he might become the natural instrument of Grace, so that Grace might build upon Nature, for "How shall they believe him, of whom they have not heard? And how shall they hear, without a preacher?"

Missiological Anthropology rests on a solid theological basis. In fact, one can justly wonder how theologically sound a mission approach is that is not thoroughly permeated with anthropological principles.

MISSIONARY CONTRIBUTION TO ANTHROPOLOGY

One of England's great missionary-anthropologists, Edward W. Smith, in his presidential address after having been elected president of the Royal Anthropological Institute declared: "Because of the missionary's contribution to anthropology, as well as because of the utility of this science for the missionary in his daily activity, social anthropology might almost be considered a missionary science" (Smith, 1934). Smith was not exaggerating the great debt anthropologists owe missionaries for the contributions made to their science. In fact, from the very beginning of Mission History to our own times the main observers of cultures were missionaries. Much of the folklore of northern and eastern Europe (e.g. the Kelts, Germans, Slavs, and Greenlanders) is derived from early missionary sources such as De situ Daniae by Canon Adam of Bremen (d. 1076), the Chronicon Slavorum by Helmold of Lübeck, and the various chronicles by Monk Regino (907–967), Nestor (c. 1100), Bishop Thietmar of Merseburg (d. 1019), and Bishop Kadlubek of Cracow (c. 1210). The observations of missionaries during the following three centuries have been even more abundant. Well known to historians are the observations of missionaries to the Orient such as John de Plano, Carpini, William Ruysbroeck, Prince Hayton, John of Corvino, John of Marignola, and Jordanus Catalani. Then came the period of the great discoveries (1500–1800). The first descriptions of the inhabitants of the Americas, Oceania, and Africa of this period are again mostly of missionary origin, e.g., Christoval Molino, Jose d'Acosta, Dobrizhoffer, de Charlevoix, and Ribeirade. In fact, the very first strictly anthropological study ever made was that of the French Jesuit Joseph Francois Lafitau (1670–1740), the author of the four-volume ethnography entitled Moeurs des sauvages américains comparées aux moeurs des premiers temps (Paris, 1724).

Among the better-known missionary-ethnographers of the 19th century was the Protestant Bishop R. H. Codrington, the author of the classic The Melanesians, first printed at Oxford in 1891 and recently (1957) reprinted by the Human Relations Area Files of New Haven.

The greatest stimulus came in the beginning of this century with the young missionary organization, the Society of the Divine Word. It was the conviction of its founder, Father Arnold Janssen, and one of its members, Father Wilhelm Schmidt, that no one was in a better position to gather information about the various cultures throughout the world than the missionary, provided that he had some training in Ethnology and continued to receive guidance while in the field. The missionary, they felt, enjoyed many advantages over the non-missionary ethnographer: he usually had the full confidence of his people; he knew their language; he also remained among them for a much longer time than any professional ethnographer could ever hope to remain while on an occasional field trip. The real stimulus came with the founding of the journal *Anthropos* in 1906, about which Robert H. Lowie, one of America's leading anthropologists, wrote: "Ethnology owes much to Schmidt for the establishment of *Anthropos*, a journal second to none in the field . . ." (1937:192). Or as Dr. Elkin, one of Australia's leading anthropologists, expressed it:

> The establishment of an international anthropological journal, *Anthropos*, by a missionary order, the Society of the Divine Word, and its maintenance for the past forty-five years has itself been a remarkable contribution to anthropology, and the foundation more recently (in 1937) of a similar journal, the *Annali Lateranensi*, by the Pontificio Museo is also very welcome. Through these media, the anthropological and linguistics studies of Roman Catholic missionaries are made available to the scientific world . . . (1953:8).

The energetic Father Schmidt soon stirred up interest in ethnographic research among Catholic missionaries of various religious orders, but perhaps among no group was the response so enthusiastic as among Father Schmidt's own confreres. He trained many of them himself while professor of Linguistics and Ethnology at St. Gabriel's mission seminary near Vienna, encouraged them to report back from the field, and constantly corresponded with them. In 1921 he became lecturer of Ethnology at the University of Vienna. He later became head of the Department of Anthropology of the University of Fribourg. At both universities he had the opportunity to train professional missionary anthropologists, some of whom became instructors of missionaries at various training centers and universities of Europe and America. The establishment of the Anthropos Institute at Mödling near Vienna in 1932 (later transferred to Fribourg and now located near Bonn, Germany) facilitated the publication of the journal and other anthropological works and provided a center for research, training, and guidance. Field trips by professionally trained ethnologists associated with the Anthropos Institute have been numerous indeed (Rahmann, 1956: 7–10). Veteran missionaries have been given opportunities to receive professional training in Anthropology. Although the Anthropos publications were not intended to be outlets exclusively for missionary-anthropologists, a great portion of the 57 large volumes of the journal and of perhaps as many volumes of the various linguistic and ethnological monograph series of the Institute has come from the pen of missionaries. Many books and articles inspired by the Anthropos movement have, of course, been published elsewhere. Father Wilhelm Schmidt's own monumental (12 volumes) *Der Ursprung der Gottesidee* was given to a German publishing company. Father Schmidt and his early associates will go down in anthropological history as among the most prolific writers of their time. Father Schmidt has authored more than 600 books and articles; Father Martin Gusinde, S.V.D., 150; Father Wilhelm Koppers, S.V.D., 200; Father Paul Schebesta, S.V.D., 130.

Thanks to the inspiration received from Father Schmidt, other culturological journals soon appeared, all of which were edited or edited and published by the Divine Word Missionaries: the *Wiener Beiträge zur Kulturgeschichte und Linguistik* was edited for many years by Father Schmidt's closest collaborator, Father Wilhelm Koppers, S.V.D., of the University of Vienna; the *Monumenta Serica, Journal of Oriental Studies*, was published by the Catholic University of Peking, a Divine Word university, at first in China and then, after the seizure of the university by the Communists, in Japan; the *Folklore Studies* is likewise edited and maintained by the Divine Word Missionaries in Japan; the *Annali Lateranensi* of the Lateran Museum in Rome was edited by Father Wilhelm Schmidt from 1937 to 1939 and by Father M. Schulien, S.V.D., since 1940.

Of this activity R. Firth, perhaps the best-known anthropologist of England today, has the following evaluation to make:

His [Fr. Schmidt's] foundation of the Journal *Anthropos* was one of the milestones in the development of more systematic anthropological records from exotic cultures, and the stimulus that he gave to field-workers in cultural anthropology and linguistics is difficult to measure because of its pervasiveness (Henninger, 1956:56).

Father Schmidt's influence has been confined mainly to Europe and therefore also mainly to *European* missionaries. In the United States the chief promoter was Monsignor Montgomery Cooper, the founder of the Catholic Anthropological Conference (now the Catholic Anthropological Association) with headquarters at the Catholic University of America, Washington, D. C. The Association publishes the *Anthropological Quarterly* and has the following aims: (1) "anthropological research and publication by missionaries and professional anthropologists, and (2) anthropological training among candidates for mission work." As in the case of the *Anthropos*, the *Anthropological Quarterly* invites scientific contributions from both missionaries as well as professional anthropologists. Although the results had by Monsignor Cooper in America can hardly compare with those of Father Schmidt in Europe, American mission-sending societies have in recent years become more and more aware of the role of Anthropology in missionary work and missionary training. This new awareness is due mainly to the promotion of the Mission Secretariat in Washington, D. C., and such universities as Fordham and the Catholic University of America.

The main promoters of Anthropology among American Protestant missionaries are Eugene Nida and William Smalley. Nida is executive secretary of the American Bible Society and the author of a number of useful books and articles of missiological interest, notably his *Customs and Cultures* and *Message and Mission*. Smalley is the editor of *Practical Anthropology*, a very useful, non-technical journal for Protestant missionaries. The chief Protestant training centers in Anthropology are the Kennedy School of Missions (Hartford Seminary Foundation, Hartford, Connecticut) and Wheaton College of Wheaton, Illinois. However, the main contribution of American Protestant missionaries has been in the field of Linguistics rather than Social Anthropology or Ethnography, and their achievements have been considerable, thanks especially to the training program of the Summer Institute of Linguistics.

It has been with purpose that so much space has been devoted to the consideration of missionary contributions to Anthropology. One of the aims of the present course is to enable the missionary to make at least some small contribution to Anthropology and to co-operate with such organizations as the Anthropos Institute and the Catholic Anthropological Association.

In concluding this section it might be well to point out that any contribution made to the "Science of Man" is a contribution to the "Science of the Missions." A truly scientific mission strategy presupposes that the mission personnel has learned to make exact inquiries into the mind and ways of the society concerned, knows how to verbalize experience, and actually records the experience. All this, of course, requires anthropological training. Although we have emphasized the importance of being able to stand on one's own feet when called upon to do so, by no means was it our intention to imply that missionaries should not learn from one another. Mission work is essentially teamwork, and nothing could be more detrimental to the team than to make each member learn everything "the hard way, the way I had to learn it." Missionaries are like an army, the efficiency of which will be very low unless the experience of the various branches of the armed forces as well as of the individual soldier are pooled.

The ideal method of sharing missionary experience would be through actual publication, and if Applied Missionary Anthropology is to reach maturity, publication is indispensable. Very often, however, actual publication is not feasible; nevertheless, missionary experience should be recorded, not only as personal notes preserved in one's own files but multiplied in some way at least. Papers read at missionary conferences, proceedings of larger meetings, or even private studies should be made available to fellow-missionaries and visiting social scientists. They should, by all means, be kept on file at the mission headquarters and made accessible especially to the newcomer.

Moreover, cultures are greatly variable and their dynamics are complicated so that often a single life-span is hardly enough to reach definite conclusions regarding certain more difficult but vital questions. Such ethnological and missiological problems must be studied "diachronically," that is, over longer periods of time. Now, any such prolonged inquiry will require careful recording and preservation of data; in a word, it will call for the sharing of knowledge.

Furthermore, almost any inquiry into so complicated a matter as culture needs checking and re-checking, not only by the original inquirer but also by others. Only by verbalizing, recording, and sharing data will testing and re-testing by others be made possible.

It is indeed unfortunate that, as is sometimes the case, when a missionary must leave his area for reasons of health or to assume a more responsible position elsewhere, his successor is obliged to begin the study of the local cultural context as if it had never been studied before. With reliable ethnological and missiological data on hand, the newcomer could easily continue where his predecessor left off; he might thus build upon the valuable experience of his predecessor instead of repeating mistakes that had been made before. Only if experience is shared will Applied Missionary Anthropology progress. Through contributions to the "Science of Man" and the "Science of the Missions" the modern apostle can not only prolong his missionary usefulness but extend it well beyond old age and the grave.

SELECTED READINGS

1. **What Is Anthropology?**
    1) E. Adamson Hoebel, *Man in the Primitive World*, pp. 3–16.
    2) F. M. Keesing, *Cultural Anthropology*, pp. 1–15.
    * 3) M. J. Herskovits, *Man and His Works*, pp. 3–14.
    4) A. L. Kroeber, *Anthropology*, pp. 1–13.
    5) Beals and Hoijer, *An Introduction to Anthropology*, pp. 1–20.
    6) *Encyclopedia of Social Science* under "Anthropology," II, 73–110.

2. **Why Anthropology?**
    * 1) R. Firth, *Human Types: An Introduction to Social Anthropology*.
    * 2) C. Kluckhohn, *Mirror for Man: The Relation of Anthropology to Modern Life*.
    3) A. L. Kroeber, ed., *Anthropology Today*, pp. 741–894.
    4) Scott Gilbert, "Tanganyika and the Peace Corps: Unanswered Questions," *Human Organization*, XXI (Winter, 1962–63), 286–289.
    N.B. For additional readings, see pages 3–4, notes 2 and 3.

3. **Relation of Anthropology to Other Sciences**
    1) A. L. Kroeber, "So-called Social Science," *The Nature of Culture*, pp. 66–78.
    2) Sol Tax, "The Integration of Anthropology," *Current Anthropology* (Thomas, ed.), pp. 313–328.
    3) R. Redfield, "Relations of Anthropology to the Social Sciences and to the Humanities," *Anthropology Today* (Kroeber, ed.), pp. 728–738.

4) R. Redfield, "The Art of Social Science," *American Journal of Sociology*, LIV (1948), 181–190.
5) R. Benedict, "Anthropology and the Humanities," *American Anthropologist*, L (1948), 585–593.

N.B. See also *Current Anthropology*, IV (1963), 138–154.

4. Missionary Contribution to Anthropology

1) A. Rosenstiel, "Anthropology and the Missionary," *Journal of the Royal Anthropological Institute*, LXXXIX (1959), 107–115.
* 2) W. A. Smalley, "Anthropological Study and Missionary Scholarship," *Practical Anthropology*, VII (1960), 113–123.

5. Father Wilhelm Schmidt, S.V.D., and the Anthropos Movement

* 1) R. H. Lowie, *History of Ethnological Theory*, pp. 188–193.
* 2) M. Gusinde, "Wilhelm Schmidt, S.V.D., 1868–1954," *American Anthropologist*, LVI (1954), 868–870.
3) P. Schebesta, "Pater Wilhelm Schmidt, S.V.D., 1868–1954," *Man*, LIV (1954), 89–90.

Numerous articles available in German, e.g., *Anthropos*, XLIX (1954), 385–432, 627–658; LI (1956), 1–18, 19–61; LII (1957), 263–276.

6. What Methods Does Anthropology Use to Achieve Its Aims?

1) R. F. Spencer, ed., *Method and Perspective in Anthropology*.
2) *Notes and Queries on Anthropology*, Royal Anthropological Institute of Great Britain and Ireland, sixth edition, pp. 3–16, 36–62.
* 3) A. L. Kroeber, ed., *Anthropology Today*, pp. 401–475.
* 4) J. J. Honigmann, *The World of Man*, pp. 23–109.
5) W. Schmidt, *The Culture Historical Method of Ethnology* (a highly technical and difficult exposition of the culture-historical method).
6) R. Firth, ed., *Man and Culture: An Evaluation of the Work of Malinowski*.
7) A. R. Radcliffe-Brown, *A Natural Science of Society*.
8) A. L. Kroeber, *The Nature of Culture*, pp. 139–151.
* 9) R. Piddington, *An Introduction to Social Anthropology*, II, 525–563.
10) R. N. Adams and J. J. Preiss, eds., *Human Organization Research*.
11) Sister M. Inez Hilger, *Field Guide to the Ethnological Study of Child Life*.
12) G. O. Lang, "Theoretical Methods and Approaches," *Anthropological Quarterly*, XXXII (1959), 41–66.

7. History of Anthropological Thought

* 1) R. H. Lowie, *The History of Ethnological Theory*.

2) Sol Tax, "From Lafitau to Radcliffe-Brown," *Social Anthropology of North American Indians* (F. Eggan, ed.), pp. 445–481.

* 3) A. L. Kroeber, "History of Anthropological Thought," in William L. Thomas (ed.), *Current Anthropology*, pp. 293–312.

4) A. Wallace, ed., *Selected Papers of the Fifth International Congress of Anthropological and Ethnological Sciences, Philadelphia, September 1–9, 1956*, Section I, "Current Status of Anthropological and Ethnological Studies," pp. 11–86.

5) J. Gillin, *The Ways of Men*, pp. 1–20.

6) Beals and Hoijer, *An Introduction to Anthropology*, pp. 12–15, 600–621.

7) L. A. White, *The Science of Culture*, pp. 55–117.

8. Specialized Fields of Anthropology

(This section of the Selected Readings is intended as a general orientation in the available introductory literature and only for browsing purposes.)

Perhaps the best over-all introductory manual in Physical Anthropology is M. F. Ashley Montagu's *An Introduction to Physical Anthropology*. For the anthropometric and biometric techniques, see also Kelso and Ewing, *Introduction to Physical Anthropology Laboratory Manual*, and Beals and Hoijer, *An Introduction to Anthropology*, pp. 81–111. For human genetics, see Hoebel, Jennings, and Smith, *Readings in Anthropology*, pp. 59–87, and Beals and Hoijer, *op. cit.*, pp. 55–80. For a discussion on evolution, see W. E. LeGros Clark, *History of the Primates: An Introduction to the Study of Fossil Man*. For a simplified treatise on Prehistoric Archaeology, see K. P. Oakley, *Man the Toolmaker*; R. J. Braidwood, *Prehistoric Men*; Grahame Clark, *Archaeology and Society*. For archaeological dating techniques, see Frederick E. Zeuner's *Dating the Past*. For modern archaeological developments, see the various articles in A. L. Kroeber, ed., *Anthropology Today* and William L. Thomas, ed., *Current Anthropology*. A basic Linguistics library for practical missionary training purposes would include at least the following introductory manuals: E. Nida, *Learning a Foreign Language*; R. Lado, *Linguistics across Cultures*; H. A. Gleason, *An Introduction to Descriptive Linguistics*; C. F. Hockett, *A Course in Modern Linguistics*; W. A. Smalley, *Manual of Articulatory Phonetics*; K. L. Pike, *Phonemics: A Technique for Reducing Languages to Writing*; E. G. Pike and staff, *Laboratory Manual for Pike's Phonemics*; K. L. Pike, *Tone Languages*; Elson and Pickett, *Beginning Morphology and Syntax*; W. Merrifield, *Laboratory Manual for Morphology and Syntax*; S. Gudschinsky, *Handbook of Literacy*; E. Nida, *Bible Translating*; E. Nida, *God's Word in Man's Language*; E. Nida, *Message and Mission*; R. Knox, *The Trials of a Translator*; N. Brooks, *Language and Lan-*

guage Learning; E. W. Stevick, Helping People Learn English; C. C. Fries, The Structure of English; P. Roberts, English Sentences; W. N. Francis, Structure of American English; H. Hoijer, ed., Language in Culture; R. A. Hall, Jr., Linguistics and Your Language; L. Bloomfield, Language; K. L. and E. V. Pike, Live Issues in Descriptive Linguistics Analysis; M. Joos, Readings in Linguistics; E. Sapir, Language: An Introduction to the Study of Speech; E. Sapir, Culture, Language, and Personality; C. C. Fries, Teaching and Learning English as a Foreign Language. For literature on highly specialized fields of Anthropology, see the following examples: E. Adamson Hoebel, The Law of Primitive Man; J. J. Honigmann, Culture and Personality; R. Nettl, Music in Primitive Culture; P. Radin, Primitive Man as Philosopher; W. Koppers, Primitive Man and His World Picture; Lessa and Vogt, Reader in Comparative Religion; M. J. Herskovits, Economic Anthropology.

REVIEW QUESTIONS

1. What is Anthropology? (pp. 23–24)
2. Show how Anthropology subdivides into specialized fields (p. 24) and define the various branches (pp. 24–29). What orientation (historical or scientific) does each branch have? (p. 27)
3. How does a course in Applied Anthropology for Missionaries differ from a course in Missiology? (pp. 31–32)
4. Give a brief outline of Applied Missionary Anthropology. (pp. 34–38)
5. What are the three basic procedures followed in Applied Missionary Anthropology? (p. 39)
6. Indicate the reasons for saying that the method followed in Applied Missionary Anthropology is theoretically (pp. 39–41), practically (pp. 42–43), and theologically (pp. 43–46) sound.
7. What contribution have missionaries made to Anthropology? (pp. 46–51)

TOPICS FOR CLASSROOM DISCUSSION AND PAPERS

1. So you are going to the Congo. Why don't you just leave the poor people alone? They were happy without the missionaries, why fill their minds with all sorts of religious scruples? Missionaries have no right to disrupt the lives of peoples in the Congo or anywhere else. (Comment on the last sentence.)
2. Show how unfounded the "anti-anthropologist" spirit really is and how the missionary and professional social scientist should co-operate. For thoughts on the subject read J. M. Hickmann, "Understanding the Jugglers," Practical Anthropology, VIII (1961), 217–220; H. W.

Fehderau, "Missionary Endeavor and Anthropology," *Practical Anthropology*, VIII (1961), 221–223; J. O. Buswell III, "Anthropologist and Administrator," *Practical Anthropology*, VIII (1961), 157–167.

3. Browse through the *Anthropological Quarterly*, *Worldmission*, and *Christ to the World* and pick out at least ten topics treated in these journals that are of special interest to a missionary-anthropologist.

4. Debate: The advancement of Anthropology should be left to the professional anthropologist.

II.

THE NATURE OF CULTURE

CHAPTER THREE

CULTURE: A DESIGN FOR LIVING

ACCORDING to Kroeber, one of America's most respected anthropologists, "the most significant accomplishment of anthropology in the first half of the twentieth century has been the extension and clarification of the concept of culture" (1950:87). The concept of culture is also the anthropologist's most significant contribution to the missionary endeavor. Nothing could be more fundamental than a proper understanding of the term. A failure to grasp the nature of culture would be a failure to grasp much of the nature of missionary work itself.

The claim just made remains true despite the fact that there is still much that anthropologists cannot tell us about the nature of culture. Anthropologists still argue among themselves about how culture is to be defined and what some of its essential characteristics are (see Selected Readings, p. 71). Perhaps the clearest analysis available is that of Kluckhohn and Kelly, "The Concept of Culture" (1945:78–106). Also useful is the presentation of Kroeber and Kluckhohn made in 1952 in which they undertake the triple task (1) of making available "in one place for purposes of reference a collection of definitions [of culture] by anthropologists, sociologists, psychologists, philosophers and others . . . ," (2) of documenting "the gradual emergence and refinement of the concept . . . ," and (3) of assisting "other investigators in reaching agreement and greater precision in definition by pointing out and commenting upon agreements and disagreements in the definitions thus far propounded" (1952:4). The authors bring together no less than 164 different definitions (1952:38–40), but, as they say, actually "close to three hundred definitions" are used throughout the book (1952:149).

To define culture, therefore, is no easy matter. In fact, there seem to be as many definitions as there are anthropologists. One of the earliest definitions was that of E. B. Taylor: "Culture or civilization is that complex whole which includes knowledge, belief, art, morals, law, customs, and any other capabilities and habits acquired by man as a member of society" (1874:1). Lowie defined culture in much the same manner: Culture is "the sum total of what an individual acquires from his society — those beliefs, customs, artistic norms, food-habits, and crafts which come to him not by his own creative activity but as a legacy from the past, conveyed by formal or informal education" (1937:3). Some of the definitions formulated are as simple as "total social heredity" and "tradition," while others are far more complicated. Kluckhohn proposed the simplified formula "culture is the total life way of a people, the social legacy the individual acquires from his group" (1949a:17). Gillin suggested that "culture consists of patterned and functionally interrelated customs common to specifiable individual human beings composing specifiable social groups or categories" (1948:181). Keesing sums up culture as "the totality of man's learned, accumulated experience which is socially transmitted, or, more briefly, the behavior acquired through social learning" (1958:18).

A good definition does not pretend to exhaust the meaning of a term; rather, it aims merely to indicate as concisely as possible the essential notes of the given concept. The particular wording will depend largely on what one wishes to emphasize and how explicit one wishes to be in regard to what otherwise might justifiably be merely implied. Although clear concepts are more important than clear definitions, a good definition does serve a purpose and cannot be ignored; it serves as a quick and handy reference, prevents much misunderstanding, and serves as a reference point for further discussion and clarification.

The definitions cited above emphasize the following characteristics of culture: culture is a *way of life*; culture is the *total* plan for living; it is functionally organized into a *system*; it is *acquired through learning*; it is the way of life of a *social group*, not of an individual as such. The present chapter (entitled "Culture a Design for Living") aims to clarify the first three characteristics mentioned; the following two chapters ("Culture and the Individual" and "Culture and Society") deal with the remaining notes of culture.

CULTURE AS A WAY OF LIFE

Culture is a design for living. It is a *plan according to which society adapts itself to its physical, social, and ideational environ-*

ment. A plan for coping with the physical environment would include such matters as food production and all technological knowledge and skill. Political systems, kinship and family organization, and law are examples of social adaptation, a plan according to which one is to interact with his fellows. Man copes with his ideational environment through knowledge, art, magic, science, philosophy, and religion. Cultures are but different answers to essentially the same human problems (Chapter Twelve).

Although we speak of culture elements as being forms of adaptation and therefore responses to human needs, we do not thereby subscribe to blind cultural determinism. Frequently two social groups in more or less similar environments will follow entirely distinct methods of coping with the problem associated with those environments. Environment may indeed limit culture but it by no means determines it. At most one can say that at times a high correlation exists between environment and certain aspects of culture.

Nor are we to imply that the responses to the human needs are always successful. Cultures are *only as a rule* successful designs for living. They generally bring a distinct lessening of tensions and provide the organization, balance, security, and satisfaction necessary for human existence. The fact is that some adaptive patterns actually give rise to new problems and create tensions and frustrations rather than dissipate them. When we speak of culture as being a way of life or a manner of coping with human problems we prescind from the success or objectivity of the solutions provided by the particular culture. Culture is merely the way a given society *tries* to be successful. Culture is only a blueprint or plan promising success (Kluckhohn and Kelly, 1945:86).

The details of the blueprint or plan for living will differ from society to society, and no two ways of life will be exactly alike. Cultures are indeed greatly variable; cultures are, in fact, unique (Herskovits, 1950:18–19). Some of the blueprints are, of course, more similar in their details than others. The non-literate food-gatherers, for example, have strikingly similar economic, social, and religious patterns, whether these so-called "true primitives" are found in the rain forests of Africa, in Northern Luzon, in Southeast Asia, or America; in fact, their cultures are so similar that Father Wilhelm Schmidt built his "oldest level of culture" on these "otherwise inexplainable" similarities. Societies with a pastoral-nomadic economy likewise have ways of life that agree in many points.

CULTURE AS A TOTAL DESIGN

The design, blueprint, or plan for living called "culture" is essentially complete: it is a "complex whole" (Tylor), "the sum total" (Lowie and Linton), "all designs" (Kluckhohn), and "the totality" (Keesing). Culture embraces all facets of life. To the anthropologist a prosaic garbage heap is as much an element of culture as the masterpieces of Beethoven, Dante, and Michelangelo. To the anthropologist, a hungry cannibal savagely devouring a piece of leg of man (and thus following his "design for living") is no less "cultured" than a great authority on etiquette like Emily Post daintily nibbling on a piece of leg of lamb. A culture is an essentially complete and detailed plan embracing all aspects or needs of human life, whatever the responses to these needs may be.

The totality of which we speak embraces the *overt* as well as *covert* responses, the *manifest* as well as the *implicit*, the *theoretical* or *ideal* as well as the *actual* or *real*, the *universals, alternatives,* and *specialties.* These terms will need, of course, further clarification.

A design for living includes more than such *manifest* items as food-getting, housing, clothing, ornamentation, eating habits, mating practices, marriage, family organization, kinship system, status, social class, ownership, inheritance, trade, government, war, law, religion, magic, and language. Culture embraces all these items but much more. Such patterns are easily observable; they are therefore said to be "manifest" and are called "behavioral patterns." But culture is more than the what, when, how, and where of behavior; it also includes the structuring or organization of parts. Not only does it include the manifest or explicit elements but also the implicit, the systematic arrangement of the constituents of culture, for culture is a *system* as the words "design," "blueprint," and "plan" imply. In fact, this particular facet of culture is so important that a large portion of the present book (Part III) will be devoted to it. This "underlying," "latent," or "implicit" arrangement of a lifeway is referred to as the "ideal patterns." The organization of a culture is not immediately manifest, nor are the individuals following such patterns always able to describe how the numberless elements are organized into a system. Rather, the anthropologist gets at these ideal patterns by careful inquiries and analysis: (1) he must discover the *function* of the various cultural constituents (the role each part plays and what purpose it serves toward the maintenance of the whole life-way); (2) he must discover how the constituents are arranged into a single whole (*integration*); (3) he must also inquire into the "motivation" that unifies the culture content into a single whole, "the values, goals, and premises," "the philosophy," "the psychology," or "mentality" of the people in question — in a word, the *configuration* of the particular culture. In other words, the plan for living (the "blueprint" called "culture") indicates not only the type of material to be used (culture content) but also how this building material is to be organized (internal patterning). In fact, no two cultures have an identical ordering of parts. It is theoretically possible for two cultures to consist of the same content but to be quite differently organized, just as it is possible to have two buildings of similar materials but of an entirely different appearance.

Overt culture embraces all the socially shared ideas (patterns) that become externalized through movement and muscular activity, while *covert* culture includes the latent patterns of belief, thought, and evaluation.

The totality of a life-way includes not only actual behavior but also theoretical standards, in other words both the *ideal* as well as the *real* culture. Man is not a mere automaton or slave of culture. Since he is endowed with a free will and subject to considerable selfish pressures, personal preferences, imperfections, and weaknesses and has had an experience that is exclusively *his*, he will be moved at times to act contrary to the "rules" (*i.e.*, culture) of his social group. A norm may be observed quite scrupulously in public but disregarded in private. The theoretically ideal may, in fact, sometimes constitute the exception rather than the rule in actual life. Sometimes the ideal is never realized. Gunner Myrdal's *An American Dilemma* (New York, 1944) clearly shows how American practice sometimes deviates from American ideals, a fact no less true of other societies. In many societies, for example, the "ideal" punishment for a wife's infidelity is mutilation. Thus, in the Caucasus, it used to be the custom to cut her nose off as a form of revenge and as a lesson to the rest of the community. The fact is that many, if not most, adultresses were pardoned and spared the humiliating disfiguration (Luzbetak, 1951:169). Or again, as Christians we are to love our enemies and do good to those who hate us. In actual life, however, such an ideal is perhaps more the exception than the rule. Anthropologists, therefore, frequently speak of a people's "self-image" or of the "ideal personality type," which might be defined as the culturally determined conceptualization of a "good" person.

The remaining terms, to be explained fully in the following chapter, might be defined thus: *universals* are those patterns which are expected of every normal member of a given society; *specialties* are the patterns expected only of certain groups within the society; *alternatives* are facultative patterns.

SUMMARY AND SELECTED MISSIOLOGICAL APPLICATION

Summary

Culture as a design for living is a plan for coping with a particular society's physical, social, and ideational environment. It is a complete and more or less successful adaptive system, which includes the total content as well as the organization of the content.

Selected Missiological Applications

1. Culture Is Essentially an Adaptive System

1) If the missionary keeps in mind that every culture, whatever its form may be, is an honest attempt to cope with human problems, customs will cease to be "ridiculous." They may be "pagan," and approval may be impossible; but realizing that the society is "doing its best" in its struggle with its physical, social, and ideational environment, the missioner should find it relatively easy to appreciate the adaptive effort made. In a word, *the basis of missionary empathy is the understanding of culture as an adaptive system.*

2) *The missioner who has learned to look upon a people's way of life as an adaptive system will be less inclined to become discouraged in the face of opposition and lack of co-operation.* To repeat a very common complaint of missionaries — "I just can't understand my people. They have hardly been baptized and they're off to their old pagan ways." Looking at the situation from a purely natural point of view, one might rightly ask: "And why shouldn't they go back to their old ways? To the society in question survival itself may sometimes seem to depend on certain traditional adaptive patterns" (see pp. 294–295). Certain traditional patterns for which

Christianity does not yet serve as a satisfactory substitute are clung to with as much vehemence as life itself. No matter how unscientific or untheological the non-Christian adaptive system may be, it is the only way of life with which the society has really had experience and therefore can fully trust. It is the only system or design for living that has till now been able to produce harmony in the lives of the people, the only system that has so far provided the necessary security and succeeded in giving meaning to life. Although the Gospel was meant for all nations, nevertheless, in the given psycho-cultural circumstances it may be more "natural" for the society to suspect and resist the missionary's message than to receive it with open arms. Not ill will but the natural instinct of self-preservation may be at the basis of much of the suspicion, resistance, and rejection of the Gospel. The problem consists not only in a weak Faith (with a capital letter) but also in a very strong faith (with a small letter) — faith in the "trustworthy" traditional design for living.

3) *The missionary's message, whether spiritual or socio-economic, must at all times be focused on the local culture as an adaptive system.* The missionary's message from the pulpit, in the confessional, in the classroom, over the radio, in the daily newspaper, or perhaps in a simple mimeographed catechism must be presented not as a list of isolated and arbitrary laws but as suggestions that can perfect the traditional adaptive system. Christianity should be presented as Divine Wisdom intended to teach all mankind how to adapt itself to the problems of life in a truly meaningful and successful way. Christian doctrines and practices, and, for that matter, any innovation which the missioner may want to introduce should not be left dangling in the air but geared into the adaptive system in question and presented as something that will actually complete and perfect it. The Gospel will not be accepted (and this is true also of medical practices and improved agricultural techniques) unless these new "wares" are presented as *missing* in the accepted design for living — missing in the sense that the traditional adaptive system requires their presence. The missioner is trying to "sell" something that is intended primarily for the adaptive system, and so he must "advertise." The Gospel will not be accepted unless the non-Christian feels that it is related in a vital way to his everyday life. New agricultural methods and products, however superior to the traditional ways they may be, will not be

accepted unless shown to fill some felt-need. In his address to the Second World Congress of Lay Apostles (October 6, 1957), Pius XII wisely reminded Asian and African indigenous teachers to "take greater care not to separate doctrine from life itself."

The proper sequence to be followed in religious as well as secular education should be determined not so much by some favorite catechism or widely used textbook in Europe and America as by the felt-needs of the people instructed. One of the very first tasks of any new missionary should be to study the traditional adaptive system so as to learn from it what the particular felt-needs are. The non-Christian will accept only so much of the Gospel as *he* feels he needs. One of the chief reasons for the spread of Communism is the ability of its proponents to present it as a *real* necessity. The missioner, too, if he *is* to be successful, must teach with focus on the actual felt-needs of his people. Oscar Lewis (1959:159) points out, for example, how a certain Catholic Mexican gave as reason for his joining the spiritists the fact that now religious rites are no longer held in Latin and therefore understandable to him and that spiritists "help people in trouble. They cure sickness and fight black magic with white." The needs of this Mexican were not filled by the Catholicism as preached by the missionary, who was too impersonal, taken up with ritual without making it understandable and meaningful, preaching too many moral sermons that were mere lists of do's and don'ts, with little to say about "what do I get out of this." In northeast Brazil, known for its poverty and Communism, a Catholic recently told an American reporter visiting the area: "See, God gave me all these children, all twelve of them, but I have to go to the Communists to feed them."

The many still unrecognized but nonetheless objective needs must eventually be felt too, but psychologically and pedagogically such objective but still-unfelt needs must wait their turn before they are accepted and integrated into the existing design for living. The normal pedagogical and psychological progression is from the known to the unknown, from the assumed to the still-unrecognized, from the felt to the still-unfelt. The starting point in instructing non-Christians is the non-Christian set of premises, values, and goals; from these existing assumptions, emotionally charged attitudes, **and** driving forces the missioner leads the non-Christian to new conclusions, new premises, new attitudes, and new motivations, **and from** there he progresses farther and farther, but always from the already-felt to the still-unfelt. Communists have mastered this principle so well that some of the deepest and most insipid theories of Marx and Lenin have been grasped even by simplest societies. Although in recent years much headway has been made in mission catechetical and pastoral methods, this basic anthropological, psychological, and pedagogical principle of starting and progressing in accord with felt-needs as much as possible has not been sufficiently emphasized even though the approach is centuries-old. St. Augustine, the great knower of the heart and ways of Man, expressed this basic principle in his *De Doctrina Christiana:* a man, he said, will be moved to action

> if what you promise is what he likes, if the danger of which you speak appears real, if your censures are directed against something he hates, if your recommendations are in harmony with what he embraces, if he regrets what you say is regrettable, if he rejoices over what you claim is a reason for joy, if his heart is sympathetic toward those whose misery you describe, if he avoids those who you advise should be avoided . . . not merely imparting knowledge about things that ought to be done but rather moving them to do that which they already know must be done (*De Doctrina Christiana*, IV, 12).

St. Augustine thus implicitly agrees with the modern missiologist that the most usable stepping-stones from paganism to Christianity are none other than the existing "pagan" needs as found in the existing adaptive system. St. Paul, who was singularly blessed with an anthropological sense, was likewise a believer in the principle just enunciated:

> For passing by, and seeing your idols, I found the altar also, on which was written: To the unknown God. What therefore you worship, without knowing it, that I preach to you . . . (Acts 17:20–23).

Modern Catechetics emphasizes the importance of making Christ the constant focus. The closer a doctrine is to this focus the more important it is theologically as well as for practical Christian living (see pp. 40–41). Without deliberately omitting any aspect of Christ's mission and teaching, the missioner appreciating the principle of felt-needs would seek a *starting-point* in his instruction that would be most in accord with the existing felt-needs. To a non-Christian society that feels no sense of guilt the work of Redemption as a starting-point or a point of emphasis would not be very meaningful. On the other hand, the person of Christ would contain many values highly appreciated by the non-Christian (cf. Noble, 1962:220). Thus a missionary could lead his flock from an appreciation of the *person* of Christ to the culturally more-difficult and less-appealing aspects of Christology.

2. CULTURE AS A TOTAL DESIGN FOR LIVING

It has already been pointed out (see pp. 5–6) that nothing less than the totality of culture is the object of missionary accommodation, a fact that will be fully explained in the present course. To carry out this official policy of the Church the missioner will need more than zeal, generosity, humility, and good intentions; he will have to know the full object of accommodation, for otherwise how can he know in what he is to accommodate? *The total object of missionary accommodation embraces the total design for living and all that this totality implies.* Accommodation that is limited to content (especially if it is restricted to certain aspects of the content) is indeed a very superficial form of accommodation: the total content as well as all that will be said in the present course about the nature, organization, and dynamics of culture constitutes the full object of missionary accommodation (Part II–IV).

3. CULTURE AS A UNIQUE DESIGN FOR LIVING

One of the most common pitfalls in any cross-cultural activity is the tendency to lose sight of the uniqueness of cultures. Every design for living has, so to speak, a personality or individuality of its own. There is a rather general tendency in any observer of foreign ways to give *identical* interpretations to behavioral patterns whenever and wherever even superficial similarities are found. Identical details, identical usages, identical functions, and identical values are attributed to similar customs. Thus, although the high value placed on virginity in some parts of the world has an economic rather than a moral or religious basis, the unwary outsider, observing the high esteem of the people for bridal integrity, will admire them for their high moral standards when actually they should be praised for their good economic and purely materialistic sense — the bride-price happens to be much higher for a virgin than a non-virgin. Similarly, just because the Chinese use candles and incense as a part of their funeral rites, the missioner may be greatly tempted to regard the usage as religious in character and to condemn the practice as "superstitious." After all, as the reasoning goes, are not candles and incense by their very nature religious in character? Or again, the word "immediately" is believed to have the same meaning in Mexico as it has in the United States. How can "immediately" mean anything but "immediately"?

All this may seem like the repetition of the obvious, yet, in actual mission life very few anthropological principles are violated as frequently as the present one: a way of life is always to be regarded as distinct and unique. We tend to interpret and evaluate with our own measuring-rod all cultural forms that happen to be somewhat similar to our own. In the Spanish culture, for example, a bullfight is a reputable sport, a most pleasant form of entertainment, a kind of ballet, a victory of art over brute force, a pageant of bravery, a fiesta brava indeed. However, to some Americans (measured, of course, with an American yardstick) bullfighting is an "unjustifiable, unfair, and positively cruel slaughter of a helpless and stupid animal by one having the great advantage of a human mind, the help of other men, and of weapons far superior to even the sharpest bovine horns." The unfairness of such interpretations becomes clear as soon as we are the victims of nonsensical ethnocentric deductions about our way of life. Two sophisticated Frenchman watching an American football game might very well be inclined to say: "American football is not a sport at all, but sheer brute force, not art but savagery, not exciting entertainment but an endless series of interruptions called 'huddles.'" The two French spectators would be drawing conclusions about American football on the basis of what their soccer would be like if played in such a "rough" and "unsportsmanly" fashion and with as many "interruptions." But measure American football with an American measuring-rod and you have a great sport indeed.

A previous acquaintance with one culture may be a great help in understanding a similar culture; at the same time, however, such an acquaintance may be a source of preconceived ideas. If the present principle is ignored, such a previous acquaintance can actually be misleading. The Chinese and Japanese are Orientals, but the Chinese are not Japanese, nor are the Japanese Chinese. Previous acquaintance with an Oriental culture will be helpful in understanding another Oriental culture, but, at the same time, it may be misleading if the uniqueness of cultures is not constantly kept in sight. Columbians, Brazilians, and Mexicans are all Latin Americans, and despite the underlying similarity in their cultures, their ways of life are distinct. Acquaintance with one Latin American people may help one to understand another Latin American people but it can also be a source of preconceived ideas and a stumbling-block. To an inquiry made by the author regarding the problem of missionary adjustment in Mexico not a few Mexican bishops and religious superiors remarked: "You North Americans are generally well disposed when you come to our country as missionaries; at least, you want to be 'de-Yankeeized' whether you succeed or not. The trouble is that your culture is so different from ours that North American missionaries have a tough job ahead of them. But they can learn our ways. It is quite different with the Spaniards. The Spaniards come from a background similar to ours, but just because their way of life is so similar to ours they imagine that there is no difference at all between Spain and Mexico, and consequently they never really learn to know us." The recognition of the uniqueness of cultures is the first step toward understanding them.

Cultural similarities are not cultural identities, and similar form does not imply identical meaning, function, and usage, even in cultures that outwardly look very much alike. Just because one has worked for many years as missionary in northern Mexico one does not thereby become an authority on the Yucatan, Guatemala, Honduras, Nicaragua, El Salvador, Costa Rica, or Panama. Cultures are indeed unique.

SELECTED READINGS

1. **What Is Culture?**
    1) C. Kluckhohn, Mirror for Man, pp. 16–44.
    2) B. Malinowski, "Culture," in Encyclopedia for Social Sciences.
    3) A. L. Kroeber, Anthropology, pp. 252–310.
    * 4) M. J. Herskovits, Man and His Works, pp. 15–79.
    5) R. Linton, The Tree of Culture, pp. 29–40; The Study of Man, pp. 80–90.
    6) E. Adamson Hoebel, "The Nature of Culture," in Man, Culture, and Society, Shapiro, ed., pp. 168–181.
    7) F. M. Keesing, Cultural Anthropology, pp. 17–29.
    * 8) Kluckhohn and Kelly, "The Concept of Culture," in The Science of Man in the World Crisis, Linton, ed., pp. 78–106.
    9) W. Schmidt, The Cultural Historical Method of Ethnology, pp. 138, 141, 229, 249, 253, 276, 283, 340.

2. **Difficulties Involved in Defining Culture**
    * 1) Kroeber and Kluckhohn, *Culture: A Critical Review of Concepts and Definitions.*
    2) L. J. Goldstein, "On Defining Culture," *American Anthropologist,* LIX (1957), 1075–1079.
    3) D. Bidney, "On the Concept of Culture and Some Cultural Fallacies," *American Anthropologist,* XXXIX (1942), 449–457.
    4) A. Blumenthal, "A New Definition of Culture," *American Anthropologist,* XLII (1940), 571–586.
    5) L. A. White, "The Concept of Culture," *American Anthropologist,* LXI (1959), 227–251. See also White's review of Kroeber and Kluckhohn in *American Anthropologist,* LVI (1954), 461–471.

REVIEW QUESTIONS

1. Define culture and from your definition indicate the essential characteristics involved. (pp. 59–60)
2. What is meant by the term "adaptive system"? How is culture an adaptive system? (pp. 60–62)
3. Cultures are more or less complete and successful. Explain. (pp. 62–64)
4. Cultures are unique. Explain. (pp. 68–70)
5. Define and indicate which, if any, terms are synonymous: culture pattern, behavioral pattern, ideal pattern, real pattern, manifest culture, explicit culture, overt, covert, latent, implicit culture. (pp. 62–63)
6. Define: function, integration, configuration. (pp. 62–63)
7. What theoretical fact underlies missionary empathy? (p. 64)
8. How can the appreciation of the fact that culture is an adaptive system help the missionary from becoming discouraged? How will such an appreciation help him understand the suspicion and rejection of the Gospel by his people? (pp. 64–65)
9. Why should the missionary keep his message focused on culture as an adaptive system? (pp. 65–66)
10. What do we understand by "felt-needs"? What bearing do felt-needs have on the sequence to be followed in instructing the non-Christian world? (pp. 66–68)
11. What is the full object of the missionary policy of accommodation? (p. 68)
12. What mistake is made when the missionary forgets that the culture of his people is unique? (pp. 68–70)

TOPICS FOR CLASSROOM DISCUSSION AND PAPERS

1. Show how ancestor worship is a form of adaptation. What felt-needs does ancestor worship fill?
2. Prepare a critical analysis of Don Adams' "Cultural Pitfalls of a Foreign Educational Advisor," Peabody Journal of Education, XXXVI (1959), reprinted in Practical Anthropology, IX (1962), 179–184.
3. What principle does the missionary disregard when he says: "My native language is Italian. Italian is so similar to Spanish that there is no reason why I should waste so much time trying to master the little insignificant differences in the language."

CHAPTER FOUR

CULTURE AND THE
INDIVIDUAL

BEES and ants carry out their social roles and, in fact, their entire mode of life without any previous training; for them being born is the same as being socialized. With bees and ants socialization is instinctive. Their way of coping with environment and of surviving is purely biological, a matter of heredity and genes. Man, on the other hand, could not survive by himself; he must *learn* how to survive and how to cope with his physical, social, and ideational environment. The process of learning a culture is known as "enculturation."

Since culture is not biologically inherited but acquired through learning, a Chinaman acts like a Chinaman because he was "taught" to act like a Chinaman. He thinks, speaks, feels, and acts in "Chinese fashion" not because he happens to have Chinese blood in his veins or has some sort of Chinese genes responsible for the peculiar behavior but because he has not learned to think, speak, feel, or act in any other manner, the way an African Bushman or Hottentot acts, or, for that matter, a Texan.

What is not learned but hereditary cannot be regarded as cultural. The fact that an American eats and that there is a physiological difference between American men and women does not constitute a part of American culture. On the other hand, that Americans make and eat ice cream and that American women use lipstick and the men do not *is* a part of the American life-way.

HOW CULTURE IS ACQUIRED

At birth man is cultureless, as cultureless as a mouse, and would remain cultureless if it were not for the process of acquiring or learning a way of life called "enculturation." Enculturation is sometimes referred to as "socialization." However, the two terms are not perfectly synonymous. "Enculturation" embraces the learning of *all* aspects of culture, including technology, art, and religion, while "socialization" focuses on those patterns by means of which the individual becomes a member of his social group, adapts himself to his fellows, achieves status, and acquires a role in society.

Enculturation is a kind of indoctrination, insofar as it makes one blind to other possible ways of behaving. The individual learns his lessons so well that, in spite of his intellect and free will, his actions, assumptions, motivations, values, the things he makes and does, the speech he uses, and the very thoughts he thinks seldom conflict with those of his group. He learns the "standard" behavior and abides by it. The accepted behavior becomes so automatic and natural that the individual takes his culture for granted and as "normal," that is, normal for any human being, little realizing that there may be other ways of thinking, speaking, and acting that are just as "proper." If while learning the "proper" ways he happens to be reminded that some people do have other behavioral patterns, these patterns are presented as "strange," "boorish," or even "savage," and definitely "undesirable" or at least "not quite right." The "correct" speech-sounds and those that seem to be "normal" and "pleasing" are those of one's own dialect. Many Europeans regard stone houses as fit human habitations, but wooden houses, very common in the United States, the most prosperous land in the world, as suitable only for animals. In our culture we are taught quite early in life to eat with a spoon or fork; to eat with our fingers is "primitive" and "savage." However, we seem to forget our own principles when we eat olives, popcorn, peanuts, or even a piece of bread: we eat such things with our fingers like "primitives" and "savages." Germans are shocked to see Americans eat sweet corn on the cob, for, to the German, corn is food for horses and pigs, not human beings. We are shocked and nauseated at the way some Melanesians season their pork: the chef chews ginger and salt and then spits the seasoning on the meat. The acceptable way of kneading dough in some isolated areas of Europe is with the feet, and it is also easier to crush cabbage for sauerkraut by treading on it right in the barrel. That is the way the tastiest sauerkraut is made — so they say. The Navaho Indians are nauseated at the very thought of eating something so slimy and smelly as fish, while Marc Connely's *Green Pastures* portrays the Negro heaven as the place where one is assured of a first-class fish-fry at least once a week for all eternity. Thus the Negro heaven becomes the Navaho hell.

Some people relish horsemeat — not Americans, of course, but people nonetheless. And somehow, donkey gets into some Italian salami, giving it that extra "kick." Americans, to be sure, would bring the "unscrupulous" butcher to court for trying to "poison" them by selling horseburger with a false hamburger label. T-bone steaks delight the American palate, but, as unbelievable as it may seem, they disgust the Hindu. It would be hard to imagine ourselves nibbling on a piece of roast poodle or southern-fried dachshund, or enjoying a cat casserole made with rice and chunks of Felix, that faithful old feline that has almost become a part of the family and has provided the whole neighborhood with dozens of his kind. But even in some civilized countries roast tom-cat is as appetizing as roast tom-turkey; and among some Indians of Mexico, dogs are bred primarily for butchering. In some parts of Africa the people are nauseated at the very thought of drinking such "disgusting" animal secretions as milk but find rats, snakes, and worms quite delicious. In the Caucasus a guest of honor is given a special delicacy, the cooked eyes of a ram. An American would find it rather heroic to eat even the tenderest eyes of any animal as a kind of *hors d'oeuvre*, while an Eskimo would not find it strange at all, for birds' eyes are a special Eskimo delicacy too.

Putting the cross-cultural menu aside — if we were to go to India we would find it rather strange that, just because someone's father happened to be a sweeper, he had no choice but to be a sweeper too. The caste system is regarded by most unsophisticated people of India and elsewhere in the Hindu world as something that makes sense, something highly proper and even sacred, while to the non-Hindu the system generally appears totally incomprehensible and positively unjust. No matter how broadminded we might be, we would be greatly tempted to scold, if not discharge our cook who consistently refused to sweep the rice he had spilled on the floor. Despite our broadmindedness, we would be inclined to forget that our Hindu cook happened to be a non-sweeperbearer and that consequently our orders were entirely unreasonable and baffling.

Not everything that is learned from one's society is to be regarded as relative. Many things are learned that are objectively true, fully in accord with reason, philosophy, science, and theology. On the other hand, it is also true that we learn things from our society that at times can hardly be justified scientifically, morally, or theologically, for instance, racial prejudice.

Much that is relative is learned as if it were absolute, as if it had a value as universal as mankind. We imagine, for example, that the normal way to rest is to sit on a "comfortable" chair. But what is comfortable in one culture may be quite uncomfortable in another. To many, if not most, primitives no chair can really be comfortable; to them the proper way to rest is to squat, recline on a hard mat or on the ground itself, or to stand on one foot like a long-legged water fowl, first resting one limb, then the other. It may seem ridiculous for a father of a newborn child to lie in bed and for days to moan and groan from "birth pains," while the mother must soon after delivery resume her work in the garden. Still, this practice, known as *couvade*, is as natural and meaningful to some societies as handing out cigars is to us. On the other hand, we take cosmetics, chewing gum, the wearing of trousers, dating and going steady, and a thousand other customs as something entirely normal for any human being, little realizing that these very same customs may appear improper and even disgusting to other societies. If the Eiffel Tower were located in the heart of Washington, it would be an extremely easy matter to convince the still unconvinced Frenchmen that the construction is but a monstrosity. Or as Schopenhauer suggested — if we were to ask an ancient Greek what he thought of the magnificent Gothic cathedrals of Europe, he would unhesitatingly reply that they were barbaric to the extreme.

In fact, we sometimes regard as psychopathic (as forms of hysteria or compulsion) patterns that are really normal, that is, normal in the sense that they are psychological states deliberately acquired through much effort and regarded by the society as highly desirable accomplishments. The convulsions and unconsciousness freely brought about by a witchdoctor or a shaman are not forms of insanity but genuine achievements, praiseworthy in their native context.

The number of "proper" things which an individual must learn is great indeed. In early childhood one is taught the fundamentals of the "proper" way to eat (with clean hands, using a spoon or fork, sitting at the table rather than squatting on the floor around a large common bowl and eating with one's fingers or chop-sticks); the child learns the correct way to speak (to avoid baby-talk, to say "fought" instead of the expected "fighted," "disobeyed" instead of "distobeyed"); the child soon learns the fundamentals of personal cleanliness and how to take care of the needs of nature in a dignified and approved manner. As years go on, the child learns to dress without much attention from others. The child soon takes pride in knowing how to tie its shoelace, without help of others and according to a very definite and approved pattern. The necktie, too, must be fastened in a specific way, although many ways are theoretically possible. The hair must be combed "properly." The individual is endlessly learning "the" way to do things, "the" way to speak and even to feel and think. Before long the individual masters his lesson so well that to think, speak, feel, or act in any other way requires effort and considerable violence to self. Culture becomes a kind of second nature to the individual. Enculturation thus has a very deep effect on the behavior and personality of the individual. From early childhood — in fact from the day one is born — one is drilled to conform to recognized ways. Companions and elders take great pains to teach the individual what is "practical," "useful," "correct," "true," "polite," and "disciplined." The individual is punished and ridiculed for parting from approved ways, praised and rewarded for "proper" and "correct" behavior, a training that at least intermittently continues till death.

The process of enculturation is, in fact, so thorough and subtle that even one's emotional reactions and muscular movements reflect one's cultural conditioning. Americans sometimes regard Chinese as "sheepish" and "suspicious," while the Chinese get the impression that Americans are "proud" and that they act "as if they owned the world." Ethnic groups are sometimes recognized by their culturally determined facial expression. Even the facial movements of an angry person, his breathing and the volume, tempo, and rhythm of his speech (and, of course, the particular choice of epithets) vary from culture to culture depending on what the particular society considers to be the "proper" way of becoming infuriated. Enculturation is so thorough and subtle that it has actually conditioned some of our glands, involuntary muscles, and nervous system. Americans would invariably vomit or be terribly nauseated if a plateful of worms were placed before them, while at the very same sight the faces of some Africans would beam with delight and expectation. We laugh, shed tears, and faint at the "proper" times — "proper" perhaps in America, but not necessarily "proper" in Japan, Lappland, or Fiji. The patterns of behavior that one learns in the process of enculturation may therefore be, as Kluckhohn and Kelly put it, "rational, irrational, and nonrational" (cf. 1945: 89–90, 97).

To admit this thoroughness of cultural conditioning is not necessarily a denial of the human will. By admitting the importance of the role of culture in human behavior, we by no means imply that the individual is a helpless slave of culture; he is not an automaton. Even homogeneous societies allow a certain amount of facultative patterns, and because the individual shows independence in following or not following prescribed patterns anthropologists had to introduce the distinction of real and ideal culture (see pp. 62–63). Moreover, patterns are not so specific as one might be inclined to imagine but are rather a range of possible ways of behaving. Above all, since one of the most important characteristics of culture is its tendency to change (see p. 195), and since change can occur only if the bearers of the culture step beyond the range of permissible variability, there can be no doubt whatsoever that the individual is not a slave of culture. Culture offers only "potential guides" for the solution of human problems; culture only "tends to be shared" (Kluckhohn and Kelly, 1945:97–98). The individual can and does part from standard and approved ways. Man is molded by his culture and pressured by it but not chained to it.

THE NATURE OF CULTURE LEARNING

There are three distinct ways in which a design for living is learned. (1) First of all, there is much that the individual learns by direct and conscious instruction called "education." "Schooling" is only a special form of education, namely when the education is given by a socially appointed educator at a given place and time. (2) Much is learned by deliberate observation and imitation, as when a small child tries to eat with a spoon in imitation of its elders. (3) Finally, there is also much that is learned unconsciously through unconscious imitation and a kind of absorption. This third manner of acquiring culture is perhaps more important than most people realize. It is a very natural way of learning; for instance, most language learning is achieved through absorption rather than positive effort on the part of the learner, elders, playmates, or teachers. In fact, unconscious copying of behavior is a very natural process indeed. We claim that we are able to judge a person's character by the company he keeps, for we presume that one is bound to absorb the evil ways of one's companions. For the same reason, children are admonished that "one rotten apple can spoil a barrel of good ones." Parents, in turn, are reminded that "words teach but example draws." An Italian is not given special instructions on how to gesticulate; nor does he practice his profuse and expressive gestures before a mirror. Nevertheless, somehow practically every Italian one meets seems to be as eloquent with his hands as he is with his tongue. He learns his Italian gestures by unconscious imitation. We are not taught expressly how and when to shed tears, when to faint or vomit; weeping, fainting, and vomiting are frequently responses to unconscious absorption of patterns, not responses to deliberate imitation or teaching. Unconscious absorption of "proper" behavior, therefore, can hardly be overemphasized; it is a very important way of learning a culture (Kluckhohn and Kelly, 1945: 89–90).

Cultural transmission would be impossible were it not for man's symbolic behavior. Animals have never succeeded in developing the least sign of true culture. Why should culture be distinctively human? Why does Kroeber define culture as "that which the human species has and other social species lack"? (1948:253.) The answer is simple: animals do not have a culture because they cannot learn it; they are incapable of symbolic behavior which cultural learning presupposes. We do not say that animals cannot learn at all. After all, dogs learn tricks, and parrots, like children, sometimes say the cleverest things. Nevertheless, there is an essential difference between animal and human learning; and the difference is not only in degree but in kind also.

At first sight it would seem that at least the more manlike animals, the anthropoids, would be able to learn the same way as does man and, that at least in regard to the anthropoid, the difference in learning would be in degree rather than in kind. Do not the many experiments carried out by such students of primates as Hooton, Köhler, and the Yerkes prove that anthropoids use and make tools and that they can even reason? Do they not learn much the same way as do human beings? Chimpanzees, for example, learn to play with toys with even greater dexterity than above-normal children. A common sight in circuses is the line of vivacious monkeys and chimpanzees pedaling their bicycles in an endless circle with as much enthusiasm and skill as any children in the neighborhood.

Apes may hurl coconuts, sticks, and stones in self-defense. When an ape finds a nut too difficult to crack with his hands or teeth he may have learned to use a stone. When a banana is beyond his reach he may have learned how to use a stick to bring the banana closer; and if one stick is not long enough, he may have learned enough arithmetic to join two sticks together. Or, in order to reach his food the more clever anthropoid may have learned to make a kind of ladder for himself by piling one box on top of the other. Chimpanzees have learned to sharpen a stick with their teeth for given purposes. They have been taught to distinguish good "money" (actually chips that fit a slot machine) from counterfeits (chips that do not) and to store their "wealth" in a kind of a "bank" for a "rainy day," so to speak, later to be deposited into the slot machine and to receive food (raisins) in return. In fact, the first American astronaut was an anthropoid. (Cf. Köhler, 1925; R. Yerkes and A. Yerkes, 1929; W. Kellogg and L. Kellogg, 1933; Titiev, 1959: 92–103.)

We might rightly suppose that, after an anthropoid has acquired a bit of new knowledge, either by imitation, accident, or by the trial-and-error approach, his fellows might imitate him and participate in his experience, luck, or precociousness. If monkeys can imitate human beings why should they not be able to imitate one another? A classic example is that of the ape who invented the amusing pastime of teasing chickens. The game consisted in poking a stick at helpless chickens in order to make them hop, cackle, and flap their wings in a frantic attempt to escape the teaser. Soon the inventor's relatives joined in the fun; and fun it was, for everybody except the poor helpless fowl. This game may sound like the transmission of group experience through the kind of learning called for in our concept of culture; however, there is a very essential element missing in the type of learning just described, an element essential for cultural transmission.

All these well-known examples of anthropoid "intelligence" and ability to learn consist in imitating what was actually seen, heard, or felt, in remembering the sensory image and associating it with a new sensory stimulus similar to the first experience. If all chickens were to emigrate from the realm of the anthropoids, the apes would never be able to "explain" their amusing "chicken game" to their offspring, for the learning of even the most intelligent ape is limited to imitating an actual *hic et nunc* sense experience.

Man, on the other hand, is able to prescind from the *hic et nunc*. He can abstract the "whatness," the "quiddity" or essence of things and events. He is able to prescind from all that is particular about a given stone, tree, house, or, for that matter, from all that is particular about any chicken which he might eventually want to tease. He is able to retain in his mind that which is common to all stones, all trees, all houses, all sticks, and all chickens. In other words, he is able to form ideas. This he is able to do because he has something distinctively human, his intellect.

But man can do more than form and preserve ideas for himself. He has the power of sharing his abstract ideas and knowledge with his fellows. He is able to describe a game without actually performing it, while others can get the gist of the game without necessarily seeing it played. Herein lies the essential difference between human and purely-animal learning.

Transmission of culture requires a transmission of ideas. Ideas are transmitted by the group to the individual by means of symbols understood by the entire group. Man is able to create symbols: his abstract ideas he can attach to colors, sounds, actions, objects, and the like, which symbols are used to represent those ideas, inasmuch as they have acquired a specific "meaning." The object meant need not be physically present and it need not be actually here and now perceived by the senses. In its place man is able to use these arbitrary symbols, the chief of which are the articulate sounds known as "language," to represent the ideas he has formed. Symbolic behavior peculiar to man enables him to have and to transmit ways, goals, premises, values, and a whole philosophy of life. Through such symbolic behavior and learning each generation contributes to the growth of group experience, preserving it in the form of "culture." In a word, culture presupposes the power of abstraction and symbolic behavior.

SUMMARY AND SELECTED MISSIOLOGICAL APPLICATIONS

Summary

A culture is not genetically inherited; it is acquired after birth through learning. This learning is possible only because man is capable of abstract ideas and symbolic behavior, the chief of which is language. The process of learning a way of life is called "enculturation," and every normal member of society goes through the process. Culture is acquired through education, deliberate imitation, and unconscious absorption. This process is pervasive (embracing all aspects of life); it is subtle (affecting even the finest details of behavior, attitude, and belief); it is deep and thorough (often requiring violence to self, to speak, think, feel, or act contrary to the "proper" or approved norms). Enculturation, however, does not make the individual an automaton; he can and does part from the approved ways.

Selected Missiological Applications

1. THE THOROUGHNESS OF ENCULTURATION

1) *Enculturation is habit-formation aiming to make the individual a master of his society's design for living.* It aims to make culture a kind of "second nature" to the individual. As far as the individual is concerned, culture is a socially transmitted system of habits — habits that may be neutral, in harmony, or in conflict with Christian attitudes and behavior. The missionary would do well, therefore, not only to investigate the particular set of habits in question but also to review the principles learned in Psychology regarding habit-formation. He would also do well to review his Moral Theology regarding the influence of habit on behavior and the corresponding diminution of culpability, the morality of evil habits innocently acquired, and the morality of living in unavoidable conditions that make the overcoming of undesirable habits extremely difficult — to mention only a few of the many pertinent topics connected with the morality of habit-formation. It often happens that in order to overcome one habit the person may have to gain control of a dozen others, and these in turn each may call for the subjugation of still other habits. This is particularly true in regard to culturally acquired habits because, as we shall see (Part III), culture is structured; the various cultural patterns fortify one another. Consequently, the mastery of one undesirable habit may necessitate a struggle with many other habits, some of which may have an important and continuous role to play in the life of the individual and the society. Add to this difficulty the fact of social control (see pp. 301–304) and one can readily understand the force which a former non-Christian life may sometimes have even on willing

and serious converts. Baptismal waters, as Theology tells us, bring the graces necessary for living a good Christian and moral life, but Baptism does not neutralize the natural force of former habits. Both the missionary and the convert should realize that the struggle of a new Christian is very often not with isolated temptations but with deep-rooted and mutually fortified habits — habits of thought, speech, judgment, desire, feeling, and action — habits innocently acquired in the process of enculturation.

I was once staying with a close missionary friend of mine. He was evidently trying to impress me with his "apostolic" methods when he began to scold his head catechist before a large group of school children for a scandal given. I listened to the missionary as he mercilessly condemned the catechist and at the same time tried to teach the offender and the children a practical lesson in Christian morality. His "powerful" oratory and his would-be pedagogy, however, failed to impress me. "I am human and you are human," he shouted, "and the Law of God is the same for me as it is for you. If I can keep His Law, you can too." As is only too evident, the argumentation of the impatient missionary overlooked a very important difference between the otherwise identical human beings which he compared. The catechist could have rightly objected, "But Father, I have *habits* to overcome, while you have only isolated temptations to worry about."

There are a number of very practical conclusions that might be drawn from what has been said about culture-learning as a process of acquiring habits. (1) A thorough and systematic investigation must be made in each mission area regarding the nature and force of such habits. Eventually a set of practical norms might be drawn up for the use of the confessor, counselor, and educator. (2) A proper appreciation of the influence of a non-Christian enculturation should give the missionary limitless patience; it should engender in him true understanding and sympathy. "Learn of Me because I am meek and humble of heart" (Matt. 11:29) should be the motto written on the inside of every confessional, counselor's office, and classroom throughout the mission world and especially on every missionary's heart. (3) The realization that the struggle may be with habits, rather than ill will or indifference, should enable the missioner better to understand the difficulty of his task and what really is involved in trying to Christianize a people cast in an un-Christian or even anti-Christian mold.

2) It has been pointed out that, despite the tremendous influence which culture has on human behavior, *the individual is by no means a slave of culture*. Besides the supernatural means that are always at the missioner's disposal, there are many human tools that can and should be used to accelerate a change in the socially transmitted set of habits. Such a change is always possible provided that the correct key to the desired change is found (see pp. 269–312). Moreover, enculturation need not be looked upon only as a *handicap* with which the missioner must struggle. Why not *take advantage* of the fact of enculturation? Because the non-Christian has been enculturated, he has acquired also many naturally *good* habits, habits that the missionary must discover and build upon.

2. The Problem of Missionary Adjustment

As a member of a distinct social group the missioner has learned to adjust himself to the human needs of *his* specific environment. When, as missionary, he leaves the physical, social, and ideational conditions in which and for which he was enculturated, he becomes very much like a fish out of water. He must now either adjust himself to the new environment and become a kind of "amphibian" or toss about frantically and hopelessly until he succumbs to cultural exhaustion and suffocation. If he be wise, he will choose the first course, the road to apostolic success through empathy and identification with his adopted people. If, on the other hand, he prefers the road going in the opposite direction, with the current as it were, he will infallibly end in "culture shock" and failure.

1) **Culture Jolts.** Before any attempt is made to describe a healthy adjustment and culture shock, it might be well first to depict at some length the situation to which a missioner must adjust himself. We shall, therefore, first describe the endless jolts met in a "strange" cultural milieu, the disappointments, frustrations, and perplexities to which the missionary must either adjust himself or suffer the consequence of culture shock.

To illustrate how constant such jolts can be and how frequently internal as well as external adjustments are called for, a number of rather commonplace missionary situations will be described. It should be noted that these examples represent categories of situations rather than isolated incidents and that their actual occurrence should therefore be multiplied many times over.

The adjustment to the new physical environment, such as the

climate and food, can be passed over rather rapidly, not because this type of adjustment is easy or unimportant but because the necessity of such an adjustment is usually self-evident. The examples that follow refer mainly to a social and ideational adjustment.

I recall, for instance, the jolts I used to receive in New Guinea almost every time I entered my kitchen. Infallibly I found my native cook doing something that normally should have brought on me a complete nervous breakdown. In fact, I still cannot understand why I do not now suffer from a kind of mental disorder that might be called "cuisinophobia novaguinensis" and have not given up eating altogether. For example, as I walked one day into the kitchen I was struck by the unusually thick coat of mud and grease on my cook's hands and face. "Before you go any further with my breakfast," I scolded him, "you better get down to the river and wash yourself." The cook, completely perplexed at my "nonsensical" order, replied, "Why should I wash? I only slept last night!" In plain Kanaka logic, there was no reason for going through the "ritual" (and agony) of washing. It is difficult to say who received the greater culture jolt, the cook or I. On another occasion I was surprised to learn how my potatoes were being peeled. I had been under the impression that there was only one way of peeling potatoes, the way anybody does back home, that is, with a knife. But I was wrong: the cook found it much easier to peel potatoes with his fingernails. I had noticed for some time that my potatoes were corrugated but I did not know why. Now the mystery was finally solved. Or again, while setting the table one morning, my cook noticed that some of the eggs of a previous breakfast still clung stubbornly to my plate; he also noticed that I was watching to see what he would do. A bit of saliva plus a dirty finger, and presto, the plate was "clean"! Although examples from the kitchen might be multiplied indefinitely (from boiling canned beer to putting ice-cubes in warm water "because ice melts faster that way") there is still one more culinary episode worth mentioning. I can never forget the mental jolt I received when I learned for the first time the measures taken by my cook to keep my bread fresh. He had observed how the wife of a neighboring government official used to wrap her bread in cloth. My cook, Kaspanga by name, was a fast learner, so he decided to adopt the same practice. The jolt this time was like a lightning bolt: the cloth Kaspanga used was his own dirty "laplap," a cotton loincloth that had been worn by him during the daytime and by my loaf of bread at night. After this incident it was not hard for me to understand why an old, experienced missionary warned me upon my arrival in New Guinea that the Commandment I would be tempted against most frequently would be the Fifth — "Thou shalt not kill!" *Adjusting oneself to native concepts of hygiene, whether in the kitchen or elsewhere, is a major problem in many, if not most mission countries.*

Etiquette is another such source of endless culture jolts. For some reason or other, logic seems to be found exclusively in the etiquette of one's own society. "Some American missionaries in Japan blow their noses as if they wanted to blow their heads off," according to an impression made on a young Japanese cleric studying in the United States. "In Japan we don't do such things. To us loud nose blowing is disgusting," he explained. Loud nose blowing is to the Japanese what belching is to the American — just not the proper thing to do. An American husband would embarrass his wife if, after a large piece of his favorite dessert, say watermelon, he would fail to muffle his every belch. In America, burping in polite society is outlawed and the urge must be supressed or the burp must somehow be smuggled in unnoticed. In China, however, things are quite different. A husband's enthusiastic and repeated belching in an exclusive Peking restaurant would please both the wife and the proprietor, the wife regarding the belching as a polite way of saying "Very delicious indeed!" and the proprietor regarding the manly burps as free advertising and a case of good judgment. One should not look for logic in etiquette, for etiquette has function not logic, at least not universally accepted logic. To illustrate the point somewhat further — the missionary's feeling and common-sense or "logic" might tell him that the "proper" thing to do when invited to dinner would be not to refuse the invitation, unless unavoidable, and to appear at the specified time and place. However, the really proper thing might be, as we are frequently reminded in books on proper conduct overseas, to come half an hour or even an hour later than scheduled, or perhaps not to appear at all, or after having refused the invitation, to come anyway and that not alone but accompanied by family and a large group of friends. A Superior General of a missionary order after returning to the United States from an official visitation to the Orient remarked, "The Japanese are an extremely polite people, but that is exactly what made my stay so unpleasant; I always felt that I was doing the wrong thing. As much as I tried,

I just couldn't figure out what was the correct thing to do." Adjustment to native etiquette will always be a major source of jolts, confusion, and headaches.

Closely associated with etiquette are the rules of friendship. Like
etiquette, "*friendliness*" *is to no small measure culturally defined
and therefore a source of jolts.* Smiles, gestures, exchange of
"friendly" greetings, pleasantries, handshakes, a pat on the back, a
wink, or an innocent caress of a small child — all these "friendly"
signs are not always such outside the missionary's home-country.
Take, for example, the "proper" way of shaking hands. The American missioner has learned that he must shake hands "like a man,"
firmly, and not as if he were handing someone a dead fish. It may
happen, however, that in certain societies the "dead-fish" handshake
is the more proper and that a firm American handshake embar-
rasses people, while an informal pat on the back may even
scandalize them. To be genuinely friendly will call for endless
adjustments to native norms of friendliness.

*Culture jolts can come even from such things as cheers, noise,
and tone of voice.* Stamping of feet, hissing, and interrupting a
speech with "Bravo!" may be forms of audience approval in certain
countries but such approval invariably jars the American lecturer or
performer. On the other hand, to a European, whistling is a form of
jeering rather than cheering. Even the tone of voice one uses in
ordinary conversation may offend. A missionary Brother in an
Argentinian trade school was nicknamed by the students "Venerable
Brother Don't-Shout." According to the local custom of the Argen-
tinians, the "proper" way to speak is to do so "in such a way that
you can be heard," in any case, much louder than was customary
in the little Bavarian village from which the Brother hailed. Whenever the missionary Brother was asked a question, he would infallibly
interrupt the interrogator with the words "Don't shout! I'm not
deaf!" Evidently Brother Don't-Shout received a culture jolt every
time an Argentinian schoolboy opened his mouth. In other cultures
the missionary may be constantly annoyed by the fact that "the
people don't speak loud enough," or perhaps "they speak too fast,"
or "they constantly giggle when they speak." A missionary from
Africa did not realize how naïve his remarks were when he told
his American audience in Boston: "Our native language is not
difficult in itself. The only trouble is that the people slur their words
and swallow half their syllables. But with a bit of training from our

good Irish Sisters they gradually overcome this rather general speech defect."

Like the loudness of voice so the distance between speakers engaged in a conversation may call for considerable adjustment. Just how far should you be from the person with whom you are speaking? In Melanesia I have seen persons half a mile apart carry on prolonged conversations. I can also never forget how annoyed I would sometimes become in New Guinea when I would call to my gardener to come to me for instructions, expecting him to leave the sweet potato patch and to come to me immediately so that I might tell him what work was still to be done and how it was to be done; but instead my gardener would wait patiently, resting comfortably on his hoe in the shade of a tree several hundred yards away expecting me to shout my long and complicated instructions to him. In fact, I even discharged my first gardener for "stubbornly refusing to come when I called him." On the other hand, in some countries of Latin America one gets the impression that the people actually "crawl all over you" and that they "breathe down your neck" when they speak to you; they keep poking you and pulling your sleeve as if you had fallen asleep or were not interested in what they were saying, and the more you draw back the closer they get to you and the more persistent does their tugging become. The comfortable conversational distance in South America is anything but a comfortable conversational distance in North America (cf. E. T. Hall 1959:204–209).

The value attached to time will likewise be an endless source of culture jolts. What does it mean to hurry? When is a person on time? When is he prompt? What should the missionary's reaction be when someone fails to keep an appointment? How long may the missionary keep one waiting? How serious must the reason be before the missionary may be disturbed? When may one be disturbed while reading, eating, recreating, entertaining a guest, resting, sleeping? The answers to all these questions will be found to be closely associated with the culturally defined value attached to time. E. T. Hall describes how a band of South Pacific natives once called on an American official at two o'clock in the morning for a relatively insignificant matter. Evidently the natives did not know the great value the American sleeping public attaches to 2 a.m. In Ghana important announcements must be made as early in the morning as possible, so that the missionary should not be surprised if at times he is awakened at an "ungodly" hour to hear some "insignificant" news.

After almost four years in New Guinea I discovered that my nickname was "Padre Wait-A-Minute." Just as Brother Don't-Shout had been receiving jolts from the Argentinian custom of "yelling," so I must have been receiving similar jolts from what I imagined was "impatience" on the part of the New Guinea kanakas. Words like "exactly" and "punctually" may mean one thing to the missionary and quite another to his flock, and the value attached to exactness and punctuality, as the missionary understands these terms, may differ considerably from the value the local people attach to such exactness and punctuality. "Mass will begin promptly at eight o'clock" may mean just that to the missioner, but to his flock "eight o'clock" may mean "between eight and nine," or, as in some parts of Melanesia, "while the sun is still rather low." Italian punctuality is not Swiss punctuality. In New Guinea I again and again reminded my native head-teacher that the morning recess was to last "only thirty minutes" and I even provided a very loud alarm clock for the school so that it would be "next to impossible" not to know when the half-hour would be up; but, as I eventually learned, not all "thirty minutes" are thirty minutes long. "Exactly half an hour" means one thing in the United States and quite another in New Guinea. "Long-range" planning in the United States may be only "short-term" planning in China. A "leisurely" pace in the United States may be "top speed" and "on the double" in Trinidad, Haiti, or the Orient. While in the United States the child is repeatedly reminded not to put off until tomorrow what could be done today, the Latin American child is "taught" not to do today what might possibly be put off until tomorrow. The mañana spirit calls for a change not so much in the people who believe in it but rather in the missionary whose enculturation is geared to a life of speed.

Still another long series of jolts can be expected from the constant "infringements" on the missionary's territorial and other rights. Squirrels have their trees; birds have their own nests; many animals have their exclusive mates; all societies have more or less clearly delineated territorial boundaries. In a word, animals and men alike seem to recognize certain rights of their fellows, territorial and otherwise (E. T. Hall, 1959:68, 187–188). But just where "exclusively mine" begins and where it ends depends very much on one's culture. Once I have used a toothbrush it becomes "exclusively mine." But not necessarily so. A planter in Melanesia told me the amusing story of how his cook would regularly make use of his master's toothbrush when the latter stepped out of the house. It was only after the planter noticed the Pepsodent-sweet breath and smile that he became quite suspicious and learned that the cook had been brushing his teeth for months with his master's toothpaste and toothbrush. In the New Guinea highland area if you throw away a piece of chewing gum that you have had in your mouth for some time, you may see that same piece of gum pass from one kanaka's mouth to another, like an Indian peace-pipe. Missionaries quite commonly complain that their people "have no sense of privacy." "Peeping Toms" in Western countries will sooner or later end in jail or in a mental institution, but a "Peeping Tom" in America may be just an "Ordinary Joe" in another country, where peeping may be an acceptable and quite popular, if not national pastime. The missioner's bathroom may be the only bit of private space that may be allowed him. The passengers in an Italian streetcar shock or at least amuse the tourists by what seems to be "a complete lack of respect" for the territoriality of other passengers. An uninhibited poke in the ribs plus a not-too-sweet "permesso" or "scusi" and you wedge your way with your elbow from one end of the crowded streetcar to the other, ramming through twenty and more passengers with no regard for age, sex, social status, or broken ribs. Different attitudes toward territoriality can become particularly shocking when both sexes are involved. In some countries, for example, it is shocking to have co-educational schools or even to have men and women sit on the same side of the church. The territoriality of "his" and "hers" may go far beyond public lavatories. (Cf. E. T. Hall, 1959:52, 60, 67–69, 187–209, 214.)

Another major source of jolts are the various cultural incongruities. (1) Which foods, for instance, go together and which do not? Beer and ice cream do not mix, but most likely they would if our culture would not make these two foods incompatible. South Americans do not hesitate to put sugar in their milk, while to the North American milk and sugar appear incongruous except with cereal. Sweet cranberry sauce with roast turkey or mint jelly with lamb, very common combinations on the American table, are unthinkable in most European countries, for sweets and meat do not mix. Milk in coffee seems to make sense in Germany, as almost anywhere else in the world, but milk in tea does not. On the other hand, in Britain tea without milk is almost unthinkable. (2) When is meat "raw" and fit only for wild beasts and savages and when is it "cooked" and compatible with civilization? To Americans, eating "raw" bacon looks almost "savage," but to the Germans, "raw" bacon is not raw at all, but since it is smoked it is already "cooked" and, in fact, bacon tastes best "before all its flavor is fried out." On the other hand, Americans do not consider themselves "savage" when they order their steaks "nice and rare." (3) Which foods are compatible with maturity and manliness? In some European countries sweets are looked upon as fit exclusively for children. Sometimes dark beer is for women, light for men; sweet wine is for women, dry for men. (4) Certain foods may be looked upon as seasonal and therefore out of place at any other time. Thus certain foods, such as fruit cake or chocolate eggs, are associated with Christmas or Easter and are not normally seen outside the "proper" seasons. In some countries ice cream is for the summer only. (5) What behavior is compatible with dignity and one's social status? We could hardly imagine seeing two nuns walking down a busy street eating an ice cream cone. The Bells of St. Mary's, a Hollywood production, jarred not only the European but also the American audience when it showed a Sister boxing with one of her schoolboys, for boxing and Sisters do not mix. It would be incongruous for a nun to ride a bicycle through New York City traffic, but it may be quite congruous in some mission countries. In the United States it is not an unusual sight to see a nun driving a car (not to say speeding); elsewhere cars and Sisters are so incompatible that an excommunication might be involved. In some mission countries it is incompatible for an employer, missionary or otherwise, to carry a heavy load. (6) What behavior is compatible with good health, adulthood, and diligence? "Don't act like a child!" may have quite a different meaning in two distinct cultures. Sleeping at noon is regarded as normal for everyone in such countries as Spain, but elsewhere siestas are not a sign of normality, health, and good sense but rather associated with some justifying reason such as illness and childhood, or with laziness. (7) Behavior compatible with masculinity and femininity is also to a large extent culturally determined. In Western countries the men are expected to carry the heavy loads; elsewhere for men to carry anything heavier and less dignified than a gun or knife or axe is unthinkable. In some cultures it is incongruous for men to wear anything resembling a skirt and for women to wear anything resembling trousers. But it is only a sign of ethnocentrism to insist that the skirt is by its very nature a woman's garb or that trousers are by their very nature for men only. It was necessary for Pope Nicholas I to instruct the early missionaries sent to Bulgaria not to hesitate to baptize the women of that country even though they insisted on wearing trousers (Mansi, XV, 421, *Resp. ad Bulg.*, No. 59). The Scotch and the Irish see nothing incongruous about a kilt and masculinity. Nor do the Fijians consider the skirt-like uniform of their police feminine; nor do the Arabs and Ghanaians consider the garb worn by the menfolk as "women's dresses." In Western countries judges, university professors, graduates, and choir members, despite their masculinity, insist on wearing gowns. Today only the ultra-conservative element in our society would condemn girls for wearing gym suits when playing basketball, snowsuits when skiing, overalls when working in a factory, or shorts when playing tennis. Even language may be at times regarded as compatible or incompatible with masculinity or femininity, depending, of course, on the particular language and culture. Thus, in our American society even the most furious woman is not supposed to use the same forceful language that a furious sailor or truck driver normally employs; nor may the sailor or truck driver use the language of a woman and refer to his new hat as "my darling hat." In Japan it seems to be more proper for women to laugh with a kind of "hohoho," that is, with rounded lips, since they are expected to observe the custom of not opening their mouths more than necessary; in fact, women are expected to place their hands to their mouths when laughing, very much the way we are expected to do when yawning. (8) The "ridiculous" and the "sublime" are incongruous but only in the same culture. What is "ridiculous" in Europe, however, need not be "ridiculous" elsewhere. (9) It is far from incongruous for a maid in an American home to tidy up the kitchen after serving a meal, but it may be utterly unthinkable in a society governed by strict occupational caste rules. However, one need not leave the American shores to find such incongruities in task-performance: one need but observe how the AFL-CIO operates. A union carpenter may not put a single trowel of mortar on a single brick. (10) A given behavior may be regarded incompatible with certain places and times. In Western societies it is incongruous for a man to walk into church with his hat on or barefooted, while in the Near East it would be unthinkable for a man to enter a mosque with his shoes on or bareheaded. In some areas of Africa it is considered extremely offensive to speak to someone who is on his way to a public lavatory. Certain behavior may be incompatible with a home or certain furniture within the home, such as the fireplace or table, as the following example clearly shows. Soon after World War II the United States Government made a special effort to teach the Japanese the meaning of democracy, and one of the measures taken was to send guest lecturers to Japanese colleges. A certain American lecturer, who enjoyed considerable repute in the United States and had received an excellent buildup before his arrival in Japan, was particularly conscious of his democratic mission. He felt that the best way to teach democracy was by demonstration. When he entered the lecture room for the first time he made sure that his face reflected the happiness and friendliness of a true democracy — he was all smiles. Before beginning his lecture he encouraged his listeners to feel at home — as in a true democracy — and to take off their coats just as they would at home. He even passed cigarettes around the room and took one himself. With a very generous and democratic gesture he began to light the cigarettes. He refused to sit behind the desk as if he were an emperor sitting on his throne; instead, he paced up and down the room, leisurely smoking his cigarette. His listeners responded quite favorably the first five minutes; but then, all of a sudden, they began to rise from their seats noisily discussing something in Japanese which the lecturer did not understand. Why the riot? What did the lecturer say that he should not have said? He inquired apologetically, but in vain. The riot could not be halted. In desperation the lecturer went to the administrator's office, who, in turn, called for one of the rioting students. After questioning the student the administrator came politely but disappointedly to the lecturer, explaining in poor but unmistakable English, "Sir, in Japan table sacred; man's democratic bottom not!" The American lecturer in his enthusiasm for democracy and his eagerness to impress his audience by demonstration rather than mere words had nonchalantly sat on the teacher's desk, an incongruity which the Japanese students took as a very serious insult.

The local language can likewise be an endless source of culture jolts. In fact, one of the most basic causes of culture shock is the inability to communicate in the language of the people (Smalley, 1963:54–55), a subject almost too evident to mention. It may not be out of place, however, to point out the difficulties arising from the culturological rather than structural aspects of a language. The American finds it difficult to understand, for instance, why the clergy indigenous to a particular country should resent being referred to as "the native clergy." He fails to appreciate the important fact that the term "native" may have anything but a flattering connotation. What the American usage happens to be should be of little concern to him; what matters is the local connotation. On the other hand, non-American speakers of English may not see anything derogatory in the term "nigger," an expression extremely painful to the American Negro. In Latin America, a citizen of the United States should not "usurp" the title Americano but should refer to himself as a Norteamericano. To speak of the Heart of Jesus seems quite natural to the missioner, but to be understood he may have to speak of the "Sacred Entrails of Jesus" instead. To speak of a pig with as much affection as we speak of a lamb, or to speak of donkeys with as much respect as we speak of horses will call for adjustment. An innocent word like "bloody" will make any decent British mother shudder when she hears her ten-year-old child use it; while the American mother, no less respectable, would merely brush the expression off as "just one of those slangy words the kids are using these days." Some missionaries in Melanesia, especially shy nuns, find it difficult to overcome the shock of using words that are vulgar in English but entirely innocent in Pidgin English. Unless they adjust themselves to the Pidgin usage of such four-letter words they may find it rather difficult to express themselves in the classroom or even the pulpit.

The most painful of culture jolts and certainly among the most difficult to adjust to are those originating in the local value-system (Chapter Seven). As is well known, face-saving in the Orient is an extremely forceful drive difficult for the non-Oriental to appreciate and to use as guide for his decisions and interpersonal relations with the local people. How will my Japanese teachers, Formosan medical assistants, or Korean technicians react to my suggestion, direction, or even correction? To interact with the Orientals, especially those in authority or who are highly respected by others, will be difficult because the underlying value-system of the Oriental and the non-Oriental in regard to face-saving is so vastly different. In Japan, for instance, since every educated Japanese is expected to know English, it would be a grave insult to the edu-

cated audience for an American lecturer to hire a native speaker
to serve as interpreter. On the other hand, the American lecturer
may be jolted throughout his talk by the lack of response and the
feeling that the audience is missing half of what is being said
(cf. E. T. Hall, 1959:16).

Interpersonal relations are made difficult indeed because the
basic assumptions of the missionary differ, at times essentially,
from those of his flock. A missionary is generally a kind of "pope
and emperor" on his station and is endlessly issuing "edicts." His
orders may nevertheless be repeatedly disregarded; his seriously
intended suggestions may be taken lightly or even as a joke. His
intention may be to impress his congregation or to teach by means
of a good example, but his kindness and generosity are interpreted
as naïveté. In his attempt to discourage materialism, he refuses to
haggle with peddlers coming to his door and gives them the price
they set; but instead of convincing his flock of the evils of greed,
he merely convinces them that he is a very inefficient, not to say
stupid, administrator. A Superior of a convent in India, who was
suffering from complete culture exhaustion, wrote her Mother Provincial begging to be relieved of her responsibilities because, as she
expressed it: "Reverend Mother, it is no use. No matter what I do
for my Indian Sisters I am always 'wrong.' When I try to show them
what is to be done I am 'rude.' When I am frank with them I am
'naïve' for being so open with my subordinates. When I am natural
and friendly toward occasional visitors I am 'boorish.' When I am
serious they say that I am only bluffing. I don't know what to do
except to give up and admit that the task which Reverend Mother
assigned to me is simply beyond my capacity."

The examples mentioned above, though they were many, did not
aim to exhaust the occasions for culture jolts but rather to show how
constant, real, and diversified they can be. The missionary must
either adjust himself to these jolts or run the risk of succumb-
ing to them.

2) **Successful Adjustment to Culture Jolts.** Various degrees of
adjustment are possible, ranging from a rather imperfect empathy
to a perfect identification. A businessman or government official
overseas can be satisfied with his adjustment to a foreign culture and
society if the people of the area in which he happens to be regard
him as their "close and understanding friend." A missionary, however, cannot be satisfied with anything less than the most perfect

kind of adjustment, complete identification or at least as perfect an identification as possible. He cannot be satisfied with being merely a "good friend," for his vocation demands of him to be "all things to all men" (1 Cor. 9:22) and to "empty himself" (Phil. 2:6–7) of the ways most natural to him and thus become one with his adopted people. Not "our dear friend" but "one of us" is what the local people must say of their missionary.

When speaking of apostolic identification we have two distinct elements in mind: there is (1) *empathy*, a sympathetic understanding of the local customary ways and psychology, an understanding that allows for no exceptions, and (2) *actual adoption* (internal approval and external usage) of native ways and values, which, however, must at all times be within the limits of sound reason, prudence, Science, Faith, and the aims of missionary work. Actual adoption of native ways, therefore, is not blind but selective. Since it has as a specific aim the acceleration and thorough and permanent integration of the Gospel with the native life-way, any internal approval or external usage that delays Christianization, gives rise to syncretistic beliefs and practices or that eventually will lead to abortive results is out of place in genuine apostolic identification. Otherwise, the sacrifice of one's way of thinking, feeling, speaking, and doing in favor of the ways and values of the local people is complete, a true holocaust. It is the missionary's main answer to Christ's invitation "Take up your cross and follow Me." It is the missionary's most painful and unquestionably most generous sacrifice. As emphasized in the very opening chapter, the missionary who claims that he has never felt the weight of this sacrifice is most likely the one who has never made the sacrifice. To be tolerant toward opposing attitudes and "unreasonable" behavior, to go against one's learned ways, to re-educate oneself after deep habits of thought, speech, feeling, and action have been formed into a "second nature," constantly to carry one's "missionary cross" may indeed be a slow but genuine martyrdom.

Apostolic identification, as we have just seen, does not mean blind approval and total adoption of native ways; there are definite limits beyond which the missionary may not go and regarding which he may not compromise. However, as far as empathy ("feeling with" or "understanding") is concerned there is no limit. Empathy means that the missioner fully understands and appreciates, as the local people do, the reasons behind their way of life. A missionary with true empathy views all native ways and values not through his colored glasses known as "enculturation" but in full native context. Without approving polygamy the missionary must understand why his people are polygamists, and without tolerating fetishism or promiscuity he must understand why his people venerate fetishes and are promiscuous. Empathy means that I understand why my people are what they are no matter what they are. Although empathy is internal, it is nonetheless clearly perceptible to the local people, and it is a prerequisite for genuine apostolic identification.

3) **Culture Shock.** A healthy adjustment to culture jolts and to the physical, social, and ideational environment for which the missionary's society has not prepared him is, as we have just explained, always selective, prudent, scientifically, philosophically, and theologically sound, and in harmony with the aims of mission work. On the other hand, a reaction that is blind and unreasoned, a reaction that is but a subconscious flight or escape from a culturally disagreeable environment leads to culture shock. As the following diagram shows, the culture-shocked person takes flight in one of two directions: he either clings blindly and immovably to his original ways or he blindly and indiscriminately renounces his former ways and values in favor of the ways and values that are responsible for the culture shock to which he is falling prey.

FIGURE 2

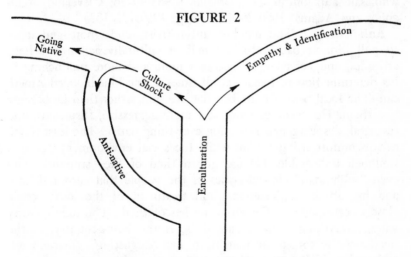

A diagrammatic sketch of possible forms of adjustment to a new cultural environment.

Those caught in the first current cling to their original ways and values as if they never left their original cultural milieu and become more and more aggressively anti-native, while those caught in the second current "go native."

It should be noted that the term "culture shock" does not refer to the numberless individual surprises or jolts described above and inescapable in a strange cultural environment. Here the term "shock" should be taken in the same sense as when one speaks of a soldier being "shell-shocked." In other words "shock" denotes a "breakdown," an "attack," a "stroke," or "exhaustion" resulting from improper adjustment to cultural frustrations and jolts.

The unavoidable jolts which one receives in a new cultural environment must be faced wisely and generously through empathy and apostolic identification, otherwise they will drive the unadjusted individual more and more to complete frustration. Such an individual becomes more and more convinced of his inadequacy in coping with the unfamiliar and unsympathetic cultural environment. He is like a child lost in a large crowd at a State Fair, perplexed no matter in what direction he turns. The culture-shocked individual has "stage fright," the stage being the strange cultural requirements that overwhelm him and make him speechless. In this predicament he will either "go native" or resort to wholesale antagonism. (Cf. Smalley, 1963:49–56; Cleveland, Mangone, and Adams, 1960:26–45; Oberg, 1960:177–182).

Anti-nativism. The budding anti-nativist tends more and more to pull himself back into his shell of culturally acquired beliefs, attitudes, and behavior; he becomes more and more unflinching in his determination to remain at all times a true blue-blooded American. The local people must become like him rather than he become like them. He becomes more and more aggressive, suspicious, and resentful, despising and ridiculing everything native. The least physical discomfort irritates him, while the social environment becomes well-nigh unbearable. He has grown tired of the "stupidity" and even "subhuman" characteristics of the people that surround him, and his utterances, reactions, and treatment of the local people closely correspond to the image he has of them. The only country where everything is as it should be is the home-country. If the missionary is forced to remain in his "disgusting" environment, each culture jolt widens the wound, making him more and more nostalgic and anti-native. It does not take much imagination to visualize how incompatible with apostolic work even a less serious case of anti-nativism can be. Many an exchange student becomes anti-American not so much because he has been mistreated in the United States but because he has succumbed to this type of culture shock.

Going Native. Going native is a form of identification too, but it is not apostolic; rather, it is a neurotic longing for security and an exaggerated hunger for belonging. This unbalanced craving for acceptance drives the unwary individual to approve and to accept as his own, indiscriminately and blindly, any and all local ways and values. The foreigner who reacts to culture shock in this manner generally begins by extolling beyond merit the religious, moral, and cultural status of the very environment that is causing the shock. Before long, more or less inordinate friendships with indigenous families or individuals are formed. The hunger for belonging keeps gnawing within him while his own culture looms like a giant wall between himself and those by whom he would want to be fully accepted. At first sight it may seem that there is only an accidental difference between apostolic identification and going native. The difference, however, is not only in degree but in kind. Unlike going native, apostolic identification does not aim at acceptance or belonging for its own sake; one is not *driven* to apostolic identification. It has a purpose, the spread of the Gospel and the welfare of the local people. While going native is selfish, apostolic identification is selfless, altruistic. While going native is a blind and indiscriminate reaction to cultural tensions, apostolic identification is positively willed, discriminating, always in accord with Faith, Science, reason, prudence, and the aims of the Missions.

The term "going native" does not necessarily refer to extremely primitive conditions. Rather, the danger of cultural shock (whether going native or becoming anti-native) may be the greatest in more advanced cultural surroundings. "When in Rome live as the Romans do" may be a wise maxim, but "going Roman" is highly unwise and to a large extent neurotic.

4) **Cultural Adjustment and Native Expectations.** Although the prime norms for judging which native ways and values should actually be approved and adopted by the missionary are Faith, Science, reason, prudence, and the aims of mission work, the attitude of the local people is a very important secondary criterion telling the American missionary just how American or un-American

he should be. Unless the particular culture expressly requires it and unless the local people actually expect certain behavior and are pleased with its adoption by foreigners, healthy identification does not mean running around in a gee-string or sari, a fez or turban; it does not necessarily mean eating rats and beetles or restricting one's diet to rice and yams. I recall, for instance, how my simple New Guinea kanakas used to ridicule a certain Australian gold-prospector for walking barefooted and eating only native foods. In reference to these externals they used to call him by the very derogatory name of "bush-kanaka" or "wildman," although they themselves have not yet completely emerged from the Stone Age and eat only sweet potatoes and never wear shoes. Native expectations, therefore, are an important criterion for judging what ought to be adopted and what not. To offer another example of the necessity of complying with native expectations — Americans, for instance, do not as a general rule learn a foreign language easily; nevertheless, they expect foreigners to speak faultless English almost the moment they set their foot on American soil. Justified or not, this is an expectation which immigrants to the United States would have to reckon with even more seriously than they normally do. Or again — my little house in New Guinea, although made of native materials (bamboo), had quite a bit of sophistication about it: curtains, table cloth, imported Chinese mats on the floor, plastic windows, painted doors and framework in gaudy red, all details as non-native as the missionary himself. Nevertheless, the people welcomed my exotic "palace." It was something they always wanted to see in their territory. To put it in their own words: "Father's new house makes our tribe look important." Father Ricci, in adopting mandarin rather than coolie ways, did so because he reckoned with the people's expectations: his choice was not a blind reaction to culture jolts but a wise way of winning the approval and respect of the people, using a well-planned mode of attack fully in accord with Chinese norms and expectations.

5) **Proper Missionary Adjustment Exemplified.** In concluding this important section on proper adjustment to a strange culture it might be well to illustrate in a concrete form what such an adjustment would imply, especially in regard to matters which the missioner could not very well approve of or adopt. What, for instance, would be the proper way for a missionary to adjust himself in regard to such commonplace matters as bodily cleanliness? As far

as the missionary's own personal cleanliness and the tidiness about his own house, mission station, school, or hospital are concerned, he would definitely not imitate the local people, unless they themselves were models of cleanliness. Hygiene makes sense anywhere in the world — that is, to the extent that hygiene is possible in the given circumstances. In fact, even the most simple people expect their missionary to be different in this regard. Cleanliness will never offend; dirt may. Thus, for example, the New Guinea highlanders would certainly have thought less of me if I had adopted their bathing habits and seldom, if ever, washed. They realized very well that I had sufficient warm water (the mountain streams are usually icy cold), sufficient soap, towels, and the necessary privacy, all of which they did not have. I would have been a fool in their eyes for not making good use of such facilities.

But what about the bodily cleanliness of the missioner's people? Should he refuse to eat their "dirty" food? Should he refuse to speak to anyone that does not first wash himself and is spotlessly clean? The answer to these questions has already been given in the preceding sections on empathy, identification, and native expectations. In most mission areas, besides being an example of cleanliness to his flock and instructing both young and old regarding the importance of hygiene, the missioner will simply have to bear up with the unsanitary conditions that surround him. It was not easy for me to keep smiling when a group of dirty kanakas would come to me in quest of medical or other help. To bear up with their dirt and smell would, in fact, have been impossible if I had not achieved at least some degree of empathy and if I had not taught myself to "feel" about the dirt and smell as my people felt about such matters. In some areas of New Guinea the natives seem never to wash except when they are caught in the rain. Since they have no clothing (and the mountain air can be quite chilly even for the well-clothed missionary) the people cope with their physical environment as best they can — by smearing their bodies with rancid lard and soot. Needless to say, the resulting odors sometimes defy description, odors emanating from the old lard and perspiration as well as those absorbed from the smoke-filled huts and the fires around which the kanakas squat for hours on end. In such a situation it is not easy for the missioner, whose culture worships cleanliness as godliness and abhors body odors like leprosy itself, to "feel" about smell and dirt in his practical dealings with the native population as a New Guinea highlander does. In fact, it may take considerable violence to self to listen patiently to their endless domestic and other difficulties without, so to speak, noticing the stench that makes breathing difficult and fills one's house with swarms of flies and lice. The missionary has indeed the required apostolic empathy if he can nevertheless say: "These are my people and those are their ways." They must also be my ways as far as sympathy and understanding are concerned. Since it is impossible for me to supply my people with sufficient blankets, soap, towels, and clothing (especially sufficient for a change whenever the clothes become dirty or wet), and since it is impossible for me to introduce overnight, as it were, a complete clothing industry and effect other economic and social changes which such an industry would entail, I will, for the time being, let my people cope with the climate the best they can — yes, with their traditional, albeit smelly, lard and soot. In fact, to come to think of it, their smelly lard and soot happen to be the most practical way of coping with the climate in the given circumstances. I do not approve of dirt as such, but I do understand why my people are dirty, and if I were in their circumstances I would be no different. In my dealings with them, therefore, their dirt and smell must mean as little to me as it means to them. This does not mean that I should not take the elementary precautions, whenever necessary, of peeling fresh fruit, boiling or filtering the water I drink, using insecticides, screening, and netting. In fact, I would be more unlike my people if I were to refuse to make use of insecticide and mosquito netting; after all, my people have a natural "insecticide" and "netting" around their bodies — their natural immunity to many local diseases. I should never unnecessarily expose myself to serious health hazards, such as cholera, typhoid, amoebic dysentery, or hepatitis, for to do so would be to go against the principle of good reason, prudence, Science, and even Faith. I would also be acting contrary to the expectations of my people, for every sane man, however primitive he may be, takes whatever precautions he can against disease. On the other hand, if it be a choice between gaining the good will and co-operation of the local people or suffering a little headache or a minor diarrhetic discomfort, I will choose the headache and the diarrhea. This is the very advice given to the Peace Corps volunteers in their manual, Working Effectively Overseas (Spector and Preston, 1961:6–8), advice that makes very good missiological sense as well.

In short, while working toward a desired change I will adhere to the dictates of prudence and good judgment, remembering at all times that there is only one substitute for still-unachieved missionary goals — patient understanding called "empathy." Such still-unachieved missionary goals include not only bodily cleanliness and hygiene but also other, far more serious matters, such as the rightful position of women, superstition, child marriages, and polygamy. In matters that have a purely culturally defined value, there is generally nothing else for me to do than actually to adopt such values and practices myself as long as they are in accord with prudence, Faith, Science, the aims of the Missions, and the expectations of the local people.

It is vital for missionary success not to be frightened into inactivity by the strange cultural environment and by the difficulties of adjusting to it. The strangeness should not frighten me but rather be looked upon as a challenge just as the unknown lands were in the age of the great discoveries or as outer space is today. I will take the culture jolts in stride, and by studying the ways and values of the local people I will anticipate such jolts; in fact, I will cushion the jolts through empathy and, whenever possible, I will try to neutralize them by advance internal acceptance. I will not wait until I master the whole strange life-way before I begin to put my knowledge of it into practice. Learning a strange culture is like learning a strange language: I do not keep my mouth shut until I have memorized the entire dictionary and mastered every phonological and grammatical pattern. On the contrary, I use as much of the language as I happen to know at the moment. I do not worry about what I still do not know and still must learn. *Fear of the strange culture would be, in fact, as detrimental to my apostolic work as the disregard for cultural differences itself.* Fear that leads to inactivity is like the fear of making a mistake in pronunciation or grammar. If the fear be so great that it keeps me from speaking, I will never learn the language. A foreign language is learned by using as much of it as is known at the time and by handling the unknown as best as one can. In much the same way, I will master a strange culture not only by studying it but by studying and *using* it — by using as much of it as I happen to know, by handling the unknown as best as I can, and by learning from mistakes — always learning more and more and *using* what I already know.

3. THE NEED FOR AN INDIGENOUS LEADERSHIP IN THE LIGHT OF ENCULTURATION

The deep effect of enculturation on the individual constitutes one of the most basic reasons for developing native leadership in the Missions. From the earliest times the official policy of the Church has been to choose leaders from among the local people. St. Paul, for instance, ordered Titus (Tit. 1:5) to ordain native Cretans for the Cretan community. From its very inception the Sacred Congregation for the Propagation of the Faith has urged mission bishops to ordain and establish a complete, self-sufficient native clergy wherever and whenever possible. In fact, the numberless documents coming from the Holy See clearly prove that the development of native leadership is not a matter of choice but a command. Pius XI could hardly have been more insistent than he was when he said:

> We are convinced that, unless you provide to the very best of your ability for native priests, your apostolate will remain crippled and the establishment of a fully-organized Church in your territories will encounter still further delay . . . you should not conclude that the role of the local clergy is merely to help the foreign missionaries in lesser matters or in some minor fashion to supplement their work (*Rerum Ecclesiae*:22, 24).

Unfortunately, the instructions of the Holy See have only too often been disregarded or at least not taken seriously enough. At times only a token native leadership was set up and merely tolerated. As Benedict XV complained in his *Maximum Illud:*

> . . . it is a deplorable fact that, even after the Popes have insisted upon it, there still remain sections of the world that have heard the Faith preached for several centuries, and still have a local clergy that is of inferior quality. It is also true that there are countries that have been deeply penetrated by the light of the Faith, and have, besides, reached such a level of civilization that they produce eminent men in all the fields of secular life — and yet, though they have lived under the strengthening influence of the Church and the gospel for hundreds of years, they still cannot produce Bishops for their spiritual government or priests for their spiritual guidance (*Maximum Illud*:17).

There are many practical reasons for this insistence on local leadership; among others, the insufficiency of foreign missionaries and the necessity of adapting mission methods to the demands of both nationalism and international politics, especially in times of war and revolution. The most important reason, however, is the fact that the very purpose of the Missions is the establishment of the Church, and establishment of the Church presupposes native leadership. In the words of Pius XII:

> The primary object of missionary activity, as everyone knows, is to bring the shining light of Christian truth to new peoples and to form new Christians. To attain, however, this object, the ultimate one, missionaries must unremittingly endeavor to establish the Church firmly among other peoples and to endow them with their own native hierarchy (Evangelii Praecones:32).

Native leadership has the great advantage of being culturally conditioned for the environment in which it operates: properly formed native leadership understands its people, speaks the local tongue, masters and shares the local life-way. Properly formed leadership is blessed with an inborn empathy. The culture jolts are non-existent. The problem of effective communication, of using the premises and motivations that have a genuine meaning and force with the local people, practically disappears from mission work as soon as there is formed a sufficient and capable indigenous leadership. It is then that Christianity can be presented to the people in the true terms of their daily lives. With a well-trained leadership established, the problem of making proper accommodations ceases to be a problem: while the foreign missionary may have to make positive effort to suggest or to effect a worthwhile accommodation, the native leader, if properly formed, has to make positive effort not to make proper accommodations. The same two points stressed here, sc., the natural effectiveness of native leadership and the necessity of proper formation of native leaders, have been stressed by Benedict XV:

> There is one final, and very important, point for anyone who has charge of a mission. He must make it his special concern to secure and train local candidates for the sacred ministry. In this policy lies the greatest hope of the new churches. For the local priest, one with his people by birth, by nature, by his sympathies and his aspirations, is remarkably effective in appealing to their mentality and thus attracting them to the Faith. Far better than anyone else he knows the kind of argument they will listen to, and as a result, he often has easy access to places where a foreign priest would not be tolerated.
>
> If, however, the indigenous clergy is to achieve the results We hope for, it is absolutely necessary that they be well trained and well prepared. We do not mean a rudimentary and slipshod preparation, the

bare minimum for ordination. No, their education should be complete and finished, excellent in all its phases, the same kind of education for the priesthood that a European would receive. For the local clergy is not to be trained merely to perform the humbler duties of the ministry, acting as the assistants of foreign priests. On the contrary, they must take up God's work as equals, so that some day they will be able to enter upon the spiritual leadership of their people (Maximum Illud:14–15).

On the other hand, it would be very naïve to imagine that the establishment of a clergy indigenous to the country would in itself be the full solution to mission problems. Enculturation in the native (non-Christian) way of life rather than in the foreign but Christian culture may have a number of disadvantages. Baptism does not neutralize the past influence of an un-Christian background; nor does mere membership in a pious lay movement or Ordination itself rid the convert completely of his culturally acquired un-Christian prejudices and habits, some of which may be a definite liability. Then, too, local leadership, especially during the transitional period of a mission country from the status of an "underdeveloped" nation to that of a full-fledged equal of a recognized worldpower, may suffer, as is sometimes the case, from excessive nationalism and corresponding prejudices. On principle, whatever is foreign is looked upon as *ipso facto* despicable, and thus local non-Christian practices and attitudes that serve as a drag in the process of Christianization may be preferred to genuinely Christian, although foreign, ways and values that would accelerate the process rather than hold it back. An inferiority complex may develop, which, in turn, may lead to a "persecution complex," making the native leader excessively critical of all foreign guidance. Often projects that are well beyond native leadership are undertaken. The inferiority complex may urge the native leader to set a pace well beyond his means and available personnel. Finally, even within a society there are subsocieties each with its own peculiar ways and values. Thus, the fact that someone is native-born may make him immune to *cultural* jolts and prejudices but not to *subcultural* jolts, *subcultural* prejudices and misunderstandings. Thus, a native bishop coming from an upper class may be blind to the needs of the masses belonging to a lower class. In fact, it is theoretically possible for a native leader to be more prejudiced against his own people than a foreigner.

These difficulties connected with native leadership are mentioned merely to emphasize the need for proper formation. The Missions do not need so much a native leadership as a well-trained and well-formed native leadership. In training native leaders it is vital that they are not "de-nativized" in the seminary. Without being forced to cling to and perpetuate their "primitive" ways in a rapidly changing world, they should be taught true humility, a humility that will enable them to see and to love their people as they really are, in the state or level in which they actually are, and not as the seminarian would wish his people would be. The apostolic approach of a native leader must be realistic, even though at times somewhat humiliating. The apostolic approach of a native leader must be realistic, dictated by the actual situation of the people rather than by the inferiority complex of the leader, an inferiority complex that may have been nurtured by the policies of the seminary and by the attitude of the foreign missionaries. It is no exaggeration to say that any future native leader could profit as much from a course in Applied Missionary Anthropology as any foreign missionary. Pope John XXIII, quoting the *Maximum Illud* of Benedict XV, was fully aware of the danger of "de-nativization" of a potential local leader when he said:

> In the training of all [indigenous] seminarians it is opportune to follow the wise norm that this training should not be given "in an ambient that is too far removed from the world" for in that case "they will find themselves in serious difficulties in their relations with the people and the cultured classes when they go out among them and it will often happen that they will err in their dealings with the faithful or that they will form a poor opinion of the training that they have received . . . it is opportune to insist upon following the local manner of life without, however, neglecting those conveniences of the technical and material order that have now become the patrimony of all civilized people and which represent progress in the standard of living as well as a safeguard to physical health.
>
> . . . this Apostolic See has always recommended the special study of Missiology, not only for the foreign clergy but also for the native clergy (*Princeps Pastorum*:14, 16).

Isolated cases of a local people rejecting its own clergy and preferring foreign missionaries have been reported; however, in such exceptional cases, it should be remembered, the local people were not opposed to a native leadership as such but to the *de facto* type of native pastors imposed upon them. The native clergy was definitely inferior to the foreign missionary intellectually and perhaps morally, snobbish, or coming from a despised area or social group, or possessing some other undesirable qualities. Such exceptions merely prove that a people will not be satisfied with just any native leadership: it must be a well-formed leadership, possessing not only the necessary Christian qualities but also those demanded by the native value-system.

A strong *lay* apostolate and leadership is no less important than a strong local clergy. The native lay apostolate, like the native clergy, enjoys the advantage of identical cultural conditioning. The Legion of Mary, for example, has an outstanding record in the Missions, even among the most primitive tribes. Not seldom where even the best-trained foreign missionary has failed, a simple, uneducated local Christian has succeeded because, unlike the foreign missionary, he was able to feel, speak, and argue in the only terms that made sense to the non-Christian. Enculturation was not the handicap to him that it was to the foreigner; rather, sharing the same way of life with his non-Christian brothers, he was able to communicate the Gospel much more effectively than the best trained foreign apostle.

SELECTED READINGS

1. **How Is Culture Acquired?**
   1) A. L. Kroeber, *Anthropology*, pp. 288–290.
   2) M. J. Herskovits, *Man and His Works*, pp. 43–45.
   * 3) J. J. Honigmann, *Culture and Personality*, pp. 201–223.
   4) H. M. Johnson, *Sociology: A Systematic Introduction*, pp. 111–145.
   5) Broom and Selznick, *Sociology*, pp. 79–111.

2. **Proper Adjustment to a New Cultural Milieu**
   1) Wm. D. Reyburn, "Identification in the Missionary Task," *Practical Anthropology*, VII (1960), 1–15.
   * 2) D. V. Hart, "Overseas Americans in Southeast Asia: Fact in Fiction," *Practical Anthropology*, IX (1962), 60–84.
   * 3) E. A. Nida, "The Ugly Missionary," *Practical Anthropology*, VII (1960), 74–78.
   * 4) E. T. Hall, *The Silent Language*.
   * 5) W. Lederer and E. Burdick, *The Ugly American*.
   * 6) Cleveland, Mangone, and Adams, *The Overseas Americans*, pp. 26–45.
   7) P. Spector and H. O. Preston, *Working Effectively Overseas*.
   * 8) H. Cleveland and G. Mangone, eds., *The Art of Overseasmanship*.

9) J. Rosengrant, et al., Assignment: Overseas. See especially G. Mangone, "Cultural Empathy," pp. 38–50, and E. A. Nida, "Many Cultures are Our Own Witness," pp. 51–65.

10) D. G. Haring, Personal Character and Cultural Milieu.

* 11) K. Oberg, "Cultural Shock: Adjustment to New Cultural Environments," Practical Anthropology, VII (1960), 177–182.

* 12) E. T. Hall and William Foote Whyte, "Intercultural Communication: A Guide to Men of Action," Human Organization, XIX (1960), 5–12.

* 13) W. A. Smalley, "Culture Shock, Language Shock, and the Shock of Self-Discovery," Practical Anthropology, X (1963), 49–56.

3. Cultural Relativism

1) D. Bidney, "The Concept of Value in Modern Anthropology," in Anthropology Today (Kroeber, ed.), pp. 682–699.

2) F. M. Keesing, Cultural Anthropology, pp. 180–184.

4. Leadership and Enculturation

* 1) R. V. Lawlor, "Church Tradition and Current Policy on Local Leadership in Mission Lands," in Local Leadership in Mission Lands (Ewing, ed.), pp. 4–26.

2) M. T. Gilligan, "Preparing the Local Laity for Leadership," in Local Leadership in Mission Lands (Ewing, ed.), pp. 117–137.

3) J. Homes-Siedle, "The New Outlook for the Foreign Missionary in Developing Local Leadership," in Local Leadership in Mission Lands (Ewing, ed.), pp. 138–146.

N.B. See also other useful articles on the subject in Local Leadership in Mission Lands.

REVIEW QUESTIONS

1. How does living by culture differ from living by instinct? (p. 73)
2. Define "enculturation." How does enculturation differ from socialization? (pp. 73–74)
3. Enculturation is a kind of indoctrination. To what extent is this statement true? Is man a slave of culture? (pp. 74–76, 78)
4. Describe the thoroughness of enculturation. (pp. 76–78)
5. What is the difference between human learning and animal learning? (pp. 79–81)
6. Learning a culture consists in acquiring habits. What practical missiological application might be drawn from this fact? (pp. 82–84)
7. Name some categories of culture jolts. How does a culture jolt differ from culture shock? (pp. 84–95)

8. How is a successful adjustment to a "strange" culture achieved? (pp. 95–97, 100–104)
9. What is meant by "going native"? How does it differ from apostolic identification? (p. 99)
10. Describe anti-nativism. (pp. 98–99)
11. What part should native expectations play in missionary adjustment? (pp. 99–100)
12. Does the Church tolerate or insist on native leadership? What anthropological principle underlies the policy of the Church regarding local leadership? (pp. 104–106)
13. What are some of the problems associated with native leadership and how can these problems be solved? (pp. 106–108)

TOPICS FOR CLASSROOM DISCUSSION AND PAPERS

1. Read the Mission Encyclicals indicated on p. 20 and summarize what is said about local leadership. Point out the anthropological wisdom contained in the Encyclicals.
2. The local clergy of your mission are subconsciously ashamed of the "primitive" ways of their people. How does such a feeling manifest itself? How does it arise? How does such a feeling keep the local clergy from choosing the best apostolic approaches?
3. Can the indigenous clergy profit from a course in Applied Missionary Anthropology?
4. Present a critical analysis of Don Adams' "Cultural Pitfalls of a Foreign Educational Adviser," *Peabody Journal of Education*, XXXVI (1959), reprinted in *Practical Anthropology*, IX (1962), 179–184.
5. Summarize and comment on Wm. D. Reyburn's article, "Africanization and African Studies," *Practical Anthropology*, IX (1962), 97–110.
6. Review Wm. L. Wonderly, "Indian Work and Church-Mission Integration," *Practical Anthropology*, VIII (1961), 193–199. In what points do you agree with the author? In what points do you disagree? Give your anthropological reasons.
7. Describe in concrete terms the identification which you as a white pastor of a colored parish in a northern U.S.A. diocese would have to achieve.

CHAPTER FIVE

CULTURE AND SOCIETY

CULTURE AS A SOCIETAL POSSESSION

CULTURE is conceived as the way of life of a *social group*, not of an individual as such. It is the way a *society* copes with its physical, social, and ideational environment. In other words, culture is a *society's* regularized or standardized design for living. "Society" can be defined as a permanently organized aggregate of persons sharing a common way of life and group consciousness. As the definition implies, the unifying elements in any human society are a common culture and group consciousness, which two facts constitute the essential difference between purely animal aggregations (such as a pack of wolves, a herd of buffalo, a flock of sparrows, a colony of ants or bees) and a human society. The first requisite for a human society (culture) is impossible among animals, for, as we have seen in the preceding chapter, animals are incapable of abstract ideas and symbolic behavior. The group consciousness typical of human societies is likewise impossible among animals because the *esprit de corps* in question is conscious and intentional, while animal aggregations never go beyond the purely organic and instinctive. When we speak of culture, therefore, we are really speaking of a design for living of a particular social group, although actually it is the individual rather than the group as such that carries out the design.

Idiosyncrasies

Since culture is a *societal* possession, behavior that is peculiar to an individual as such is by that very fact not cultural. In Anthropology such peculiarities are known as "idiosyncrasies." It should be noted, however, that not all idiosyncrasies are oddities, as the common usage of the term implies. For example, any invention or discovery prior to its acceptance by a society is an idiosyncrasy, although not necessarily an oddity. Similarly, although millions may speak the same dialect, no two individuals will pronounce the same word exactly alike. Such personal differences in pronunciation are not cultural; they are idiosyncrasies. Personal skill, personal doubts, and personally acquired phobias are all idiosyncrasies and therefore not cultural. That such individual differences should occur is unavoidable, since they are due to unavoidable differences in experience, health, physique, emotional responses, muscular control, vision and general sharpness of senses, and intelligence.

Universals

Some patterns are expected of every normal member of society, for example the vernacular language. Such patterns are known as "universals." It should be noted, however, that in anthropological literature the term "universal" is sometimes used not only in the sense just mentioned but also in the sense of "basic to human nature" or "common to all men and cultures."

Specialties

Some patterns characterize the members of a specialized subgroup within the society, say, a particular occupation, a certain age, one of the sexes, or a social class. In most, if not all, societies, playing with dolls is normal behavior only for children, only for small children, and usually only for small children of the female sex. There is much that American menfolk know and women do not, and, of course, vice versa. The husband may not know all the particulars about washing the family clothes (what to starch and bleach and how much soap, starch, bleach, and bluing to use), but whenever the washing machine refuses to function it is the husband, not the wife, who knows what to do; he is the "jack-of-all-trades" around the house. After a preliminary diagnosis, the clever husband may either try to repair the washing machine himself or he may call on someone who knows even more about broken washers than he; he may call an expert repairman, a specialist in the truest sense of the word. Astrophysics and jet-planes are a part of our culture, but not everyone is expected to be an astrophysicist or a jet-pilot. The ways of specialized groups within a society are known as "specialties." Even in the simplest societies certain types of work may be regarded as normal for men, while other types may be normal only for women; even in such simple societies adults will normally not behave as small children, since certain patterns are tabooed after childhood.

Alternatives

An individual is sometimes free to choose from among a number of possible ways of behaving. In America people may live in a bungalow, a ranch-style home, a trailer, an apartment, or a hotel. When we go to a barber shop we can have our sideburns merely trimmed or cut rather close. We can wear a shirt of a number of possible styles and colors. We may travel by air or train or bus or automobile. Travel by horse and buggy, except perhaps for fun or in a parade, is no longer an alternate mode of travel in the United States, especially not on our modern expressways. In our pluralistic society we are also free to choose our religion and school of philosophy or art. Such facultative but nonetheless approved patterns are referred to by anthropologists as "alternatives."

Because universals, specialties, and alternatives are socially approved, and therefore transmitted, they are true elements of culture; idiosyncrasies, being personal traits, are not. Individual peculiarities, however, may and frequently do become integral parts of a society's way of life. New English expressions begin as idiosyncrasies — President Roosevelt's "chislers" or President Truman's "red-herring" for instance — and eventually they become universals. New agricultural and medical practices begin as idiosyncrasies and through education and promotion they may become alternatives or universals. In mission countries Christianity begins as an idiosyncracy, or, to be more exact, as a set of idiosyncrasies; Christian ways, by being accepted by a small community, become specialties; eventually they become alternatives, and finally, the Christian ways and values may become the accepted ways and values of the whole society.

CULTURE PATTERNS

We have been describing culture as a "design," "blueprint," or "plan" for living because it does not consist of concrete artifacts and actual behavior but of mental details which anthropologists call "patterns." Patterns are the society's standards, norms, or regularized guidelines for coping with life's demands. Patterns are not things or specific actions but rather plans as to how one is to make things and how to act. Without such norms or standards life in a human society would be impossible. The members of the social group must agree on their "laws" and "by-laws" (the patterns), otherwise confusion rather than harmony and co-operation would be the chief characteristic of social behavior.

It should be noted that culture patterns consist in a *range of possible behavior* rather than in specific and definite modes of behaving. Patterns might be compared to the rules of a game. Although all players observe the same rules, no two players play exactly alike. As long as the members of a society stay within the range of approved behavior, it remains possible for them to interpret and predict one another's speech, products, moods, reactions, and other behavior and to work harmoniously together (cf. Flannery, 1960: 87–92; Honigmann, 1954:211–212).

THE LOCUS OF CULTURE

Although there is still some controversy about the locus of culture, facts favor the more common and more recent view that culture is located (as the words "design," "blueprint," and "plan for living" imply) not in the external world but in the mind.

In discussing this point one should carefully distinguish between "culture" as it exists in the mind of the anthropologist or anyone else who, like the anthropologist, speaks of the *total* design for living and as it exists in the minds of individuals who share the particular design. As already intimated, as far as the *bearers of culture* are concerned, culture does not consist of visible, tangible tools, weapons, and houses; culture does not consist of actual lessons given to children and the youths, or to apprentice barbers, magicians, and philosophers; it does not consist of ritual acts that *de facto* take place. Culture as such exists only in the form of *ideas* in the mind of the individual bearer of culture, *ideas* of tools, weapons, houses, marriage and burial customs, rituals, and the like. Culture is therefore rightly regarded as "the socially shared mental content" (cf. Barnett, 1953:1–16).

But where does "culture" exist as the *anthropologist* conceives it? Where is the total socially shared design for living? Such a "culture" exists only in the mind of the anthropologist. No individual in a society masters the total socially shared design for living; much less is the individual able to carry out the entire design for living. Even in very simple societies no individual can master the numberless details of the culture. Some behaviors are, moreover, contradictory and mutually exclusive. The totality as such is an abstraction of the anthropologist. It is a "thing of the mind" but, at the same time, "founded on reality." The concept is very much like the concept of "gravity" in the case of the physicist or "genes" in the case of the biologist or "grammar" in the case of the linguist. It is a useful construct, an abstract summation of a society's shared mental content which may or may not have outward expression. It is a "thing of the mind" but not a mere figment of the imagination, no more than the physicist's construct "gravity," and the biologist's "gene," or the linguist's "grammar," for the anthropologist's "culture" is founded on psychological *reality*, mental processes that actually take place.

It should be noted that when in the present course we speak of objects and actions as being parts of culture we do so figuratively and refer not to the concrete outward behavior as such (things and actions that are unique in time and space) but to the psychological patterns in the minds of the bearers of culture.

CULTURE A SOCIAL HEREDITY

Culture is superorganic and supraindividual, transcending the individual; it will continue even after the present bearers of culture pass away. Culture is a continuum, a tradition, or social heredity. These terms, however, suggest too much passivity on the part of the living bearers of culture and therefore require further explanation.

Culture is indeed a tradition and may be regarded as social heredity; however, culture is not dead but very much alive. Culture is dynamic — dynamic because the individuals following the particular design for living are very much alive and active. Even non-literate food-gatherers are constantly changing their way of life, slowly and imperceptibly perhaps, but changing nonetheless. It has been well said that "the only completely static cultures are the dead ones" (Herkovits, 1950:20). Cultures are constantly changing because the bearers of culture, the architects of the cultural blueprint, are active. They are not only following the plan but constantly modifying it, "improving" and adjusting their ways to the whims and demands of their environment, adjusting to the demands of the various human drives, adjusting their "plan for living" in accord with the society's growth in experience and in accord with numberless historical accidents. Details of the "blueprint" that pass the acid-test of time become more or less "established," giving the entire culture the appearance of being basically conservative and traditional. In a word, we may indeed look upon culture as a "tradition," but only if we do not overlook the dynamic nature of culture. Culture is a "social heredity," but it is not a finished product. Culture is not only a "plan" but also a "planning."

THE EXTENT OF CULTURAL AND SOCIETAL BOUNDARIES

Are there as many cultures as there are societies, and vice versa? Do the boundaries of a society coincide perfectly with those of a given culture? May we, therefore, define "society" simply as "a cultural group"? Can discrete societies possess identical cultures? To answer these questions one must keep in mind that the term "culture" is used in a number of different senses.

1) Sometimes the anthropologist does use the term to designate the way of life of a particular society. Culture is, after all, a "tradition," an embodiment of the history of a particular society. Since no two societies can have identical experiences and histories, it follows quite logically that their ways of life can never be perfectly the same. In this sense a culture is as unique as the society, and the society is as unique as its culture; in this sense the boundaries coincide.

2) Sometimes the term "culture" is used when it would be more proper to speak of "subcultures." A society may include a number of subgroups, each with its own traditions or subculture. This is particularly true of the more complex societies. We speak of "subsocieties" and "subcultures" because the social groups in question are partly dependent on and partly independent of larger units. Subsocieties have not only their own histories and group consciousness but also a common history and a common group consciousness with individuals of the other subsocieties with whom they co-operate and together form a larger unit. Subcultures have had their own historical development and have their own ways and values, their own customs and mentality, but at the same time they are only a part of an over-all culture and have only a part of the total design for living of the larger group. In the United States we have one society and one way of life, which, however, embraces a relatively large number

of subsocieties and subcultures. The Jews, Protestants, and Catholics constitute distinct subgroups within the American society. They possess distinct traditions, have their own *esprit de corps*, but at the same time they share a common American tradition and group spirit.

In view of what has been said about universals, specialties, and alternatives, it should be noted that subcultural patterns are but specialties. Since the individual is not free to accept or reject such patterns, subcultural patterns are definitely not to be regarded as alternatives; nor are they universals, for they are normal only for the particular subgroup in question.

3) Sometimes anthropologists will speak of "a culture" when they more properly should speak of "cultures" in the plural, for they refer to a group of similar but distinct ways of life. Thus, each "culture area" consists of several distinct cultures, but because they occur in a given geographical territory and include behavioral patterns that happen to be similar in some significant aspects, anthropologists group them together and speak of the Plains Culture (singular!), or the California Culture, the North Plateau Culture, the North Pacific Culture, the Eskimo Culture, etc. They also may speak of the "Western Culture" or "Western Civilization," meaning the many distinct cultures of Europe and America.

SUMMARY AND SELECTED MISSIOLOGICAL APPLICATIONS

Summary

1) Culture is a societal possession; it is the way a society (not an individual) copes with its physical, social, and ideational environment. Idiosyncrasies, inasmuch as they are personal traits, are not cultural; on the other hand, since specialties, alternatives, and universals are socially transmitted, they are cultural.

2) A culture is made up of "patterns," i.e., standards, norms, or regularized guidelines for behavior. Culture is not made up of concrete artifacts and actual behavior but is "a thing of the mind." Patterns consist in a range of possibilities rather than in specific ways of behaving.

3) Although culture is "tradition," it is dynamic; it tends to persist but at the same time it tends to change.

4) Depending on one's frame of reference, the boundaries of "culture" and "society" will or will not coincide.

5) Frequently societies and cultures are divided into subsocieties and subcultures.

Selected Missiological Applications

1. CULTURE AS A CONTINUUM AND A SOCIETAL POSSESSION: ITS BEARING ON MISSIONARY METHODS

Culture is a societal possession and as such is supra-individual and a continuum. The individuals of a society will sooner or later cease to be, but the society and the culture will live on. A mission policy that overlooks or does not sufficiently appreciate the significance of the continuity of culture is shortsighted indeed. Mission policies and the corresponding activities of missionaries must aim beyond the present willing individual; they must aim at culture itself, at the institutions in the society. A mission fully appreciating the socio-cultural approach may not see the results of its various activities immediately (for instance, the results of native seminaries and universities), but the results will be there, results that will automatically continue from generation to generation and over the entire society. Pope John XXIII, speaking of the socio-cultural approach, calls such missionary undertakings "real and urgent needs" which, he says, should not be neglected "even if at times 'He who sows is not the one who reaps'" (Princeps Pastorum:17).

The individual approach is focused on the individual as an individual, with no regard for the individual's position in his society and his capacity to accelerate a desired change. Missionaries following this approach wrongly judge success by the number of baptized individuals. The socio-cultural approach rightly keeps in mind that the individual is more than an individual, that he is a member of an interacting group and a bearer of culture. In other words, since the socio-cultural approach is particularly interested in the society and in its particular design for living rather than exclusively in the individual as an individual, the missionary following this approach will always consider in his plan of attack the various positions occupied by individuals in the society, the roles they play, and the relation of such roles to culture persistence and change. He does not merely leave the door to Christianity or socio-economic betterment wide open to any willing individual who, so to speak, happens to be passing by. The socio-cultural approach does not merely leave doors open; rather, it is a positive and farsighted approach. The missionary goes out into the highways and byways extending *special* invitations to those individuals who in the given society, culture, and time are most vital for the establishment of the Church inasmuch as they occupy positions that enable them to Christianize roles and institutions.

The socio-cultural approach, without closing the door to anyone, wisely and necessarily discriminates in the use of the limited time, means, and personnel available. Logistics in missionary work are no less important than in war. Missionaries, like soldiers, must be placed in the most *strategic* positions, not in the most agreeable ones; *they must be assigned to tasks and posts that bring socially and culturally meaningful results.* One might, for instance, question the advisability of concentrating the clergy in a few monasteries in Quito, while there is an unbelievable shortage of priests throughout Ecuador. One might also question the advisability of concentrating all one's effort on willing children and submissive women, exactly the ones who may have the least to say about the way of life of the people. The children, it is true, will some day grow up and will assume adult roles, but roles that, to a large extent, may be kept un-Christian by the senior adults whom the missionary has been ignoring as "no-hopers." One often hears missionaries say: "We believe in concentrating on the children, for they are the hope of the future. Some day they will take over; only then can we expect to have genuine Christians. In the meantime, let the older generation go its way. After all, that is what the Communists are doing, and they are successful." There is a serious fallacy hidden in such reasoning; it is also not true that Communists believe in such a policy. When the children, the so-called "hope of the future," grow up they will indeed assume adult roles, which, theoretically speaking, they may be able to Christianize, but the fact is that they often find themselves unable to do so on account of the superior authority and pressure of their non-Christian seniors, the more influential adults whom the missionary has been ignoring as "no-hopers." The very institutions which the missionary presumed would be Christianized by the new generation may force the young Christian adults back into their former un-Christian ways, the end-result of missionary activity being syncretism and a community of "baptized pagans." A vicious circle indeed. The problem of second and third generation Christians is only too well known. To obviate this danger, Communists by devious means manage to occupy *culturally and socially meaningful* posts, the strategic positions of educators, editors, union leaders, student organizers, and at the right moment sweep down upon the *institutions*, which they first Communize and then hand over to the younger generation. The immediate target of Communism is not, as is often falsely supposed, the pliable child — the so-called "man of tomorrow" and "the hope of the future" — but the roles and institutions of today. The general approaches followed by the Communist and the wise missionary are very similar; the difference lies in the fact that while the Communist does not hesitate to employ force, hatred, deceit, subversion, political pressure, and other unethical means, the missionary must limit himself to strictly ethical methods and achieve his goals through communication and free choice.

It is sometimes said that Satan is an excellent psychologist. This may be true, but he must also be given credit for being an expert applied anthropologist as well. He seems to know the nature of culture and that man is to no small measure a creature of his culture. By setting up a way of life diametrically opposed to Christianity, Communism for instance, Satan's work can without much attention on his part be endlessly perpetuated, for it becomes a continuum with the culture itself.

2. The Concept of Subculture: Its Bearing on Apostolic Techniques

1) *The concept of subculture has an important bearing on practical apologetics and communication.* American Protestantism and American Catholicism are both subcultural forms of Americanism. When explaining Catholic views to our separated brethren, or when attempting to bring about the highly desirable unity among Christians, one should not lose sight of the fact that in such activity one is obliged to cross subcultural boundaries even if one does not leave the American shores. To understand our separated brethren and to be effective in our communication with them, it is of utmost importance to keep in mind that we are separated not only in faith but also culturally; to reach the non-Catholic, the Catholic must cross subcultural boundaries. He must apply essentially the same anthropological principles and techniques here as he would in a strange, far-off land. The Protestant wishing to understand

the Catholic must likewise realize that he does not speak the same cultural language. Today, when there are as many Protestants as Catholics reading papal and episcopal statements summarized or reprinted in full in newspapers and leading secular magazines, it has become imperative for Catholics to use a language understood by Protestants and Catholics alike. Catholic public relations has until now been geared almost exclusively to the Catholic subcultures and is to no small measure responsible for much of the ignorance, confusion, fears, and suspicion of even broadminded Protestants, who are understandably concerned about the rapidly growing influence of American Catholicism. One need not be a Paul Blanshard or a member of his Protestants and Others United for the Separation of Church and State to misinterpret the Codex of Canon Law, for the Codex, besides being couched in strictly legalistic terms, is intended expressly for the Catholic subcultures of the world and not the non-Catholic. In fact, the Codex is not intended for the Eastern Rite Catholics either; nor is it quite understandable to them. The presence of Protestant and Orthodox observers at the Second Vatican Council and the establishment of a special Secretariat for the Promotion of Christian Unity will, no doubt, go a long way toward communicating official Catholic views in language less likely to be misunderstood by the non-Catholic world.

2) *The notion of "subculture" casts important light on the subject of accommodation* (Chapter Thirteen). The policy of accommodation is not to be restricted to so-called "pagan" or "primitive" peoples; it is no less in place in highly civilized and Christian countries like the United States, England, and Germany. Accommodation is in place whenever and wherever we are dealing with a culture or subculture that happens to be different from our own. It is indeed strange that Catholics sometimes tend to be more sympathetic toward non-Christian cultures and ideals than toward their fellow-Christians. Protestants entering the Church should be encouraged to retain the many laudable aspects of their (subcultural) backgrounds, even in preference to some of the so-called "Catholic" ways. In a word, in dealing with our separated brethren, compromise of principle will always be impossible, but accommodation will always be in place.

3) *The theoretical distinction of "subcultures" and "specialties" takes on a very practical aspect when viewed from the angle of effective mass communication.* Missionaries engaged in mass communi-

cation such as radio, television, and newspapers would do well to keep in mind that cultures are frequently divided into many sub-cultures, each with its peculiar content, structure, and inner logic. Tragic mistakes are sometimes made by government as well as mission personnel engaged in mass communication by forgetting that it is quite possible to reach a very limited subgroup without in the least influencing the rest of society. The elite may be reached while at the same time the masses may be completely overlooked; the city people may be reached while the farmers may be forgotten. Each subsociety has its own way of life and underlying assumptions, values, and goals, and unless the communication is geared accordingly it will fail to inform, convince, and persuade.

3. Group Consciousness and Group Conflicts Among Mission Personnel

Culture, we have said, is a *societal* possession. Any social group will have a set of shared ideas (a culture, subculture, or specialties) as well as an *esprit de corps* or group consciousness. The present missiological application deals with the many possible group contacts and group conflicts that may occur on the mission field. The groupings may be based on difference in culture, subculture, or on such specialties as one invariably finds in different age-groups, occupations, or among individuals of a slightly different social background. The aim here is to understand group conflict and to reduce the dangers associated with such conflicts. A proper diagnosis is always half the cure. A missionary is called upon not only to adjust himself to a new cultural environment (see pp. 84–103) but also to adjust himself to and co-operate closely with individuals having behaviors, group loyalties, and group interests that are different from his own. Just as it is possible for a missioner to suffer culture shock so it is quite possible (and perhaps even more so) to suffer "social shock."

A proper understanding of group conflict presupposes especially the following four basic principles: (1) there is a deep-rooted craving in man to form in-groups and out-groups based on shared ways, values, and interests, whether cultural, subcultural, or based on more limited specialties; (2) whenever an in-group contacts an out-group, conflict between the two groups becomes possible; (3) there is particular danger of conflict as soon as the groups begin to feel that a dominant or majority versus a minority relationship has arisen or is arising; (4) excessive group-consciousness (whether on the cultural, subcultural, or on the more limited level of specialties) invariably leads to conflict unless successfully restrained.

1) *There is a deep-rooted craving in man to form in-groups and out-groups* based on shared ways and values, whether on the cultural, subcultural, or specialties level. It should be noted from the outset that in-groups and out-groups are not necessarily *organized* into opposing factions; rather, they are internal groups who happen to think and behave alike. Such internal feeling may, of course, lead to the formation of cliques and factions, but that is not our present concern. The individuals who share a common behavior and a common set of values and interests are referred to by the pronoun "we" and therefore constitute the "we-group," while the opposing side is known as the "they-group."

Man is a social being and instinctively takes sides, entering in his mind this camp or that camp, depending on the ways and values that he considers to be his. He instinctively aligns himself with others into an endless series of we's and they's: the Gentiles align themselves against the Jews; the Catholics align themselves against the Protestants; the Irish align themselves against the British. As teenagers we aligned ourselves against our "unreasonable" parents; and earlier still, while the gang-instinct was still alive in us, it was "us boys" and "them lousy girls." Such a tendency to form into groups of we's and they's does not disappear with the pronouncement of the three vows, Ordination, or the departure for the Missions. The tendency to form in-groups and out-groups is, in fact, very much alive in every missionary. The better he understands and appreciates the fact that this natural tendency exists also in him (and not only in the other fellow) the better are his chances of avoiding "group shock." The first step toward group harmony and co-operation on the mission front is to have every missionary, from the bishop down to the recently arrived lay-missionary, admit the existence of such a natural tendency in *himself.*

2) *Whenever an in-group contacts an out-group, conflict between the two groups becomes possible.* In the Missions there are many such internal groupings possible. To mention only a few of them — there are: (1) the "privileged" clerics and the "underprivileged" Brothers and Sisters; (2) the "all-important" religious and the "unappreciated" lay-missionaries; (3) the "hard-working" bush missionaries and the "lazy" school staffs; (4) the "progressive" Ameri-

can missionaries and the "narrowminded" Italians; (5) the "naïve" Americans and the "not-quite-so-naïve" Europeans; (6) the "born-geniuses" from abroad and the "not-yet-quite-civilized" local staff; (7) the "before-the-war" missionaries and the "after-the-war" missionaries; (8) the "know-it-all" new missionaries and the "will-never-learn" old missionaries. We might, of course, continue in this fashion almost indefinitely. A former missionary from China teaching Moral Theology at a mission seminary in the United States used to tell his fellow-professors that he finally had infallible proof that he was middle-aged. "The old professors," he would say, "come to me to complain about the young professors, and the young professors come to me to complain about the old professors." From these examples we can readily see that the in-groups can be quite varied and that it is possible to belong to a dozen or more of such we's and they's. Conflict is possible as soon as there is contact between groups that follow either different cultures (e.g., native versus non-native), or different subcultures (e.g., upper class versus lower class), or different specialized ways (e.g., medical missionaries versus missionary educators, or the kitchen staff versus the laundry staff in the same hospital).

Generally speaking, the wider the sharing of behavior, the more serious the problem. The most serious conflicts are those affecting entire nationalities. There are some relatively small mission dioceses and vicariates with missionaries from a dozen or more distinct countries and cultures, each with its own, unavoidable national consciousness and loyalty. Whether missionary or not, one is inclined to favor his own cultural group: an Irishman will as a rule prefer an Irishman to an Englishman, an Austrian will as a rule prefer an Austrian to a Prussian, a Brazilian will as a rule prefer a Brazilian to a Portuguese, a Latin American will prefer another Latin American to a Spaniard. It should not surprise anyone if he should find among the clergy of the Philippine Islands a Filipino in-group and a foreign out-group; or in Japan, an indigenous in-group and an American or European out-group; or, for that matter, in the diocese of Los Angeles or San Diego an in-group of "American Irish" and an out-group of "foreign-born Irish." We are interested in *all* group contacts and conflicts, whatever the basis of the grouping.

We are not group conscious to any appreciable degree until we come in direct contact with an out-group. The second step toward a proper understanding of group problems, therefore, is to realize that wherever and whenever there is contact there may be conflict.

3) There is particular danger of group conflict as soon as the groups begin to feel a dominant versus a minority relationship. The sociologist does not necessarily speak of numbers when he speaks of a "minority." That group is considered "dominant" or "the majority" which is recognized as the stronger and more influential. Although a dominant and minority status is often unavoidable and even necessary, such a situation, justified or not, predisposes the groups to conflict. Trouble may be brewing as soon as groups begin to feel uncomfortable on account of relative weakness or a real or imaginary unimportance. It is quite human to "feel bad" about having to play second fiddle all the time simply because one belongs to the "wrong" group. The "minor" roles assigned to lay-missionaries, often unavoidable on account of their relatively short stay in the Missions, may give the group the impression that they are not trusted, considered incapable, unreliable, definitely inferior, and unwanted. The indigenous clergy may give the same impression to the handful of American priests who have volunteered to assist the local priests of Brazil or Bolivia. Whether the impression created is true or not, whether it is justified or not, matters little; the effects are the same — the creation of a "majority" and a "minority" group, a situation favorable for conflict.

Human beings instinctively crave for recognition and appreciation. Particularly dangerous are the undeniable slurs, open remarks, inconsiderateness, and other signs of a lack of appreciation of a minority group. A minority group is excessively sensitive and predisposed to unfair criticism, rash judgment, and needless misunderstanding, facts that the dominant group should ever keep in mind. A minority group tends to develop a kind of persecution complex: it begins to consider itself the "underdog" of the diocese, hospital, or school; it is the "Cinderella" of the Missions. Missionaries involved in school work may consider themselves as the neglected segment of the Missions, unimportant and discriminated against; the medical missionaries may feel that their work is not being appreciated by the bishop and the rest of the mission personnel. As the persecution complex grows, the danger of conflict grows also. The dominant group is no longer respected; it is often unjustifiably condemned and even ridiculed. Although such an attitude in the religious or missionary life can hardly be justified, for the religious and missionary are to live above the natural level, the feeling and reaction is quite human and expected. In any case, it should be understood and fully reckoned with.

The third step toward a proper understanding of group problems in the Missions, therefore, is to recognize that a minority status, whether real or imaginary, necessary or not, justified or not, makes the danger of group conflict particularly serious.

4) *Unless successfully restrained, group-centeredness (whether on the cultural or subcultural level, or on the level of specialties) invariably leads to group conflict.* By "excessive group-centeredness" we mean the natural tendency in man to evaluate one's own in-group and its behavior and interests as superior to those of other groups. This feeling of superiority is generally subconscious, but only too often expressed in word or action. "Our form of government is the best in the world." "We are the most moral and cultured people of all Europe." "Our educational system makes the local universities look like kindergartens." "Our cooking cannot be equalled." "We are the wittiest people in the world." "Thank goodness, we don't have such ugly customs as one finds in America. Imagine, women smoking and using lipstick and fingernail polish!"

To understand the nationality problems in the Missions, whether among the foreign missionaries or between the indigenous on the one hand and the foreign clergy on the other, in fact, to understand any problem involving groups, one must fully grasp the role of ethnocentrism and all forms of excessive group-centeredness. Every nationality and every specialized group (e.g., the medical missionaries, missionary educators, bush missionaries, or a particular religious order) will tend, to some degree at least, to regard itself as well as its activities and methods as all-important, at the same time minimizing the roles of other groups. *Esprit de corps,* good and even necessary at times, may become an occasion for group conflict through excess and lack of restraint.

Group-centeredness becomes particularly dangerous when it drives the group, as it only too often does, to re-educate the out-group. "To make everyone as good as myself!" What an ideal! The British want to Anglicize all non-Britishers; the Germans want to Germanize every non-German; the Americans feel it their God-given mission to Americanize every non-American. Everyone wants to re-educate everybody else "according to his own image and likeness." This urge may become a kind of duty, a mission, or obsession, and even an all-out crusade. After World War II the American military government tried to impose the American life-way on occupied Germany. According to a report, it even tried to introduce the American educational system, including the good old American spelling-bees. However, since German is written quite consistently and almost phonemically, spelling-bees just could not eliminate any of the participants. One almost has to be a moron to misspell a German word. This urge to make everyone like oneself is natural and human and therefore that it should crop up among mission personnel is to be expected. This urge is in the American, in the Spaniard, in the German, in the Frenchman, and even in the New Guinea cannibal. Awareness of one's own group-centeredness and a positive effort to appreciate the good in others will go a long way toward reducing the danger of nationality and other group problems in the Missions.

A minority group will often refuse to be thus re-educated, that is, Americanized, Germanized, or re-enculturated according to any other pattern. The mere placement of indigenous Superiors, especially if de-nativized, is no solution to nationality problems in a diocese, seminary, convent, hospital, or school, if the general policy of the institution insists on keeping the institution American, German, Spanish, Italian, French — in a word, non-native. Dislike of things foreign is often not so much an imperfection or wickedness as something purely human. On the other hand, it is also well to remember, even the most charitable and most humble missionary will have a certain amount of excess group-centeredness within himself. Even if all the missionaries of a given country were Saints, the American Saints would feel it their sacred duty to make their parishioners the best Christians possible and therefore would unwittingly tend to make them American in certain respects. This is unavoidable. The same would be true of the German group of hypothetical Saints; the same would be true also of the French, Spanish, and Italian hypothetical Saints. The tendency is present and it should not be denied. Rather, one should constantly be aware of its presence and try to keep it in control. Although Christian values are the same the world over, they are nonetheless colored by the underlying value-system of the particular culture, and it is the coloring that will cause our different groups of hypothetical Saints trouble. The Bible frequently speaks of God as if He were a man, a being in human form. However, such anthropomorphism will differ from culture to culture. Without realizing it the zealous American Christian tends to transform God into an American, just as the devout Spaniard tends to picture God not only in human terms but as a Spaniard. Both the American and European believe in charity and friendliness. The American, however, may prefer charity and friendliness (Christian virtues universally accepted and valid) that are less formal even when dealing with strangers, while the European may insist on a type of charity and friendliness that is heavily colored with European etiquette and formality. American Catholics consider it quite laudable to have their national flag displayed in church next to the altar, for to them it is a sign of their devotion to country, a Christian virtue and duty; the German Catholics and others also believe in love of country but consider the flag as a kind of political symbol, and to display it next to the altar is almost blasphemous. Each group of hypothetical Saints will be convinced that *its* value-judgments alone are correct; each group feels also that it has the duty to make mankind God-like. Now, if you bring such groups together, do not be surprised if there is a clash every now and then, yes, even among Saints — zealous, devout individuals who somehow do not realize that even their asceticism has been influenced by their culture, for even the particular way we love God is colored by our cultural background.

Group-centeredness is very much alive in missionaries because it is very much alive in normal human beings. It urges the missionary, so to speak, to thank God that he is "not like the rest of men." It urges him to usurp the Creator's authority and to try to re-mold others according to the image and likeness of a particular group. More than any other factor excessive group-centeredness is responsible for group conflict. The consciousness of this group-centeredness, an appreciation of the good and the importance of other groups, and more broadmindedness — in a word, a bit more catholicism — would go a long way toward the realization of that ideal *Ut unum sint!*

If a solution is to be found for the group problems that are unavoidable in so vast an undertaking as the Missions, and if there is to be a genuine spirit of co-operation among the numberless soldiers of Christ, the road to harmony and co-operation will be found not only in spiritual writings on obedience, charity, and humility but also in books on human behavior — on culture and social psychology. There is also a need for an honest examination of conscience — Superior as well as subject, religious as well as lay-missionary, the indigenous apostle as well as the foreign. Not *tua culpa* but *mea culpa!* The group cannot be cured unless each member admits that he too suffers from excessive group-centeredness. A broadminded missionary will say to himself: "I will at all times try to see the beauty in the Creator's human kaleidoscope. I will at all times try to appreciate the variety of flowers in God's human garden; they are all attractive, even if they are not all roses like myself. If God is delighted with differences in human beings, I must be too. I will at all times, therefore, try to see the Divine Humor in allowing mankind to be so varied — so different from me."

One might be tempted to say that the best solution to group conflict is to avoid group contact. Such a segregationist view is both unrealistic and defeatistic. The Missions, like the Kingdom of God itself, are necessarily made up of countless social groups and must remain so. Moreover, group contact can occur on many levels and the same individual may belong to a number of groups: avoidance of contact and conflict by segregation is impossible because it is impossible to cut up an individual into a dozen pieces corresponding to his dozen different in-groups. Then there is the fact that missionary strength actually consists in unity and diversity, not in segregation. The vastness and complexity of mission work calls for many specialized groups, professional and otherwise; it calls for recruits from all social strata and from all nations. The task of spreading the Gospel is the task of all religious congregations and orders, of diocesan clergy, and of the laity, each group with its *esprit de corps*, ways, and values. Diversity contributes to strength not only because of numbers but also because no group (e.g., American or Dutch missionaries, the Jesuits, Maryknoll, Columbans, or Divine Word Missionaries) has all the answers. Inbreeding is harmful to any missionary training program, policy, or practical approach. Co-operation between missionary groups (not segregation), diversity and unity rather than isolation, constitutes the secret to effective missionary action.

SELECTED READINGS

1. **Culture and Society**
   * 1) R. Linton, *The Study of Man*, pp. 91–112.
     2) Kroeber and Kluckhohn, *Culture: A Critical Review of Concepts and Definitions*, pp. 41–82, 145–179.

2. **Subcultures and Specialties**
     1) M. J. Herskovits, *Man and His Works*, pp. 574–577.

* 2) R. Redfield, *Peasant Society and Culture.*
* 3) R. Redfield, *Folk Culture of the Yucatan.*
  4) R. Linton, *The Study of Man,* pp. 272–285.
  5) A. K. Cohen, *Delinquent Boys: The Culture of the Gang.*
  6) M. Zborowski and E. Herzog, *Life Is with People: The Jewish Little-Town of Eastern Europe.*
* 7) M. Kenny, "Twentieth Century Spanish Expatriates in Cuba: A Sub-Culture," *Anthropological Quarterly,* XXXIV (1961), 85–93.
* 8) M. Kenny, "Twentieth Century Spanish Expatriates in Mexico: An Urban Sub-Culture," *Anthropological Quarterly,* XXXV (1962), 169–180.
* 9) R. Redfield, *The Little Community.*
  10) O. Lewis, *Life in a Mexican Village.*
  11) O. Lewis, *Five Families: Mexican Case Studies in the Culture of Poverty.*

REVIEW QUESTIONS

1. What do we mean when we say that culture is a societal possession? Is it not the individual rather than the society that acts? (p. 111)
2. Define "society." How does it differ from an animal aggregation? (p. 111)
3. What is the difference between an "idiosyncrasy" and a "specialty"? What are "alternatives"? "universals"? (pp. 111–113) Which of these is not cultural and why? (pp. 111–113)
4. What is a "pattern"? (pp. 113–114)
5. Where is culture located, in the mind or the external world? (pp. 114–115)
6. What do you like (or dislike) about defining culture as "tradition" or "social heredity"? (pp. 115–116)
7. What is the "imperative of selection"? (pp. 115–116)
8. Do cultural and societal boundaries coincide? (pp. 116–117)
9. What is a "subculture"? (pp. 116–117)
10. How does the socio-cultural approach differ from the individual approach? (pp. 118–120)
11. What bearing does the concept of "subculture" have on practical apostolic work? (pp. 120–122)
12. Indicate at least six different types of group conflicts that are possible on the mission field. How can the danger of group conflict be lessened? (pp. 122–129)

TOPICS FOR CLASSROOM DISCUSSION AND PAPERS

1. How can one's asceticism be colored by one's cultural background? Give as many examples as possible.

2. Elaborate on the statement that Communists believe in a socio-cultural rather than an individual approach.
3. Read a book on Catholic-Protestant relations and show how and why Catholics and Protestants fail to understand each other. (*Anthropological* reasons only!)
4. What accommodations might be made in dealing with Protestants entering the Church?
5. Formulate a definition of culture by yourself and be prepared to defend your choice of words, or choose one of the many definitions of recognized anthropologists and show its incompleteness or inexactness.
6. Compare Oscar Lewis' *Tepoztlán: Village in Mexico* with Robert Redfields' *Tepoztlán: A Mexican Village*.
7. What answer would you give to a young priest who says that he is not interested in Cultural Anthropology because "my future work will infallibly be in a Colored parish down South: I'm not going to Kenya or Vietnam; I'm staying right in my own backyard!"?
8. Comment on "Evangelization and Team Spirit," *Christ to the World*, III (1958), 283–294. What culturological basis does the article possess?

III.

THE ORGANIZATION OF CULTURE

CHAPTER SIX

STRUCTURAL INTEGRATION

CULTURES have not only a content but also a peculiar organization of that content; cultures are peculiarly integrated wholes. At present we are interested not so much in the content of culture as in the manner in which the content is organized into a *system*. We are interested, as it were, not in automobile *parts* but in how these parts go together to form a self-moving vehicle. We are interested not so much in a "dictionary" as in a "grammar" of culture.

The cultural integration of which we speak is effected in two ways — through function and configuration. Function is responsible for the structural integration (the subject of the present chapter) while configuration is responsible for the psychological integration (the subject of Chapter Seven). In Chapter Eight we shall combine both aspects into a single picture and point out the possible degrees of "oneness."

THE NOTION OF STRUCTURAL INTEGRATION

Ideally speaking, as anthropologists generally point out, culture should be described in a single comprehensive sweep, for it is a single "organic" entity. Culture is not like a freight train that might be described car by car; culture is not like a chain that might be examined link by link. Much less may we describe it as we might the various items on sale in a hardware store. Culture is not an assembled freight train or a chain of patterns; much less is it a mere random collection of human ways. It is more like a complicated machine in full operation, or like a living organism, like the human body, whose parts cannot be properly understood except in relation to all other parts and to the whole. We must look at culture as a *whole*, with interconnected parts, each part with its specific and over-all function.

However, to describe culture in one single sweep is an impossible

ideal, for culture is too complicated an assemblage of closely interrelated, functionally organized parts and groups of parts. Instead,
anthropologists must content themselves with describing their complicated cultural machine or organism by focusing their attention
on one part at a time, or on a definite system of parts which
happen to be more intimately connected with each other than
with the other parts, constantly, however, relating the parts to
each other and to the whole. In a word, to speak of "parts" of
culture is to speak of the whole of culture in a practical, even if
not ideal manner.

Not only is a good mechanic acquainted with the different parts
of an automobile and knows the technical names of all the nuts
and bolts, washers, plates, rods, cylinders, tubes, wires, and whatever goes to make up a car, but in one glance, as it were, he also
sees these parts in their relation to the other parts; he sees what each
part is for and what it does for the whole (function); he knows the
arrangement of the parts (structure), how the parts are organized
to higher and higher complexity, into larger and larger units, and
finally into a whole called "automobile." A physician, too, looks at
the human body not as a conglomeration of parts but as functionally
organized subsystems that are further organized into larger and
larger units, such as the circulatory system, the nervous system, and
the like. These systems, in turn, are intimately interwoven into an
integrated structure called the "human body" (Luzbetak, 1961:
167–168).

Although every comparison limps (and the present one is no
exception), one may nevertheless profitably compare the structure
of culture to that of a machine or human body. However, in so doing
we must keep in mind that the extent to which a particular way of
life will resemble a machine or organism will vary from culture to
culture and that some parts of culture may be functionless or, as
already pointed out, they may cause stress rather than ease tensions
(see p. 61; Honigmann, 1959:177–179).

A culture, therefore, is divided and subdivided into smaller and
smaller purposefully organized units. These units are: institutions,
complexes, traits, and items. A culture trait is that minimal constituent of a way of life which is functionally organized and regarded
as having an independent existence. A trait, therefore, has three
essential characteristics: (1) it is minimal; (2) it is functionally
organized with other parts of culture; (3) it has its own existence in

spite of the fact that it is a part of a larger unit. A trait is composed of *items*. Unlike traits, items are not regarded as having an existence that is independent of the action, thought, or artefact of which they are parts; that is, they have a significance only as constituents of traits. Traits unite into complexes, complexes into institutions, institutions into the total life-way or culture. A culture *complex* is a group of interrelated traits having a common immediate function. Complexes interwoven so as to achieve a common response to a basic human need are known as *institutions*. Institutions are small behavioral systems in themselves that might very well be compared to the nervous, circulatory, or digestive systems of the human body or to the ignition, fuel, cooling, or lubricating systems of an automobile.

We might best use Linton's classical example to illustrate these terms (1936:399–400). Taking the Comanche bow as a starting-point, Linton shows how this particular trait embodies such items as the Osage orangewood taken from the heart of the tree, rectangular cross-section, high polish, a more or less definite length, and a sinew bowstring tied in a distinctly Comanche manner. These items are essential for a genuine Comanche bow, although they have very little significance in themselves. Now the bow (a trait) combines with several other traits (the arrow, bowcase, quiver, and a particular method of shooting) into what might be called a "bow-and-arrow complex." Each of these traits might be broken down into smaller units, which we have called "items." The arrow, for instance, would include such items as the arrowhead, the shaft, the wings, and the notch for the bowstring. The bow-and-arrow complex unites with other complexes, such as the horse-complex, the tracking-complex, and others, which together form the hunting-institution. The hunting-institution combines with other economic, social and ideational activites to form the Comanche culture.

As Linton himself admitted, his example is an extreme simplification. At times it may not be easy to draw clearcut lines between the various units and subunits, leaving considerable room for subjective interpretations. In any case, the divisions should be based on the structure of the culture in question and not on any other.

The same item is usually not shared by or linked to distinct traits, whereas the same trait may, and frequently does, occur in combination with distinct complexes and institutions. For instance, a bow functioning as an instrument for providing food belongs to an economic institution; a masterful use of the same instrument may single out an individual and give him authority and prestige. Since the bow has such an important economic and social value it will most likely be an important subject in the educational system and a special concern of the local magician and priest. The bow thus becomes linked to a large number of distinct economic, social, and ideational activities.

Items themselves may be further subdivided into constituent parts; however, since such parts lack cultural significance, that is, since they are not geared into the structure itself, they are not parts of culture. They are like the molecules, atoms, neutrons, and electrons of parts that make up a machine; they are organized among themselves but they are not geared into the machine as such. The molecules, atoms, neutrons, and electrons are not mechanically significant just as the components of items are not culturally significant.

FUNCTION

The linkages through which structural integration is achieved are known as "functions." A functional linkage is the purpose, specific or general, which a culture trait, complex, or institution serves. The notion, still imperfect in many ways, is nonetheless useful, and anthropologists are constantly making use of the concept even though some do not even mention the word "function." They may instead speak of culture elements as being "prerequisites" for other culture constituents; they may say that certain complexes have special "tasks" to perform, or that they "confer" status, "ensure" prestige, or do some other "service" for the individual and society. Or, a custom may be presented as "filling certain human needs." Sometimes anthropologists may refer to function negatively by speaking in terms of "repercussions." Sometimes function is presented as an "association" or "interrelationship" in a given structure, or as an "expression" or "reflection" of certain values held by the society (cf. Firth, 1955:237–258).

Following Linton's suggestion (1940:402–404), some anthropologists distinguish between form, meaning, use, and function. In other words, instead of speaking only of form and function, function is broken down into three aspects, sc., meaning, use, and "function" ("function," in this case, being understood in a restricted sense) (cf. Beals, Hoijer, 1953:620–621; Keesing, 1958:155).

Form is the shape, size, manner of production or execution, and everything else that makes the custom observable, e.g., the shape, dimensions, and material of an axe; the type of singing, drumming, costuming, and movements in a dance.

Meaning is the totality of subjective associations attached to the form — the various connotations and associated values. Everything in a culture, therefore, has a "price-tag" attached to it. Since among some isolated primitive tribes steel implements are rare, steel axes may be associated with a special value, making the tool "precious." A custom may be greatly respected on account of an historical association which it may happen to have with the founder of a nation or a religion. Form is observable, meaning is not; form is easily diffused, subjective associations and connotations and values are not. In America, for example, tin cans are associated with filthy alleys, garbage heaps, slums, and hobo camps, but in the Pacific, where prestige-giving plywood floors are gradually replacing the traditional bamboo, tin cans are used as spittoons and have the meaning of progress and of preferred status. In America an outright donation may mean that you are charitable; elsewhere, such an act may mean that you are drunk or completely out of your mind, or that you are challenging the humiliated recipient, or that the object offered is worthless. A missionary will react to polygamy as to something immoral, scandalous, and disgusting; a Mohammedan, on the other hand, will react to the very same practice as something highly moral, prestige-giving, approved by Allah, and therefore very laudable. The Seven Day Adventist despises the Pope, while the Catholic speaks of him with the deepest respect, love, and devotion — as of Christ's representative on earth.

The tea-loving Australian lecturer Dr. Fred Schwarz, trying a bit of Australian humor on his supposedly coffee-loving American audience, once described the drink as a concoction made from castor oil beans soaked in shellac. The castor oil, he claimed, was responsible for the flavor, while the shellac explained the color. "And," he added, "it takes idiots to drink it." The lecturer was dumfounded when his audience broke out in riotous applause, taking the would-be joke quite seriously and in keeping with the meaning which the particular American group gave to coffee. The audience happened to be a group of coffee-haters who regarded coffee-drinking as sinful (Schwarz, 1960:137–138). In other words, the same object may have quite a different meaning in different cultures or subcultures, for cultures are indeed a "silent language," a system of behavior with meaning (E. T. Hall, 1959).

Use is the particular purpose for which a society employs a cultural form. An axe, for instance, may be used for chopping firewood; it may be used for twirling in a dance, or as a kind of walking-stick; it may be used as an essential part of a man's costume; it may be used as a weapon by the warriors defending the tribe. Similarly, fire may have a great variety of uses depending on the particular culture. Fire may be used for cooking, heating, lighting, for burning rubbish, for chasing mosquitoes, for creating an atmosphere as in campfire singing or in an ultra-modern temperature-controlled home, for smoke signals, and for Liturgy.

Function (in the restricted or specialized sense of Linton) implies a much broader relationship of the form within the structure of the particular culture than is implied by use. Function means the place which the custom occupies in the total culture rather than in the immediate context as in the case of use. Thus, the axe in relation to the whole culture may be a way of filling an economic need, as in the case of an agricultural society that uses the axes to clear a forest for farming. In another culture the axe may function as a means of filling aesthetic needs. The term "function," used in this restricted rather than generic sense, in regard to initiation rites would refer to such broad purposes as social stability, solidarity, security, co-operation between the young and the old, and education.

FUNCTIONALISM

Function entered anthropological literature in the 1920's as a result of the popularity enjoyed by Gestalt psychology, reflecting the trend in both philosophy and science toward a "holistic" viewpoint. Bronislaw Malinowski in his *Argonauts of the Western Pacific* (London, 1922) and Alfred Radcliffe-Brown in his *The Andaman Islanders* (London, 1922) quite independently arrived at the conclusion that cultures can be properly understood only if their constituent parts are viewed as interrelated and as having very definite purposes or "functions" as regards the whole.

Malinowski and Radcliffe-Brown differed somewhat in their use of the concept of "function." The latter emphasized the role played by culture patterns in maintaining the *whole*, while Malinowski viewed function more as the role culture patterns played in filling human needs. Malinowski exaggerated the cohesiveness and integration of cultures, while Radcliffe-Brown rightly recognized degrees of integration. While Malinowski's focus was on function in *culture*, Radcliffe-Brown's interest was centered on function in *society* (what culture does for a social group rather than how culture operates in itself). Malinowski refused to consider culture except on a single time-level, while Radcliffe-Brown studied culture also from a "diachronic" viewpoint (Keesing, 1958:152–154).

Malinowski, Radcliffe-Brown, and their early followers have been responsible not only for the valuable concept of function but for the development of practical field techniques as well. Today their influence is most strongly felt in Anglo-Saxon countries, especially in Britain, so much so that R. Firth does not hesitate to say that "all British social anthropology today is functionalist" (1955:247). Today, under the leadership of such outstanding anthropologists as Fortes, Evans-Pritchard, and Firth, functionalism is broadening its interests, improving its techniques, and clarifying its concepts and terminology (Firth, 1955:237–258). Although there is still much to be done before the final word can be said about the functional nature of culture, the approach throws considerable light on problems facing the modern applied anthropologists. In fact, the approach followed in the present course is to a large extent "functional."

SUMMARY AND SELECTED MISSIOLOGICAL APPLICATIONS

Summary

1) Culture is not a mere lifeless heap of unrelated parts: it is a *system* and more like a living organism or a complicated machine in full operation. Culture has a content as well as an organization of that content. Culture is structurally organized or integrated by means of function; it is psychologically integrated by means of configuration. "Function" refers to the role each part plays in relation to the other parts and the whole. The interrelation we call "structure." "Integration" is the "oneness" of culture.

2) Culture may be divided and subdivided into smaller and smaller functionally organized units: institutions, complexes, traits, and items.

3) Besides form, cultural "parts" have use, meaning, and function

understood in a specific sense. Use consists in the way a society employs the trait, complex, or activity; meaning embraces all the associations, connotations, and values attached to a custom; function taken in the restricted sense is the purpose a custom serves or the relationship it has in the total (rather than the immediate) cultural context.

FIGURE 3

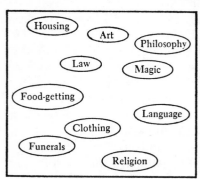

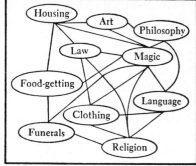

A "photographic" or "journalistic" description of a culture.

A "functional" description of culture.

Selected Missiological Applications

1. THE NECESSITY OF A FUNCTIONAL APPROACH TO THE STUDY OF CULTURE

Whatever segment of culture the missioner may wish to examine, he will have to refer the segment to other segments of the culture and to the whole life-way. Even the most detailed photographic description of, let us say, a bus-stop on a New York street will not tell a simple Pacific Islander, who has never before seen city life or a bus or a bus-stop, what a bus-stop really is. A mere photographic portrayal, no matter how detailed, is not an *anthropological* picture, the kind of picture that would tell one the way of a *people*. Besides the form of the bus-stop, its use, meaning, and function must be described and its relation to other elements of the life-way of New Yorkers would have to be shown (see Figure 3). It would be necessary to show the Pacific Islander how the bus-stop is a culture trait of a bus-service complex, which together with other transportation services, such as the subway, taxi, plane, and train, fills an important need — transportation. It would be necessary also to show how transportation is connected with other aspects of American city-life. Buses bring people to work, school, clubs, government offices, to homes of friends and relatives, to art museums and concerts, and to churches. Consequently, the bus-stop is indirectly linked to the economic, social, and psychological life-way of New Yorkers from many sides. The Pacific Islander might be reminded also that bus service provides considerable employment, for which New Yorkers are paid salaries, with which salaries they are able to buy food, provide shelter, clothing, and education for their families, support their churches, and make a government possible through taxation.

A missionary who studies native dwellings, agricultural techniques, weddings, and funeral customs "photographically" may be given credit for having an innocent and a partially useful hobby, but he certainly would not be following a scientific approach to the understanding of his people. Houses, gardens, weddings, and funerals must be studied in all their details but *as they are functionally interlocked with the infinitude of human ways.* The author's previous treatment of the subject (Luzbetak, 1961:167–169) may throw some useful light on the unfortunate tendency to view cultural elements as independent and unrelated customs.

> The mistake referred to consists not so much in not being interested in the *whole* culture but rather in not being interested in the culture *as a whole.* . . . Today there can be no valid excuse for missionary techniques and policies based on the false premise that cultures are nothing but a conglomeration of human ways.

> Mere "photographic" or "journalistic" descriptions of native housing, farming, engagement ceremonies, weddings, folkmedicine, so-called "superstitions," music, dancing, and art — mere "photographic" or "journalistic" descriptions provide only a very superficial knowledge of the ways and mentality of a people; and missionary policies and techniques based on such limited knowledge will of necessity be as imperfect as the knowledge itself. . . .

> To an American, a pig is nothing more than a potential sausage or canned ham and a source of income for certain individuals. To the New Guinea native, the pig is incomparably more, for the animal is intermeshed with practically every aspect of native life. In fact, native life would be impossible without the pig . . . without the pig the native religion would be impossible. The pig is the chief source of security, for the pig must be sacrificed to placate pork-hungry an-

cestors and deceased relatives on whom the well-being of the clan-members depends. No child is born into the world successfully and no tribal battle is won except through pig-sacrifices. The pig has also a very important economic and social role to play. Pigs, for instance, are exchanged for the precious pearl shell, and form the most important part of the family wealth. Although pork is eaten on a feast-or-famine basis, it is the main and usually the only source of animal-protein in the native diet. An exchange of pork seals friendships between individuals, families, lineages, and larger social groups. In fact, a friend is referred to literally as "my fellow-pork-eater." Distribution of pork climaxes all major festivities, such as birth ceremonies, engagements, weddings, and food-exchange between friendly groups. Without pigs it would be impossible for a boy to be initiated into the tribe and thus become a fullfledged member of his social group, with all rights and privileges annexed to such membership. The number and quality of pigs give the owner prestige. A pigless adult would, in fact, be a kind of Stone Age tramp or hobo. A woman's value as wife is measured by her skill in caring for pigs, and one of the major tests which a young woman must go through during her trial-marriage is that of pig-raising. It is impossible to acquire a wife except with pigs as an essential, if not main, part of the bridewealth. One can hardly imagine the number of functional linkages that would be severed if the Government or the missionaries (as one of the religious bodies on the island is actually trying to do) were effectively to outlaw the raising of pigs. The pig is interwebbed with practically every aspect of native life, and in dealing with the people the missionary would have to look upon the pig not as he would at a photograph of the animal but in full cultural context, with all linkages (economic, social, and ideational) in view.

Similarly, to understand polygamy, the missionary will have to view the practice not as he would a photograph of a polygamous trio but rather as plural marriages are related to prestige, to friendship between families and tribes, to wealth, daily routine, comfort, animal husbandry, feuding, tribal loyalty, ancestor worship, and to all other associated aspects of life. Radio and television are linked to hundreds of different aspects of American life: education, sports, politics, religion, recreation, law enforcement, shipping, taxi service, fuel delivery, various repair services, rocketry, and many other elements in American culture — not to mention the infinite variety of products advertised by the sponsors of radio and television programs. The radio and television set are more than electronic devices producing sound or sound and picture. To understand these devices, one must understand how they are interlocked within the structure of American living.

2. PRACTICAL HINTS AS TO THE MANNER OF
INQUIRING INTO FUNCTION

To discover the various functions of culture patterns and to see how the patterns are interwebbed will call for keen observation, painstaking investigation, clever questioning, considerable reflection, and careful analysis. To ask outright: "Why do you do that?" or "What's that for?" or "What is the meaning of this ceremony or object?" may at times produce the information desired (manifest functions), but very often functions are latent and such direct questioning is naïve, for the functions are not known to the society in question. They are like the grammatical patterns of a language, used by the native speaker but latent. More often than not, functions must be "dug out" with considerable effort on the part of the investigator. Function, moreover, may be objective or merely supposed. A charm, for example, may be worn "in order to keep evil spirits away," a subjective reason for wearing it; objectively it functions as a source of security and peace of mind.

A practical approach to the study of function is to observe culture *in action* and, if possible, to arrive at function *negatively*. By observing and inquiring into actual cases of deviation from a particular custom one arrives at actual (not merely attributed) consequences of such deviations. Imagination, rationalization, and philosophizing on the part of the missionary or his informant are all very poor substitutes for actual case studies.

In practical field work a negative approach may prove to be far more rewarding than any other, for it is generally easier to observe "bad" effects, tensions, disorganization, and disaster than to observe positively what the purpose of a custom is supposed to be and what it does for the culture and society. The indirect approach recommended might be best described through illustrations. A convert's excuse for not living up to Christian principles may indicate that needs formerly filled by traditional un-Christian ways are *de facto* not being filled by the new Christian mode of life. The convert may insist on participating in dances considered by the missioner as immoral; the convert does so not because he is an indecent individual or does not respect Christian standards as such but because he values a particular *function* of the traditional dance, such as prestige for instance. Such dances may also function as a normal procedure in courtship, and the excuse given may be: "If I don't take part in our traditional dances I shall never be able to get married." Domestic and tribal disputes can likewise provide indirect information about the function of cultural patterns. A husband or wife, for instance, may be accused of not fulfilling his or her role (function). Or again, the many "childish" fears that the missionary may have to allay, the many worries that upset adults, and the various personal conflicts arising from the incompatibility of certain Christian and traditional ways will all cast light on the why of behavior: the new Christian standard is perhaps not filling legitimate and morally justifiable needs, such as prestige, friendship, and family loyalty. Similarly, dissatisfaction with and criticism of Christian ways will indirectly reveal certain traditional uses, meanings, and functions, Christianity being criticized precisely because it does not serve the traditional and valued purposes.

Although we have been emphasizing the importance of observing and inquiring about actual cases, we need not exclude hypothetical situations from our inquiries. Such hypothetical cases may not provide scientific evidence, but they will provide useful clues to such evidence. Observers of custom, especially trained anthropologists, have their own little "tricks" or ways of discovering and following up clues. A school teacher could, for instance, suggest many a topic for a composition which would provide useful clues to function. Writing about "What Pigs Mean to a Kanaka," a New Guinea schoolboy gave his imagination free rein and pointed out negatively numberless consequences which an epidemic would have if it were to exterminate the animal. Such a composition could provide, as it actually did, a number of very useful clues as to the why of pig-raising.

At times the missionary will have to inquire into functions that will turn out to be rather embarrassing to the informant. As a general rule, one should not unduly press the informant; instead, it might be far better, for the time being at least, to be satisfied with knowing that the topic is embarrassing, a fact which is in itself useful information. Instead of pressing the question farther than etiquette and prudence will allow, the inquirer should put it aside and, in the meantime, try to gather as much background information as possible. The realization that the inquirer is acquainted with the background of the embarrassing inquiry may make the informant less self-conscious and less hesitant.

At the least sign of embarrassment it was my practice while in the highlands of New Guinea to speak of "the olden times," that is, *before* the arrival of the government and the missionaries in the area, in this manner suggesting that the informant's behavior as well as that of his tribesmen may have changed considerably. The mere suggestion that I was not accusing the informant or his group of a custom Europeans, especially government officials and missionaries, would normally disapprove of would remove the barrier of secrecy and would at least provide clues to the embarrassing inquiry. I would then follow up the clues by discussing the customs of *neighboring* groups whose life-way I rightly suspected to be very similar to those of the local people. Discussing *others* is always less embarrassing. For this reason it was my policy to have a few employees (a cook, a gardener, and a teacher) who were "outsiders," that is, belonging to neighboring but friendly tribes. They were well acquainted with the ways of the local people, and, in fact, were closely bound to them through intermarriage. Although these "outsiders" would be somewhat reluctant to speak about their own more or less secret customs, they showed very little inhibition when asked about the local people; in fact, they even volunteered information about them. Armed with valuable clues from "pre-missionary" times, from neighboring practices, and from information about the local people provided by outside informants, I was thus able to suggest questions to my regular local informants that made them suspect that I practically knew the answer, and they no longer hesitated or felt embarrassed. Cross-examination and checking with other independent sources provided the evidence sought. Such interviews were, of course, as much as possible about *actual* incidents rather than hypothetical cases. The student must be warned, however, that there is no rigid formula for field research: the actual choice of techniques must be decided right on the spot — in the field and at the moment of inquiry — constantly keeping in mind the personality of the inquirer as well as that of the informant.

There are two very common tendencies that make the study of function difficult: (1) manifest functions of the missionary's culture tend to be transferred to similar forms in the local culture; (2) latent functions tend to be completely overlooked. To counteract these tendencies the missioner must make a positive effort to develop an awareness of function and structure by studying the local culture from a functional viewpoint. This awareness should be

148   THE ORGANIZATION OF CULTURE

sharpened by studying the works of anthropologists who emphasize function and structure. Recommended especially are R. Firth's *Elements of Social Organization* (London, 1951) and R. Piddington's *An Introduction to Social Anthropology* (London, 1950, 1957).

3. STRUCTURAL INTEGRATION AND ITS BEARING ON GENERAL MISSIONARY POLICIES

We have emphasized the importance of placing mission personnel in strategic, that is, in culturally and socially meaningful positions (see pp. 118–120). The meaning of "strategic" becomes clearer in the light of what has been said about structural integration. The Church in Latin America, for instance, is appealing to Europe and North America for priests and religious instructors. The more enlightened leaders in the Church as well as the more enlightened missionaries answering the appeal realize that priests and religious instructors are not the full answer to Latin American problems. Culture is an integrated whole, and religion is of necessity intimately interlocked with social and economic aspects of life. Latin America needs more than priests and religious instructors; it needs an army of highly qualified professionally trained specialists, dedicated experts in practically every field of knowledge — economists, social psychologists, educators, sociologists, social workers, urbanization experts, anthropologists, dieticians, agronomists, technicians — dedicated Christian specialists who would make religious instruction and priestly work possible and worthwhile (Luzbetak, 1961:169; Korb, 1961:115). This same reasoning justifies the vast outlay in money and personnel necessary to maintain schools in mission countries, especially colleges and universities, which at first sight seem merely to be competing with parallel secular institutions and systems of education.

> To effect a change in one aspect of culture (religion), the Missions must deal with the whole culture and with culture as a whole. Instead of condemning ancestor worship from the housetops, . . . [the] missionary might be far more effective if he would for a moment forget about ancestor worship as such and instead introduce for young and old alike an educational program on sanitation and hygiene. By convincing the people that disease comes from germs, viruses, organic defects, and biological degeneration, he would at the same time prove to them that sickness does not come from vengeful ancestors, and

thus he would in the most effective way possible remove the very basis for ancestor worship. By the same token, the unsound medical practices which the government health authorities seek to eradicate will tend to be perpetuated unless the native belief in ancestor worship is eradicated (Luzbetak, 1961:169–170).

A sound missionary policy will, moreover, call for sound predictions. Businessmen and governments, people of the world, choose policies in accord with what they feel is a wise prediction. Why should not the modern apostle be as wise as "the children of this world"? When dealing with men, we are, of course, dealing with beings endowed with a free will, so that scientific predictions in the form of rigid and infallible laws are impossible. Moreover, factors involved in any human behavior are so numerous and their interplay is so subtle that infallibility in prediction is out of the question. Then, too, there is the fact that Applied Anthropology is still a very young field of knowledge — in fact, it is still in its infancy — and there is much we do not know about culture change. Nevertheless, a grasp of functional linkages may indicate the most probable course events may take, for a kind of chain reaction may sometimes be suspected well in advance.

A classic case of how a knowledge of functional linkages could have prevented a catastrophe is that of the introduction of the steel axe among the Yir Yoront aborigines of southwest Australia. The change from stone to steel did not have the results hoped for by the missionaries and European settlers who helped to introduce the new axe. The new implement, far superior to the old-fashioned counterpart, made the latter obsolete, and every custom and value attached to the onetime all-important stone axe also disappeared. The whites had hoped that the steel axe would advance native technology, improve the standard of living, and give the aborigines more leisure for aesthetic activities. However, the standard of living remained the same, while the steel axe, the new time-saving device, merely served to make the men lazy and to forget the arts they once mastered. The making of the stone axe formerly gave the menfolk a certain amount of self-reliance and prestige; it fostered friendship through trade and made the old men important in the eyes of the other members of the tribe. The stone axe was regarded as the chief symbol of masculinity. The missionaries and European planters, not realizing this fact and eager to improve the socio-economic situation of their people, began to distribute the steel axe to women and children as prizes, rewards, and wages in complete disregard of functional linkages. The old men, the onetime respected segment of society, were not considered "good" material for Christianity and were more or less ignored. Formerly women were permitted at most only to borrow an axe from their husbands — that is, if they were considered ideal wives and were found worthy of the honor of using such a noble and genuinely masculine tool. Now, however, women could not only use but actually possess axes as their own, axes far superior to the ones their husbands had. While children could easily become the lawful owners of the new prestige-giving implement, their fathers, "the no-hopers," could not, for the Europeans distributing the steel axes would have nothing to do with them. As wife and children grew more and more independent, insubordination set in and the former head of the family grew more and more insecure. There was confusion of age, sex, and kinship roles and serious disorganization resulted. Ownership in general became more and more confused, resulting in stealing and other disorders. As the stone axe, once a source of prestige and pride, became a mark of shame, the old festivals in which trading of stone axe heads and initiation of the youth took place lost their excitement and glamor; in fact, life itself seemed to have lost its zest and the idea of suicide, unknown before, became a not-too-rare means of ending a confused, insecure, and disorganized life. Formerly the Yir Yoront had a closely-knit totemistic system of ideas, values, and sentiment that permeated practically everything they did; a normal change in their culture always occurred in accord with their totemistic philosophy. Attempts to find totemistic myths upon which to base the rapid changes taking place as a result of the introduction of the steel axe could not keep pace with the demoralizing trend. A serious psychological and moral void was thus created, threatening total disintegration of the Yir Yoront culture and annihilation of the people themselves (Sharp, 1952). Although hindsight is easier than foresight, much of this tragic disintegration and demoralization could have been prevented if the functional linkages between the stone axe and the rest of the culture content would have been analyzed and traced and if the new steel implement had been selectively distributed in accord with the demands of the existing linkages.

4. Structural Integration and the Medical Missionary

The medical missionary's professional training may be quite sufficient for work in his own cultural milieu, but as soon as he crosses cultural boundaries, additional talent, knowledge, skill, and character traits are called for. Principles of hygiene that are easily grasped in the missioner's home-country may become extremely complicated in the "strange" network of cultural patterns on the mission front. Such "self-evident" recommendations as boiling water in order to avoid cholera and other serious diseases are self-evident only in the cultural setting in which the missionary was brought up. "Commonsense" rules like boiling water may lose all their simplicity in the alien context, for water may have many "strange" functional linkages: water may be interwebbed with the economic, social, and religious life-way of the local people in a very complicated and intense manner. Water may be linked with magic, kinship obligations, moral codes, ritual purifications, etiquette, friendship, daily routine, status, and many other aspects of the local people's beliefs and behavior. It may be theoretically easy to boil water, but to limit one's drinking exclusively to boiled water may be extremely difficult. A friend who does not care about boiling water offers his comrade a drink; refusal to accept the water may be a serious insult and may mean the end of a close and important friendship. One might hesitate to boil the water not because it is a difficult chore but because a water-spirit might be offended. Routine may make boiling water as difficult as it is for us to brush our teeth after every meal, the best means of preventing dental decay. The medical missionary must be able to see health factors not as they are found in his home-country, in the test tube of a modern laboratory, or perhaps as described for him in a reputable and widely used medical manual or journal but as health factors actually occur in the particular socio-cultural structure.

5. Structural Integration and the Agricultural and Technological Specialist in the Missions

As in the case of missionary medical work, new agricultural and technological efforts will call for more than a knowledge of Agronomy and Technology. The introduction of such "simple" matters as hybrid corn, manuring, drainage, shading, mulching, and erosion control may be simple only in theory and out of cultural context. A certain agronomist working for the U. S. Government among the Taos seemed certain of success until one day he tried to put into practice a very basic and almost self-evident principle with which every agriculture specialist would agree — early-spring ploughing. Unfortunately this almost self-evident principle made good sense only in Agronomy but not in Anthropology. The agronomist had, in fact, little appreciation for native ways; much less was he concerned about any possible linkages between the Taosian economic life and other aspects of culture. After all, was he not sent to the Taos by the government to change their ways, to teach rather than to learn? And was it not true that his only interest was agriculture, not native religious beliefs, especially since he represented a government that believed in strict separation of church and state? Such an attitude made the specialist totally blind to the important connection between Taosian religion and agriculture. The native religion portrays Mother Earth as pregnant in Spring, a belief which the Taos not only took for granted but imagined that everyone else accepted as true. The agronomist, however, was so taken up with his agricultural theory that he completely failed to observe that the Taos never drove their wagons to town in early Spring and that their horses did not wear horseshoes during this period, and, in fact, that the people themselves very religiously avoided the use of shoes with hard soles. The expert did not realize that Mother Earth was pregnant in Spring and that, as a consequence, one could not be careful enough when walking over Her. In fact, the onetime greatly-admired friend of the Taos went so far as to suggest that they adopt the "unthinkable" and "insane" practice of digging into Mother Earth with a deep, sharp plough while She was pregnant (E. T. Hall, 1959:102–103). Needless to say that the expert was no longer considered an expert and that his influence was at an end.

6. Structural Integration and Pastoral Problems

Moral and canonical pastoral problems will never be satisfactorily solved in isolation; they must be studied and analyzed as they occur in the total cultural context with all functional linkages in view. Among the most common of such problems and at the same time perhaps the most difficult are those regarding marriage, e.g., polygamy, child and trial marriages, and the existence and non-existence of a natural marriage bond. Polygamy fills a number of very definite needs and is generally linked with a wide variety of economic, social, and religious elements. Monogamy most likely will not replace plural marriages until these various needs are somehow provided for. Or again, in some mission areas it is extremely difficult to determine the exact moment when two individuals become husband and wife. Actually they may be only in the process of being married — a process that may extend over many years. An inquiry into functional linkages of unmistakable marriages would provide much of the necessary evidence for the existence or non-existence of a natural marriage bond. In other words, the canonist in his attempt to solve a marriage case may have to study such matters as native funerals, property rights, and penal laws, and other seemingly unrelated cultural patterns. Where, for example, would an unmistakably married woman be buried, at her husband's burial grounds or in the cemetery of her original village? If this doubtfully married woman were to die, where would she be buried? What property rights does a fully married woman enjoy? Does this doubtfully married individual enjoy such rights? What are the penalties connected with adultery in the case of an unmistakably married woman? If the doubtfully married woman were to commit adultery, how would she be punished? What spirits does a fully married woman worship, her husband's or her own? What about the doubtfully married individual? In other words, we are not saying that any single question proposed above will be sufficient to solve the case regarding the existence or non-existence of a natural marriage bond but that a very important source of evidence will be found in the various linkages associated with indisputably valid marriage contracts. Similarly, in keeping baptismal and other parish records, the missionaries should make meaningful entries, meaningful in the structure of the local culture rather than in America or Europe. For instance, it is quite conceivable that the place of burial assigned by custom to every individual the moment he is born may be a far more meaningful entry in the baptismal or marriage record than the place of birth and the family name itself.

7. Structural Integration and Counseling

Common-sense demands that the counselor understand the problem which he is called upon to help solve. Problems, however, are never isolated but deeply intermeshed in a complicated psychological and socio-cultural network. The solution offered, in order to be workable, must take this network into consideration and actually be geared into it. A confessor will not be able to understand the problem of his polygamist penitent, nor will he be able to offer any valid advice unless he see polygamy as the polygamist sees it — tied in with prestige, duty to family or tribe, loyalty to ancestors, security, marital taboos, and many other possible functions. An outright suggestion that the polygamist give up his unlawful wives can hardly be looked upon as a form of counseling. The only advice that will make sense to the polygamist is the advice that appreciates the various functional linkages that make plural marriages desirable.

This important section on the significance of cultural linkages in the Missions might be best concluded by comparing apostolic work to a ball of tangled strings. If human behavior were not so interwebbed, the religious and socio-economic activities of missionaries would indeed be simple.

> Cultures are like a ball of tangled strings, one strand representing the economic life, another social institutions, another aesthetic and religious patterns. At different points the various strings are tied in knots, at some points more tightly than others. In order to untie one knot of any particular string, one must study the whole tangle; and just as no two tangles are alike, no two cultures are exactly alike. One must study the particular tangled whole and see which string must be tackled first, which knot must be untied now and which later, which string must be pulled and which relaxed, and which, in order to achieve the desired end, must be completely severed. Missionary work closely resembles this situation: to a large extent it consists in untangling cultural knots (Luzbetak 1961:171).

SELECTED READINGS

1. The Notion of Structural Integration
      1) M. J. Herskovits, Man and His Works, pp. 214–221.
      2) J. J. Honigmann, The World of Man, pp. 171–180.
  *   3) R. Linton, The Study of Man, pp. 401–421.

2. Functionalism
  *   1) R. Firth, ed., Man and Culture: An Evaluation of the Work of Malinowski.

* 2) R. Firth, "Function," in *Current Anthropology* (Thomas, ed.), pp. 237–258. (See Firth's well-chosen bibliography!)
  3) R. Firth, *Elements of Social Organization.*
  4) E. E. Evans-Pritchard, *Social Anthropology.*
  5) E. E. Evans-Pritchard, *The Institutions of Primitive Society.*
  6) S. F. Nadel, *The Foundations of Social Anthropology.*
  7) R. Piddington, *An Introduction to Social Anthropology.*
* 8) R. H. Lowie, *The History of Ethnological Theory*, pp. 230–249.
* 9) B. Malinowski, *Argonauts of the Western Pacific.*
  10) B. Malinowski, *A Scientific Theory of Culture and Other Essays.*
  11) A. R. Radcliffe-Brown, *The Andaman Islanders.*
* 12) A. R. Radcliffe-Brown, *Structure and Function in Primitive Society.*
  13) A. R. Radcliffe-Brown, "On the Concept of Function in Social Science," *American Anthropologist*, XXXVII (1935), 394–395.

3. **Structural Integration and Missionary Work**

* 1) G. M. Korb, "The Scientific Scrutiny of Mission Methods," *The American Ecclesiastical Review*, CXLIV (1961), 114–121.
  2) A. Rosentiel, "Social Change and the Missionary," *Practical Anthropology*, VIII (1961), 15–24.
  3) W. D. Reyburn, "Polygamy, Economy, and Christianity in the Eastern Cameroun," *Practical Anthropology*, VI (1959), 1–19.
* 4) E. H. Spicer, *Human Problems in Technological Change.*
  5) B. D. Paul, ed., *Health, Culture, and Community.*

  N.B. For other useful readings see page 3, note 2. See also the various articles in the *C.I.F. Reports*, Center of Intercultural Information, Cuernavaca, Mexico.

REVIEW QUESTIONS

1. What are the two integrating factors in culture? (p. 135)
2. How is culture integrated structurally? (pp. 135–137)
3. Define and illustrate: institutions, complexes, traits, items. (pp. 137–138)
4. What is meant by "function"? Describe the three different types. (pp. 138–140)
5. Give a short historical sketch of Functionalism. (pp. 140–141)
6. What is the difference between a "photographic" and a "functional" description? (pp. 141–144)
7. How would you go about studying functions? (pp. 145–148)

8. What bearing does structural integration have on general mission policies? (pp. 148–150)
9. Why should the medical missionary be concerned about functional linkages? (p. 151)
10. Why should the missionary agronomist be interested in non-agricultural beliefs and practices? (pp. 151–152)
11. How does a knowledge of function help the missionary in his pastoral (moral and canonical) problems? (pp. 152–153)
\ 12. Why should the counselor be interested in structural integration? (pp. 153–154)

TOPICS FOR CLASSROOM DISCUSSION AND PAPERS

\ 1. Describe an American birthday party in terms of "institutions," "complexes," "traits," and "items."
2. What are the functions of polygamy? What bearing do these functions have on practical missionary techniques? Consult general anthropological textbooks, e.g., Honigmann's *The World of Man*, for function of plural marriages. See also W. D. Reyburn, "Polygamy, Economy, and Christianity in the Eastern Cameroun," *Practical Anthropology*, VI (1959), 1–19.
3. Have missionaries disregarded the functional nature of culture in the past? What about the Jesuit Reductions? Fr. Ricci? Cardinal Lavigerie?
4. Describe some of the main aspects of the structure of Mohammedanism. Show how an analysis of functional linkages in Mohammedanism could indicate what practical steps a missionary may have to take in dealing with Islam.
5. Syncretism (*i.e.*, an untenable combination of paganism and Christianity) is an evident sign that the missionaries have not succeeded in filling important needs. If you agree, explain and illustrate the statement.
6. Go through the back numbers of the *Worldmission, Mission Bulletin, C.I.F. Reports*, or *Christ to the World* and comment on any article dealing with function.

CHAPTER SEVEN

PSYCHOLOGICAL INTEGRATION

AN ORGANISM is more than its functioning parts; it has, in addition, a principle of life. Culture is likewise more than its functionally organized parts; it too has a "soul" that gives direction to the functions. Philosophers and historians have long emphasized the existence of such a "soul." Anthropologists have taken up the idea and offered various theories to explain the nature of this principle of life or "configuration" as they called it. Ruth Benedict, who was particularly interested in cultural configurations, saw a *single*, all-pervading principle, while M. E. Opler, whose theory we follow, suggests that each culture has not just one principle but a *set* of related underlying "themes."

THE NOTION OF CONFIGURATION

Of all the human potentialities in adjusting to needs, a society will select certain ways of thought, attitude, and action and reject the others. This selection is not haphazard but usually will be in harmony with the "soul" of the culture. Moreover, whatever is selected and incorporated into the culture will tend to be further modified in accord with the particular configuration (see pp. 214–220).

Configurations are the dominant, underlying premises, values, and goals which permeate the various aspects of a culture and give it its "oneness." This unifying psychological trend has been called by various names: *Geist, genius, philosophy of life, mentality, psychology, Weltanschauung, worldview,* and *inner logic*. Sumner spoke of "ethos" while Sapir preferred the terms "patterning" or "style" of cultures. Ruth Benedict spoke of a "mainspring" and "patterns." The particular choice of term generally depends on the particular aspect of the dominant characteristics or tendencies in culture which one wishes to emphasize (Keesing, 1958:159). (1) When the "soul" is viewed as being responsible for the *oneness* of culture, the configuration or dominant tendencies are called "the

157

total-culture pattern," "the focus of culture," "the plot," "the set," "the climax," "the orientation," "the emotional and intellectual mainsprings" of culture, "integrating factors," and the like. (2) When these dominant trends are viewed as *the starting-points in the thought process* of a given society, they are called "premises," "postulates," "assumptions," "master-ideas," "ideas," "themes," "hypotheses," "inner logic," and so forth. (3) When the dominant tendencies are viewed as *emotionally charged attitudes*, they are called "values," "value-attitudes," "attitudes," and "interests." (4) When such dominant tendencies are viewed as the approved *motivating forces* in action, they are called "goals," "ideals," "sanctions," and "purposes."

Premises

Human psychology is the same the world over, no matter how simple or how sophisticated the society. The psychic unity of mankind is a fact. However, in spite of the identical psychological laws and processes involved in human emotions, attitudes, reasoning, and actions, we cannot predict the behavior of a people on the basis of what we would do in a similar situation. The thought-process may be the same for all human beings, but the actual starting-point in reasoning will differ from culture to culture. Lévy-Bruhl's "prelogical mentality" (*Primitive Mentality*, New York, 1923) has been debunked, and even Lévy-Bruhl himself recanted before he died (Koppers, 1950:1–7). The reasoning itself will be the same for all peoples; the difference is in the premises. To arrive at the mentality of his people, the missionary will have to discover their basic premises, their underlying assumptions, or postulates, otherwise effective communication will be impossible.

Values and Goals

Values are the underlying, emotionally charged attitudes, e.g., face-saving in the Orient, freedom of speech and worship in America, material progress in Russia, etc.

Goals are the underlying motivations for action. What may serve as a very effective goal or drive in one culture or subculture may appear utterly senseless and ineffective in another. What may make the missionary blush may lead an Oriental to take his own life.

THEORIES REGARDING CONFIGURATION

Ruth Benedict's Patterns of Culture

Of all proponents of configurational theories Ruth Benedict was perhaps the most enthusiastic, and her *Patterns of Culture* (New York, 1934) has become a classic. She claimed that "a culture, like an individual, is a more or less consistent pattern of thought and action." This "consistent pattern," she explained, was due to "drives" peculiar to the culture. At first Ruth Benedict greatly exaggerated the consistency of such "drives" and was consequently attacked by her colleagues, at times mercilessly. The litany of epithets included such charges as: "purely intuitive," "subjective to an extreme," "blind insistence on an attractive but unreal consistency," "a distortion," "guess-work," "oversimplification," "poetry," "unscientific, unfactual mysticism." In face of such overwhelming criticism, Ruth Benedict modified her earlier views and in her *Patterns of Culture* admitted degrees of psychological integration and consistency. The terminology used by Benedict was borrowed from Psychology. She described the Navaho culture as a typical introvert system: individualistic, self-centered, nonconformist, excessive to an extreme, and aggressive — in a word, typically "Dionysian." The neighboring Pueblo Indians were described by Benedict as typically "Apollonian," that is, highly group-conscious rather than individualistic or self-centered, conformist, with emphasis on externals such as ritual, restrained rather than excessive or aggressive. The terms "Dionysian" and "Appollonian" were taken from Nietzsche and represented a single, unified, all-pervading trend in the culture. It was Benedict's contention that all behavior (whether economic, social, or ideational) will follow the current set by the configuration in question.

Opler's Theme Theory

Far more useful than Benedict's all-pervading configurations is Opler's theme theory. Cultures do not have one, but several closely-related and interrelated "themes," which give direction and thus unite the various culture elements into an integrated whole. Opler defines a theme as a "position, declared or implied, and usually controlling behavior or stimulating activity, which is tacitly approved or openly promoted in a society" (1945:198–200). Cultures do not have one all-pervading *Geist* but a more or less philosophically consistent set of interrelated premises, values, and goals. Such premises, values, and goals are usually latent rather than manifest and the individuals concerned are generally not aware of such themes. As in the case of functions, themes will therefore have to be "dug out" by the anthropologist with much painstaking work and careful research.

A considerable amount of valuable clues to the underlying set of themes may be found by inquiring into the following: (1) the self-image of the society and whom the society considers to be "a good person"; (2) the violent resistance to certain innovations; (3) the native educational content and motivations, the constant lessons and warnings given to small children, the instructions given to the youths during the initiation rites; (4) arguments between tribesmen, quarrels between husband and wife; (5) the scolding, reprimands, and praise given especially to the young; (6) the factors that contribute to a feeling of security; (7) the factors that contribute to a preferred status; (8) the content and motivation contained in the arguments of native agitators; (9) the reasons for dissatisfaction and criticism; (10) the object of violent hate and condemnation; (11) the assumptions, motivations, and general line of reasoning observed in tribal meetings and court sessions; (12) the behavior which the more severe sanctions aim to control; (13) the type of sanctions feared most; (14) the more serious worries; (15) the severest insults and the most painful type of ridicule; (16) chief aspirations; (17) occasions for war; (18) motives for suicide (cf. Keesing, 1958:159–168). These are but a few of the many clues that may lead to the discovery of the set of basic psychological themes underlying a culture. Inquiries into the suggested topics should as much as possible be based on actual cases rather than on the imagination of the field worker or his informant. By constant inquiry and observation and careful analysis the missionary should formulate for himself a list of what appears to be his people's basic themes, interrelated assumptions, attitudes, and motivations, which he can tentatively assume to best represent the "psychology," "inner logic," or "soul" of the society. This picture, however, should be constantly checked and reviewed, made clearer through new observations and details, and revised wherever and whenever necessary; it should never be hung up as a finished painting, no matter how long the missioner may be in the field. It should be noted that the set of themes is only *more or less* consistent, and therefore the presence of some opposing or even contradictory themes is not excluded.

National Character and Modal Personality Studies

Without underestimating the psychological fact that each individual has a unique character arising from his particular physical makeup and personal experiences, anthropologists and sociologists have become increasingly interested in discovering so-called *societal personalities*, the common core of character traits which arise from the particular life-way and which are shared by the bearers of the given culture (Kardiner, 1945; Mead, 1953; Honigmann, 1954; Hsu, 1961; Kaplan, 1961). Such "typical" personalities have been variously conceived, e.g., as the personality type most in accord with the given configuration, as the "ideal man," and as the statistically most frequent character. These "representative" personalities or generalized temperaments have also been variously called, e.g., "modal personality types," "basic" or "communal" personalities, and "social characters."

Some anthropologists and sociologists have attempted the very difficult task of analyzing the social characters of complex societies (nations). Thus, attempts have been made to describe the "national character" of the Americans, British, Russians, French, Norwegians, Chinese, Japanese, Jews, and others (see *Selected Readings* and *Topical Bibliography* under "Culture, Personality, and Society"). Studies on national character, as controversial as they may be, provided that they are based on sound anthropological, sociological, and psychological principles, make useful reading insofar as they indicate valuable sources of information and practical clues to the mystery of a people's mentality. The study of national character is, of course, of only recent development, and, especially in regard to more complex societies, the pictures drawn must be taken with "a grain of salt."

SUMMARY AND SELECTED MISSIOLOGICAL APPLICATIONS

Summary

The "oneness" of a culture is effected structurally by means of functions, psychologically through the particular configuration or "soul" of the culture. Normally configurations are not single, all-pervading principles but rather a number or set of closely related and more or less consistent tendencies called "themes" which give direction and produce unity in the culture.

When the configuration of culture is looked upon as a starting point in the reasoning process, the anthropologist speaks of "premises," "postulates," or "assumptions"; when it is looked upon as a starting-point for emotions and attitudes, the anthropologist speaks of "values"; when it is looked upon as a starting-point for persuasion and action, the anthropologist speaks of "goals" or "drives."

Selected Missiological Applications

1. THE LOCAL MENTALITY AND THE NEW MISSIONARY

In many, if not most mission areas, newcomers upon their arrival are given an orientation course, and almost invariably the "peculiarities" of the local people's psychology are discussed. Even if such orientations turn out to be only a briefing or a summary of general impressions rather than the result of careful, thorough, and scientifically accurate analysis, they are generally worthwhile and may keep the newcomer from making many, and at times irreparable initial mistakes. Bishop Leo Scharmach, M.S.C., of Rabaul, New Britain, offers his new missionaries a *Manuale Missionariorum* (Kokopo, 1953), the first part of which is a "Compendium of the Psychology of Local Natives." Although presented in simple, non-technical terms and in traditional phraseology, the *Manuale* is a useful sketch of the psychology of the Rabaul people. The Bishops of the Society of the Divine Word in Indonesia have preferred to embody the mentality of their people right in with the various rules and directives of the vicariates and prefectures concerned, thus acquainting the new missionary with the psychology of the people indirectly but in a practical and concrete manner — in the form of a privately distributed *Manuale Pastorale* (Steyl, Holland, 1957). Whatever approach may be followed, an orientation in the psychology of the particular mission territory should be given before the newcomer sets out to do any work among a people whose basic assumptions, values, and goals may differ from his like night and day. The mentality of the local people should be frequently discussed informally with missionaries, government officials, planters, and other foreigners who have spent a considerable amount of time in the area. Their many concrete experiences and mistakes will provide much of the necessary initial knowledge in an informal but practical way. Such information, of course, is meant to be only a minimal introduction that must be constantly expanded.

2. A MISSIONARY APPROACH GEARED TO THE LOCAL SET OF THEMES

A popular topic of discussion at almost any gathering of missionaries is the "strange" or "peculiar" mentality of the local people. Surprise is often expressed at the extent to which their "philosophy" shapes practically all their thoughts, emotions, and actions. Missionaries point out how even after accepting Christianity their converts still tend to cling to "their way of thinking." Missionaries rightly feel that if they could properly understand the mentality about which they are so concerned, it would be a relatively easy matter to communicate effectively; it would simplify the difficult task of counseling; it would be a relatively easy matter to discover the arguments that would effectively persuade the wary and skeptical individual who hesitates to accept the socio-economic improvements which the missioner wishes to introduce; above all, the truths of the Gospel could be presented in terms that could be understood and appreciated. Although Anthropology is not yet in a position to offer the modern apostle a completely satisfactory method of analyzing the mind of a society, especially in highly civilized and heterogeneous countries like our own or in more sophisticated and rapidly changing urban areas of Africa, India, and other parts of the world, the missioner can nevertheless profit from what anthropologists do have to offer. As we have seen in the present chapter, modern anthropological theory tells us that a society seems to have a basic set of interrelated and more or less consistent "themes" that permeate native thought, sentiment, and action. Using the clues suggested above (see pp. 160–161), the missioner might draw up a list of such "themes" and tentatively assume that they represent what he has been referring to as his people's "strange mentality." This list, as already emphasized, should never be hung up as a finished painting; nevertheless, the missioner should make use of as much knowledge as he has at the moment. Just as the set of "themes" guides all that the local people thinks, feels, and does, so this same set, as far as possible, should guide the missionary in whatever he says or does in his dealing with his flock. The local configurational system should to a very large extent determine the approach he follows in his catechetical instructions and sermons, in the advice and admonitions he gives, in all his interpersonal relations, and in promoting socio-economic and other ideas. Some excellent examples of what we mean by "the psychology" or "soul" of a people are available, e.g., C. Kluckhohn's "The Philosophy of the Navaho Indians," published in F. S. Northrop (ed.), *Ideological Differences and World Order* (New Haven, 1949); P. Tempels, *La philosophie bantoue* (Paris, 1949).

To illustrate what we mean by a list of underlying "themes" and to show how such an analysis can serve as a constant guideline for practical apostolic work, we offer the following partial sketch of the Middle Wahgi (New Guinea) mentality. The sketch is intended merely as an illustration of the theme-theory in general rather than as the final word on Middle Wahgi themes (Luzbetak 1961:173–176).

Assumption I: The ultimate norm for "good" and "bad," "right" and "wrong" is the clan.

> CoroLLARY A: *"Outsiders" do not have rights.*
>> Practice 1: It is not wrong to steal from a non-clan-member. One may injure, rape, murder an "outsider" if he can do so without being apprehended.
>> Practice 2: Such acts become wrong only if the clan suffers harm, e.g., through an unwanted war or feud.
> CoroLLARY B: *The clan is always right.* To disagree with one's "brothers" is a betrayal of the clan, a most shameful act.
> CoroLLARY C: *Personal rights and advantages are subservient to that of the clan.*
>> Practice 1: No personal advantage is to be sought at the expense of the clan.
>> Practice 2: Women should be satisfied with their relatively inferior status, for they thereby serve the clan.
>> Practice 3: Forced marriages occur primarily for the good of the group, e.g., to strengthen a friendship that exists between two clans.
>> Practice 4: An individual may be expected to confess a crime which he did not commit so that the culprit, who is more vital for clan-life, might escape imprisonment.
> CoroLLARY D, E, F, etc.

Assumption II: Security is found in the clan alone.

> CoroLLARY A: *Group prosperity and prestige is all-important.*

Practice 1: Brotherly co-operation is expected of all clan-members at all crises and important phases of life, e.g., by contributing to the bridewealth, helping another in constructing a house, participating in the various customs associated with a birth, engagement, wedding, funeral.

Practice 2: Selfishness is frowned upon; sharing one's fortune or success with others is expected.

Practice 3: Willingness to defend one's clan and to die for it if necessary is a basic obligation. Bravery in battle is regarded as a great virtue; cowardice in battle may constitute an impediment to marriage.

Practice 4: Since the good of the clan has precedence over personal good, competition within the clan is frowned upon. On the other hand competition is expected between clans, e.g., in outdoing another clan during a festival or football game.

COROLLARY B: *Every member of the clan is vitally important to the group.*

Practice 1: An offense to one member is an offense to all.

Practice 2: The group assumes the guilt and consequences of the actions of the individual members, e.g., feuding, hostage taking.

Practice 3: Disregard of tradition by one or a few members may bring down the anger of the ancestors on all.

Practice 4: The education of the young is the responsibility of all.

Practice 5: The clan will go to war for the sake of any single individual whose life is threatened.

Assumption III: Successful living consists in close co-operation among all members of the clan, living as well as departed and still-unborn.

COROLLARY A: *Co-operation among the living is emphasized.*

Practice 1: Games are mainly recreational and educational rather than competitive unless the games are between distinct clans.

Practice 2: Instructions given during the initiation of the youth emphasize the importance of co-operation.

Practice 3: Not individual action but group action brings results.

Practice 4: See Assumption II, Corollary A, Practices 1, 2, and 3.

COROLLARY B: *The living members of the clan are utterly dependent on the departed; the very survival of the living depends on the all-powerful deceased relatives of the other world, e.g., health, sickness, gardens, successful birth, victory in battle, etc.*

Practice 1: Traditional ceremonial dances, mock-battles with traditional enemies, feasts, and pig-sacrifices are not only social affairs but also religious, aiming to please the dead and to win their favor.

Practice 2: Elaborate funeral and memorial rites, chopping off fingers to prove one's sympathy for the departed, consultation of spirit-mediums, and other practices reflect the utter dependence of the living on the power and influence of the departed.

COROLLARY C: *The departed members of the clan are utterly de-
pendent on the living for their happiness in the land of the ances-
tors, the other world.*
Practice 1: The departed constantly threaten the living with all
    sorts of misfortunes so that the living would be mindful of them.
Practice 2: The Middle Wahgi ancestor worship is primarily a
    religion of fear.
Practice 3: The happiness of the dead depends especially on the
    number of pigs sacrificed in their honor. Pig-sacrifices take place
    on a small as well as large scale.

Assumption IV: Man's most important material possession is the pig.
Without the pig native life would be impossible (see pp. 143–144).

One should note how closely related and interwebbed the various
assumptions actually are. Although a few other themes might be
suggested, there is a distinct emphasis on clan-concepts and clan-
values. The various themes give direction to the whole Middle
Waghi way of life. These relatively consistent group-oriented assumptions, attitudes, and drives permeate practically everything the
society thinks, says, feels, and does. Such psychological integration
should suggest to the missionary the advisability of building his
religious and socio-economic activities and general apostolic policies
as much as possible on *group*-concepts and *group*-values. The following concrete program of action for the Middle Wahgi illustrates
how practical missiological techniques might be built upon a
thematic analysis.

Since the various assumptions or themes are so group-centered, it
might be advisable to present Christian beliefs and practices in
terms of group-concepts and group-values as far as such a procedure
is theologically possible — and possible it is, in the light of the
doctrine of the Mystical Body of Christ. Instead of the meaningless
loanword "ekklesia" for "Church" it might be well to employ the
term "Christ's *Clan*" instead. We call the Church "*Christ's* Clan"
in order to give Christ the central position that is rightfully His.
In fact, "member of Christ's Clan" is a very close translation of
"Christian." Christ is the inner core of the missionary message
and the focus of Christian living, not a kind of excuse or a would-be
justification for a distorted piety. "*I* am the Way, and the Truth, and
the Life" (John 14:6); "Without *Me* you can do nothing" (John
15:5). In other words, a doctrine should be given as much emphasis

as it is close to or distant from this focus. The structure of Christ's Clan, therefore, will be presented in terms of this focus.

One becomes a member of Christ's Clan through Baptism, a washing ceremony of adoption, through which one is reborn and shares the common Life of the Clan. Membership in Christ's Clan brings many rights and privileges, the greatest of which is the sharing in the Clan Life (Sanctifying Grace). Through union with Christ, the Head of the Clan, and through close communication with other members of the Clan, this Life is increased, and one becomes more and more fully a member of the Clan. With any clan rights and privileges go also clan duties and obligations; hence, the members of Christ's Clan have a number of obligations. However, the cost of membership is far below the advantages derived.

All the desirable qualities one would wish one's natural clan are to be found in an eminent degree in Christ's Clan. Since there is nothing one could wish for more than to belong to a clan that is numerous, rich, enjoying great prestige, and powerful, it would be well to point out to the new Christian that Christ's Clan has all these qualities beyond compare. It is, for instance, very numerous, since it is not limited to any given area, between certain nearby rivers or mountain ranges, but includes "brothers" and "sisters" all over the world. Like the natural clan, it includes not only the living but also those in the other world (the Church Militant, the Church Suffering, and the Church Triumphant). The Saints are the Clan-heroes, some of whom died in battle (martyrs), while others were outstanding through their singular attachment to the Clan-ideals. Saints are human like ourselves, our true "brothers" and "sisters" who now live in the Clan's true home with Christ. We have to imitate their bravery in trials and difficulties and their devotion to our Clan Head and Clan-ideals. Since they are our "brothers" and "sisters" they are deeply interested in us, and we should be interested in them especially by imitating them. The Blessed Virgin Mary is the most outstanding, purely-human member of the Clan, and there is no member whom Christ could love more, for she was His mother. Since she is so dear to Him she must also be dear to us. In fact, Christ gave her to us as the Mother of the Clan. Christ's Clan, however, is not only numerous and has all these wonderful members but is also rich and powerful, for it shares the treasures and power of the Head, Who, unlike the other members, is God with the Father and the Holy Spirit. The privileges we enjoy as members of the Clan had once been foolishly thrown away by our first parents, Adam and Eve, but the Head of the Clan, the Son of God, Who lived from all eternity with the Father and the Holy Spirit, assumed flesh, was born of a Virgin, and through His Birth, Death, and Resurrection restored all. We lose these rights and privileges of the Clan through sin, best translated as "a betrayal of our Clan," "an insult to the Head of our Clan," or "insult to our Great Father," or in some similar manner. Christ is the Head of the Clan and is visibly represented on earth by the Holy Father in Rome.

Other doctrines can be easily explained in such group-concepts and group-values too, e.g., the Sacraments, the Decalogue, and the Bible. Liturgy, presented as a group-activity, will have a special appeal in such a group-oriented society.

The fact that every Christian is responsible for spreading the Faith will be easily grasped if presented as a clan-obligation — an obligation of being interested not only in oneself and in actual members but also in potential or still-unborn members, an obligation already felt toward the natural clan. The lay-apostolate and vocations to the priesthood and religious life make best sense in terms of clan-growth rather than in any other terms. In fact, in such a deeply group-oriented society it would seem best to gear all mission techniques and policies to group-concepts and group-values, as far as this is possible. It would, therefore, seem far more desirable to make use of the existing clan structure than to rely on willing individuals in organizing religious and social festivals, in establishing and conducting schools, and in building roads and hospitals.

Our presentation of Catholic doctrine in terms of the Middle Wahgi mentality was not intended to be in any way complete but rather to serve as an illustration. A considerable amount of caution and reorientation would, of course, be necessary so as to avoid theological misconceptions and improper emphases. Such reorientation might be done best of all not by abandoning the clan-idea for fear of misinterpretation and syncretism but rather by explaining Catholic beliefs and practices by means of contrast, by pointing out the differences between the natural and supernatural clan — by means of positive confrontation.

To sum up what has been said about psychological integration and its bearing on mission methods we can rightly say that in dealing with a "strange" culture the missionary must simultaneously use two minds, that of the local people and his own.

SELECTED READINGS

1. **Configurations of Culture**
   * 1) R. Benedict, *Patterns of Culture.*
   2) R. Piddington, *An Introduction to Social Anthropology*, Vol. 2, pp. 597–646.
   3) M. J. Herskovits, *Man and His Works*, pp. 221–226.
   4) M. E. Opler, "Themes as Dynamic Forces in Culture," *American Journal of Sociology*, LI (1945), 198–206.
   * 5) M. E. Opler, "An Application of the Theory of Themes in Culture," *Journal of the Washington Academy of Sciences*, XXXVI (1946), 137–165.
   * 6) F. M. Keesing, *Cultural Anthropology*, pp. 155–172.

2. **Modal Personality Studies**
   * 1) G. Gorer, "The Concept of National Character," in *Personality in Nature, Society, and Culture*, C. Kluckhohn and H. A. Murray, eds., revised edition, pp. 246–259.
   2) S. M. Lipset and L. Lowenthal, eds., *Culture and Social Character.*
   3) M. Mead, "The Study of National Character," in Lerner and Lasswell, eds., *The Policy Sciences: Recent Developments in Scope and Method*, pp. 75–85.
   * 4) M. Mead, "National Character," in Kroeber, ed., *Anthropology Today*, pp. 642–667.
   5) B. Kaplan, *Studying Personality Cross-Culturally.*
   6) G. Gorer, *The American People.*
   7) M. Mead, *The American Character.*
   8) W. L. Warner, *Democracy in Jonesville.*
   * 9) C. Dubois, "The Dominant Value Profile of American Culture," *American Anthropologist*, LVII (1955), 1232–1239.
   10) F. L. K. Hsu, *Americans and Chinese: Two Ways of Life.*
   11) G. Gorer, "Themes in Japanese Culture," *Transactions of the New York Academy of Sciences*, Second Series, V (1943), 106–124.
   12) R. Benedict, *The Chrysanthemum and the Sword: Patterns of Japanese Culture.*
   13) G. Gorer and J. Rickman, *The People of Great Russia.*

REVIEW QUESTIONS

1. What do we understand by "configurations"? What other terms do anthropologists use? (pp. 157–158)

2. What did Ruth Benedict understand by "patterns" in her *Patterns of Culture?* How does the use of the term differ from our previous use of the term? (pp. 159, 113–114)
3. How does the "theme theory" differ from Ruth Benedict's "patterns"? (pp. 159–160)
4. Indicate some of the possible sources of information regarding the underlying premises, values, and goals of a culture? (p. 160)
5. What is meant by "national character" and "modal personality type"? (p. 161)
6. How would you go about acquiring a preliminary knowledge about the mentality of a "strange" society? (pp. 162–163)
7. How would you go about perfecting this knowledge? How would you make use of such a knowledge in mission work? (pp. 163–169)

TOPICS FOR CLASSROOM DISCUSSION AND PAPERS

1. Are group conversions possible today? advisable? Give a critical analysis of C. F. Vicedom, "An Example of Group Conversion," *Practical Anthropology*, IX (1962), 123–128.
2. Read some simple treatises on Communism and draw up a list of Communist themes. (Consult, for instance, F. Schwarz, *You Can Trust the Communist*, or M. Djilas, *The New Class: An Analysis of the Communist System*. For a more penetrating study see C. J. McFadden, *The Philosophy of Communism*.)
3. Read C. Kluckhohn's "The Philosophy of the Navaho Indians," Father P. Tempels' *La philosophie bantoue*, or one of the books on national character cited in the Selected Readings and draw up a brief outline of a course in religion geared to the particular mentality.
4. What bearing would the group-concepts and group-values of the Middle Wahgi tribes have on your approach in a socio-economic project? (Consult E. H. Spicer, ed., *Human Problems in Technological Change* and some studies on Community Development for additional ideas.)
5. Read and comment on William A. Kaschmitter, M.M., "How Different is the Oriental," *Worldmission*, VI (1955), No. 1, 62–69.
6. Compare two Oriental philosophies and point out some of the main differences. See Selected Readings.
7. Write a critical book review of Geoffrey Parrinder's *West African Psychology* (London, 1951).

CHAPTER EIGHT

DEGREES OF INTEGRATION

SOME terms connote completeness and perfection, such as "round," "square," and "level." Whatever is round is always perfectly round, and one thing cannot be more round than another. In much the same way, the terms "integrated" and "one," which we have been using in reference to culture, may likewise suggest completeness and perfection. When we speak of the "oneness" of culture and say that a life-way is an "integrated whole" we may, perhaps, be saying too much, unless we somehow qualify our statement. The present chapter aims to rectify any possible suggestion that cultures are *totally and perfectly* "one" and "integrated."

NORMS FOR DETERMINING THE DEGREE OF INTEGRATION

No culture is perfectly integrated, and no culture operates with 100 percent efficiency. The operation of "cultural machines" is never perfectly smooth, and one "machine" may operate more smoothly than another. In fact, cultures may sometimes become quite disorganized and even disintegrate (see pp. 223–228). What are the essential requirements for the "oneness" and "integration" of culture? What criteria might we use to judge the degree of integration? A way of life resembles the "oneness" of an organism to the degree that the culture content, the various functions, and themes are interrelated, consistent, and balanced (cf. Gillin, 1948:515–526).

Relatedness of Parts

By "relatedness" we mean any functional or logical connection of traits, complexes, or institutions within a given culture. "Connection," as understood here, implies "dependence." A church hymn, baseball, and a pony-tail hairdo are elements of our culture but they are independent of one another. The Inca culture was so thoroughly interrelated through functional linkages that the removal of one major component (the Inca leadership) caused the entire culture to disintegrate. We have already seen how loosely linked pig-raising is in Western economy, whereas in Melanesia the pig is so thoroughly intertwined with other aspects of culture that if the animal were to be taken away from the New Guinea highlander native life itself would be jeopardized (see pp. 143–144).

Consistency

Mere relatedness of parts and the existence of functional linkages do not guarantee smoothness of operation: two wrong gears that touch may indeed be "related," but they will cause trouble rather than add to the efficiency of the machine. The relatedness must be harmonious; the functions and themes must be consistent. Early dating and marriage in highly civilized countries are incompatible with the complicated economic and social patterns that call for considerable education and maturity. Our social patterns requiring a widow to go to work to earn a living for herself and her children are incompatible with the role of motherhood and the rearing of children. Other things being equal, that culture is more thoroughly integrated in which there is more harmony among the various cultural components.

Reciprocity

In a thoroughly integrated life-way one will find not only that the various components are related and that they are consistent with one another but that, to a greater or lesser degree, they also mutually support one another. Such a balance or reciprocity exists, for example, when management and labor not only do not interfere with one another's goals but actually support each other in a kind of symbiosis.

SYNTHESIS

Although the Functionalist "theory of needs" (cf. Piddington, 1950:219–235) does not fully explain the presence of all the elements that may occur in a given life-way and although the theory is not sufficiently concerned with the dynamism of culture, it does help one visualize cultural "oneness" as it actually occurs at any given moment in its many degrees and in its numberless varieties. The present section aims to synthesize what has been said about integration in this as well as in the two preceding chapters.

One of the chief tasks of Cultural Anthropology is to study a society's mode of solving human needs — needs that are common to all mankind. Functionalists reduce such needs to three categories: (1) the primary needs, (2) the derived needs, and (3) the integrative needs. In the following description one should note the infinite variety of possible structures and configurations as well as the many possible degrees of relatedness, consistency, and reciprocity.

Primary Needs

The primary needs are those which the human organism shares with other animals. Such needs are known also as "biological imperatives" and include: (1) the need for food, (2) the needs associated with physiological processes, (3) the need for protection against climate, (4) the needs connected with the sex drive, and (5) the needs associated with reproduction.

1. THE NEED FOR FOOD

In the case of animals the biological need for food is quite satisfactorily filled through instinct. Animals normally do not starve because they are endowed with certain instincts peculiar to their species. In the case of man, not instinct but the culture satisfies this biological need. It does so by "teaching" the individual specific ways of food-getting: gathering, hunting, fishing, agriculture, animal husbandry. It also provides specific tools, techniques, and oranization which food-getting involves — at times very complicated techniques and organization, such as those of highly civilized societies.

Culture, however, does not merely provide *isolated* means of survival; rather, the responses to the need for food are a part of a *system* of survival. The various responses to the need for food may be linked not only with one another but also with the rest of culture, the intensity of such interwebbing depending on the particular culture. Hunting, for example, may be organized on a communal basis and may be interwebbed with the existing social structure. Hunting may also be closely related with sex taboos and magical rites performed before the hunters set out on their expedition; after the hunt the animals caught may be divided according to specific social priorities or obligations; skill shown during the hunting trip may give the hunter prestige that may go far beyond hunting activities. Since hunting is an important means of livelihood and since it is a major source of prestige, it will be an important item in the native educational system and may be an important consideration in choosing a political leader or a marriage-mate. Thus hunting, as a response to the need for food, may become closely interwebbed with various social and magico-religious patterns. The set of underlying assumptions, values, and goals makes such interwebbing "logical." One should also note how the elements connected with hunting can mutually reinforce each other: hunting techniques may be supported by educational patterns while educational patterns may be upheld and further developed by hunting techniques.

2. Needs Associated With Physiological Processes

Because man is an animal he needs rest and sleep, and waste must be removed from his body; but since he is a cultural animal, he responds to these needs not merely by instinct but by his learned ways. In response to the need for rest his culture may provide techniques for weaving mats or manufacturing inner-spring mattresses. The answer to the need for urinating and defecating is the construction of toilets and sewage systems.

Here again one should observe how the responses, whatever their form may be, are linked with other responses and tend to be in harmony with them. Not only do cultures provide a dignified method of eliminating waste products from the system but at the same time satisfy the moral needs of the society by separating the sexes and providing privacy. The particular form of response to the need for sanitation may be quite consistent with and may support the aesthetic tastes of the society as well as the particular magico-religious beliefs and practices. If the feces happen to be an object sought by a sorcerer, the culture may provide methods of defecating that will not "endanger" the life of the individual. The responses will most likely be consistent with the inner logic of the particular culture.

3. Protection Against the Climate

Man, like all animals, needs protection against the climate; however, he copes with the climate not as he is urged by instinct but as he learns to do so from his social group. He learns from his society how to build a shelter, how to make a fire, and how to cover his body with some sort of protective "clothing." At the same time, however, the society does not fail to take into account the rest of its life-way. Clothing, for instance, will generally be "modest," that is, in accord with the moral standards; it will also tend to be in accord with good native taste and consequently will be linked with the particular aesthetic values; clothing frequently respects status and occupational differences in society. Thus the response to the need for protection against climate may be linked with various economic, social, and religious patterns into a more or less consistent network permeated by basic assumptions, attitudes, and goals. In much the same way as clothing, houses will not only serve as a protection against the climate but will also uphold and stimulate native art; they will respect the social standards, such as the separation of sexes and the subdivisions of a polygamous family; they will single out the head of the village or the chief. Some houses will serve the economic needs of the community, others the social (club houses), others the religious (churches). The set of underlying assumptions, values, and goals will in various ways and in various degrees be manifest in any settlement large or small, primitive or highly sophisticated. In a word, the responses to the need for coping with the climate are, again, not isolated responses but elements of a unified system or design for living.

4. Sex Drives

Unlike other animals, man, the rational being, responds to sex not by instinct alone but also rationally and socially. Every human society provides means of sexual satisfaction and at the same time sets up well-defined restrictions. In so doing, the society generally respects (to various degrees) the total life-way, especially the particular moral, aesthetic, and magico-religious values. Marriage is the usual response to sex, in fact, a universal human answer; but even in marriage sex will be restrained in accord with other human needs and the particular philosophy of life. Thus, marital relations may be tabooed during planting time "lest the fertility of the soil suffer"; it may be tabooed before a hunting trip as a form of magic or supplication to a deity to ensure success in hunting; it may be tabooed during pregnancy and lactation "for the good of the child." Sex restrictions as well as the approved use of sex aim to support such social needs as the dignity of the woman, the stability of the family, and the proper care and education of children. The socially approved responses to sex are, therefore, generally consistent with the rest of the life-way, being supported by and supporting other aspects of the culture. The sex responses of a society tend to be functionally organized and in accord with the underlying assumptions, values, and goals of the particular society.

5. Reproduction

Reproduction is still another basic human need embracing such responses as a recognition of parenthood (whether by means of the *couvade* or by handing out cigars), infant and child care, and the many practices associated with pregnancy, delivery, and lactation. The particular form which the responses take will again be more or less in harmony with the society's aesthetic tastes, economic, social, and religious norms, and will be more or less guided by the inner logic and underlying values and goals of the society in question.

6. Good Health

Man's constant and quite varied struggle to maintain good health is another primary response to a biological need. Hygiene, sanitation, medicaments, surgical techniques, and weapons are all adaptations to this primary drive. Such responses will once again tend to be in harmony with other aspects of culture which they reciprocally support, e.g., good health may be best assured through a moral life and magical or religious rites.

Derived Needs

The second class of imperatives is termed "derived" because the various needs are "derived" or arise from man's social nature. Man cannot survive except collectively. His organized collective living is, as a result, responsible for a whole set of tensions which societies satisfy by such responses as education, language, economic systems, leadership, co-operation, laws, and politics. Once again it must be emphasized that the particular choice of adaptation will as a rule be more or less in harmony with the rest of culture, linked with and mutually supported by the various other constituents of culture and the underlying philosophy. The derived needs include: (1) the need of organization for collective activity, (2) the need for communication, (3) the need for material satisfaction, (4) the need for social control, and (5) the need for an educational system.

1. The Need for Collective Activities

Collective activities presuppose organization; organization, in turn, presupposes co-operation and leadership. Thus, within the family we find a division of labor based on sex and age; various roles are assigned to the members of the family in child-rearing, weddings, and funerals. Like the family, larger social units are likewise characterized by co-operation and leadership, e.g., in warfare, government, religious and social festivities, and food-getting. These distinct collective responses are, again, not isolated responses but constituents of a system of adaptation, in line with the rest of the culture content and the underlying psychology. Thus, for example, in case of war, the weapons, shields, and fortifications will be in harmony with the technology of the particular society and will be "blessed" in accord with the native religious or magical beliefs and practices. Social and religious sanctions may be attached to cowardly use of the weapons, while prestige and economic reward may be won through outstanding bravery in battle. The "commander-in-chief" may be chosen on the basis of a "supernatural" call or dream.

2. The Need for Communication

The main response to this particular derived need is language. In accord with the general theory of linkages, consistency, and reciprocity of responses, there is a close relation between linguistic patterns and modes of thought and behavior, so much so, that a whole new field of Anthropology has developed in recent years around this close relationship (Hoijer, 1954).

3. The Need for Social Control

If a group of individuals is to live in close contact with one another and achieve success in its common efforts, social control becomes essential. There must be sanctions that will force the uncooperative and rebellious individuals, the drones, parasites, and saboteurs, to share the burden of collective living. The main negative controls include: commands, physical punishment, gossip, ridicule, fines, scolding, threats, taboos, and the like; the main positive controls are education, rewards, praise, admiration, a sense of security, art, and ceremony. Once again there is a constant interwebbing among the various responses and the general direction will be given by the underlying premises, attitudes, and drives. Education and praise (two forms of social control) will most likely harmonize with religious beliefs and the value-system of the people; the rewards will correspond to the existing social and economic values.

Integrative Needs

The third category of needs is called "integrative" because the needs in question do not seem to be absolutely necessary for the purely biological or social nature of man but rather emanate from man's intellectual and moral nature. In response to such needs societies have magico-religious and aesthetic patterns, knowledge and philosophies, and recreational and ceremonial activities. Again, one should keep in mind that these responses are but elements of a single entity, of a system. The integrative needs include: (1) the need for a feeling of right and wrong; (2) the need for expressing collective sentiment; (3) the need for a feeling of confidence; (4) the need for aesthetic expression; (5) the need for recreation.

1. The Need for a Feeling of Right and Wrong

This need is filled by "conscience," the inner feeling over and above the imposed social controls. Conscience tells the individual what is to be regarded as "good" and what is to be regarded as "bad," what is "right" and what is "wrong," what is "just" and what is "unjust." The particular form in which this feeling actually appears in different societies will be in general harmony with the society's basic assumptions, values, and goals as well as with the rest of its life-way. Thus, for example, to sell one's wife or children into slavery would not cause qualms of conscience in a society where the absolute *patria potestas* is in force. Similarly, the feeling regarding what is and what is not "incest" will greatly depend on the cultural interpretation of blood-relationship.

2. The Need for Expressing Collective Sentiment and the Need for a Feeling of Confidence

Man feels a distinct need for confidence and collective sentiment, and societies answer these cravings by their various magico-religious systems. Although we do not wish to imply that such responses are the full explanation for religion, magico-religious responses, however unobjective they may be at times, provide the necessary courage and security especially in times of danger, uncertainty, crises, frustrations, and death. Magico-religious systems are the answers to the unknown and mysterious; from them the societies derive the suprahuman powers for which they long and which they desperately need. Such responses will, again, be more or less consistent with the content of culture and its configuration. Such responses and those with which they are related are often in a reciprocally beneficial relationship; thus, for instance, the educator may teach his pupils to respect religion, while one of the important lessons religion teaches the believer may be the necessity of respecting the educator. Magico-religious systems may be closely intermeshed with laws and sanctions, with rank and social roles, with medicine, war, art, ceremony, recreation, and food production — in a word, with practically every aspect of life. Some cultures, of course, are more "religious" than others, that is, they are more interwebbed with religious beliefs and practices, and the underlying philosophy of life may be more supernaturally oriented.

3. The Need for Recreation and for Aesthetic Expression

A normal and healthy individual usually has a surplus of physical as well as psychological energy that seeks expression. The corresponding recreational and aesthetic responses will reveal at least a certain amount of harmony and interlocking with other aspects of culture. Games, for instance, are frequently not only recreational but also educational and teach the players the economic, social, and religious patterns that they must master as adults. Games will also teach co-operation and leadership. Aesthetic activities, such as carving, music, and dance, generally harmonize with the rest of culture and the psychology of a people; in fact, the basic reason for the difficulty one generally experiences in appreciating foreign art is that the art is closely connected with a life-way that is not understood.

SUMMARY AND SELECTED MISSIOLOGICAL APPLICATIONS

Summary

No culture is perfectly integrated and no two cultures are equally integrated. The degree of integration can be judged by the relatedness consistency, and reciprocity of cultural parts, that is, the relatedness, consistency, and reciprocity of content, function, and inner logic.

Selected Missiological Applications

The missionary cannot be satisfied with anything less than a Christianity that is in the truest sense of the word an integral part of the local life-way, a twenty-four-a-day affair. "All whatsoever you do in word or in work," says St. Paul, "do all in the name of the Lord Jesus Christ" (Col. 3:17). In the present chapter three criteria have been proposed for judging the thoroughness of cultural integration, criteria indicating to the missioner how thoroughly his message has become a part of native living: (1) the number of linkages between the missionary's message and the native life-way; (2) the degree of consistency and (3) extent of reciprocity between the two.

1. The Apostolic Principle of Cultural Relatedness

As a rule of thumb one might say that those policies and techniques are to be preferred which are most likely to establish strong linkages between the new Christian ways and the existing cultural structure. Moreover, existing linkages are, as a rule, not to be severed without replacing them with new ones, that is, either Christianity itself must be so presented as to fill the needs formerly filled by the supplanted pre-Christian behavior or some other innovation in addition to the Christian message should be introduced. It is, therefore, vital for the missioner to study the functions of the native religious beliefs and practices in all their ramifications. If, for example, the native religion plays an important role in the economic life of the people — in the form of fertility rites perhaps or rain magic — the missionary should not be satisfied with merely condemning the old ways but should positively strive to provide a theologically sound substitute which will function as a source of economic security. If, as is frequently the case, the native religion functions as an essential source of familial and tribal solidarity and security, such functions must be taken fully into account. In his instructions on Baptism, for instance, the missionary might very well stress even more forcefully than he would in his home-country the fact that this Sacrament makes one a child of God, entitled to special love and protection of an *Almighty, All-wise,* and *All-good* Father. In communicating Christianity the missionary might place very special emphasis on doctrines that are able to provide the desired security and feeling of belonging, e.g., the doctrine of the

Mystical Body of Christ. In coining new theological and practical catechetical terminology, instead of using meaningless words derived from the Latin or Greek, he might choose genuinely native idioms laden with connotations and sentiment that will contribute toward the desired linkages. It has already been suggested, for example, that in areas where group-consciousness is dominant, the Church might very well be referred to as "Christ's Clan" or "Christ's Tribe." Baptism can be described as an adoption into a *powerful* society, against which even "the gates of hell" cannot prevail. The Head of the Church is the Son of the *Almighty*. The Head is deeply interested in all the members of the Mystical Body, and each member contributes to the welfare of the other members. Christ comes to the individual in a very special manner in Holy Communion. The relationship between Christ and the Christian is personal and real. Security and solidarity can be further instilled by proper and meaningful instruction regarding Grace and the place of the Holy Spirit in the life of the individual and the whole Mystical Body.

Severed functions must never be ignored, otherwise the corresponding needs will be filled in some other, un-Christian (usually traditional) way. Thus, for some North American Indians, Baptism is nothing more than a form of magic, and an individual may be "baptized" as often as he falls ill. In Guatemala pagan rites by so-called Christians may take place right in front of the parish church with no one really taking it amiss. Syncretism is an evident sign that the missionaries have not succeeded in filling felt-needs. We are not blaming anyone but merely pointing out the sad fact that for some justifiable or unjustifiable reason missionaries have not succeeded in filling native needs, and, as a result, the new Christians are forced, so to speak, to perpetuate their traditional pagan responses to such needs.

The existence of syncretism in not a few mission countries does not prove that the Gospel is unable to fill such needs. "All whatsoever you do . . . do *all* in the name of the Lord Jesus Christ" (Col. 3:17) is a basic Christian doctrine, for Christianity is as broad as human life itself. Moreover, a glance through the *Roman Ritual* would be sufficient to prove that the Church is deeply interested in linking religion with every important phase of life and every aspect of it. In the *Ritual* we find, for example, beautiful prayers and blessings for those about to undertake a journey; there is also a blessing of homes, of the marriage bed, of the stable, of the gardens, food, horses, cattle and other animals, bridges, wells, vehicles, fishing boats and other vessels; there is a special prayer and blessing for the expectant mother, for infants, children, youth, sick and infirm; there is a blessing for schools and hospitals; and there is even a blessing *ad omnia*, which might very well be understood literally "for all things," for, according, to St. Paul's teaching just quoted, God is interested in all aspects of human life. The Liturgical Year, if properly linked to local traditions, can bind the new religion with the traditional ways. Specially organized dances in full native costume may single out Christmas or the Feast of Corpus Christi as special days for rejoicing in the Lord and dancing in His sight. With proper precautions fiestas need not make "fiesta-Christians" of anyone or encourage drunkenness; rather, they can serve as a healthy link between the new and the old. The various intentions for which Holy Mass might be offered or a para-liturgical service might be held, e.g., for the cessation of a pestilence, for rain, or for peace, may contribute considerably to the desired linkages. It is all a matter of interest in the particular needs and demands of native life and an appreciation of the universal adaptability of the Gospel to all human needs.

2. The Apostolic Principle of Cultural Consistency

The second criterion suggested for judging the degree of integration is the consistency or harmony with the culture-whole, *i.e.*, the content, the structure, and the inner logic. The more consistent the Christian expectations are with the traditional expectations, the higher the degree of integration.

Evangelization of necessity introduces a certain imbalance in the native life-way. As we shall see in discussing the dynamics of culture (see pp. 214–220), just as water seeks its own level, so culture spontaneously seeks consistency and harmony. If an innovation turns out to be inconsistent with the particular cultural content, structure, and underlying philosophy it is either modified and made consistent, or the culture-whole begins, so to speak, to shift and shuffle itself until consistency is achieved, or, as is perhaps generally the case, both processes take place. Of interest to the missioner is the fact that newly introduced Christian beliefs and practices tend to be "nativized" and, if they become untenable on moral or theological grounds, we speak of them as becoming "paganized" or syncretistic. A major missionary task is to "engineer" or direct this unavoidable integrating tendency, so that during the process no necessary element of Christianity is lost or distorted.

The policy of accommodation, therefore, is not one-sided — as if the adjustment were to be made exclusively on the side of the Church and the missionary. Actually, the policy calls for a mutual "give-and-take." The Church must adjust itself to the local life-way while the new Christians must adjust themselves to the ways of the Church. In his first epistle to the Corinthians St. Paul compares mission work to nursing tender plants. Comparing his own apostolic labors with those of his colleague Apollo, he says:

> What then is Apollo, and what is Paul? The ministers of Him whom you have believed. . . . I have planted, Apollo watered, but God gave the increase (1 Cor. 3:4–6).

St. Paul realized, however, that evangelization has also a starker and somewhat less paternalistic aspect. Evangelization consists in more than tenderly planting, gently watering, faithfully weeding, and carefully cultivating, for mission work actually implies a kind of "cultural surgery." St. Paul speaks also of "engrafting" Christ (Rom. 11:19, 24), and "grafting" when speaking of a society is "cultural surgery." The same thought is conveyed when the Apostle speaks of the necessity of ridding oneself of "the old man" and "putting on the new" (Col. 3:9–10). Christ went even further when He pointed out that to save one's soul it may be necessary to "cut off" limbs and "pluck out" eyes:

> And if thy right eye scandalize thee, pluck it out and cast it from thee. For it is expedient for thee that one of thy members should perish, rather than that thy whole body be cast into hell. And if thy right hand scandalize thee, cut it off, and cast it from thee: for it is expedient for thee that one of thy members should perish, rather than that thy whole body go into hell (Matt. 5:29–30).

Applied to a non-Christian society these startling analogies certainly call for nothing less than "cultural surgery." If a cultural trait, complex, or institution "scandalize" (i.e., prove to be inconsistent with Christianity and therefore a stumbling block), the society must "cut it off" or "pluck it out." Compromise is impossible when "surgery" happens to be the only means of saving the true and full meaning of the Gospel.

It should be noted that evangelization will unavoidably interfere

also with the smoothly running *social* system. Missionaries may regard themselves as harbingers of peace but they should not forget
that before peace there must be war. Evangelization unavoidably
brings along with it a certain amount of social disorganization besides unbalancing the culture. Although Christ was the "Prince of
Peace" (Is. 9:16) and although after His Resurrection He could
wish His faithful followers nothing more precious than peace, He
nevertheless had to say of Himself:

> Think ye, that I am come to give peace on earth? I tell you, no; but
> separation. For there shall be from henceforth five in one house
> divided: three against two, and two against three. The father shall
> be divided against the son, and the son against his father, and the
> mother against the daughter, and the daughter against the mother,
> and the mother in law against her daughter in law, and the daughter
> in law against her mother in law (Luke 12:51–53).

Evangelization, as Christ warned, would inevitably involve a certain
amount of interference with the smooth operation of a non-Christian society and culture. A polygamist in giving up his second,
third, and fourth wife may thereby impoverish his family, lower
his own status and that of his family for generations to come, and
antagonize his wives and their families — to mention only a few of
the possible disorganizing features of monogamy.

Christ and St. Paul did not wish to say that the preacher of the
Gospel is to be ruthless in his method. Rather, their intent was to
show that, in order to bring about consistency and harmony between
Christianity and traditional ways, compromise was impossible even
if only an "iota" was concerned (Matt. 5:13–19). "Cultural surgery," as much as one may dislike the term, is unavoidable at times.
The acceptance of the Gospel presupposes a cross, the greatest of
which is the "folly" of giving up one's traditional ways and values.

> The kingdom of heaven is like unto a treasure hidden in a field.
> Which a man having found, hid it, and for joy thereof goeth, and
> selleth all that he hath, and buyeth that field. Again the kingdom of
> heaven is like to a merchant seeking good pearls. Who when he had
> found one pearl of great price, went his way, and sold all that he had,
> and bought it (Matt. 13:44–46).

The missionary has no choice in the matter; he must, at times,
play the disagreeable role of "culture surgeon." However, he must
be a "surgeon" that is deeply sympathetic, one who is constantly
aware of the complexity and consequences of cultural intermeshing.

Evangelization, direct as well as indirect, will at times call for total removal of an existing custom and the transplanting of a Christian pattern instead. As in surgery, so in apostolic work, the removal as well as the engrafting and healing processes call for a genuine, far-seeing appreciation of the interwebbing of the various parts of the cultural organism. Like a conscientious and sympathetic physician, the missioner must make the operation as painless as possible. His every action must be well-planned and well-timed; and just as he now insists on a period of careful preparation for the operation, so he must later on insist on a careful convalescence, a patient waiting for complete health and balance. He will resort to "surgery" only because after careful study and consultation with others he finds "surgery" unavoidable. He does not hesitate to seek advice of experts whenever his own knowledge appears inadequate. Above all, he is fully aware of the total set of "organic" connections in culture and society, lest the removal of a diseased portion of the "body" cause more disorganization than necessary or a disorganization far more destructive than the cure of the disease warrants. Like a good "surgeon," he is deeply concerned about every linkage he must sever; he appreciates the consequences of each severing; and, as far as his knowledge and skill will allow him, he tries to compensate and supplement every interference with the existing structure of the organism.

The missionary must, at times, be uncompromising, while the would-be Christian is called upon to make many and great sacrifices of his traditional ways and values. The price demanded by Christ is high, and the missionary has no authority to lower the price. However, like Christ, the missionary must be profoundly sympathetic, fully aware that the new Christian is paying a great price for "the pearl of great price" and that the convert sincere about his Faith is actually willing to "sell all that he has" (Matt. 13:44-46). Perhaps an appropriate addition to every missionary's daily examination of conscience would be: (1) Am I demanding of my people as much as Christ wants me to demand of them? (2) Do I appreciate the sacrifices my people are making in order to live up to their baptismal vows? Only an understanding of the socio-cultural linkages will make it possible for the missioner to answer the second question and to understand what pressures, difficulties, and sacrifices true conversion calls for.

The Church, like Christ Himself, has always been uncompromising whenever principle was involved. The Church would sooner lose an entire nation than sacrifice a single principle of faith or morals. In the Malabar Rites dispute the Church was ready to lose a large portion of the missionworld rather than compromise a single iota of what She felt was the Law of God. Benedict XIV writing to the Bishop of Peking in 1744 sets the official policy of the Church in the following words:

> Let it be known to everyone that in matters pertaining to religious truth, when it is a question of superstition or idolatry, sympathy or tolerance is utterly impossible, as Tertullian put it: "Any such tolerance is itself a form of idolatry" (Collectanea, I:349).

On the other hand, the Church wants the missionary to introduce that form of Christianity which would be consistent with the particular way of life and in accord with the "soul" of the people. The very fact that the Church has set up a special Congregation to tend to the matters of the Missions and has given missionaries special privileges and faculties shows the eagerness of the Church to make Christian expectations harmonize with the local way of life as much as possible. The Collectanea and other documents abound in concrete examples of how the Church has been striving for such harmony. The best evidence, however, is the importance the Second Vatican Council has placed on the nativization of the Church in mission areas.

Harmonization of Christian expectations with native ways and values promotes integration. The Friday abstinence rule is unheard of in most mission areas, precisely because the Church realizes that such a rule just does not make sense in the given situation; it does not fit into the life-way of most mission countries. There, meat is usually a rarity, and means of preserving meat are non-existent. In such countries meatless days are the norm rather than the exception, so that every day of the year is a "Friday." Communion fast until recent times imposed on all Catholics the obligation of abstaining from food and drink from midnight until after the reception of Holy Communion, the reason being respect for the Eucharist and to promote devotion. This rule, however, was quite inconsistent with the type of life which the faithful had to lead in many mission countries. In some mission areas the faithful had to walk many miles to church, up and down steep mountain trails, with the hot tropical sun beating upon their naked bodies.

To expect the Christians to be frequent communicants and at the same time to live in such conditions was perhaps a case of an unnecessary inconsistency between Christian and traditional ways. Not to allow the faithful even a sip of water or coconut milk during the long walk to church was somewhat inconsistent with actual living conditions. Then, too, it often would happen that the missionary's arrival at an out-station where Holy Communion would be distributed was delayed, thus also delaying the distribution of Holy Communion and prolonging of the Communion fast. When the missionary would finally arrive, there would often be a long line of penitents waiting for confession, which had to be attended to before the missionary could begin Holy Mass. In other words, the recent changes regarding Communion fast are a good instance of how the ways of the Church that have nothing to do with divine law as such can and should be brought into harmony with the actual life-way of the faithful. On the other hand, the new Holy Week liturgy with the change from morning services to that of the afternoon and evening may prove incompatible with certain local conditions. For example, afternoon and evening services may conflict with the local economic way of life, as would be the case if the community had to tend to its livestock at this time or if other necessary chores would conflict with afternoon or evening services. Such services might also conflict with the local physical environment; for instance, Easter may fall during the rainy season, and daily cold rains might be expected in the given area in the afternoon or evening, making the crossing of mountain streams dangerous and perhaps inviting serious colds and even pneumonia. In such cases, the so-called "spirit of the early Church" should give way to the needs of the modern Church.

It is not always easy to recognize inconsistency between Christian and traditional expectations. A missionary's counsels, instructions, and suggestions may involve many, even though perhaps non-vital discrepancies between the two ways. Among the Navaho, for instance, blue is considered a "good" color while red represents something "wicked." Some years ago the Indian Service tried to introduce democracy among the Indians. Democracy, of course, implied free elections, for democracy and voting always go together. However, many of the Navaho Indians were illiterate, so that voting turned out to be a major problem. The solution suggested was to choose colors instead of names. This would have indeed been a splendid solution if the official in charge had not chosen colors that were inconsistent with the democracy he wished to introduce: he chose blue to represent one party and red to represent the other, unmistakably telling the "free" voters which party was "good" (blue) and which was "bad" (red) (E. T. Hall, 1959:133). In some parts of Africa and elsewhere white rather than black symbolizes mourning. To drape a coffin in black may be a rather "insignificant" matter; still, such "insignificant" inconsistencies destroy the supranational image of the Church. The main harmony to be sought, of course, is that between Christian expectations and the particular cultural configurations, a topic already fully discussed in the preceding chapter.

There are three distinct steps, each constituting a special problem, connected with any attempt to harmonize native ways with Christianity: (1) the recognition of disharmony and inconsistency between the two ways; (2) the unbiased decision as to who must make the adjustment, the Church or the local people; (3) the discovery of the most suitable method of making the necessary adjustment. The problem of recognizing disharmony has been discussed in the section on enculturation and referred to practically throughout the present course. The second problem was treated at some length in the section on missionary adjustment (pp. 84–103). The third problem of effecting and directing culture change has been partly treated in the chapters dealing with integration and will be more fully discussed in those dealing with dynamics of culture.

3. The Apostolic Principle of Cultural Reciprocity

The third norm for judging the degree of integration is reciprocity, that is, the way the different elements of a culture mutually reinforce each other. The greater the reciprocity, the more integrated the culture. Applying this norm to apostolic work, the degree of reciprocity between the essential Christian ways and native patterns will indicate how thoroughly or how superficially Christianity has been integrated into the local culture. Reciprocity is not something that will come of itself; it must be encouraged by the policies and techniques adopted. The alert missionary will constantly strive to establish reinforcing relationships between what he introduces and what his people value, believe in, and are actually doing. If, instead of insisting on Western norms for judging leadership, the missionary makes use of native values as much as possible in appointing heads for the various mission undertakings, he will by that very fact bolster up a traditional pattern, which, in turn, will tend to strengthen the newly-formed ties with Christianity. Or again, if mission schools show interest in the felt-needs of the local people, by so doing, they will support the native life-way, a fact which the pupils, parents, and government will surely notice and appreciate, and in return may support the educational effort of the missionaries. Or, as is the case among some Melanesian tribes — native psychology spontaneously seeks a mythological basis for a change in custom; in such a case it is conceivable that it may be wise at times to make use of this form of rationalization, justification of behavior, or philosophizing. These tribes claim that as long as it can be shown that the ancestors behaved in a certain manner or at least foresaw a change in a particular custom, it is right and laudable to accept the corresponding new ways. Such associations with ancestral behavior give the society a sense of satisfaction and security. Without denying the inherent dangers in such a procedure, it is nevertheless quite conceivable that such rationalization might be usefully employed by the missioner. If the tradition should claim, for instance, that the ancestors had at least a vague notion of a Supreme Being, the missionary might, with due caution, be able to support such a tradition (Aufenanger, 1960–61:67), while the tradition might very well assist him in introducing the belief in God. His opening sermon might begin with the simple question and proposition: "Your ancestors, as you yourselves claim, worshipped the Supreme Being. Why don't you? I am His messenger. If you will listen to me I shall tell you about Him." Here the missioner would be linking belief in God to native assumptions and values as found in tradition, reciprocally supporting local tradition and in turn being supported by it.

4. THE IMPERATIVE OF SELECTION AND APOSTOLIC WORK: A WARNING

Although we have considered at some length the idea of integrating the missionary message with the native life-way by means of approaches that take relatedness, consistency, and reciprocity into account, we have so far said little about a very real and serious danger involved. It is quite possible, and in fact not uncommon, for a newly-converted society to select and to integrate according to the "imperative of selection" (see pp. 273–275) relatively minor elements of the missionary message, while the really essential beliefs and practices of Christianity remain on the periphery of the native life-way. The essentials remain on the periphery even over generations, while the minor beliefs and practices become more and more deeply integrated. Such minor beliefs and practices, having, as they often do, greater appeal and consistency with the traditional ways, may be accepted wholeheartedly, emphasized and even overemphasized by the local people. Their missionary may be wrongly encouraged by their enthusiasm, mistaking it for "a lively Christian spirit in accord with their mentality." What is actually being integrated and encouraged by the missionary may be nothing more than a distorted form of Christianity. St. Anthony or St. Francis of Assisi may be far more appealing to the local people and far more consistent with the native culture than the Holy Spirit; the Blessed Virgin may be far more appealing than her Divine Son; processions and "holy" fiestas may be far more appealing than Holy Mass or the Sacred Scriptures; lighting candles may be far more appealing than the observance of the Ten Commandments; Christ's Infancy may be far more appealing than His Death and Resurrection; the Crucifix may be far more appealing than He Who died on the Cross. According to the imperative of selection, the more appealing and the more consistent beliefs and practices will tend to be integrated into the traditional life-way and will be proportionately more meaningful. The integration which we have been advocating is the one that is directed and not left to the imperative of selection. The process of integration must be so directed that the Good News remains theologically sound both in substance as well as in emphasis. Not what the local people prefer but what happens to be the true content of the Christian Message is the object of cultural integration, and the various items of that content must at all times retain their theologically defined proportions. Untheological emphasis is almost as undesirable as untheological content.

SELECTED READINGS

1. **Norms for Determining the Degree of Integration**
   * 1) J. Gillin, *The Ways of Men*, pp. 515–531.
     2) J. W. Rowe, *The Inca Culture at the Time of the Conquest*, in J. H. Steward, ed., *Handbook of South American Indians*, 1946.

*   3) E. E. Hoyt, "Integration of Culture: A Review of Concepts,"
     Current Anthropology, II (1961), 407–426.

2. The Theory of Needs
*   1) R. Piddington, *An Introduction to Social Anthropology*, Vol.
     1, pp. 219–244.
     N.B. See the Selected Readings on Functionalism, pp. 154–155.

3. Integration and Apostolic Techniques
1) A. Schaefer, S.V.D., "A Post Turns into the Cross," *Worldmission*, XI (1960–1961), No. 4, 41–47.
2) H. Aufenanger, S.V.D., "Primitivity along the Sepik," *Worldmission*, XI (1960–1961), No. 4, 58–68.
N.B. See also Selected Readings on "Accommodation," p. 353.

REVIEW QUESTIONS

1. Are all cultures perfectly integrated? Can one culture be more thoroughly integrated than another (p. 171)
2. What are the three norms for judging the degree of integration? (pp. 171–172)
3. What is meant by "the theory of needs"? (pp. 172–173)
4. What are the three categories of needs and give a few examples for each category? (pp. 173–179)
5. Describe the "oneness" of cultures in the light of the theory of needs. (pp. 173–179)
6. How can the missionary relate Christianity to the native life-way? (pp. 180–182)
7. How can he make Christianity consistent with the local culture? (pp. 182–188)
8. How can the missionary put the "principle of reciprocity" into practice? (pp. 188–189)
9. What bearing does the "imperative of selection" have on practical apostolic techniques? (pp. 189–190)

TOPICS FOR CLASSROOM DISCUSSION AND PAPERS

1. How might the medical missionary relate his message to the local culture? How might he make it consistent with the local life-way? How can he apply the principle of reciprocity?
2. From what has been said in the present chapter what light may have been cast on the syncretism and so-called "ignorance" of many Latin American areas?

IV.

DYNAMICS OF CULTURE

CHAPTER NINE

CULTURE DYNAMICS:
GENERAL NOTIONS

CULTURE is indeed anything but a heap of unrelated elements. Culture, as emphasized in the preceding chapters, is an integrated system composed of functionally organized elements that unite into larger and larger units and finally into a single whole; in fact, these units constitute a kind of living organism with a "soul." Like any true living organism, cultures have a double tendency — the tendency to persist and at the same time to change. New elements are constantly being added; other elements are constantly being lost, substituted, or fused. This changing is not haphazard but rather in harmony with the culture-whole. Cultures are constantly changing because the individuals of a society, the "architects of culture," are constantly modifying their cultural plans, "improving" and adjusting their ways to the whims and demands of their physical, social, and ideational environment. One change in the blueprint may necessitate other changes so as to restore the balance and harmony that through change has been disrupted. Sometimes change gets out of control and disorganization sets in. Some cultures may change more rapidly and more thoroughly than others, but *all* cultures change, even the most primitive and isolated. Some societies tend to change in regard to one or the other aspect of life, while in other aspects they may be ultra-conservative.

RESEARCH IN CULTURE DYNAMICS

What is culture change? What actually takes place when a culture changes? How, when, where, why, at what rate, and to what extent are cultural elements added, lost, substituted, and fused? Many questions have still not been answered by anthropologists, for Anthropology is a young science, and like any science it too will have many more problems to solve than it will have solutions to offer. Nevertheless, our knowledge of culture dynamics is significant and is rapidly increasing. A glance through Keesing's excellent bibliographical survey (Stanford, 1953a) or a brief examination of the wealth of information in some of the more recent textbooks (Kroeber, 1948:344–537; Herskovits, 1950:459–621; Piddington, 1957:647–748; Keesing, 1958:381–418; Honigmann, 1959: 171–283) or a brief examination of Barnett's full-length study (New York, Toronto, London, 1953) will be sufficient to convince anyone of the progress being made. Methods of inquiry are constantly being perfected, and while older approaches and concepts are being re-examined, reformulated, and refined (Firth, 1955; Nadel, 1951; Koppers, 1955; Haekel, 1959; Heine-Geldern, 1960; Steward, 1956; Hallowell, 1955), new light is steadily being cast on the problem — a problem that has fascinated anthropologists from the day Anthropology was born (Redfield, 1953b; Linton, ed., 1940; Hodgen, 1952; Bidney, 1953a; Rouse, 1953; Spindler and Goldschmidt, 1952, etc.; see Selected Readings).

THE LOCUS OF CULTURE CHANGE

One might be tempted to brush aside any discussion regarding the locus of culture change as something purely speculative and of little relevance as far as Applied Anthropology is concerned. The fact is that very few considerations could be more vital than the question: When culture changes where does the change take place?

When culture changes it is not so much the houses, farming techniques, wedding customs, dances, funerals, and religious rites that change as the ideas (the patterns) of houses, farms, weddings, dances, and religion. When cultures change, socially acquired sets of ideas change.

The shared ideas of a society, which we call "culture," as such exist only in the mind, not on streets, farms, or in places of worship. To change cultures, therefore, means to propagate new ideas. Culture change takes place according to psychological laws.

Since we are dealing with psychological laws, there is no essential difference between a culture change affecting tractors and farm techniques on the one hand and a culture change affecting culture elements of a more abstract nature on the other, say philosophy, art, or religion, for psychologically all ideas are the same.

Although deeply involved in psychology, the agent of culture change and the applied anthropologist are more than "psychologists." They must view psychological laws in the light of culturological and sociological concepts, theories, and principles. The student of culture change is concerned not only with ideas as such but with ideas held in common within a particular social group — ideas that are, so to speak, imposed on the individual through the process of enculturation, insisted upon by the social group by means of social controls, and made "necessary" by reason of the "organic" structure of culture. When speaking of culture change, therefore, we are actually speaking about laws of thinking, feeling, evaluating: how thoughts, attitudes, and goals change; how they fuse; how they grow and diminish; how they may eventually disappear. However, as anthropologists we are not dealing with just any thoughts, attitudes, and values but those shared with one's society. We are in the complex psycho-socio-culturological field, for culture is essentially "the socially defined mental content" (Barnett, 1953:1–16).

PERSISTENCE AND CHANGE

On the one hand cultures tend to remain stable, on the other hand they tend to change. In psychological terms the individuals of a society tend to retain certain socially shared ideas in their original form, while other ideas are given up in favor of new ones. Persistence and change are interdependent concepts, so much so that it is impossible to speak of the one without speaking of the other: they are simply the front and back sides of the same coin, the positive and negative aspects of culture dynamics.

VARIATION AND CHANGE

A culture pattern, say of a particular house-form, a specific gardening technique, or of a certain ritual, is really not so definite as one might be inclined to believe. Culture patterns actually consist in ranges of possible ways of behaving. An individual becomes an innovator only when he steps beyond the permissible, socially approved limits of variability.

KINDS OF CULTURE CHANGE

As to Extent

First of all, persistence and change might be described in terms of the extent to which changes take place (after Honigmann, 1959: 181–185). *General persistence* is operative whenever the members of a society are intent on limiting or resisting change in a wide area of life. The Amish are a classic example of general persistence, for anything typical of this world (anything "worldly") is frowned upon. God's chosen people are not of this world and therefore must not conform to it, whether it be in matters pertaining to travel, clothing, haircuts, or modern conveniences. Even the lapels and buttons seen on "worldly" coats must not be found on the apparel of the Amish. Cars, bicycles, television sets, radios, phonographs, and pianos are all for "worldlings," not for the Amish. Positive effort is made to inculcate in the young a dislike of radical change. Particularly "dangerous" is a "worldly" secondary education through high school and college, for it threatens the very foundation of the Amish-way (Honigmann, 1959:181–182).

Sectional persistence, on the other hand, affects only certain aspects of culture, the so-called "hard" parts of a way of life, which are particularly resistant to change. The American way of life shows clear sectional persistence: there is almost a passion for technological change but at the same time a distinct sectional persistence regarding sports, political organization, religious attitudes, and certain other aspects of life.

Token or *partial persistence* is a special form of sectional persistence, referring to a custom that is carried out with reduced frequency or only in restricted situations. For instance, nowadays in American cities a wake is generally held in a funeral home rather than in the parlor of the relatives of the deceased as was the custom only some decades ago. The use of horses is generally restricted to military funerals.

Survivals are culture traits or complexes that have with the passage of time changed their function and have become mere conventions or formalities. In the last analysis they are but a type of token persistence. Thus the custom of coloring eggs on Easter and the use of the mistletoe during the Christmas season are the remains of old superstitions and represent token persistence. The fake slit on lapels and the useless buttons on the sleeves of coats persist as survivals of onetime functioning parts of a man's apparel. The maniple was originally a kind of towel, now no longer functioning as such.

As to Rate of Change

A *revolution* is, as Kroeber defines it (1948:408), a "change suddenly precipitated with more or less violence, affecting a considerable total portion of a culture, and due to an accumulation of arrears, or lag, in progressive change." Classic examples are the Industrial and Bolshevik Revolutions and the spread of Christianity throughout Europe. The opposite extreme of a revolutionary change is *style*, a short-lived and rather insignificant modification in a single cultural element, as, for example, the relatively minor changes that occur every year in new car models. A *long-term trend* is likewise an insignificant modification in a single cultural element, but, unlike style, it continues for a long time. *Cultural drift* is the process whereby "minor alterations slowly change the character and form of a way of life, but where the continuity of the event is apparent" — to borrow Herskovits' definition — contrasting with *historic accidents*, "the more abrupt innovations, whether arising from within a culture or coming from outside a given society" (Herskovits, 1950:581).

As to the Object of Change

Culture change may occur in the content, structure, or configuration; it may affect the form, meaning, use, or function of the trait, complex, institution, or of even a wider range of customary behavior.

As to the Manner of Change

Change occurs through (1) substitution, (2) loss with no replacement, (3) incrementation with no displacement, (4) fusion.

1. SUBSTITUTION

Substitution consists in the dislodging of traditional elements by new ones. Gas light has thus been dislodged by electricity. Corporal punishment has disappeared from American schools and courts, and, to a large extent, from the homes, with other methods of disciplining taking the place of the traditional rod.

Substitution may be *complete* or it may be *partial*. Complete displacement is not so common as one might be inclined to imagine.

Our modern military academies teach the cadets the principles of nuclear warfare, rocketry, and jet-propulsion, but they still insist on drilling the cadets in the techniques involved in manipulating old-fashioned swords, an art still necessary in the modern armed forces for ceremonial purposes. Similarly, the horse has been only partially displaced in our age of speed: horses are still used in parades and in connection with many of the burial services at the Arlington cemetery; New York policemen still find the horse a useful animal, in certain situations superior to any modern vehicle; and large ranches are still maintained in Wyoming to provide the horses necessary for such purposes as races, rodeos, and circuses. In fact, we have not as yet completely emerged from the Stone Age: if for some reason or other we need a hammer but cannot find one, we do not hesitate to use any suitable stone to do the job. Armor is still used on the stage, in museums, and in mansions for decorative purposes. Home-made cakes and pies have been partially displaced by ready-mixes and frozen pastries. Home-made bread has been almost completely displaced by bakery-made bread, and home-made ice cream has become as rare as home-made shoes. Asbestos and vinyl tile have partially replaced linoleum, and the ballpoint pen has partially displaced both the pencil and the pen.

That displacement should be partial rather than complete is largely due to the fact that innovations, as a rule, are unable to fill all the functions of the corresponding traditional pattern. Electricity, to mention an instance, has not been able to dislodge the old-fashioned kerosene lamp on camping trips where electrification is impossible or still impractical. Or, again, among some primitive peoples the highly appreciated steel knife is found less suitable for butchering than the simple traditional bamboo implement. Similarly, the digging-stick is preferred to the finest steel implement when it comes to digging out sweet potatoes, for the steel spade is found to be too sharp and unwieldly and would do too much damage to the small, still-unripe potatoes as well as the roots and vines, making an all-year-round harvest impossible. On the other hand, if the novelty seems to fill a need more satisfactorily than the traditional pattern, the tendency is for the new to dislodge the old. The safety razor has thus practically displaced the old straight-razor, except in the case of professional barbers and professional cutthroats.

2. Loss

Loss consists in the dislodging of a traditional pattern without at the same time providing a substitute. Very often loss is the consequence of a chain-reaction. Piercing of the sides of the nose to hold decorative nasal appendages may disappear completely with the disappearance of the ornaments. In the same way, it is quite conceivable that missionary work may dislodge marital stability and tribal discipline by dislodging belief in magic. Such total disappearance of a custom may come also from the repeated disregard of certain taboos in imitation of a neighboring society. Or again, a myth may somehow be shattered, and with the myth everything connected with it may disappear. Long convalescence after an operation is rapidly disappearing from medical practice. Such a prolonged convalescence is, at least after certain operations, a medical myth, shattered during World War II when there was a great shortage of doctors and hospital space, forcing the patient to leave the hospital as soon as possible.

3. Incrementation

Incrementation takes place by introducing additional elements into the culture without a corresponding displacement. When television became a part of the American way of life such increments appeared on the American scene as TV antennas, factories that manufactured TV sets, stores and salesmen that sold them, and repairmen that maintained them. Television called for special TV rooms and nooks as modern features for the modern home, while the furniture industry had to develop special "TV chairs." Almost every newspaper in the country had to publish a special "TV Guide" for the week and include a special daily TV column as a regular feature. New "TV stars" had also to be created. Television required an army of specialized photographers, engineers, entertainers, choreographers, news commentators, script writers, directors, and sponsors, called the "television industry." Laws and special commissions had to be created to regulate programing and advertising. Of course, besides incrementation, television has brought much substitution into the American way of life by partially displacing movie attendance, radio listening, and other recreational and social patterns.

4. FUSION

Fusion is the amalgamation of an innovation with an analogous traditional pattern. Perhaps one of the clearest examples of fusion is Neo-Melanesian, commonly known as "Pidgin English," a true language that has resulted from the attempted communication between the native and the white man in Melanesia. The language is "English" inasmuch as the vocabulary has a semblance in form to corresponding words in English. But it is only a semblance of being a kind of "English," for in phonological and grammatical structure and in meaning the language is perhaps as much Melanesian as it is English. The word *han* is evidently derived from the English word "hand," but it has many other meanings and is much more generic than its English counterpart, reflecting the Melansian culture rather than the English. In combination with other words derived from English but in accord with Melanesian thinking we have:

brukim han (lit., "break the hand") = to make a fist, to fracture one's hand or arm

han bilong pam (lit., "hand belonging to a pump") = pump handle

han bilong em i-nogut (lit., "hand belonging to him [or her] is no good") = she is menstruating. (This evidently is a euphemism. Since during the period of menstruation a woman is not allowed to cook and is forbidden to touch certain things, she is, as it were, without a healthy hand.)

han bilong diwai (lit., "the hand of a tree") = branch

han bilong singlis (lit., "the hand belonging to a shirt") = sleeve

han pensil (lit., "a pencil-hand") = fingerprint of an illiterate on a contract form

han wara (lit., "hand of a water") = a tributary of a river or stream

paitim han (lit., "fight the hand") = to clap

plentihan (lit., "plenty hands") = a centipede

sekan long haus lotu (lit., "Shake-hand in prayer-house") = to get married

han bilong pik, bilong dok, bilong pusi (lit., "hand belonging to a pig, dog, cat") = the foreleg of a pig, dog, cat (The Melanesian pictures animals not as having four legs but, like human beings, with two hands and two feet) (Mihalic, 1957:41–42; see also R. A. Hall, 1943 and 1954).

SUMMARY AND SELECTED MISSIOLOGICAL APPLICATIONS

Summary

Some cultures tend to change more rapidly than others, but all cultures change, for all cultures have a double tendency — the tendency to persist as well as to change.

Essentially culture change consists in a modification in the socially approved set of ideas. The locus of change, therefore, is in the mind of the individual member of society. Culture change presupposes innovators, individuals who step beyond the permissible, socially approved limits of variability.

There are various kinds of changes possible: revolutions, styles, long-term trends, cultural drifts. Persistence may be general or sectional. Culture change may occur in the content, structure, or configuration of the particular life-way; it may affect the form, meaning, function, or value of a trait, complex, or institution, or of even the whole culture. Change can occur through substitution, loss, incrementation, or fusion.

Selected Missiological Applications

1. THE MISSIONARY AND CULTURE DYNAMICS

The primary aim of missionary work is to establish the Church where it does not yet exist and to consolidate it where it is not yet fully established. In anthropological and therefore purely human and natural terms, the establishment and consolidation of the Church is essentially a matter of culture change.

Nothing, however, could be more naïve than to suppose that a grasp of anthropological theory will infallibly enable the missionary to steer the course of history at will. Even the most thorough understanding of culture dynamics (which no sane anthropologist would claim for himself) is not a guarantee that the missionary will succeed in establishing the Church in any non-Christian society. Life is too complicated a matter to make "human engineering" as simple and as certain as other types of engineering; and, of course, there is still much — very much — that Anthropology does not know about culture change.

Despite these limitations, a grasp of the theory regarding culture dynamics as is available today will cast considerable light on missionary work, especially if this theory be integrated with what has been said earlier about the nature and organization of cultures. Such knowledge will not enable the missioner to determine the course of history, but it will help him better to understand why history takes the course it does; and without turning the missionary into a prophet, such knowledge will enable him to base his approach on the most logical predictions. As already pointed out (see pp. 149–150), any sane enterprise (business, governmental, or otherwise) will be deeply interested in "foreseeing" the future and will base its policies on sensible predictions. Although even the most clever businessman cannot prophesy the future with absolute certainty, he does rely on diagnosis and foresight. There will always be an element of gamble in his work, but the choice is not between knowing infallibly what the future has in store but between a blind gamble on the one hand and a wise and reasonable calculation on the other. Again the truth is borne out that "the children of this world are wiser in their generation than the children of light" (Luke 16:8). Only too often missionary policies and approaches are based on tradition and guesswork rather than on exact investigation and analysis.

Countless missionary years and lives are, humanly speaking, wasted, and countless dollars are foolishly disposed of in the modern missionary effort because not enough research enters into missionary methods. Every industry has its team of research workers whose sole task is to discover more effective and more efficient ways of manufacturing and marketing the product in question. The Missions today need a few less salesmen and more research workers than are employed by this "industry." Mission research centers must be established with mission-minded specialists co-operating in every modern skill and scientific field. But, no matter what field one may have in mind, underlying the practical application of the field in question will always be the theory of culture dynamics. *Research into culture dynamics is perhaps the most urgent and most basic missionary research called for.*

2. Missionary Work in the Light of the Locus of Cultural Change

The locus of culture change is the individual *mind.* When culture changes, we have said (see pp. 196–197), it is the set of ideas which the individual shares with the members of his society that changes. Culture being "the socially defined mental content" (Barnett), the target of any agent of culture change is the mental content in question, and his approach must correspond to this aim. To be effective, techniques employed by the missionary in bringing about socio-economic or religious changes must be aimed at the mind of the people. Essentially, missionary techniques are those of Psychology — communication and education in particular.

The consciousness that the missionary is trying to alter the socially defined mental content will set the whole tone to missionary work. Since he is dealing with the acceptance of ideas, it is not the number of ploughs, the size of hospitals, or the sophistication of religious architecture that tell one how much progress is being made in agriculture, health, and religion; one must look into the mind and heart of the people. What ideas do the individuals have concerning agriculture, health, and religion? Things may and often do reflect ideas, but they need not. A few sophisticated rich individuals can flood the country with things without affecting the ideas of the people. The beautiful Spanish churches throughout Latin America can hardly be regarded as evidence that the ideas of the people are genuinely Catholic. A few sophisticated hospitals or schools may be used by developing countries to advertise the "progress" being made, but, de facto, such buildings need not reflect the beliefs, practices, and values of the masses. Any agency can, so to speak, "dump" things on a community, but ideas can enter only through proper communication. Since World War II the United States has delivered shiploads of things to Southeast Asia but possibly not more than a handful of ideas.

The missionary is, therefore, primarily an educator, and his main tool is communication. His job is not so much to deliver things as to communicate ideas. He is not a delivery man who drops tractors on farms or medicines and bandages at various points called "dispensaries" and "hospitals." As a missionary his task is not to drop off God and His Law on the pagan's doorstep but to communicate. His every policy must aim at effective communication, and progress in mission work must be judged by the amount of progress made in communication. Although charity must be a mark of every missionary, he is not to limit himself to doing things for his flock but rather he is to teach them how to do things for themselves. This is the greatest form of charity, the type of charity that can bring about culture change.

To illustrate the point — what, for instance, would be my task as a medical missionary? As a medical *missionary* my ultimate goal would, of course, be the Christianization of the local people; as a *medical* missionary my primary goal would be not so much to nurse and to heal the suffering individual that comes to my clinic as it would be to influence the ideas of the society regarding health and illness. This does not mean that I am not to be sensitive to the suffering of the particular patient or to the immediate needs of the community. Even while demonstrating Christian charity through medical work — while dispensing medicines, bandaging sores, washing the feverish body of a dying person — a medical missionary true to the primary goal of his profession will not lose himself in paternalism. The primary aim of the medical missionary's activity is educational — in a word, cultural. No matter how much good medical activities may accomplish for the suffering individual, medical missionaries will fail to achieve the most important part of their task if they disregard the educational nature of their work of mercy.

This emphasis on communication and education in medical and other missionary work, rather than on the particular immediate good derived, should help determine the over-all policy of the modern apostolate. The goal is not only to help the suffering people but rather to help them help themselves. The suffering people of the world do not need alms as much as they need opportunities.

Although universities and ultra-modern hospitals have a definite place in the missionworld, effective communication, not sophistication, must be of primary mission interest. In some circumstances simple steel hoes or small ploughs may be far more important educationally, and therefore missiologically, than sophisticated farm machinery. Several small and relatively "primitive" clinics may in certain situations have greater educational value than expensive, ultra-modern duplicates of an American or European hospital. If the changing of ideas rather than the shipment of things is the aim of the missionary nurse, educator, or agronomist, the policies followed will emphasize the educational suitability of techniques rather than their sophistication.

3. The Modern Missionary and Revolution

"Revolution" was mentioned among the different types of culture change (see p. 199). Missionaries only too often seem to forget that the leisurely pace of their predecessors has completely gone out of style with the modern world. We are living in a revolutionary age. Changes formerly requiring decades and centuries are taking place overnight as it were. Missionary methods to be successful must be geared to this breakneck speed of our times. Unfortunately, no one, including missionaries, has really been prepared for revolutionary change. Missionaries know very little indeed about revolutions and revolutionary methods. The mission research centers suggested above must therefore include experts primarily concerned with revolutionary methods, ethical methods that can serve the cause of Christ during this revolutionary period. Today, revolutionary methods are no longer a matter of choice but of necessity: in the mad race forced upon the missionary there is no choice, unless, of course, the missionary does not mind being left behind in the dust.

SELECTED READINGS

1. **Bibliographies and Surveys of Literature on Cultural Dynamics**
    * 1) F. M. Keesing, *Culture Change: An Analysis and Bibliography of Anthropological Sources to 1952*, pp. 1–94.
      2) B. J. Siegel, ed., *Acculturation: Critical Abstracts, North America.*
      3) R. Beals, "Acculturation," in *Anthropology Today* (Kroeber, ed.), pp. 639–641.
      4) J. Macklin, "Culture Change," in *Review of Sociology: Analysis of a Decade* (Gittler, ed.), pp. 531–545.

2. **General Coverage of Culture Dynamic Theory**
    * 1) J. J. Honigmann, *The World of Man*, pp. 181–283.
    * 2) F. M. Keesing, *Cultural Anthropology*, pp. 381–418.
      3) M. J. Herskovits, *Man and His Works*, pp. 459–607.
      4) J. Gillin, *The Ways of Men*, pp. 532–569.
      5) A. L. Kroeber, *Anthropology*, pp. 344–571.
      6) G. P. Murdock, "How Culture Changes," in *Man, Culture, and Society* (Shapiro, ed.), pp. 247–260.

3. **Specific Approaches to the Study of Culture Change**
    a. FROM THE POINT OF VIEW OF INNOVATION
       1) H. G. Barnett, *Innovation.*
    b. FROM THE STUDY OF HISTORY
       1) A. Lesser, "Evolution in Social Anthropology," *Southwestern Journal of Anthropology*, VIII (1952), 134–146.
       2) M. T. Hodgen, *Change and History*, in *Viking Fund Publications*, XVIII (1952).

3) B. J. Siegel, "The Meaning of History in Anthropology as Exemplified by Near Eastern Culture Materials," *Southwestern Journal of Anthropology*, III (1947), 50–56.

4) I. Rouse, "The Strategy of Culture History," in *Anthropology Today* (Kroeber, ed.), pp. 57–76.

5) G. Foster, *Culture and Conquest: America's Spanish Heritage*.

c. THE CULTURE-HISTORICAL SCHOOL AND CULTURE CHANGE

* 1) W. Koppers, "Diffusion: Transmission and Acceptance," in *Current Anthropology* (Thomas, ed.), pp. 169–184.

* 2) R. Heine-Geldern, "Recent Developments in Ethnological Theory in Europe," in *Selected Papers of the Fifth International Congress* (Wallace, ed.), 49–53.

3) J. Haekel, "Zur gegenwärtigen Forschungssituation der Wiener Schule der Ethnologie," in *Beiträge, Symposium 1958, Wenner-Gren Foundation*.

N.B. See also the various articles evaluating Father Wilhelm Schmidt's culture-historical contributions, in *Anthropos*, XLIX (1954), 385–432, 627–658; LI (1956), 1–18, 19–61; LII (1957), 263–276.

d. THE FUNCTIONALIST INTERPRETATION OF CULTURE DYNAMICS

1) M. Gluckman, *An Analysis of the Sociological Theories of Bronislaw Malinowski*, in *Rhodes-Livingstone Papers*, Capetown, 1949.

2) B. Malinowski, *The Dynamics of Culture Change: An Inquiry into Race Relations in Africa*.

3) R. Piddington, *An Introduction to Social Anthropology*, Vol. 2, pp. 647–748.

4) R. Firth, *Elements of Social Organization*.

5) S. F. Nadel, *The Foundations of Social Anthropology*.

6) M. Fortes, "Time and Social Structure: An Ashanti Case Study," *Social Structure: Studies Presented to A. R. Radcliffe-Brown* (Fortes, ed.), pp. 54–84.

e. MODERN EVOLUTIONISTS AND CULTURE CHANGE

1) J. H. Steward, "Cultural Causality and Law: A Trial Formulation of the Development of Early Civilizations," *American Anthropologist*, LI (1949), 1–27.

2) J. H. Steward, "Evolution and Process," *Anthropology Today* (Kroeber, ed.), pp. 313–327.

3) J. H. Steward, *The Theory of Culture Change*.

4) V. Gordon Childe, *Man Makes Himself*.

5) L. White, "Energy and the Evolution of Culture," *American Anthropologist*, XLV (1943), 335–356.

6) *Evolution and Anthropology: A Centennial Appraisal*, The Anthropological Society of Washington, 1959, pp. 106–157.

f. ECLECTIC AND OTHER APPROACHES TO CULTURE CHANGE

1) W. Goldschmidt, *Man's Way*.

2) G. E. Spindler and W. Goldschmidt, "Experimental Design

in the Study of Culture Change," *Southwestern Journal of Anthropology*, VIII (1953), 68–83.

3) J. B. Watson, "Four Approaches to Culture Change," *Social Forces*, XXXII (1953), 137–145.

4) A. Holmberg, "Adventures in Culture Change," in *Method and Perspective in Anthropology* (Spencer, ed.), pp. 103–113.

* 5) R. Redfield, *The Primitive World and Its Transformation*.

* 6) R. Linton, ed., *Acculturation in Seven American Indian Tribes*.

* 7) R. A. Hackenberg, "Process Formation in Applied Anthropology," *Human Organization*, XXI (Winter, 1962–1963), 235–238.

8) D. Bidney, *Theoretical Anthropology*, pp. 182–285.

REVIEW QUESTIONS

1. Do all cultures change? Are some cultures static? (p. 195)
2. Is any progress being made in the study of culture dynamics? (pp. 195–196)
3. Where does culture change take place, in the mind or outside the mind? (pp. 196–197)
4. When does an individual become an "innovator"? (p. 197)
5. What do we understand by "general persistence"? "sectional persistence"? "token persistence"? "survivals"? (pp. 198–199)
6. What is a "revolution"? a "style"? "long-term trend"? a "cultural drift"? (p. 199)
7. What is the object of culture change? (p. 199)
8. Describe the four different ways in which culture can change. (pp. 199–202)
9. Why should the missioner be interested in culture dynamics? in the locus of culture? in revolution? (pp. 204–207)

TOPICS FOR CLASSROOM DISCUSSION AND PAPERS

1. Describe our "revolutionary times" referred to on page 207. The description should be from an anthropologist's point of view.
2. From the section "Specific Approaches to the Study of Culture Change" in the Selected Readings, choose and describe one of the viewpoints.
3. Draw up a list of revolutions, styles, and long-term trends.

CHAPTER TEN

THE PROCESSES BY WHICH CULTURES CHANGE

CULTURES consist of socially approved standards, regulated tendencies, norms, or patterns; they do not consist of concrete objects or individual actions. Consequently, when speaking of the *nature* of culture our emphasis was on *society*, now that our interest is focused on culture *change*, our emphasis must pass over to the *individual* and to the individual's actual behavior. The individual becomes our prime concern because the only way a culture can possibly change is through actual deviations from the socially shared patterns. This deviation must be given social approval, again by *individuals*, and thus become the norm.

The present chapter examines the processes involved in culture change, while the next chapter will deal with the factors that encourage or discourage deviation and social approval.

Culture change can be considered under three distinct aspects: (1) the primary or innovative aspect includes the processes that give rise to or create change; (2) the secondary or integrative aspect refers to the processes that are activated by the primary and which attempt to fit the novelty into the existing culture-whole; (3) the terminal aspect refers to the over-all result of change, e.g., equilibrium or disequilibrium.

THE PRIMARY ASPECT OF CULTURE CHANGE

Origination

We speak of "origination" whenever the change arises through processes from within the society, and of "diffusion" whenever borrowing from without the society is in question. Origination and diffusion are primary processes inasmuch as they initiate change.

Anthropologists generally speak of two forms of origination: the one they call "invention" and the other "discovery." However, this distinction seems to confuse the issue rather than clarify it and does not seem particularly useful for a proper understanding of culture dynamics. Some such more or less arbitrary distinctions are: invention is intentional while discovery is accidental; discovery consists in new knowledge while invention consists in the new application of old knowledge; invention is an idea which is given an overt or tangible expression while discovery has no such tangible expression; discovery is an original awareness while invention presupposes no such awareness. To avoid unnecessary multiplication of distinctions, it seems better to adhere to the popular usage of the terms "discovery" and "invention" or to limit oneself to the general term "origination."

"Origination" includes "discovery" and "invention" no matter how one may wish to define the terms, as long as the innovation arises from within the society rather than from without. Origination can be intentional or accidental. Even the simplest societies do a certain amount of deliberate experimentation or "research," while many of the great inventions of highly civilized peoples were pure accidents, e.g., vulcanization, penicillin, and shock treatment. The Communist art of brainwashing was accidently discovered by Pavlov when the dogs he had been experimenting on were rescued in a flood. The confusion, physical pain, exhaustion, and fear completely disoriented the dogs, giving Pavlov and the Communists the key to brainwashing. The relatively simple Maori discovered a substitute fiber to replace the bark cloth which had formerly been obtained from trees growing in their original homeland but not in New Zealand where they migrated. This discovery was made through deliberate experimentation and research. The essential element in the concept of "origination," therefore, is the fact that it is an *internal* process, not due to borrowing from another culture.

Originations do not take place in leaps and bounds, but, to some extent at least, are built upon previous knowledge and experience. In other words, originations have antecedents, and only by way of exception do innovations occur with little or no connection with the past. Even if every Neanderthal had been an Einstein, the Neanderthals would never have discovered the theory of relativity, for they lacked the necessary cultural background. It is quite true that some individuals have extraordinary foresight and that they are "ahead of their times," but even their foresight is to no small measure built upon previous cultural inventory. If Jules Verne had been a Stone Age Australian aborigine he probably would not have been dreaming about trips to the moon — much less writing about them. General William Mitchell would not have predicted the "unthinkable" flights over the ocean or the "impossible" attack on Pearl Harbor by the Japanese if he had not been a good pilot and military genius with an excellent training in the then-modern warfare. But both Jules Verne and William Mitchell were unusual men, with extraordinary foresight; normally, origination is a much slower and a much less drastic process.

Origination need not be a unique event in history, as is sometimes supposed, for two independent inventions are quite possible. Kroeber in his exposition of simultaneous originations gives no less than twenty-six remarkable examples of concurrent inventions and discoveries (1948:342): the telescope of Jansen, Lippershey, and Metius in 1608; sunspots discovered by Fabricius, Galileo, Harriott, and Scheiner in 1611; logarithms by Napier in 1614 and Bürgi in 1620; calculus by Newton in 1671 and Leibnitz in 1676; nitrogen by Rutherford in 1772 and Scheele in 1773; oxygen by Priestly and Scheele in 1774; the steamboat by Jouffroy in 1783, Rumsey in 1787, Fitch in 1788, Symington in 1788; the telegraph by Henry, Morse, Steinheil, Wheatstone, and Cooke about 1837; phonograph by Cros and Edison in 1877; North Pole by Cook and Peary in 1909. To this list one might add the recent discoveries and inventions in the nuclear and military fields made by the Russians and the Americans. There are a number of reasons for simultaneous inventions and discoveries: (1) Often the number of possibilities is limited. Thus practically all human beings (and their anthropoid cousins) peel their bananas the same way and eat them from one end rather than like a cob of corn. All human beings wash with water — Cleopatra being a remarkable exception. (2) Mere coincidence is also possible. If it should be established that the word for "big toe" is the same in the Greek koiné as in a Polynesian dialect, the linguistic similarity would most likely be a mere coincidence. (3) Then, too, since the psychological make-up of human beings is basically the same, and since human needs are also the same, one might rightly expect distinct societies occasionally to stumble on the same solution. (4) Especially when societies share similar or identical ideas and have a common purpose, there is a likelihood of their coming up with similar answers, e.g., the discovery of the H-bomb by the Americans first and then by the Russians. In the latter case, despite the "outside help," there was nevertheless considerable originality involved.

A *basic origination* (also known as "developmental" or "revolutionary") is one that gives rise to a large number of other innovations, as did electricity, radio, and food production. A *secondary* or "modificational" origination is really only a further elaboration of something that already exists, e.g., a new car model.

Diffusion

Far more common than change from within a society is diffusion. In fact, most culture change can be said to be traceable to borrowing. Isolation and the corresponding reliance on independent origination merely leads to considerable stagnation. As History clearly testifies, cultures tend to grow in proportion to their exposure to cross-fertilization, while isolation, such as that to which the Australians, Tasmanians, and other primitives are or have been subjected, stifles cultural growth. History leaves no doubt that cultures situated at crossroads of contact are precisely the ones that flourish and grow most rapidly (Hoebel, 1958:607).

Diffusion can take place with no direct contact between the borrowing culture and the culture of origin, for the object itself can, so to speak, migrate. The New Guinea highlanders use pearl shell money, although they themselves have never seen the ocean. The potato was first borrowed from South America by the Spaniards in 1560, then diffused to England in 1586, Ireland in 1590, Germany in 1651, Scotland in 1683, Sweden in 1725, and Russia in 1744 (Honigmann, 1952:210).

There are various types of diffusion (after Honigmann, 1959: 212–215). (1) *Stimulus diffusion* occurs when an idea (the stimulus) is borrowed, which is then independently elaborated upon by the borrowing society. Here the classic example is the Cherokee syllabary, an elaboration of the idea of writing derived from the white man. *Pure diffusion*, on the other hand, consists in borrowing the foreign element itself, e.g., a Stone Age society accepts steel implements as a part of its way of life. (2) Diffusion may be *gradual* or *rapid*, depending on how fast or how slow the adoption of the foreign element can be achieved. (3) It may be *objective*, i.e., the object itself may diffuse, or it may be *technical*, i.e., the technique of producing the object may be adopted rather than the object itself. (4) Diffusion may be *strategic* or *non-strategic*, depending on whether the diffusion calls for extensive preparation or not. Industrialization, for example, would require extensive modifications in food production, trade, transportation, housing, education, etc. (5) Diffusion may be *active* or *passive*, depending on whether the borrowing society must participate in the diffused element or whether it can, so to speak, merely observe and enjoy the borrowed novelty, e.g., Russian ballet in the United States would be an instance of passive diffusion, whereas eating caviar and drinking vodka would be quite active. (6) Finally, diffusion, like origination, may take place in regard to form, usage, meaning, or function, and its object may be a simple trait, a complex, an institution, or even a complex of institutions.

A special form of culture change in which diffusion plays a major role is *acculturation*. At first anthropologists made no distinction between "diffusion" and "acculturation." However, in the past few decades they have been using "diffusion" to mean any direct or indirect transmission of an element from one culture to another, while (after the recommendation of Redfield, Linton, and Herskovits serving on a special committee for the Social Science Research Council) "acculturation" has taken on the meaning of "those phenomena which result when groups of individuals having different cultures come into continuous firsthand contact, with subsequent change in the original culture patterns of either or both groups." Acculturation should not be looked upon as a specific process: it is rather a special contact situation involving a whole gamut of dynamic processes. Since in such a situation the contact between the recipient and donor cultures is close, continuous, and generally extends over a longer period, acculturation merits the attention which it is receiving from the modern anthropologist.

SECONDARY ASPECTS OF CULTURE CHANGE

Secondary processes, we have said, are those which are triggered by the primary processes: the "innovative" processes trigger the "integrative." Although even the most sophisticated individual is never perfectly logical, the human mind, however simple or primitive, strives for harmony and consistency in behavior. In response to this universally valid tendency, whenever a new idea becomes a part of the socially accepted mental content called "culture," there is a certain amount of imbalance created, and a corresponding uneasiness or quest for consistency sets in. Conflicting habits of thought, attitude, and action begin to compete and interfere with one another. The secondary processes aim to restore balance and to integrate the novelty with the traditional design for living. However, as we shall see when speaking of the terminal aspects of culture change, the integrative processes are not always successful; at times they cannot keep pace with the changes taking place, and disorganization sets in.

The balancing and integrating modifications of which we speak may affect the form, meaning, usage, or function (see pp. 139–140); in fact, the very structure and configuration of the culture may be significantly altered. The novelty itself may be modified ("reinterpretation"), or additional changes may enter into the culture whole ("ramification"), or both processes may take place. The modifications are brought about through loss, accretion, substitution, and fusion (see pp. 199–202), and are usually in accord with the "imperative of selection."

Reinterpretation

Reinterpretation is sometimes called "reformulation," "contextualization," "redesigning," "reorientation," "reworking," "reconstellation," "readaptation," "recasting," and "reintegration."

1. REINTERPRETATION OF FORM

Form is usually the least likely to undergo modification. A steel spade will tend to remain a steel spade in form when taken over by a Stone Age tribe. A change in form would occur, for instance, if the Blessed Virgin were to be depicted by a native African artist as a "Black Madonna," or if in the Palm Sunday procession local flora were to be used instead of palms. Barnett points out how some years ago the Vatican called for an exhibit of Christian art from all over the world, resulting in a collection of some 600 different reinterpretations (1953:53). Reinterpretation of form is particularly clear in the case of foreign language learning: the non-native speaker invariably tends to reinterpret the phonological as well as grammatical forms of the foreign language in accord with his existing speech-habits (Lado, 1957; 1962).

2. REINTERPRETATION OF MEANING

What generally diffuses, as Linton pointed out, is the form

"stripped of most of the meanings and associations which it carried in its original context" (1955:45). In America a spade is just an ordinary tool of an unskilled laborer, while among the simple highlanders of New Guinea one can see a native lugging his newly-acquired steel spade even on long and difficult journeys — not because it is a spade but because it has been reinterpreted as a status symbol. The spade has acquired a new meaning; its owner is "getting up in the world" or at least "keeping up with the New Guinea Joneses." Newly-introduced women's clothing may sometimes be reinterpreted as having the meaning of "suitable for men." At Sari, in the Wabag area of New Guinea, I was surprised one morning to see two of my altarboys enter the sacristy sharing a woman's dress: the one boy was wearing the blouse while his friend wore the skirt, I alone being shocked, for my interpretation of a woman's dress was not their reinterpretation.

3. Reinterpretation of Usage

Here, too, New Guinea can offer numberless examples. Newspapers, for instance, are greatly appreciated by the illiterate highlanders, not for the news contained but as cigarette paper. Or again, for some time plastic saucers could not be successfully introduced by the store-keepers in New Guinea, no matter how hard they may have tried — that is, not as saucers. But as soon as a clever individual discovered a new use for the saucers and reinterpreted them accordingly, the supply was soon exhausted. He drilled a few holes into the saucers so that they might be worn on the forehead like a traditional *maiduma*-shell. Then, too, for quite some time I had been wondering why the New Guinea schoolchildren were so eager to empty my waste basket. There was really nothing of value that I was throwing away — so I thought — until one day I had to stop a fight between two boys quarrelling over some old crumpled-up carbon paper that I had been throwing away quite regularly. The schoolchildren were using the discarded carbon paper as a beauty aid to make their hair jet-black. And, again, despite the fact that these natives had no trousers to hold up they were nevertheless very eager to acquire a leather belt, either as a decorative belly band or, in the case of a few women, for purposes of abortion. Thick woolen sweaters seemed entirely out of place in the hot tropical sun, until I learned that the sweaters were intended not so much to make the body warm as to make it "beautiful."

Other examples of reinterpretation of usage commonly observed in the Pacific area are, for example: tin cans and oil drums used for cooking; blankets used for clothing; labels of canned goods and pictures cut out from a Sears Roebuck catalogue used to paste on the forehead for decorative purposes; imported Chinese fans made of dyed chicken feathers used as part of the festive headgear. There is also the story of the famous reinterpreted toilet seat picked up by a New Guinea native from a planter's junk heap and used to frame the picture of a dear friend. And finally there is the amusing story of the American missionary who discarded his long flannel winter underwear (which he had wrongly supposed would some day prove to be useful in the chilly climate of the New Guinea highlands) only to be picked up later by one of the faithful, an important individual in the tribe. Little did the missionary suspect that the following Sunday when he would turn around at Mass for the *Dominus Vobiscum* he would receive the shock of his life. And a shock it was when he beheld strutting proudly down the middle aisle the ghost-like figure of the headman of the tribe, dressed in his pastor's snowwhite underwear. Immediately after Mass, in the sight of all his gaping admirers, the native divested; then carefully rolling up his fineries he walked home with his reinterpreted longjohns under his arm, lest while plodding along the dusty trail he dirty his "brand-new tuxedo."

4. REINTERPRETATION OF FUNCTION

A form can readily diffuse without its original function. The Hawaiian *hula* is essentially a semi-sacred dance with a corresponding function; when performed on a New York stage it is stripped completely of its religious significance, and functions much the same way as any other profane, purely entertaining feature on the program (Linton, 1936:409).

Ramification

Since the various cultural constituents are intermeshed (Chapters Six to Eight), a change in one aspect of life often calls for changes in other areas through additional loss, increment, substitution, and fusion, and through still further reinterpretation. This fanning out of secondary processes into distinct but related cultural aspects we call "ramification." Thus, for instance, imported blankets, bush knives, steel axes and spades, cotton loincloths, and other Western goods not only serve corresponding purposes in the recipient primitive culture but tend to ramify as symbols of prestige, as highly desirable objects for gift exchanges, and as essential parts of the bride-wealth. The example of the introduction of the steel axe among the Yir Yoront aborigines of Australia used above to illustrate the interwebbing of culture (see pp. 149–150) is a classic case of ramification. So many changes entered the culture with the introduction of the steel implement that the culture was threatened with complete disintegration. Formerly, the Winnebago Indians had rather lax attitudes toward toilet training of children, and the philosophy behind the attitude was quite sound: No diaper, no bother! But as soon as the Indians introduced wooden floors, no diaper meant plenty of bother. Tired of constantly cleaning the floor, the Indians had to introduce two additional novelties, diapers and early toilet training, two ramifications of the new-fangled flooring (Honigmann, 1959:14). As we have seen (p. 201), television has set off similar cultural ramifications throughout the American way of life. Urbanization, industrialization, and nativism (see pp. 225–227, 248–258) are likewise associated with countless ramifications.

It should be noted that innovations do not ramify evenly, a fact responsible for many personal as well as social conflicts. Some aspects of culture will change faster than others, because, among other reasons, the "imperative of selection" (see pp. 115–116, 202, 219–220) is active. Thus the so-called double standard of some new Christian communities is but a case of uneven culture change or culture lag. In mission countries one can meet individuals who attend Christian services and religious instructions very faithfully, theoretically accept the Decalogue and other Christian practices, but at the same time may offer sacrifices to ancestors or nature gods, consult diviners, attend seances that "bring them in contact" with their ancestors, and do anything but give up their traditional promiscuity (see section on "Christo-paganism," pp. 239–248). While professing the doctrine of heaven and hell they still somehow may feel that the departed souls of their relatives have joined their ancestors and live with them in the ancestral burial place. In much the same way, modern superstitions are but anachronisms, cases of uneven culture change even in highly civilized countries. That serious personality conflicts may arise from uneven change is only too evident: Christianity, for instance, insists on monogamy (an innovation), while tribal responsibility based on traditional

values may call for an additional wife because the first is sterile
(a culture lag). Personality conflicts arising from uneven culture
change may lead to serious mental disorders, a subject worthy of
the missionary's deepest concern and serious research.

It should also be noted that the acceptance of an innovation
does not, as a rule, take place evenly throughout the community:
the educated classes may accept a novelty while the uneducated
may remain totally uninterested; the poor may wholeheartedly accept the innovation while the rich may vehemently reject it; the
professional people may welcome the change while the simple
laborers may strongly oppose it. A very common case of social conflict arising from uneven social change is that of the native-born
children on the one hand and their immigrant parents on the other.
In mission areas social conflict frequently occurs between Christian
children and their non-Christian elders, between the Christian wife
and her non-Christian husband, between the Christian families and
their non-Christian relatives (see pp. 183–184).

The tendency to reinterpret and to ramify innovations is not
haphazard but, generally speaking, in accord with the life-way of
the borrowing society. Thus the wheel, the so-called greatest invention of all times, first appeared in the Old World, and from
there diffused to Assyria, Iran, India, and then on to Egypt. In
Egypt domestication of animals was unknown at the time; on the
other hand, pottery was an important element in the culture.
Consequently, the newly introduced wheel was not utilized for
vehicles to be drawn by animals but was reinterpreted in terms of
pottery (the potter's wheel). The wheel reached northern Europe
after the domestication of animals, and therefore, in accord with
the existing way of life, the wheel was employed for transportation
purposes (Benedict, 1956:191), in which direction it also ramified.
Language, in particular, reflects the tendency to reinterpret loanwords in accord with the culture in question. The expression "God
is our Father" may not lose its essential theological significance in
a culture in which some of the Western roles of a father are replaced by those of the maternal uncle, but one can rightly expect
considerable reinterpretation on account of the difference in connotation. The word "pick-axe" in the Middle Wahgi language is
kongmam, meaning "mother-pig." When I asked the people of
the area why they should refer to the newly introduced implement
by such an amusing term, they replied: "The tool is very much

like a mother-pig. You see, when we build roads for the government, one man (the one with the 'mother-pig') roots up the ground exactly the way a real mother-pig does it, while her 'piglets' (the men with the spades) break up the clumps." To reinterpret the pick-axe in terms of a pig is quite in keeping with the important role played by the animal in the life-way of the people. Or to borrow Herskovits' excellent example — Napoleon's soldiers, we are told, were extremely hungry for acceptance by the Russians. Whenever a French soldier would meet a Russian he would immediately try to engratiate himself by referring to himself as bon ami, implying "I am your good friend." The Russians, however, did not respond favorably; they readily accepted the French form bon ami (in Russian, bonamicheski) but at the same time reinterpreted the expression to mean "scoundrel" (Herskovits, 1950:555). A devout artist, quietly painting in his studio in an old Spanish monastery, will portray the Blessed Virgin in harmony with the aesthetic and moral values of Spain, depicting his sacred subject as the ideal of moral integrity, beauty, and womanly dignity, while his Protestant Scandinavian counterpart would try to express slightly different aesthetic as well as moral values corresponding to his cultural background.

TERMINAL ASPECTS OF CHANGE

What are the over-all results (the terminal aspects) of this constant multi-directional shifting from balance to imbalance, this constant change through origination and diffusion, through selection, through reinterpretation and ramification, through the various simultaneous losses, incrementations, substitutions, and fusions occurring in a living, dynamic culture? The terminal aspects are especially: (1) development and decline, (2) elaboration and simplification, (3) growth and reduction-segregation, and (4) equilibrium and disequilibrium. Just which aspects will predominate (development or decline, elaboration or simplification, equilibrium or disequilibrium) will depend on the interplay of many factors, which will be discussed fully in the next two chapters.

Development and Decline

By "development" is meant the greater ability of a society to control its environment. The adaptive system of a society tends to. develop as its experience grows and as its contact with other cultures increases. However, generally speaking, this ability to control environment is limited to the physical world. As the society's experience grows through the generations, its ability to control the physical environment tends to grow also, e.g., climate is controlled through improved housing, heating, and clothing; distance is controlled through improved means of travel and communication; there is also an increase in the control of energy and disease. Such technical development does not necessarily imply greater control of social relationships or greater ability to cope with ideational problems. There may be a "decline" rather than a "development" in the ability of the society to cope with its social environment, e.g., the inability to reduce delinquency, strife between social classes or races, wars, etc. (Honigmann, 1959:273–279).

Elaboration

Through constant culture change the life-way may become increasingly more complex. There is more variety in the culture. It should be noted, however, that certain aspects of culture may become more elaborate while others may become more simplified.

Reduction-Segregation

As a rule, loss does not keep pace with increment, and the culture tends to grow larger and larger. To cope with this growth the culture begins to divide the rapidly expanding inventory into specialties based on occupation, age, sex, etc., or it systematizes the socially shared mental content (culture) into more generalized concepts, reducing the total knowledge and experience of the society into generalized theories, laws, disciplines, and "schools."

Equilibrium

Despite this constant shifting from balance to imbalance, and despite the growth and development, cultures, generally speaking, seem somehow to maintain a more or less satisfactory over-all balance or equilibrium. The various secondary processes, the growth itself, and the accompanying reduction-segregation constitute an effective cultural gyroscope, making the normal terminal situation that of equilibrium. This state of balance is also known as *eunomia* or *euphoria* (after Radcliffe-Brown), a "feeling of well-being" characterized by an over-all steadiness in the culture, a high morale, self-confidence, and a sense of security. Such steadiness does not make further change impossible. The term "steadiness" merely refers to the rather well-established and more or less smoothly operating state of the culture.

Nor does the term "equilibrium" carry with it any value-judgment. It is quite possible for a way of life full of theologically untenable elements to be "better" balanced than a culture with a theologically sound ideology. "Balance" calls for efficiency, not righteousness. The way of life of a Communistic society may be more balanced than that of a God-fearing people, for "balance" implies consistency and smoothness of operation, and nothing more. A harmful weed may be a healthier, stronger, and more resistant specimen of plant-life than a delicate but highly-valued flower. In fact, materialism and godlessness may be the balancing factors responsible for the *eunomia* and smoothness of operation. Prosperity, for example, if sudden and all-absorbing, may make a religiously minded society become inconsistent in its behavior and philosophy. The prosperity may trigger changes throughout the culture, affecting the family life, school system, government, and religious and moral behavior; it may also deeply affect the basic assumptions, values, and goals of the society. In such a case, materialism tends to take over and through various reformulative responses brings about cultural equilibrium.

In the case of *acculturation*, equilibrium takes on additional meaning. Cultures in an acculturative situation (close, firsthand, and more or less continuous contact) reach a state of equilibrium among themselves through a kind of symbiosis, through pluralism, or through assimilation (Honigmann, 1959:270–271). (1) In a *symbiotic* situation, each culture specializes in certain activities, the one society becoming dependent on the roles and services of the other. A fisher-folk may supply the fish for an island agricultural group, while the latter may supply much of the vegetable needs of the former. (2) In a state of *stabilized pluralism*, the societies in contact control both the borrowing and the direction of culture change, so that the particular way of life of each remains relatively intact, e.g., the *ladinos* and *indigenas* of Latin America. Modern times call for an adjustment on the part of the Church to a deeply pluralistic world. Without compromising principle, Catholics must strive toward close fraternal co-operation with secular as well as non-Catholic religious groups. (3) *Assimilation* consists in the complete blending of distinct cultures.

Disequilibrium

Sometimes the reintegrating processes fail to keep up with the growth and changes taking place. Disorganization begins to mount, decay sets in, and the culture begins to disintegrate. As sociologists speak of "social pathology," so the anthropologists rightly can speak of "cultural pathology." In fact, where the one occurs there is usually also the other.

Disintegration, so to speak, renders one's enculturation useless. In the process of enculturation the individual has learned his society's design for living — its content, meanings, usages, functions, and configurations. This learning gave the individual and the society a sense of confidence, an assurance of being able to cope with the physical, social, and ideational environment. Cultural disintegration, on the other hand, brings uncertainty, confusion, frustration, and low morale. The behavior of the members of the society becomes unpredictable. Traditional values become hazy. In a word, *dyspattern*, *dysfunction*, and *dysconfiguration* displace a patterned and functional behavior, and a behavior consistent with the underlying value-system of the people.

Cultures may become disorganized through various causes, from within as well as from without the society. History is full of tragic disappearances of cultures, even of great civilizations like those of Ancient Egypt, Greece, and Rome. Cultures decay and die from various causes: from the disappearance of the bearers of a culture (whatever the reason for the disappearance) and from cultural disorder with which the society could not cope.

1. Culture Decay and Death Through War and Conquest

Cultures have died as a result of war and conquest, as in the case of the Inca, whose highly integrated society collapsed under the pressure of the Spaniards. Two thirds of the total population of the once-great Inca empire died as a result of forced labor and from diseases introduced by their European overlords. The remainder was subjected to intolerable serfdom and a life of frustrations, with only alcoholism and debauchery to satisfy the once-proud and culturally rich Inca heart.

2. Culture Decay and Death Through Contact and Change

Describing the unfortunate effects of European contact and colonialism in Melanesia, Rivers summed up the situation as "a loss of the will to live." The expression may sound somewhat exaggerated; nevertheless, the contact did bring about so much disorganization that the Melansian had only a life of extreme boredom, disgust, frustration, and near-despair to look forward to. The Melanesians, however, were not the only people that have been subjected to the ill effects of contact and uncontrollable change. The degree of decay has, of course, varied from less serious cases of dysphoria to complete disintegration. It is a known fact, for instance, that the Tasmanians and some American Indian tribes have completely disappeared with their cultures through Western contact.

An instance of serious dyspattern, dysfunction, and dysconfiguration has been recently described by the Swiss anthropologist Alfred Bühler (1957:1–35). The native population of the Sepik area of New Guinea, despite the fact that there are only a relatively few whites in the area, has since World War I been subjected to intensive acculturative pressures. Western contact has created a vacuum rather than a successful blending of cultures through a balanced reintegration. Formerly the tambaran-houses served very important functions in the community: they were the symbols of tribal solidarity; they were the art studios and museums of the people; they were the temples, the sources of supernatural power and security; they were, in fact, the very heart of the native religion and the mainspring of the Sepik life-way itself. Christianity has so far not succeeded in serving as a satisfactory substitute for the old ideology, while the material "benefits" derived from European contact have left the native heart cold and lifeless. Patterns that formerly gave the individual prestige, such as the possession of shells, have ceased to stir up pride and admiration in the native heart, and no real substitute has been found to fill this void. With the coming of the government, plantations, and mission stations, many individuals began to dream of the day when they would be able to achieve the same material advantages as the Europeans. Full of expectation the Sepik natives flocked to plantations, government posts, and mission stations for work or education, the two roads that promised success. Today, however, serious frustration has set in and the hope of ever participating fully in the white man's world of wonder seems to have been shattered. Connected with this disillusionment is a deep feeling of inferiority. The Sepik native is subconsciously convinced that he is too far below the white man in intelligence, ability, and value, a point that had again and again been impressed upon him in one way or another by the white man. Through contact with Western civilization many changes have thus entered into native life, causing not a few patterns to fall into disuse or to lose their significance and become functionless. A cultural vacuum has thus been created, which, together with the frustration felt deeply especially by the young, has become an ideal climate for such movements as the Cargo Cult (see pp. 255–258) and, one might add, Communism.

3. DISINTEGRATION THROUGH URBANIZATION AND INDUSTRIALIZATION

Today the greatest danger of serious disintegration comes from the understandable but misguided craving for rapid and even instantaneous technological change. Industrialization and urbanization have become worldwide phenomena and worldwide problems. In Africa, Latin America, India, Japan, Indonesia, and elsewhere throughout the world an ever-increasing proportion of the population is moving into urban and industrialized localities. Thousands of individuals are daily leaving their sheltered, although usually not ideal traditional environments in favor of poverty-stricken, filthy shanty towns skirting the larger cities. Latin American cities like Caracas are a beautiful picture indeed — except for the frame, the numberless shacks that encircle the city. It is not the physical inconveniences and health conditions alone that are deplorable. The most painful consequences of urbanization are perhaps the depersonalization and deculturization that accompanies migrations to the cities. As uninviting as the conditions of the home-village may have been, there was still the comforting feeling of belonging, a sense of solidarity: there were law and order and co-operation in the community and among the kin; there was a sense of responsibility toward the needs of others and the corresponding feeling that "someone is interested and cares about me." With the abandonment of social ties, however, the migrant frequently loses his sense of responsibility toward others and finds himself socially isolated. In the traditional environment the individual had a definite status and a corresponding role

to play; in the new surroundings he is isolated, with no one worry-
ing about him, while he, in turn, feels no responsibility toward anybody else. Self-centeredness is a typical trait of a shanty town
dweller, where everyone must "stand on his own feet" and "shift
for himself." In the shanty town the family must cope with problems by itself, a difficult task and one for which it was not prepared.
Even in traditional conditions a death will always be a shock,
especially if the father or mother of the family be concerned; but
such a shock is generally softened by kinship, tribal, and community
patterns. In shanty towns, however, there is no one to soften the
shock. The problem of eking out a living in a shanty town is often
unbelievable. The mother must frequently seek employment instead of caring for her children, especially if her husband, as happens not too seldom, turns to drink or becomes a dope addict. By
moving to the city the migrant family gives up much of its old
value-system and traditional controls of behavior, so that crime,
alcoholism, debauchery, quarrels, and especially marriage and family
breakdown become, so to speak, almost as common as the shacks
in which the squatters live. Mental disorder becomes a major problem, and overcrowding seriously affects the moral life of the children.
Respect for elders and parental authority diminishes and gradually
disappears. Such conditions may, of course, not be true of every
family living in a shanty town; however, the picture portrayed is,
unfortunately, common enough to justify the gloomy and pessimistic
stereotype described (cf. Considine, 1960:176–197).

In almost any rapidly industrializing area one finds mining camps,
laborers' quarters, and so-called "company towns." Although such
"migrations" are only temporary, their effects are sometimes tragic
and permanent. In New Guinea, for instance, the young men from
the highlands are recruited for work on coastal plantations a hundred
and more miles from their homes.

. . . employment on the coast has widened the young man's horizon.
His interests now seem to extend well beyond the tribal territory. He
is now able to speak Pidgin English fluently. He has become sure of
himself and has now a better chance of succeeding on a mountain
plantation near home. He feels superior to his less-traveled brother.
However, not everything that he has learned on the coast is necessarily
a boon to him: he now knows how to gamble and has perhaps grown
fond of gambling; types of sexual perversion unheard of in the mountains may have been ordinary plantation gossip; his respect for the
white man has definitely diminished and perhaps the dangerous seed

of the Cargo Cult has been planted among the mountain people while a few of the young men were laborers on the coast. Although the anopheles mosquito is present in the mountains, especially in the Wahgi flats, the recruits return with much more malaria than they had when they went to the coast and much more than their natural resistance permits. One rightly wonders if the romance is really worth the price (Luzbetak, 1958a:73).

4. DISINTEGRATION THROUGH MIGRATIONS

As we have seen, increasingly larger and larger proportions of the world's population are moving into urban areas, making urbanization one of the chief missionary problems of our times. However, almost any type of migration will involve considerable social and cultural disorganization. In the United States the immigrant problems of today center mainly around the Puerto Ricans and Cubans as they once centered around the Italians, Slavs, and earlier still, the Germans and the Irish. Migrations call for an adjustment to new and often difficult physical, social, and ideational conditions for which the migrants have not been culturally prepared. Religious and civic organizations, national clubs, educational and other assistance offered by earlier migrants, the establishment of an organized community within a community, whether in the form of a parish or ghetto, have all helped the immigrant to adjust himself to his new situation. Such measures generally help to reduce the danger of depersonalization and other evils connected with migrations.

One of the earliest and more important studies on the subject was made in 1918 by Thomas and Znaniecki, published under the title of *The Polish Peasant in Europe and America* (New York, 1927) showing the disorganization that results from the decrease in the influence of traditional social patterns upon the individual migrant. The authors contrast traditional Polish family life as found in the home-country with that of America. In Poland the "large-family group" (*i.e.*, relatives to the fourth degree) rather than the nuclear family owned the land on which the peasants worked. The "large-family group" was closely linked to other such groups through marriage. Authority was in the hands of the older members and was duly respected by all. Interests centered around the farm and the closely interacting socio-economic group into which the individual was born. However, when the peasant migrated to America, his new ideational and socio-economic environment was a new world to him, for which he was not prepared. He had to be satisfied with a job that required no special skill and had to become a city-dweller rather than a farmer. In his new environment he lacked economic security and the solidarity which the "large-family group" provided for him in Poland. Formerly everything he did was established for him by custom; in his new country he had to plan every step for himself, in matters with which he was not familiar. He would make a decision and then hope for the best. Unlike the situation in Poland, the wife had to assume the lowly role of housekeeper, leaving the role of breadwinner to the father of the family. Paternal authority, traditional to the Poles, rapidly declined as the children and wife became more and more aware of their new freedoms. As is well known, the Polish peasant in America, despite his language difficulties and associated clannishness, has adjusted himself quite satisfactorily by adopting new American economic and social mores. He has erected parish churches and schools (some of the largest and finest in the country); he managed to build himself a relatively comfortable house in the city despite the low salary received in steel mills and coal mines; he formed social organizations with others who spoke a language he could understand and who shared his problems; he also discovered new sources of security in the American way through insurance policies and bank accounts, and within another generation or two he will be completely assimilated, and except for his name may be unrecognizable from his fellow-Americans. The transition, however, has not always been so smooth and successful as just described. Not seldom did it happen that the low salary of the unskilled immigrant forced him to become involved in heavy debts, to rely on charity, and sometimes to have recourse to drink. His American-born children were confused by the conflict which they could not help but see between the values of their American environment and the norms upheld and insisted upon by their foreign-born parents. At times moral values taught them by their parents appeared unreal or uncertain, and delinquency became a serious problem to not a few of the immigrant families (cf. Murray, 1947:839–841).

SUMMARY AND SELECTED MISSIOLOGICAL APPLICATIONS

Summary

Culture change can be brought about only through actual deviation from the standardized ways and through the social acceptance of the deviation as the new norm. There are three distinct aspects involved in culture change: the primary refers to those processes which give rise or create change; secondary processes are those that are activated by the primary and aim to integrate the innovation with the rest of culture; the terminal aspect is the over-all end-result of change, sc., equilibrium or disequilibrium, development or decline, elaboration, and reduction-segregation.

Origination is a primary process creating change from within the society, while its counterpart, diffusion, is a change from without through borrowing. Acculturation includes "those phenomena which result when groups of individuals having different cultures come into continuous firsthand contact, with subsequent change in the original culture patterns of either or both groups."

A change generally brings an imbalance into the culture which the secondary processes try to correct by modifying either the novelty or the traditional patterns or both. Such reintegration is achieved especially through reinterpretation, selection, and ramification.

Equilibrium is a terminal aspect of culture change, characterized by an over-all steadiness and consistency in the culture, a "feeling of well-being," high morale, self-confidence, and a sense of security. Disequilibrium consists in cultural disorganization, ranging from minor to complete disintegration. Serious disorganization is brought about in various ways: through war and conquest, contact between different cultures, urbanization, industrialization, migration, and other causes affecting either the culture itself or the bearers of the culture.

Selected Missiological Applications

1. The Agent of Culture Change and the Individual

The missionary as an agent of culture change, although fully aware of the necessity of following a socio-cultural rather than an individual approach (see pp. 118–120), must at the same time realize that the only way he can achieve his ends and bring about culture change is through *individuals*. There is no other way of introducing new, Christian beliefs and practices or new socio-economic ideas than by effectively persuading *individuals* to deviate from their traditional ways. There is also no other way of directing reinterpretation, controlling selection and ramification, or restoring equilibrium than through the individual bearers of culture.

The individuals who dare to part from their traditional ways are the bridge between the missionary educator, technical advisor, doctor, catechist, counselor, confessor, and preacher on the one hand and the set of socially shared patterns that the missionary wishes to alter on the other. The innovators are the bridge between the Church and the non-Christian society. Although it may sound somewhat crude to refer to pioneer Christians and potential followers of Christ as "innovators," when speaking as anthropologists we have no other choice. The fact remains that the missioner, who in cold anthropological terms bears the unsavory label of "agent of culture change," is deeply involved in "innovations" and "innovators" — the "leaven" spoken of in the Gospel (Matt. 13:33). The only way the missionary can enter and transform a society is through this "leaven." He will necessarily be dealing with individuals, not with an abstract society. Proper relations with this "leaven" will stimulate it to action, while mistakes in interpersonal relations or an inability to interact correctly may hinder it from having its desired effects. Dale Carnegie's *How to Win Friends and Influence People* and similar collections of purely human wisdom may sometimes make more missiological sense than many an *ex professo* missiological treatise. We shall treat the present topic under two heads — rapport and leadership.

1) **Rapport.** To a large extent the subject of rapport has been implicitly treated in the section on proper adjustment to a strange culture (pp. 84–103). What follows aims to supplement what has already been said and might very well be summed up in two simple axioms: (1) respect and treat the individual *as an individual* and (2) respect and treat him not only as an individual but *as a personal friend.*

To respect an individual *as an individual* is difficult enough in one's own social and cultural milieu, but it becomes doubly difficult in an environment in which subconsciously there is a hidden feeling of superiority, such as exists in a Christian toward a "pagan," a "knower and lover of God" toward an "idolator," and an educated American or European toward a "half-educated" or illiterate non-Westerner. To recognize and treat an individual as an individual — with his own temperament, talent, handicaps, and name — and not to lump all individuals together under one stereotype will be difficult especially in the beginning of one's missionary career. To a newcomer to the mission all the people look the same (they all have the same kind of skin and perhaps slanted eyes) and act in the same "strange" and "inferior" manner.

Respect for an individual as an individual means *respect for his feelings*. There is very little logic in our own feelings — why insist on logic when dealing with the feelings of "strange" people? Why accuse them of "excessive" sensitivity, when we are as sensitive as they? The only difference between ourselves and the "strange" people is the fact that their "sore spots" are in a different place. Feelings, in other words, vary not only from person to person but from culture to culture. For example, where hospitality is considered a major virtue, breach of etiquette may be extremely offensive.

Not to offend may sometimes be a very difficult problem indeed. A personal experience illustrates the point quite well. In one of the Central American countries the hostess not only prepared my meal but insisted on standing at my side while I was trying to eat the food she had prepared. She stirred and poured and almost spoonfed me. She was poor and offered the best she had. The milk was yellowish from dirt, fresh from some kind of a milk-producing animal, the species of which I could not judge from the milk. A hair still floated on the surface proclaiming the milk's freshness — fresh from the animal out in the street. The meal was the best she could offer, and it meant quite a deprivation to the rest of the household. To eat what was placed before me was not easy, but somehow I managed. It was easier to accept the hospitality than to hurt the feelings of one of the kindest persons I have ever known. At times, of course, one cannot argue with one's stomach. We have all heard of the gentleman who wrapped up a caterpillar in a lettuce leaf and then heroically and unnoticeably swallowed it so as not to offend his hostess. Without going that far, one might find some other clever solution to avoid offense, as did a certain government worker overseas who had been offered a fish head to eat, a way of singling out the guest of honor. To refuse the fish head would have been a grave insult, but to gulp it down would have been to tempt the Lord and the height of presumption. Very wisely the man suggested: "Back in America, where I come from, we have the custom of saving such delicacies for the ladies; so, if Madame Hostess wouldn't mind, it would make her humble and unworthy guest extremely happy to see her eat the fish head" (cf. Spector and Preston, 1961:46).

Respect for an individual as an individual, therefore, calls for respect for his culturally defined feelings. What might be considered "firmness" and "consistency" in dealing with one's employees in the United States might very well be regarded as "harshness" and "stubbornness" or "inconsiderateness" elsewhere. What the missioner might be inclined to judge as "snobbishness" and "discrimination" might very well be regarded as "due respect" and "reverence" by his Japanese flock. When going for an outing, for instance, the Japanese teachers may expect preferential treatment. To pile them into the same bus with their students would be looked upon as an insult, not as discrimination. Similarly, in many parts of the world the women have to carry all burdens, while the gentlemen "travel light" if not empty-handed. This may be "discrimination" and "a lack of respect" for the dignity of the woman in the United States but it is not such everywhere. Contrary to the missionary's feelings, children may have to be fed first while the adult guests may have to wait. To disregard such culturally determined attitudes is to disregard the feelings of the people and a failure to treat the individual as an individual.

An individual is made to feel as an individual especially by making him feel important and not just "one of the mob." Once again, just how and when to make a person feel important and appreciated will be determined by the norms of the local people. To the missionary who has traveled thousands of miles by plane, a short hop from one airstrip to another may mean little, but to the headman of a New Guinea clan who has had the rare fortune of receiving a free airplane ride from the government or the mission deserves to be congratulated and made to feel "big." It is, after all, a red-letter day in his life as well as in the history of his people. His flight is as important to them as astronaut Glenn's flight around the world was to the Americans or Yuri Gagarin's flight was to the Russians. The promotion of a native in an isolated primitive tribal government may objectively be a trivial matter as far as world politics are concerned, but to the individual concerned it may mean as much as it meant to President Kennedy to be elected President of the United States. Such an individual deserves to be congratulated. Missionaries visiting their out-stations or mission doctors checking their medical outposts should encourage and publicly praise the teacher or native nurse whenever praise is due, however, not using the educational and medical standards of the missionary's home-country but the realistic norms of the society in question. To know people by name and to greet them individually, by a handshake perhaps, may be applicable in many cases — an old trick duly appreciated by the vote-hungry politicians. Al Smith, for instance, had the reputation of remembering every name he heard: once introduced, he never forgot the name. His trick was a very simple one. Whenever he could not remember the name he would ask in a very friendly tone of voice: "And what was the name again?" As soon as the unfamiliar individual's name was uttered — "I'm Jones," or "I'm Martinelli," or "I'm Markewicz" — Smith would immediately interrupt the stranger with "O no, I mean your first name." The stranger was, of course, greatly flattered, and Al Smith had another vote.

Rapport demands that the individual be treated not only as an individual but as a personal friend. Without going into a long treatise on the meaning of "friendship," let it suffice to point out that friendship anywhere in the world presupposes: (1) mutual understanding, (2) common taste, (3) common interests, (4) mutual assistance, (5) mutual admiration, and (6) mutual accessibility. These will lead to mutual trust, affection, and identification. The actual details of each of these items, it should be noted, will again to a large extent be culturally defined.

(1) *Mutual Understanding.* A friend is never a stranger and a stranger is never a friend. Identification presupposes that the missionary knows his people, understands their ways, and appreciates their values. Since the entire present course aims to show the missionary how to go about breaking down the wall of strangeness that exists between individuals having different cultural backgrounds, there is really no need to speak specifically about the matter here as if it were a new, distinct problem.

It may not be out of place, however, to suggest that the missionary should make an effort not to remain a closed book to his people, for friendship is two-sided, and the understanding which friendship presupposes must be mutual. It may be well for the missionary to speak every now and then to his people about his own "strange" ways — not in a haughty manner but with view to helping them to understand the "strange" person that he happens to be. Once they realize that their missionary is "different," they will overlook many of his "naïve" remarks, "foolish" decisions, "impolite" behavior, and "rudeness." Just when and how he is to speak of his cultural background, family, and home-country will depend on the local expectations. In Japan, for instance, a spiritual man ought to be detached from things of this world, including his own family. Elsewhere, on account of the emphasis placed on family loyalty, such detachment may scandalize the people, giving them the impression that the missioner is disloyal to his family and ungrateful to his parents, the two worst sins imaginable.

(2) *Common Tastes*. Conflicting tastes, no less than strangeness, will tend to discourage friendship and identification. Since taste is to a large measure culturally defined, it is a vital matter for the missionary to discover the tastes of the local people and as much as possible make them his own. In fact, "culture" and "taste" are almost synonymous, especially in more homogeneous societies.

Missionaries, by reason of their position in the community, are obliged to make one decision after another, decisions that affect their employees, pupils, native staff, and congregation. By disregarding the tastes of those with whom the missioner must interact, he may be building up a wall between himself and the individuals with whom he should be identified. "He is not friendly at all; he is always against us" is the reference made to missionaries who fail to learn and adopt native tastes. Ignorance of local ways and values is not a valid excuse, for it is the missionary's problem and duty to discover the tastes of his people and to adopt such tastes in his dealing with them as far as Faith, science, prudence, the aims of the Missions, and the expectations of the people will allow (see pp. 347–351).

(3) *Common Interests*. Friendship and identification presuppose common interests. A missionary who knows how to share responsibility with his flock will almost spontaneously develop a common interest with them; on the other hand, the missionary who tends to conduct his activities in a cloud of mystery and with a "none-of-your-business" attitude will most likely never succeed in stirring up such an interest. It is quite true that the prime responsibility for the mission station, school, or hospital usually rests with the local missionary rather than with the local people, nevertheless, a "none-of-your-business" attitude discourages friendship. More proper would be a discussion of plans and ideas rather than an "I'll-call-you-when-I-need-your-advice" spirit or a constant "who's-the-boss-around-here" reminder. The local people should be as much as possible the missionary's partners, sharing his worries, burdens,

and glories. Mission activities should be *their* activities.

In turn, the missionary should be deeply involved in the interests of his flock — in their crops, their fiestas, and the expected additions to their families, again, as far as native etiquette and other rules of prudence allow. In a society in which the family is the center of interest, the missioner would do well to be keenly concerned about individual kin groups, much more so than pastors normally are in the missionary's home-country. In his sermons and instructions he would frequently propose rewards affecting the family; in public prayer he would make the prosperity of the family a frequent intention; in his dealing with the local community he would carefully uphold the family authority and show deep respect for the sacredness of kin ties. In a word, a missionary who wants to be regarded as a friend of his people must make their interests his own.

(4) *Mutual Assistance.* Mutual interest, however essential it may be, is not sufficient in itself; interest must be backed up by meaningful assistance. But what type of assistance is meaningful? Again, one cannot generalize too much. Paternalism is definitely not the type of charity that the people generally seek. Excessive paternalism sometimes serves merely to humiliate rather than to win friends, especially in a rapidly changing and ambitious society. As emphasized above (see pp. 204–206), truly meaningful socio-economic assistance consists in providing *opportunities* rather than in outright giving, even though the latter is at times necessary.

Although according to Christian teaching the virtue of charity is a universal value, the concrete form of an act of charity will have to be decided with the help of native norms. True charity aims to fill needs, and needs can be properly interpreted only in full cultural context. In highly civilized countries, for instance, the mentally retarded are among the most needy; they cannot survive because the economic system is very complex. However, in a South Sea island community, the economy may very well be so simple that even the most retarded individual can "make a living," that is, he can climb a coconut tree and feed himself, while even the slightest lameness that makes tree-climbing impossible may be a very serious handicap. In civilized societies physically handicapped individuals are sometimes not only able to survive but to compete and even outdo their physically sound colleagues in medicine, law, literary work, and as executives. In short, any socio-economic assistance must be evaluated with the needs of the people to be assisted in view.

The type of assistance that encourages friendship is mutual, not one-sided. The missionary must help his people, but, at the same time, they must help him. As early as possible the new Christian community should be taught its responsibility regarding the support of the local as well as the universal Church. To insist on a reasonable "give-and-take" relationship is to encourage *mutual* assistance, the type of assistance that promotes a friendly relationship and identification.

(5) *Mutual Admiration.* Friends are people we admire. Consequently, the missioner must, as far as this is possible, strive to be an individual whom his people could admire; he, in turn, must learn to admire them, a task particularly difficult when the would-be friendship is between individuals having different cultural backgrounds. If the missioner is to be admired by the local community he cannot afford not to learn their "silent language," the latent meanings in their outward behavior. Even the way a person walks communicates a message, for the particular stride may be associated with timidity, suspicious intent, or haughtiness. If the missioner does not learn his people's "silent language" he may wrongly give them the impression that he is harsh, timid, stupid, impolite, and possesses other qualities one would normally not find in a self-chosen friend.

It is particularly important to admire the "self-image" of a people. Every society has its own picture of "a good man," which it attributes to itself. In practical mission work it matters little whether the self-image misses the mark or not: it *is* the image the people have of themselves, or as they would like to appear, and, as such, this image must be respected by any foreigner who wishes to be identified with the local people. The missioner cannot begin soon enough to inquire into this image and, as far as possible, to admire it. The people of India consider themselves highly spiritual; the Chinese consider themselves highly moral; the Americans consider themselves highly democratic; the British consider themselves highly cultured. The self-image represents ideals, and ideals, even though perhaps never reached, are worthy of admiration. Respect for the self-image of a society is one of the surest ways of achieving entry into it and of winning the confidence, friendship, and co-operation of the people.

(6) *Mutual Accessibility.* Friends are mutually accessible. Habitually to brush people off and to have little or no time to listen to their worries, problems, and needs (no matter how busy one

really may be) is a serious mistake to make by anyone like the missionary whose work depends on close, friendly relations with the local community. A regular leisurely stroll through the village or market place, with an appropriate greeting for all and a short chat here and there, is one of the many ways of making oneself accessible and of promoting friendly relations. Availability restricted to regular "office hours," whether in the classroom, pulpit, confessional, or clinic, generally does not provide the type of contact that stimulates friendship; over and above such official contacts there should be time set aside for informal meetings compatible, of course, with one's state of life, prudence, and the expectations of the people.

Nothing could be more detrimental to friendly relations than not being available even during "office hours," whether through neglect of duty, selfishness, or any other unjustifiable reason. The exact meaning of "office hours," however, will be determined not only by what the missionary himself considers to be reasonable but also by the role he plays in the community and the traditional "office hours" ascribed to such a role. In some cultures a missionary is regarded as "a public servant" who must be available 24 hours of the day, even for relatively minor matters. In the United States, normally one does not phone the pastor after 9:00 p.m. or before 6:00 a.m. unless the matter is really urgent. An additional difficulty arises in mission countries from the fact that "important" and "urgent" in reference to business is culturally defined, and what the missionary may consider to be trivial may be a matter of life and death to the local people.

Accessibility, as meant here, excludes, of course, excessive familiarity. Especially in older mission areas, certain patterns regarding permissible behavior for missionaries have been developed, such as the frequency of visits to private families, lengthy conversations, and socializing in general. Such tested norms should be learned and observed by the newcomer, no matter what his views or inclinations may be. He should also remember that, to decide what is "coldness" and what is "excessive familiarity," he must use not only his own good judgment but apply local norms as well (see pp. 86–87). It would also be well to remember that all cultures seem to impose a certain "distance" on roles of respect, such as those of the teacher, leader, and persons dedicated to religion. Even in the United States, where informality is regarded as proper and desirable, a "call-me-Joe" type of teacher or priest may be popular — very popular indeed — but most likely anything but effective as a teacher or priest. It is sometimes said, and perhaps rightly so, that this culturally imposed "distance" makes those in authority and highly-respected positions the loneliest persons on earth.

Much more, of course, could be said about rapport — the proper relation between an agent of culture change and the innovators. Before concluding, however, it must be emphasized that theoretical knowledge will never be sufficient to ensure successful interpersonal relationship: rapport will be the result not of theory but of practice, not of resolutions but of established character traits. Rapport, in a word, is the result of character formation, continuous self-discipline, and spiritual growth.

2) Witness and Leadership. Rapport by itself, no matter how important and indispensable it may be, does not guarantee apostolic success; there is still another task which the missionary must carry out. He must *activate* the "leaven," for, as we have seen (pp. 210, 229–230), change can enter a culture only through actual deviations by innovators. In fact, the deviation must be accepted as the "norm" by a sufficient number of individuals. When describing the socio-cultural approach (see pp. 118–120), we pointed out how social acceptance can be best achieved through individuals who occupy culturally and socially strategic positions. Humanly speaking, they are the most important element in the "leaven" that must be activated.

Unfortunately, these basic culturological principles are sometimes not fully appreciated. Some missionaries are inclined to imagine that they alone are the workers in the vineyard of the Lord, while their congregations are regarded merely as "the fruits of missionary labor." It would be far more in accord with the parable of the leaven and with the anthropological theory enuntiated to regard the missionary merely as a kind of catalyst, ascribing to the pioneer Christians who dare to part from traditional ways the actual work of changing the society.

Sometimes such a misconception is shared by the new Christians, for they regard Baptism as an entirely personal matter, as a kind of diploma after a long and difficult course in Christian Doctrine or as a personal entry permit into the Church. Such an attitude is an unfortunate reflection of the missionary's own views and cate-chetical methods. The missionary should have been emphasizing during the entire catechumenate that Baptism is not only a personal reward but a serious commitment obliging the newly baptized to share their Faith with others. Christian witness and leadership are not of a supererogatory nature but an essential aspect of being a Christian. If the candidates for Baptism are not convinced of the missionary nature of Christianity they are not really prepared for the reception of the Sacrament. The fact that they are committed to apostolic work must again and again be impressed upon the catechumens, with almost as much force as the necessity of saving their own souls. Such an emphasis on dedication to the apostolic cause is both theologically as well as anthropologically sound — anthropologically, because the agent of culture change is only a catalyst, while the real changers of a culture are the members of the society who deviate from its traditional ways and lead others to deviate with them.

2. CHRISTO-PAGANISM

There are very few problems plaguing the Missions today that are as serious and as real as the problem of syncretism. Despite this fact, very little scientifically organized on-the-spot research and controlled experimentation have been done by missionaries and missiologists. This very unfortunate phenomenon will be best understood by keeping in mind the theory enunciated above about selection, reinterpretation, ramification, fusion, form, usage, meaning, function, and cultural consistency.

1) **Notion of Syncretism.** Fusion is the amalgamation of any innovation with an analogous element. If moral or religious behavior is involved, the amalgamation is known as *syncretism*. In a somewhat broader sense, the term is applied to the blending of any two or more conflicting religious beliefs, as has occurred for instance in Islam (cf. Schmidlin, 1933:27–28, 80–81). In a more restricted sense, as used in the present course, syncretism refers to the fusion of *Christianity* and what is commonly known as "paganism," resulting in a *theologically untenable* amalgam called "Christo-paganism."

2) **Examples of Syncretism.** The Negroes of the Caribbean area have identified many of their African deities with Catholic Saints or their representations, pictures, statues, etc. (cf. Métraux, 1959; Herskovits, 1937:635–643; Herskovits, 1941; Herskovits, 1950:553–555). In Haiti St. Anthony becomes one with the West African

Dahomean and Yoruban trickster Legba, an identification based on the fact that both St. Anthony and Legba were known as lovers of the poor. St. Patrick becomes identified with Damballa, a West

FIGURE 4

CORRESPONDENCE BETWEEN AFRICAN GODS AND CATHOLIC SAINTS IN BRAZIL, CUBA, AND HAITI*

African deities as found in:	Brazil	Cuba	Haiti
Obatala		(O) **Virgen de las Mercédes; the Most Sacred Sacrament; Christ on the Cross	
Obatala; Orisala; Orixala (Oxala)	(I) (N) (R) "Nosso Senhor de Bomfim" at Bahía; (N) Saint Anne; (R) "Senhor do Bomfim" at Río (because of the influence of Bahía")		
Grande Mambo Batala			(M) Saint Anne
Shango	(I) (N) (R) Santa Barbara at Bahía; (R) St. Michael the Archangel at Río; (R) St. Jerome (the husband of Santa Barbara) at Bahía (see Yansan below)	(O) Santa Barbara	
Elegbara, Elegua, Alegua		(O) "Animas benditas del Purgatorio"; "Anima Sola"	
Legba			(M) (H) St. Anthony; (W) (H?) St. Peter
Esu	(I)(N)(R) the Devil		
Ogun	(I) (R) St. George, at Río; (N) St. Jerome; (I) (N) (R) St. Anthony, at Bahía	(O) St. Peter	
Ogun Balandjo			(M) St. James the Elder; (H) St. Joseph
Ogun Ferraille			(H) St. James
Osun	(N) Virgin Mary; N. D. de Candeias	(O) Virgin de la Caridad del Cobre	
Yemanjá	(N) Virgin Mary; (R) N. S. de Rosario (at Bahía); N. D. de Conceição (at Río)	(O) Virgin de Regla	
Maitresse Erzulie; Erzilie; Erzilie Freda Dahomey			(M) (S) the Holy Virgin; especially the Holy Virgin of the Nativity; (P) Santa Barbara (?); (H) Mater Dolorosa
Saponam	(I) the Sacred Sacrament		

---

* Reprinted with permission from M. J. Herskovits, "African Gods and Catholic Saints in New World Religious Belief," *American Anthropologist*, XXXIX (1937), 635–643.

** In this table, the initials before the names of the saints indicate the sources from which the correspondences have been derived:

(H) Herskovits, field data (see also *Life in a Haitian Valley*, Ch. 14).
(I) Ignace.
(M) Price-Mars.
(S) Seabrook.

(W) Wirkus and Taney.
(N) Nina-Rodrigues.
(O) Ortiz.
(P) Parsons.
(R) Ramos.

African deities as found in:	Brazil	Cuba	Haiti
Osa-Osé (Oxóssi)	(I) (N) (R) St. George, at Bahía; (R) St. Sebastian, at Río	(O) St. Alberto; (occasionally) St. Hubert	
Ololu; Omolú	(R) St. Bento	(O) St. John the Baptist	
Agomme Tonnere			(M) St. John the Baptist
Ibeji (Brazil and Cuba); Marassa (Haiti)	(R) Sts. Cosmas and Damien		(H) Sts. Cosmas and Damien
Father of the Marassa			(H) St. Nicholas
Orumbila (Odumbila?)		(O) St. Francisco	
Loco	(R) St. Francisco		
Babayú Ayí		(O) St. Lazarus	
Iía	(R) The Most Sacred Sacrament		
Yaman (wife of Shango)	(R) Santa Barbara (wife of St. Jerome)		
Damballa			(W) (H) St. Patrick
Father of Damballa			(H) Moses
Pierre d'Ambala			(M) St. Peter
loa St. Pierre			(H) St. Peter
Agwe			(H) Expeditius
Roi d'Agouescau			(M) St. Louis (King of France)
Daguy Bologuay			(M) St. Joseph
la Sirène			(M) the Assumption (H) N. D. de Grâce
loa Christalline			(H) Ste. Philomena
Adamisil Wedo			(H) Ste. Anne
loa Kpanyol			(H) N. D. de Ab Gracia
Aizan			(H) Christ (?)
Simbi			(H) St. Andrew
Simbi en Deux Eaux			(H) St. Anthony the Hermit
Azaka Mede			(H) St. Andrew (?)
'Ti Jean Petro			(H) St. Anthony the Hermit (?)

African rainbow-serpent. The Blessed Virgin, frequently portrayed in regal garments, has been identified with Erzulie, a goddess of the water, who is in control of all riches. The River Jordan becomes identified with certain African rivers. In Trinidad the head of the Shouter Baptists corresponds to the African cult-head, and much of the baptism ritual is traceable to African initiatory rites (Herskovits, 1950:554).

Some traces of Christianity can be found in the Peyote Cult, also known as Peyote Religion, Peyote Way, and the Native American Church (Slotkin, 1952; 1955:202–230; 1955–1956:64–70; 1956; LaBarre, 1938). The Peyote Cult is perhaps the most widespread religion among the present-day North American Indians. It seems to have originated in Oklahoma among the Kiowa and Comanche Indians in the late nineteenth century. "Peyote," after which the religion is named, refers to a spineless cactus that grows in northern

Mexico and some southern areas of Texas. When eaten it produces an alkaloid-drug effect; it seems to have some minor curative properties, reduces fatigue, and may help concentration. The cactus is the focal point of Peyote religion: the fresh peyote or its dried tops are eaten, or sometimes a kind of tea is made and taken "sacramentally." Peyote is employed as a kind of supernatural medicine to help the ailing body in minor as well as more serious illness, in the latter case a special ritual being prescribed. Peyote is used to ward off harm and to give protection to warriors in battle. It is also supposed to give knowledge and is regarded as superior to Bible reading inasmuch as it produces an experience "with God rather than being merely knowledge about Him." In fact, the sacred plant is supposed to be a source of Revelation, for under ritual conditions it enables the communicant to have visions of God or of "some intermediary spirit like Jesus." Mere eating of the plant, however, is not sufficient for mystical experience: one must be disposed externally as well as internally — externally through bodily cleanliness, internally through humility, desire to obtain the effects of peyote, and recollection or concentration on the sacred plant. Peyote is also supposed to have telepathetic effects, enabling the communicant to understand totally unfamiliar dialects through a kind of "gift of tongues" (cf. Slotkin, 1955–1956:64–70).

A somewhat similar syncretistic belief occurs among certain southern Mexican Indians, where, however, a species of mushroom is used instead of the peyote cactus. The sacred mushroom has hallucinatory powers and, as the Mazateco Indians claim, Christ speaks to man through the mushroom. Jesus is supposed to have spat on the ground, thus miraculously creating the sacred plant, which has been perpetuated to our own times (E. Pike and F. Cowan, 1959: 145–150).

Speaking of syncretism among the Chols of Mexico, Beekman (1959:241–250) describes the custom of covering the crucifix with a black cloth during the days immediately before Easter and of removing it on Easter day, a practice intended to symbolize the Resurrection. However, this Catholic and quite sound custom has fused with ancient Chol beliefs and a traditional corn-planting ceremony. The Chols now believe that the "god" is covered so that he would think that it is dark and cloudy and thus be reminded to send sunshine in order to dry out the recently felled trees and underbrush so that the fields might be burned in preparation for planting. When, on Easter day, the cloth is removed, the "god" will see the blazing sun and send rain which the newly planted corn needs.

Guatemala (after Nida, 1961a:1–14) offers perhaps the best examples of syncretism, with its sorcerers (brujos), medicine men (curanderos), pagan sacrifices, local shrines (ermitas), and polytheism. The Guatemalan Christo-pagan believes in two gods, the Christian God and the traditional Dios Mundo, the owner of the world. The Blessed Virgin is equated with the moon deity, the symbol of benefits and fertility, while Christ is the offspring of the Virgin and God. In pre-Columbian times the "god of the dead" was the son of the moon and the sun; it was, therefore, no difficult matter to identify the Crucified Christ with the traditional "god of the dead," our Lady with the moon deity, and God with the sun, God often having been referred to by the Spanish missionaries as the "God of Heaven." Satan was easily equated with Dios Mundo, who, like Dios Mundo, is essentially wicked and referred to in Christian theology as the "Prince of the World." The Catholic custom of attaching Saints' names to persons, places, shrines, and churches also proved quite compatible with pre-Columbian paganism, for the dueños (wicked spirits) of the Guatemalan Indians had their assigned images, places, and shrines too, so that a mere transference of names was all that was necessary for a Christo-pagan blending. To the new Guatemalan Christian, prayer and supplication remained what it always had been — a form of bargaining with the supernatural being. The sixteenth-century Spanish emphasis on vows, penance, and gifts harmonized perfectly with the traditional idea of prayer. Christianity was so reinterpreted as to function the same way as the pre-Columbian religion — as a way of assuring or restoring temporal well-being. Since the Indians were particularly fond of ceremony, especially the use of fire and copal, they welcomed the Spanish religious usages which were similar to their own — abundant use of candles, gay processions and fiestas. Sorcery, common in Guatemala today, is really a blend of pre-Columbian black magic and the beliefs of early Spanish settlers and missionaries. To the modern Guatemalan Christo-pagan, the greatest sin consists in mistreating nature (as, for instance, by pulling up corn plants) and disturbing the social order (for example, through gossip or by "showing off" and acting "like a ladino"). The peccadillos ("small sins") in-

clude such "little things" as fornication, while drunkenness, polygamy, and prostitution are no sins at all; in fact, prostitutes have a
patroness, Santa María Magdalena. Sin is not evil in itself, for by
blindfolding statues one is in a position to sin with impunity, and,
at least one day a year, while Christ is in the tomb and "God is
dead," all sins are allowed.

3) **Some Possible Causes and Controls.** Religious hybridization
will be found throughout the missionworld, in both Catholic as well
as Protestant areas. It is mainly a form of undirected or misdirected
reinterpretation, selection, and ramification. The problem may, of
course, be more acute in some places than in others, and, at times,
as in Guatemala, Christo-paganism might rightly be regarded as one
of the most basic problems facing the missionary today.

The seriousness and complexity of the problem is sometimes
minimized by referring to it as "ignorance," as if a simple announce-
ment of the truth would be sufficient to put an end to undesirable
religious amalgamations. Christo-paganism is much more than ignorance; Christo-paganism is a way of life and a problem as complex
as culture itself. The advice sometimes given to newcomers by veteran
missionaries in areas where syncretism is a major problem can often
be reduced to one word — "patience" — as if patience were really a
solution. The fact is that syncretism will never vanish by itself.
Unless something more positive and meaningful than patience is
resorted to, Christo-paganism will not vanish but will become even
more deeply imbedded in the life-way of the succeeding generations.

The following suggestions are not intended as a full solution to
the problem. Much more research must be done by anthropologists,
missiologists, and the practical missionary before a fully satisfactory
answer can be given regarding the causes of syncretism and the most
effective way of counteracting and directing the forces responsible for
untenable blends of Christianity and paganism.

*Principle One: The first step toward a solution of the problem of
syncretism is an exact historical analysis.* As is generally the case in
culture change, many factors are involved in syncretism, and there
is usually a subtle interplay of factors (see next chapter): Each instance of religious hybridization must, therefore, be studied as an
historically unique development. Haitian Christo-paganism is not
Guatemalan Christo-paganism; Congolese syncretistic beliefs are not
Ghanaian syncretistic beliefs. To understand any given case of syncretism, one must study the history of both components, Christianity

as well as paganism, the original form of pagan beliefs and practices on the one hand and the type of Christianity actually preached by the missionaries and the actual policies which they followed on the other. Spanish Catholicism is not French, German, or American Catholicism, nor is Spanish Catholicism a kind of generalized "Roman Catholicism," as some non-Catholic missiologists like to call it when discussing Latin American missionary problems, syncretism in particular. Nor are Jesuit missionaries Franciscans. Similarly, Baptist missionaries are not Lutheran missionaries; Methodist and Anglican missionaries are not Jehovah Witnesses or Seven Day Adventists. Nor is the sixteenth-century political, social, and economic situation that of the twentieth century. Nor are the missionary goals of the sixteenth century and the corresponding policies and techniques those of the twentieth century; and missionaries are children of their times. In a word, the first step toward a proper understanding of a given instance of syncretism is to study the problem historically with an historian's sense of detail, proportion, and habit of interrelating events.

Principle Two: *Christo-paganism is, to a large extent, the result of undirected selection.* It has already been pointed out (pp. 189–190) that innovations, religious or otherwise, are subject to a screening process known as "the imperative of selection." There is a natural tendency for a society to select from the many possibilities those innovations which are most compatible with the rest of culture. Generally, too, only those innovations will be accepted which leave the configurational system unimpaired (see pp. 273–275). As we shall see in the following chapter, many factors are involved in the acceptance of novelties, one outweighing the other. The missionary task consists in not only communicating the Word but in directing the selection that unavoidably accompanies innovation. Untended selection leads to distortion of the content of the missionary message as well as to the distortion of the relative importance of the various aspects of that content. More time, effort, ingenuity, and strategy are required to "sell" an unsavory but essential aspect of Christianity than the attractive but nonessential.

Principle Three: *Christo-paganism is, to a large extent, the result of undirected reinterpretation.* No matter how clearly the missioner may present the catechism or interpret the Bible, his congregation will tend to reinterpret the message in accord with the local cultural inventory, structure, and configuration. The form of Christian beliefs and practices may indeed be accepted and remain unaltered, but the associated meanings, usages, and functions may be changed through reinterpretation, the reinterpretation ranging from insignificant and accidental nativization to wholesale and substantial distortion. For instance, the beautiful expression "Lamb of God" in reference to Christ leaves the Melanesian cold and unmoved, for sheep are not sacrificial animals in the native life-way; in fact, the ancestors would be terribly disappointed if such an inferior animal were offered to them. Extremely important, therefore, is the task of directing the reinterpretation that is taking place. Unfortunately, at the present stage of anthropological and missiological development relatively little can be said about concrete procedures. Of importance to remember, however, is that reinterpretation is a fact, and that reinterpretation must somehow be directed. Here, to a large measure, the missionary must use his own ingenuity.

In all intercultural communication, missionary or otherwise, there is need for less talking and more listening, less directing and more observing, less lecturing and more quizzing, less instructing and more discussing. Only in this way can the missioner hope to discover what is actually going on in the minds of his listeners and what direction his message is taking.

Once he knows the type of reinterpretation that is taking place, the missioner can more easily and more effectively proceed with the next step, that of positively confronting the traditional with the new. The difference between the traditional form, usage, meaning, and function must again and again be set up side by side with the intended substance of the missionary message. The bolder the confrontation, the more evident the differences; the more evident the difference, the less dangerous the reinterpretation.

In a word, directing reinterpretation is a very difficult task indeed, difficult but necessary. In dealing with individuals of one's own cultural environment, one need give relatively little attention to reinterpretation; however, when communicating with a "strange" people having an entirely different cultural background, one is obliged to make a major adjustment in one's communication habits.

Principle Four: One of the main reasons for syncretistic beliefs and practices is the fact that, as a rule, an innovation does not succeed in filling ALL the functions of the traditional counterpart. The more common and expected result of change is partial displacement rather than total (see pp. 199–200). The functions of polygyny, for example, would include: (1) prestige derived from the fact that a man has several wives while the majority of men must be satisfied with only one wife; (2) prestige derived from the fact that a man has a large potential offspring; (3) prestige and the satisfaction of fulfilling a social or religious obligation; (4) a means of supplying a strong labor force for the family, e.g., necessary for cattle raising; (5) a means of reducing the work load for the women; (6) a way of providing a defense for the family, e.g., in areas where feuding is common; (7) a way of providing social security for widows; (8) a way of providing companionship for women where there is a strict separation of sexes; (9) a sexual adjustment, e.g., if taboos require long abstinence; (10) a way of fostering intertribal or interfamilial friendships; (11) personal reasons, such as lust, incompatibility, revenge, etc. Since monogamy cannot fill many of these needs, polygamy will most likely not be displaced until ways are found to fill the needs in some other manner or until the functions themselves lose their value and disappear. Merely to preach against polygamy is futile. In much the same way, superstitions connected with the rearing of children will not disappear until the functions they serve are filled in some other way. In the Dominican Republic, for instance, so-called Catholic parents will insist on their male infants' wearing long hair like girls, the reason being to deceive the evil spirits who do not bother about harming girls. On the island of Kairiru off the coast of New Guinea I observed one day how a mother protected her newly-baptized infant from evil: in her netbag, besides her child and an abundance of native charms, there was also a new magical "safeguard" — a small perfume bottle of holy water. Evidently Baptism has not satisfactorily filled the function of providing security, and the sacramental was reinterpreted as just another charm. Such superstitions as wearing long hair or using holy water in a complex of charms will continue or tend to continue in the Dominican Republic and on Kairiru until the missionaries somehow succeed in filling the need for security which mothers crave for their frail infants the first months of the child's life. The proper approach to displacing existing syncretistic beliefs and practices, therefore, is first to analyze their functions and then to find ways of filling the corresponding needs with theologically tenable patterns.

Principle Five: Uneven social acceptance of Christian ways and values encourages syncretism. Generally speaking, innovations do not spread evenly through the society: some individuals or segments of society accept the innovation more quickly than others. This unevenness may be aggravated if the missionary, on principle, neglects a portion of the community or if the segment that is not interested in the Gospel constitutes the main current of communication in the given society (see pp. 297–301). The resultant ignorance of Christianity and the strong traditional non-Christian views tend to neutralize the power of the missionary's teaching. The constant and at times very close communication between the Christian and non-Christian elements of the society tends to develop Christo-pagan views. If the missionary concentrates exclusively on children, "the hope of the future," and neglects their parents he is blind to the influence of parents on children. Such neglected adults generally acquire a smattering of knowledge about Christianity, just enough to provide material for reinterpretation, and through their constant and close interpersonal relation with their children they tend to communicate their syncretism to the young, who, in turn, either accept the blurred Christo-pagan views of their parents whom they trust and admire, or, in their confusion, try to achieve psychological balance through their own half-Christian, half-pagan concoctions.

Principle Six: Christo-paganism is, to a large extent, the result of unsound catechetical approaches. We refer here to a point emphasized several times before (see pp. 41, 189–190). Nothing invites syncretism to develop more than letting the likes and dislikes of a new Christian community rather than sound Theology decide the content and emphasis of the missionary message. The kerygmatic approach of Fr. Joseph Hofinger, S.J., and his followers has won wide applause among religious educators and missionaries throughout the world and deserves the fullest support of the missionary-anthropologist. Its strong emphasis on Christ-centeredness, the Bible, Liturgy, and its concern about the relative importance of the various Christian beliefs and practices are both theologically as well as culturologically sound — excellent antidotes against syncretism.

3. NATIVISM

The occurrence of nativism is wordwide, and its effects on missionary work have often been devastating and irreparable. This specialized form of reformulation deserves a somewhat more thorough study.

The term "nativism" is used for a large variety of somewhat

similar responses, making the formulation of a definition difficult. The "Closed-door Policy" of China, the Cargo Cult of Melanesia, the atavistic movement in Siberia, the Ghost Dance of the American Indians, the Mau Mau terrorism of Kenya, and the gatherings of the Black Muslim hate-group throughout the United States are all forms of nativism. Under the term we must include also a variety of new religions and the so-called "prophetism" and "messianism" reported from all parts of the world. Nationalism itself is a type of nativism, whether it be of the mad Nazi variety or whether it be a form of rightful striving for national expression as was that of Ghandi in India, or as exists today in most of the developing nations throughout the world. The movements may range from humble acquiescence and patient prayerfulness to fierce political and socio-economic agitation, violence, and even savagery.

Nativism has always been a favorite topic for journalists, ethnographers, anthropologists, and social psychologists, and a considerable amount of material is available on the subject. Numerous attempts have been made to enucleate the essential elements common to all forms of nativism and to classify the varieties under different heads. Although much is known about specific forms of nativism, we still do not have a satisfactory definition, typology, and causal analysis. A great step forward was made by Ralph Linton in 1943 in his article "Nativistic Movements" (1943). A further advance came with A. Wallace's "Revitalization Movements" (1956).

Nativistic movements are usually, although not always, traceable to frustration and are generally a reaction against suppression by a dominant culture. Nativism, therefore, is usually an attempt to restore group integrity, self-respect, and solidarity. Such movements are either (1) basically anti-acculturative in nature and primarily aim to restore or perpetuate selected traditional ways and values or (2) they are basically pro-acculturative, aiming to hasten assimilation of selected desirable aspects of the foreign ways, at the same time, however, encouraging the preservation of certain traditional, highly appreciated values. Essential to the concept is the *conscious* striving of the people to restore or perpetuate traditional ways. The movement begins through the agitation of a forceful personality, often a kind of "prophet" or "messiah," who promises his followers the restoration of a Golden Age or the building of a Utopia. Since nativism is, as just mentioned, frequently a reaction to suppression and deprivation, and since this deprivation consists foremost in a deprivation of values, and values are embodied primarily in native religion, nativistic movements tend to be magico-religious in character. They are often anti-Christian (anti-Catholic as well as anti-Protestant), for, more often than not, it was Christianity that displaced the old religion; however, the target of nativistic reaction may be any missionizing religion, such as Hinduism, Buddhism, or Islam. The movements are usually anti-white, for the deprivation to which they are a reaction is generally traceable to colonization. The American Black Muslims are both anti-white and anti-Christian.

In order to illustrate the phenomenon and to show how real its dangers can be, a brief survey of nativism as it occurs in different parts of the world will be made (Koppers, 1959). In fact, the dangers are perhaps more real today than ever before. Almost everywhere rightful nationalism in developing countries tends to degenerate into excessive and even fanatical revivalism. Colonialism, although practically speaking dead and buried, is despised today more vehemently than ever before, and Christianity is not seldom regarded as the partner or product of colonialism.

1) **North America.** The earliest report of nativism in North America goes back to 1675 when a Pueblo medicine man declared himself to be a "prophet" and "deliverer" who would save the Indians from Spanish domination.

Another revivalistic movement occurred in the eighteenth century. After a humiliating defeat by the whites, the Delaware Indians made a serious effort to adjust themselves by becoming identified with Western ways; however, after repeated failures, frustration and nostalgia for the traditional beliefs and practices set in, with "prophets" preaching the return to the old ways and away from Christianity.

The best-known case of North American nativism is that of the so-called "Ghost Dance Movement," which consisted of eschatological and messianic elements and aimed to resurrect the slain Indians and to annihilate the whites. The "prophets" associated with the Movement promised a millennium of perfect happiness in which Europeans would have no part. The dance was a reaction to the rapidly deteriorating plight of the Indian, especially the loss of territory and the extinction of the buffalo. Its name, "Ghost Dance," refers to the belief that resurrected Indians would participate in the dance. The Ghost Dance Movement spread rapidly: it originated in 1869 among the Northern Paiute in Nevada, spreading to Northern California in 1870; in 1890 it moved eastward even beyond the Plains Indians. As the movement diffused it took on slightly different forms, at times becoming very aggressive in character, with shamans arousing the Indians to attack the white invaders as a sacred duty. The Movement finally disappeared as a result of disillusionment and of action on the part of the U. S. Government (Mooney, 1896: Barber, 1941:663–669; Barnett, 1957).

Among the more recent developments in the United States is the Black Muslim movement, a Negro hate-group that began in the 1930's when Elijah Poole, a former Georgian ploughboy, became Elijah Muhammed and received instructions from Allah to rescue the American Negro from the "slavery" of Christianity and Western culture. As Elijah Muhammed himself put it:

> The man Allah raised up from among the American so-called Negroes in the West will unite his people to Islam with the guidance of Allah with a book of Scripture for his people prepared and written by the fingers of Allah (Sokolsky, *Washington Post*, July 31, 1962).

Today the movement numbers some 70,000 Negroes, all calling themselves Muslims but not recognized as such by orthodox Islam. The members are concentrated in the metropolitan areas of the North and West; they hold their own religious services, insist on certain ethical practices such as the avoidance of illicit sexual acts and the observance of strict dietary habits, and teach Negro superiority over the white man. The chief characteristic of the movement is its resentment toward whites, who are but "devils" and therefore far inferior to the Negro. The hate-group is definitely opposed to any form of racial integration because it would mean integrating with the "devils." Christianity, being a "white" religion, is the religion of "devils" and therefore evil.

2) **Latin America.** There is evidence that even in pre-Columbian times the Indians of Mexico were acquainted with "prophets" and "messiahs." They believed in the coming of a "White Savior" from the East, a belief that makes some Americanists think that they have additional evidence of pre-Columbian Mexican contact with Christianity.

A typical messianic movement broke out in Mexico soon after the Spanish conquest of the country. The "messiahs" tried to restore the old traditions, promising complete destruction of the white overlords and the annihilation of the new religion which they brought to Mexico. A new era of abundance was to follow, and life would be spent in a true paradise in which no one would have to work and where suffering and pain would be unknown.

The earliest report of revivalism in South America is that of the Caucatal (Columbia) Indians which occurred in 1576. As in Mexico and Central America, the movement in Columbia was aimed at the Spanish conquerors and their religion. A great flood was prophesied that was to destroy all Europeans and Christianity, after which the liberated Indian territory would be transformed into a paradise.

For some four hundred years Indian tribes of Brazil and Paraguay moved back and forth across the country in quest of the "Promised Land" and the "Land of No Evil and of Immortality." The Tupinamba, for instance, in their attempt to escape the Portuguese oppression, wandered about Brazil from 1530 to 1612. Similar migrations originated in Paraguay among the descendants of the Christians once associated with the Jesuit Reductions.

3) Africa. Africa is well known for its many cases of revivalistic movement, with "prophets" and "messiahs" arising again and again from among their people as a reaction against Europeanization and Christianization. The many movements of the nineteenth and twentieth centuries were not restricted to any particular locality and ranged from acquiescence to outright terrorism. Well known are especially the Mau Mau terrorism of recent years, the many revivalistic movements of Central Africa especially since World War II, and the present-day veneration of Nkrumah as the "savior" of Ghana.

The nativistic outbreaks in Central Africa after World War II were, for the most part, mere rejuvenations of former secret societies. The famous Abako movement actually began in 1920 when a certain Simon Kimbangu, a Congolese medicine man and Protestant evangelist, declared himself to be a "prophet" and later a "messiah." Kimbangu, in imitation of Christ, chose twelve "apostles" and called his residence "Jerusalem." Europeans were regarded as "enemics of the people," while the non-co-operative Congolese were labeled as "the damned." In 1921 Kimbangu tried to take revenge on a Catholic mission which was believed to have reported his revivalistic activities to the government. Kimbangu was subsequently arrested, but somehow he managed to escape, giving credence to his claims of being an "omnipotent" messiah. That same year the "omnipotent" was again in trouble with the law and this time was condemned to death for sabotage. His sentence, however, was later commuted to life imprisonment, Kimbangu spending the rest of his "prophetic" life in an Elizabethville prison.

However, neither his imprisonment nor his death in 1951 put an end to the movement which he had begun. In fact, his followers became even more active. The movement spread rapidly and grew stronger than ever especially through mergers with other similar organizations. It is interesting to note that after Kimbangu's death many Congolese joined the Salvation Army, since, according to rumors, the "prophet" was supposed to have risen from the dead, transformed into a white man and a member of the Salvation Army.

Simon Kimbangu has remained a symbol around which nativistic movements could rally. "Sacred earth," for instance, has been brought to market places from Mkamba, the "New Jerusalem" of the "redeemer," by the cartload and sold to the Congolese believers, the money being used to promote the aims of the cult. Even after his death he was proposed to the United Nations as the most logical person to take over the leadership of independent Congo.

Kimbanguism made the Catholic Church its main target after World War II. Terrorism reached its peak shortly before Congo became independent: in the Leopoldville area the Abako was responsible for about 50 deaths, with no less than 250 wounded, of whom one fifth were Europeans.

Of particular interest is the development of African schismatic sects, almost invariably of Protestant rather than Catholic origin (Koppers, 1959:40; Andersson, 1958:262). There was, for example, the so-called "Ethiopism," named after the nativistic Ethiopian Church ("Ethiopian" meaning "African"), a movement that originated in the missions of the American Methodist Episcopal Church toward the end of the last century. The movement was put on a surer footing by Bishop Turner, an American Negro, who had been summoned to Rhodesia in 1898 to consolidate the new church. Bishop Turner made his war-cry the now-famous "Africa for the Africans." Also well known is the nativistic schism of the Hottentot Protestant Hendrik Wibooi, a second "Moses," who felt himself called to lead his people to the "Promised Land somewhere in the North."

4) **Asia.** As intimated above, revivalistic movements are not always and exclusively anti-Western and anti-Christian. In Africa, for instance, some of the uprisings have been directed against Islamic

rather than Western or Christian influence. Similarly in Asia, the target has been at times not Christian but Islamic, Hindu, Buddhistic, and Lamaistic proselytism. Thus, in 1904, the Russians and the Orthodox Church became the target of an outbreak among the Turko-Altaic people; nor should one imagine that Communism is immune to nativistic movements.

The best-known case of nativism in the Philippines is Aglipayanism, a schism started in 1902 by Aglipay, a politically-minded and highly nationalistic Filipino priest who declared himself to be the "Obispo maximo de Iglesia Catolica Filipina Independiente." As Schmidlin points out (1933:637), although much of Aglipay's success was due to the nationalistic atmosphere that prevailed immediately after the American annexation of the Islands, one must not forget such contributing factors as the confusion of the times, the great shortage of priests resulting from the deportation of Spanish missionaries, Protestant propaganda and financial support, and the "Catholic mask" put on by the Aglipayan schools and press, which misled not a few individuals who had little or no interest in Aglipay's nationalistic intentions as such.

The missions of India were not spared from revivalistic trends either (after Anathil, 1961:224–233). In the early nineteenth century, for example, there was the Brahmo Samaj movement, known for its zeal for the purification of Hinduism and for socio-economic betterment of the people of India. In 1875 Dayanand Saraswati inaugurated a reform movement very similar to the Brahmo Samaj, having as its battle cry "Back to the Vedas!" and as one of its aims the reduction of the influence of Christianity. There was also the famous Swami Vivekananda, who extolled Hinduism as the only satisfying form of religion and the Hindu Way as the only perfect life-way, condemning and despising everything Western in origin. Today, the most influential movements of an anti-Western and anti-Christian nature are such groups as the Hindu-Mahasabha.

It is interesting to note that some of the present-day religious nativism of India is not only deeply nationalistic but also syncretistic. Moreover, while claiming not to be anti-Christian or anti-any-religion it is nevertheless anti-missionary. Keeping in mind the influence of Western thought on the views of Indian nativistic leaders, one can easily understand the logic behind such an attitude. It is a compromise between a Western education on the one hand and a Hindu cultural background on the other. Mahatma Gandhi is a typical example of how Indian nativists can be deeply nationalistic without thereby being anti-Christian but positively against any type of evangelization. Mahatma Gandhi is known to have been a great admirer of Christ, having adopted many a Christian attitude and practice. He nevertheless maintained that it was "an error" to evangelize. Conversion, according to Mahatma Gandhi, was "an error which is the greatest hindrance for progress and peace" (Anathil, 1961:228). The practical conclusion he drew was: "We should not even secretly pray that anyone should be converted, but our inmost prayer should be that a Hindu should be a better Hindu and a Muslim a better Muslim and a Christian a better Christian" (Anathil, 1961:228). All religions are, therefore, equally good, and one should abide in the faith of one's forefathers. We should help others live their traditional religion more faithfully and by no means coax them to abandon it in favor of another creed.

5) **Oceania.** Most of the nativistic movements in the Pacific have taken place in Melanesia rather than in Micronesia, Polynesia, or Australia, although isolated instances have been reported from these areas as well. In Melanesia the revivalistic movements occur as much in Catholic missions as they do in Protestant. They are revivalistic, prophetic, and proacculturative and aim to accelerate rather than slow down the assimilation of certain (especially material) innovations. At the same time, however, they try to re-establish or preserve certain highly appreciated traditional values, such as those connected with ancestor worship.

The Melanesians have been in close contact with prosperous European communities, government officials, planters, and missionaries, but so far have not been allowed to participate in the material well-being of the whites; nor could they themselves develop a standard of living commensurate to that of the European. Melanesian nativism, therefore, seems to be an attempt on the one hand to explain the European material wealth and success and on the other hand the failure of the native population to achieve the same. In an attempt to equal the material attainments of the whites the Melanesian "prophets" sometimes resort to magical cults that are distinct imitations of such mystifying European ways as writing, marching, use of flags, erection of radio antennas, etc. The following examples illustrate the various reformulative responses as they occur among the Melanesians (after Belshaw, 1950:116–125).

The Tuka Cult. The Tuka Cult of Fiji of the late nineteenth century consisted essentially in the belief that the world would be turned upside down and that, as foretold by the "prophet," the Europeans would become servants of the indigenous population. The cult' also reduced the Christian God to a position below that of the local deities. Marching and drilling in the manner of European soldiers aimed to curb the expanding influence of the government.

The Vailala Madness. The so-called Vailala Madness of Papua lasted only about five years (1919–1923) and was characterized by a ritual involving trances, shaking fits, various Christian elements (e.g., confession), and some adaptations of government practices (e.g., military drills, flagpoles, and antennas through which the messages from the ancestors would be received).

The Tanna Cult. In 1940 on the island of Tanna a certain John Frum proclaimed himself to be the spirit of Karaperamun, a powerful ancestor. According to his prophecy, the whole world was to become a paradise. The volcanic cone on which the people looked day after day would become fertile, the faithful followers of the "prophet" would be forever young and healthy, and their every wish would be fulfilled. There was, however, an important condition that had to be fulfilled: all Europeans would have to be destroyed, "filthy" European money would have to be gotten rid of as soon as possible, and the people would have to return to their traditional ways of kava drinking, dancing, and polygamy, all practices forbidden them by the Presbyterian missionaries. The movement lasted about ten years.

The Naked Cult of Espiritu Santo. From 1944 to 1948 a "prophet" was proclaiming to the Espiritu Santo (New Hebrides) people that going naked and cohabiting in public was not a sin but something necessary. All private family huts were forbidden, and instead, two large communal houses were built, one for the men and one for the women. Whatever was of European origin (e.g., certain domestic animals) had to be destroyed. The people were to stop working for the Europeans; instead, they were to wait for the Americans who would bring them whatever they would desire. These American goods they would enjoy for ever and ever.

Cargo Cults. Very many of the Melanesian nativistic movements contain the element of "cargo" — ships and planes bringing highly desirable goods which are now enjoyed exclusively by the whites.

Thus in 1913 on the island of Siabai, Torres Straits, a "prophet" foretold the impending visit of the ancestors, who would arrive on a modern steamer loaded with precious cargo. The ancestors would destroy the Europeans and distribute the cargo among their faithful descendants.

About ten years later a similar rumor was heard on the island of Espiritu Santo. The "prophet" claimed that if the Europeans were to be killed, the ancestors would be so pleased that they would rise from the dead, but with white skins. The resurrected ancestors would not come emptyhanded, of that one could be absolutely certain. In preparation for their coming it would be necessary to build a large house where the ancestors could stay. It is interesting to note that during a feast connected with this movement the wife of the "prophet" and a European were killed, the only case on record of an actual murder of a white man in connection with Melanesian nativism.

There are many versions of the Cargo Cult, too many to enumerate, and new cases are constantly cropping up. The endless flow of goods, the sophisticated machinery and vehicles, especially jeeps, trucks, and airplanes, the baffling gadgetry, and the great variety of materials like steel, glass, and cement — upon all of which the native looks with an envious eye — are frequently considered as the products of Melanesian ancestors intended for their descendants, but while the cargo is en route the whites pirate the goods or somehow manage to change the addresses on the boxes so that instead of going to the "rightful" owners the cargo invariably is distributed among the Europeans. Sometimes the "prophets" call for the construction of large storehouses in preparation for the coming of the "happy days." Sometimes, too, as mentioned above, existing property must be destroyed. Of course, the expected Utopia never comes, nor do the ancestors appear — among other reasons because the whites somehow succeed in stealing the cargo or diverting the ships on which the ancestors sail.

In recent years various attempts have been made to explain the why of Cargo Cults, but we still do not have the full answer (Inglis, 1957:250–263; Stanner, 1958:1–25; Inglis, 1959:155–159; Worsley, 1957:18–31; Guiart, 1951:227–229; Keesing, 1941:235; Burridge, 1960; de Bruyn, 1951; Lawrence, 1954). One thing is certain: the movement, as far as the missionary is concerned, is dangerous, and the seeds of the Cargo Cult have already been planted throughout Melanesia, New Guinea in particular; it is a serious problem and challenge to both the government and the Missions.

Nativism, as we have just seen, is a worldwide phenomenon. It is one of the missionary's most serious problems. Unfortunately, little can be done to stem the tide of such movements until more research has been done. Although nativism may with one sweep wipe out all that missionaries have accomplished through decades or centuries of toil and untold expense and sacrifice, it is difficult indeed to understand why so few (if any) mission anthropologists, sociologists, and psychologists are investigating this most disheartening phenomenon; a diagnosis must precede the cure. It should be noted, however, that many of the suggestions made regarding syncretism (see pp. 244–248) and culture change in general are applicable to the present problem as well.

4. THE MISSIONARY AND CULTURAL DISORGANIZATION

It has been stressed again and again that in striving for a desired change the least disorganizing techniques and policies should be adopted. It has also been shown that the least disorganizing changes are those that are most in accord with the existing patterns, structure, and configuration. Our present question is: What can the individual missionary do about cultural disintegration once it has set in?

Is there really anything that the missionary can do, for instance, about the fact that more than half of the arable land of Latin America is owned by 1½ per cent of the population while the rest must be satisfied with eking out a living as serfs often for no more than 25 cents a day? What can the individual missionary do about the rapid growth of shanty towns throughout the world? One out of every five Latin Americans is a slum dweller, and shanty towns are growing twice as fast as the total population. Is there anything that the individual missionary can do about the poverty, crime, alcoholism, dope addiction, and prostitution so typical of slums? What can the missionary do as an individual about the rapid cultural and social disorganization resulting from Western contact, urbanization, industrialization, and migration? The missionary must seek an answer to these causes of social and cultural disorganization. He must find an answer to the problem, for, as someone has put it, "It is not easy to preach the love of God to a starving person."

What can the missionary do? The individual missionary can actually do little, if anything, as an individual; however, a knowledge of cultural dynamics will enable him to appreciate the complexity of the problem. Realizing the complexity of the problem the missioner will thereby be (1) more inclined to admit that the load is too heavy for the shoulders of any single individual and (2) more convinced of the strength of co-operative effort. There are many things an individual soldier cannot do that a whole army can; the same is true of restoring social and cultural order. *The problem of disintegration is far from hopeless if a sufficient number of strategically placed individuals tackle it.*

The missionary's task, then, is to get together a kind of army. (1) Where proper concern for the problem of social and cultural disintegration is lacking, the individual missionary can stir up interest among the mission staff and authorities in the dangerous disorganizing trend. (2) The problem is so immense that assistance should be sought wherever available, both as to means and personnel. Help from government, business, and private sources should be sought whenever possible and advisable. If the government and business world or a philanthropic foundation or an interfaith project are in a position to help restore cultural and social equilibrium, why not make use of such assistance? Outstanding work has been done through credit unions and through mission participation in community development programs. If the government or some other agency is in a better position to improve the health and housing conditions than the local bishop, why not welcome the assistance with open arms? If they can prepare the soil for missionary work better than the missionaries themselves, why not co-operate? In making these recommendations it is presumed that the Missions will not thereby become identified with an undesirable agency. (3) Appreciating the complexity of the problem of disorganization, the Missions should realize that they are desperately in need of new approaches, for the problems are very often new. The modern mission staff needs the assistance of specialists: professional educators, social workers, economists, technical advisors, sociologists, urbanization experts, and anthropologists. The training of missionary specialists as well as the recruiting of lay experts will go a long way toward solving the difficult problem of disorganization. (4) A bit of organizational ability and leadership would be extremely useful. Where cultural disintegration threatens, very few organizations could be more helpful than the Legion of Mary, the Young Christian Workers, the Confraternity of Christian Doctrine, the Cana Conference, the Christian Family Movement, and other well-known lay movements. One's organizational ability would also prove useful in setting up centers where migrants might receive information regarding housing, employment, purchasing, borrowing money, etc. Adult education programs and provisions for at least a minimal amount of recreation and medical care would be essential. Youth work and leadership training are particularly important in slum areas (Ewing, 1955; Burke, McCreanor, and O'Grady, 1960; Considine, 1960; Ewing, 1961:25–41; Brossard, 1961:42–46; Murphy, 1961:47–57; Reyburn, 1960:124–131).

In other words, the restoration of equilibrium lost through such causes as urbanization and migration is not a one-man job. However, one man, through his appreciation of the meaning of social and cultural disorganization and through his fighting spirit, may be ultimately responsible for the restoration of balance and a healthy climate for the bodily and spiritual development of a confused, suffering migrant or shanty town community.

There is still another type of disintegration, one that results from contact with civilization, a contact that has merely created a vacuum rather than a balanced blending of traditional and Western ways. Taking the New Guinea Sepik situation described above to illustrate the possible approach (see pp. 224–225), the applied anthropologist might make the following recommendations: (1) If the spirit houses serve a sociological function, the function must be preserved and upheld even if the spirits must go. It is just as important for the missionary to maintain the function as it is for him to put an end to the belief in spirits. While wiping out the belief in non-Christian deities the missioner must see to it that at the same time he does not wipe out but provides for the associated sense of security and solidarity. A substitute functioning as a source of security is indispensable, and Christianity if properly presented and understood is able to provide even greater security and be a deeper symbol of solidarity than the spirit houses themselves. (2) The encouragement and, if need be, the restoration of basic native interests, such as art, must be as much a concern of the missioner as the destruction of the superstition with which the art has been traditionally associated. (3) To make life worth living, prestige is indispensable. If through culture contact the traditional sources of prestige began to disappear (e.g., in the Sepik area the possession of shells and polygamy) new sources of prestige must be sought and encouraged. (4) Mass education should aim to prepare the people for the type of world in which they will actually have to live — a changing world indeed but one still basically traditional, otherwise false hopes are built up merely to be shattered and substituted by nativistic cults or Communistic dreams. In a word, the missionary's concern must be more than the non-Christian beliefs and practices: his responsibility is as wide as native life itself.

5. Social and Personality Conflicts Arising From Uneven Change

Uneven social change and cultural lag (see pp. 218–219) frequently give rise to serious social and personality conflicts, which must be treated sympathetically and reduced to a minimum (see pp. 184–188). Frequent relapses into traditional ways contrary to the teaching of the missionary are, no doubt, very disheartening; nevertheless, such relapses, whether pertaining to religious and moral matters or to socio-economic practices, must be sympathetically evaluated. The convert may be seriously torn between loyalty to new Christian principles on the one hand and loyalty to kin, tribe, or country on the other — torn by a conflict not easily appreciated by one who has never experienced the same. The convert may be torn by deeply ingrained, innocently acquired superstitious fears on the one hand and the assurance of science and the Gospel on the other. What appears foolish to the missionary and totally unreal may be terrifying and only too real to the weak and confused convert. Proper judgment of a penitent's moral guilt as well as effective counseling are impossible unless such conflicts are duly appreciated and sympathetically treated.

SELECTED READINGS

1. **Culture Processes**
   * 1) G. P. Murdock, "How Culture Changes," in *Man, Culture, and Society*, (Shapiro, ed.), pp. 247–260.
   * 2) A. L. Kroeber, *Anthropology*, pp. 344–444.
   * 3) M. J. Herskovits, *Man and His Works*, pp. 492–560.
   4) R. Linton, *The Tree of Culture*, pp. 41–48.

5) L. J. Luzbetak, "The Middle Wahgi Culture: A Study of First Contacts and Initial Selectivity," *Anthropos* (1958), 51–87.

2. Syncretism

1) E. A. Nida, "Christo-Paganism," *Practical Anthropology*, VIII (1961), 1–14.
* 2) M. J. Herskovits, "African Gods and Catholic Saints in New World Religious Belief," *American Anthropologist*, XXXIX (1937), 635–643.
3) A. Métraux, *Voodoo in Haiti*.
4) J. S. Slotkin, "The Peyote Way," *Tomorrow*, IV (1955–1956), 64–70, reprinted in *Reader in Comparative Religion* (Lessa and Vogt, eds.), pp. 482–486.
5) Wm. Madsen, *Christo-Paganism: A Study of Mexican Religious Syncretism*.
6) E. Pike and P. Cowan, "Mushroom Ritual versus Christianity," *Practical Anthropology*, VI (1959), 145–150.
7) J. Beekman, "Minimizing Religious Syncretism among the Chols," *Practical Anthropology*, VI (1959), 241–250.
* 8) W. L. Wonderly, "Pagan and Christian Concepts in a Mexican Indian Culture," *Practical Anthropology*, V (1958), 197–202.
* 9) W. LaBarre, "Twenty Years of Peyote Studies," *Current Anthropology*, I (1960), 45–60. (Good bibliography!)

3. Nativism

* 1) R. Linton, "Nativistic Movements," *American Anthropologist*, XLV (1943), pp. 230–240, reprinted in *Reader in Comparative Religion*, pp. 466–474.
* 2) A. Wallace, "Revitalization Movements," *American Anthropologist*, LVIII (1956), 264–281.
* 3) A. Lesser, "Cultural Significance of the Ghost Dance," in *Religion, Society and the Individual* (Yinger, ed.), pp. 490–496.
4) J. Mooney, "The Ghost-Dance Religion and the Sioux Outbreak of 1890," in *Bureau of American Ethnology, 14th Annual Report*, 1896, pp. 641–1110.
5) B. Barber, "Acculturation and Messianic Movements," *American Sociological Review*, VI (1941), 663–669, reprinted in *Reader in Comparative Religion* (Lessa and Vogt, eds.), pp. 474–477.
6) H. G. Barnett, *Indian Shakers: A Messianic Cult of the Pacific Northwest*.
7) E. Andersson, *Messianic Popular Movements in the Lower Congo*, Studia Ethnographia Upsaliensis, XIV.
8) L. Krader, "An Atavistic Movement in Western Siberia," *American Anthropologist*, LVIII (1956), 282–292.

9) G. M. Anathil, "Are Hindu renascent movements a help or an obstacle for spreading of Christianity in India," *Neue Zeitschrift für Missionswissenschaft*, XVII (1961), 224–233.
10) I. Leeson, *Bibliography of Cargo Cults and Other Nativistic Movements in the South Pacific*, South Pacific Commission Technical Papers, No. 30, July, 1952.
11) K. O. L. Burridge, *Mambu: A Melanesian Millennium*.
12) P. Worsley, *The Trumpet Shall Sound: A Study of "Cargo" Cults in Melanesia*.
13) M. Mead, *New Lives for Old*.
For additional material on syncretism and messianism in various parts of the world, see: S. L. Thrupp, ed., *Millennial Dreams in Action: Essays in Comparative Study*, Hague, 1962; W. E. Mühlmann, ed., *Chiliasmus und Nativismus*, Berlin, 1961; W. Koppers, "Prophetismus und Messianismus als völkerkundliches und universalgeschichtliches Problem," in *Saeculum*, X (1959), 38–47, a summary of G. Guariglia's full-length study, *Prophetismus und Heilserwartungs-Bewegungen als völkerkundliches und religionsgeschichtliches Problem*.
For more on the Melanesian Cargo Cult, consult General Bibliography: Inglis, 1957; Stanner, 1958; Inglis, 1959; Worsley, 1957; Burridge, 1960; Lawrence, 1954.

4. **Interpersonal Relations**
   * 1) H. Cleveland and G. Mangone, eds., *The Art of Overseasmanship*.
   * 2) J. Rosengrant, et al., *Assignment Overseas*, see especially contributions by G. Mangone, "Cultural Empathy," pp. 38–50, and E. Nida, "Many Cultures are Our Own Witness," pp. 51–65.
   For other material see Selected Readings, pp. 108–109, "Proper Adjustment to a New Cultural Milieu."

5. **Leadership and Co-operation**
   1) Muzafer Sherif, ed., *Intergroup Relations and Leadership: Approaches and Research in Industrial, Ethnic, Cultural and Political Areas*.
   * 2) J. Franklin Ewing, ed., *Local Leadership in Mission Lands*, Proceedings of the Fordham University Conference of Mission Specialists, January 23–24, 1954.
   3) Schmidlin, *Catholic Mission Theory*, pp. 300–332.

6. **Cultural and Social Disorganization**
   1) J. Franklin Ewing, ed., *Social Action in Mission Lands*, Proceedings of the Fordham University Conference of Mission Specialists, January 22–23, 1955. See especially V. Rev. Thomas S. Walsh, M.M., "World Problems of Urban Social Action," pp. 115–136.

   * 2) J. J. Considine, *The Missionary's Role in Socio-Economic Betterment*, pp. 166–197.

   * 3) C. J. Nuesse and T. J. Harte, *The Sociology of the Parish*.

   4) P. Abrecht, *The Churches and Rapid Social Change*.

   5) D. J. Hatton, ed., *Missiology in Africa Today: Thought-Provoking Essays by Modern Missionaries*.

   6) Burke, McCreanor, O'Grady, *Training Missionaries for Community Development: A Report on Experiences in Ghana*.

   7) W. L. Wonderly, "Urbanization: The Challenge of Latin America in Transition," *Practical Anthropology*, VII (1960), pp. 205–209.

   8) E. C. Bergel, *Urban Sociology*.

   9) UNESCO, *Urbanization of Asia and the Far East, 1957*.

   10) UNESCO, *Social Implication of Industrialization and Urbanization in Africa South of the Sahara, 1956*.

   11) J. Comhaire, *Urban Conditions in Africa*.

   12) E. Mayo, *The Social Problems of an Industrial Civilization*.

   13) R. Redfield, *From Primitive Life to Civilization*.

   * 14) G. Myrdal, *Rich Lands and Poor*.

   15) M. Mead, ed., *Cultural Patterns and Technical Change*.

   16) L. W. Shannon, *Underdeveloped Areas*.

   17) P. Ruopp, *Approaches to Community Development*.

   18) Schmidlin, *Catholic Mission Theory*, pp. 392–440.

REVIEW QUESTIONS

1. Why is emphasis placed on the individual rather than on society when speaking of culture change? After all, culture is the way of life of a society? (p. 210) What significance does this have as far as missionary techniques are concerned? (pp. 229–230)

2. What is the difference between origination and diffusion? (p. 210)

3. Culture change has three distinct aspects; describe briefly. (p. 210)

4. Can originations occur accidentally? (p. 211) Do they always, usually, or seldom have antecedents? (pp. 211–212)

5. Are simultaneous originations possible? Give reasons. (p. 212)

6. What is the difference between a basic and a secondary origination? (p. 213)

7. In what geographic situation would you expect the greatest cultural change? Why? (p. 213)

8. Describe the different types of diffusion. (pp. 213–214) What is meant by "acculturation" (p. 214)

9. Describe the chief secondary processes. (pp. 214–215, 217–220)

10. There are four kinds of reinterpretations. Describe. (pp. 215–217)

11. What is meant by "culture lag"? Give some examples. (pp. 218–219)

12. How does social conflict arise from culture change? (p. 219) What can be done about it? (p. 261)

13. What is meant by "the terminal aspect of culture change"? (pp. 220–223)
14. How do cultures disintegrate and disappear? (pp. 223–228)
15. What are some of the more important rules regarding rapport between the agent of culture change and innovators? (pp. 230–238) Indicate the cultural relativity involved.
16. Describe the necessity of witness and leadership. (pp. 238–239)
17. What is meant by "syncretism" and how might it be minimized? Give examples. (pp. 239–248)
18. What is meant by "nativism"? Give an example from America, Africa, Asia, and Oceania. What can be done to counteract excessive nativism? (pp. 248–258)
19. What can the missionary do about cultural disorganization? (pp. 258–261)

TOPICS FOR CLASSROOM DISCUSSION AND PAPERS

1. Debate: There is nothing that the missionary can do about nativism in Africa.
2. What is your explanation of the Cargo Cult in Melanesia? (See Selected Readings for bibliography.)
3. Study the various cases in E. H. Spicer, ed., *Human Problems in Technological Change*. Which of the cases seem to be least satisfactorily solved? Make your criticism as constructive as possible.
4. Describe some aspect of personality or social conflict arising from uneven culture change in Africa or the Pacific. What might be suggested to reduce the conflict? (For some preliminary ideas, see B. Hutchinson, "Some Social Consequences of Missionary Activity among South African Bantu," *Practical Anthropology*, VI [1959], 67–76.)
5. With focus on the concepts and principles discussed in the present chapter, point out the "anthropological wisdom" contained in one or more of the following papal encyclicals: *Maximum Illud* (Benedict XV), *Rerum Ecclesiae* (Pius XI), *Evangelii Praecones* (Pius XII), *Fidei Donum* (Pius XII), *Princeps Pastorum* (John XXIII), *Mater et Magistra* (John XXIII). (The first four encyclicals mentioned are available in one volume, *Catholic Missions: Four Great Encyclicals*, T. J. Burke, S.J., ed., Fordham University Press, New York, 1957.)
6. Read Dr. Thomas A. Dooley's *The Edge of Tomorrow* and show the "anthropological wisdom" in his policies and techniques. (For some preliminary ideas consult W. A. Smalley's editorial in *Practical Anthropology*, VI [1959], 90–95.)
7. Nida makes a number of generalizations about "The Roman Catholic, Communist, and Protestant Approach to Social Structure" in *Practical Anthropology*, Supplement (1960), 21–26. Which generalizations would you question?

8. Summarize the following articles and comment on the aspects pertinent to the present chapter: W. A. Smalley, "Religious Systems and Allegiance to Christ," Practical Anthropology, VII (1960), 223–226; B. Sundler, "Bantu Messiah and White Christ," Practical Anthropology, VII (1960), 170–176; Buckwalter, Grimes, Reyburn, "How Do I Adjust to Giving?" Practical Anthropology, Supplement (1960), 100–109.

9. Write a critical analysis of R. A. Felton, The Pulpit and the Plow, Friendship Press, New York, 1960. (N.B. "Critical" here means "anthropological.")

10. Write a book report on Oscar Lewis' Five Families: Mexican Case Studies in the Culture of Poverty, Basic Books, Inc., New York, 1959.

11. Carefully read the following articles by E. Nida. Point out in concise statements the anthropological principles he seems to hold. With which concepts do you agree or disagree? What about his assumptions and generalizations about "Roman Catholicism"? Do you agree with his applications? "The Indigenous Churches in Latin America," Practical Anthropology, VIII (1961), 99–105; "Communication of the Gospel to Latin Americans," Practical Anthropology, VIII (1961), 145–156; "Mariology in Latin America," Practical Anthropology, Supplement (1960), 7–15. Compare with W. J. Coleman, Latin American Catholicism — A Self-Evaluation, World Horizon Reports, Maryknoll, No. 23.

12. As a society grows more and more pluralistic through acculturation, a demand is made upon it to make various adjustments in its ways and values. What adjustments must be made in Latin America in its passage to pluralism? (For some preliminary thoughts on the subject, see Juan Luis Segundo, S.J., "The Passage to Pluralism in Latin America," C. I. F. Reports, I (1962), 313–322.)

13. In directing a desired change native leadership is vital. Write a paper on the role of native leadership, e.g.,

   1) What we can learn from the Communist approach to local leadership. (See, for instance, Douglas Hyde, "Training for Leadership: What Communists Are Doing," Christ to the World, VI [1961], 395–409; Douglas Hyde, "Training Catholics for Leadership," Christ to the World, VII [1962], 87–108; Douglas Hyde, "Lessons to be Drawn from the Communist Experience: A Stimulant for our Zeal," Christ to the World, V [1960], 371–389.)

   2) Selection and training of local leaders. (See J. Franklin Ewing, ed., Local Leadership in Mission Lands: Proceedings of the Fordham University Conference of Mission Specialists, Second Annual Meeting, January 23–24, 1954; E. A. Nida and Wm. L. Wonderly, "Selection, Preparation, and Function of Leaders in Indian Fields," Practical Anthropology, X [1963], 6–16).

   3) The use of local lay leaders. (See, for preliminary ideas, "Lay Apostolate by the Legion of Mary in Places Deprived of Priests,"

Christ to the World, II (1957), 94–101; Father Grenot, "Lay Missionary Apostolate in Dahomey," Christ to the World, I (1956), No. 4, 50–52; A. Schaefer, "How Laymen Successfully Struggled Against Superstition in New Guinea," Christ to the World, I (1956), No. 5, 42–44; Ewing, ed., Local Leadership in Mission Lands.)

14. Analyze the Christopher Leadership Handbook How to Be a Leader by Communicating Your Ideas (The Christophers, 16 E. 48th St., New York 17, N. Y.) and reword the main principles in culturological terms, keeping in mind especially what has been said in the present chapter about innovators.

15. Rapport is important in stimulating change. Develop this topic from the point of view of a missionary-anthropologist. (For some preliminary ideas see Rev. James Keller, M.M., "To Make the Lay and Missionary Apostolate More Efficient," Christ to the World, I [1956], No. 6, 88–96; Abbé Michonneau, "Visits to Families and Contact with Militants," Christ to the World, II [1957], 354–362.)

16. Discuss the disorganization that migrant laborers experience in Africa or some other mission area. What solutions would you as missionary-anthropologist suggest to such problems? (For preliminary ideas see F. Synnott, O.P., "The Apostolate to Migratory Workers," in Missiology in Africa Today, Hatton, ed., pp. 115–125; L. Coninx and A. Langenfeld, "To Bring Christ to Gold Mine Workers in Equatorial Africa," Christ to the World, III [1958], 309–321; Most Rev. Joseph Fady, W. F., D.D., "Migrant Labor in Nyasaland," Worldmission, VI [1955], 417–422.)

17. Write a paper on the "Missions and the Revolutionary World." (Read Louis and André Retif, The Mission of the Church in the World. London, Burns and Oates, 1962; also published as Vol. 102 of Twentieth Century Encyclopedia of Catholicism.)

18. Hispanism as found in the Catholicism of Spain and Latin America is a form of accomplished reinterpretation. Explain. (See Wm. J. Coleman, Latin-American Catholicism.)

19. Describe and try to analyze historically a case of syncretism in a mission country not referred to in the text (see pp. 239–244); consult, for instance,

1) G. E. Simpson, "The Shango Cult in Nigeria and in Trinidad," American Anthropologist, LXIV (1962), 1204–1219;

2) Yoshiro Ishida, "Mukyokai: Indigenous Movement in Japan," Practical Anthropology, X (1963), 21–26, 43;

3) W. E. Mühlmann, et al., Chiliasmus und Nativismus: Studien zur Psychologie, Soziologie und historischen Kasuistik der Umsturzbewegungen, Berlin, 1961;

4) Vittorio Lanternari, Movimenti Religiosi di Libertà e di Salvezza dei Popoli Oppressi, Milano, 1960;

5) S. L. Thrupp, ed., Millennial Dreams in Action: Essays in Comparative Study, Supplement No. 2, Comparative Studies in Society and History, Hague, 1962.

20. Similarity between traditional religious beliefs and practices and those preached by the missionary may lead to undesirable syncretism unless the missionary is aware of such similarities, analyzes them, and contrasts the Christian doctrine with the traditional. Show from actual cases that similarity in belief can sometimes lead to syncretism. What positive steps would you suggest? See, for instance, John G. Messenger, Jr., "The Christian Concept of Forgiveness and Anang Morality," *Practical Anthropology*, VI (1959), 97–103. See also the other recommended readings on syncretism, p. 262.

21. Cardinal Suenens appreciates the significance of what we have said about (1) revolution, (2) the lay apostolate, and (3) culture lag. Prove this statement from his *The Gospel to Every Creature* and *The Nun in the World*.

CHAPTER ELEVEN

CONDITIONS FAVORING CHANGE

WHEN speaking of conditions favoring change or resistance to change it is important to keep in mind that there is a *constant interplay* of factors — *many* factors — the one outweighing the other, and generally no single factor infallibly and by itself bringing about the change. The cumulative effect decides the actual direction in which the scale will tilt — toward the rise and acceptance of change or toward its rejection. When enumerating the various factors an attempt will be made to reduce the unavoidable overlapping to a minimum by dividing the variants involved into two categories: (1) the factors favoring change or persistence in general and (2) those favoring a special type of change, *i.e.*, origination or diffusion.

CONDITIONS FAVORING CHANGE IN GENERAL

Presence of Suitable Innovators

Unless there are suitable innovators there will be no innovation, whether the innovation is to occur from within the society (origination) or from without (diffusion). *Someone* must invent, discover, or borrow the novelty, and a sufficient number of *individuals* in the society must give their approval.

Some innovators are more suitable than others, and one society may have more such innovators than another. Certain individuals seem to possess a personality favoring change; they have a special aptitude for "being the first" or "among the first." They are disposed for experimentation and idiosyncrasies. Certain personality traits definitely incline individuals to go beyond the permissible range of variability, while other personality traits will rather encourage conservatism. Some personalities are unstable: at first they seem to reach out for the novelty but drop it as soon as they feel the least social pressure against its adoption. Certain personality traits are associated with leadership and therefore incline others to follow, whether the action of the leader be in accord with or contrary to conventional ways. Some individuals seem to possess special "talent" for being different; others never dare to be different. Before false eyelashes became part of the American culture, some bold (or eccentric) woman had to be the first to wear the almost frightening spiderlike attachments, while other women, sooner or later, had to do the same. In short, a society "blessed" with an abundance of suitable innovators at any given time will tend to change its ways more rapidly than a society that lacks individuals possessing the necessary aptitude, personality, experience, talent, and interest conducive to change. While one society may have a relatively large number of suitable innovators ("radicals," "Utopians"), another may have a relatively large number of conservatives ("ideologists") (Wallace, 1961:130–133). Other things being equal, the presence of suitable innovators favors change.

Attitude Favorable to Change

Some societies — we are no longer speaking of individuals — frown upon novelties more than others. A favorable attitude of the society toward change stimulates innovation. Such an attitude constitutes the proper climate for change. Today, China is much more favorably disposed toward political and technological innovations than a few generations ago. One can expect relatively little change in the Amish way of life despite its contact with the ways of the "worldly" non-Amish Americans, precisely because the Amish do not favor change. A society that expects and favors change will change more readily than one that considers change impossible, unthinkable, and evil.

At times expectation of change is limited to certain aspects of culture only. Some Mennonites do not expect any change at all in their ways. Catholics expect a dogmatic development or accidental clarification of their faith but no essential change, whether through loss or accretion; the Catholic doctrine must be contained in Scripture or in apostolic tradition. Americans expect change in technology but not in regard to such matters as separation of Church and State. Anticipation of change favors change.

Sometimes group pride militates against innovation, e.g., some decades ago many European villages had their own distinctive costumes, and an innovation in dress was looked upon as putting on airs and therefore frowned upon. In Guatemala one of the more serious sins that one can commit is to show off and act like a *ladino*. For a similar reason New Guinea schoolboys returning to their homes for vacation are sometimes forced to discard their cotton loincloths and dress "properly" — like "real" kanakas.

The intensity of the desire for change may vary greatly. Margaret Mead in her *New Lives for Old* (New York, 1956) describes how the people of Manus were not only favorably disposed toward change but had a craving for it, so that within a matter of twenty-five years the entire culture was transformed. A philosophy (see pp. 157–161) of a people generally fixes a value on change in general and on certain expected changes as "good," "natural," "necessary," "progressive," "highly desirable," etc. *The more "desirable" the change, the more conducive the attitude toward innovation.*

Freedom of Inquiry and Action

Some societies positively encourage improvisations and novelties, at least in regard to certain aspects of life. American women generally prefer hats and dresses that are unique in design, as original and as distinctive as their noses, but do not hesitate to adopt a Jacqueline Kennedy hairdo precisely because "everybody's doing it." While Protestants regard freedom of inquiry and difference of opinion regarding religious and moral matters as desirable, Catholics consider such freedom not permissible. What Protestants consider to be authoritarianism and suppression of individual liberty, the Catholics usually will regard as a necessary and welcome divinely instituted guidance, without which there would be but endless confusion and contradiction. Cultures differ as to the amount of independent action that is to be allowed, but no society allows complete freedom of inquiry and action. "Eccentric" and "crackpot" are labels used even in strictly scientific circles, where freedom of inquiry is supposed to be paramount; even in such circles one finds considerable reliance on the opinion of so-called "authorities" and the avoidance of ideas that are "too radical" (Barnett, 1953:68).

The greatest freedom of inquiry and action exists especially during periods of cultural and social disorganization, as is generally the case during wars and revolutions, economic depressions, migrations, rapid urbanization and industrialization (see pp. 223–228), a fact fully appreciated by Communists and other revolutionists. They usually make their attack during such times, for they realize that cultures are most vulnerable in situations such as these. Once the Communists have established themselves, they immediately deprive the society of its freedom of inquiry by setting up a police state and by taking away freedom of speech, lest through freedom of inquiry the newly-won Communistic "ideals" be lost or exchanged for other ideas. Communists fully appreciate the principle under discussion: *the greater the freedom of inquiry and action, the greater the chance for innovation.*

It should be noted that authoritarianism and bureaucracy do not make innovation impossible; rather, they generally tend to channelize the change.

The Force and Effectiveness of Social Control

An individual tends not only to conform to the socially approved ways but also to make other members of the society conform. One need but observe a group of small children at play to realize how strong this latter tendency actually is. The fight over a seat in a schoolbus is often the result of a violation of an accepted norm and of an attempt to force the "wrong-doer" to recognize and observe the norm. Children constantly keep reminding each other "That's not fair!" In order to force the rebellious playmate to conform, children frequently resort to ridicule, temporary ostracism, and an occasional black-eye. The growing child not only observes certain rules of etiquette at table but voices annoyance when others disregard such rules.

This tendency to make others conform grows and remains with the individual until death. Without even realizing it, the adult is a slave of numberless rules and at the same time is a tyrant that mercilessly imposes those very same rules on others. What could be more "nonsensical" than dressing formally on a hot summer day? A sport shirt, no necktie, and a pair of light trousers are far more comfortable than a long-sleeved, starched shirt, tight bow-tie, and a woolen tuxedo.

Over and above this personal urge to make others conform is the society's set of traditional pressures. "Social control" refers to a society's peculiar set of beliefs, precepts, and institutions, the function of which is to pressure individuals to conform to the accepted ways. Such controls can be divided into various categories: they may be *organized*, e.g., a police force, a code of laws, an educational system, or *unorganized*, e.g., ridicule, propaganda, threats;

they may be *negative*, e.g., penalties, or *positive*, e.g., rewards.

Social control will vary from society to society not only as to form but also as to severity, extent, and actual application of the pressures. *Other things being equal, the more forceful and effective the social controls, the more persistent the culture.* Aspects of culture to which little or no pressure is applied will tend to change more readily than those which the society insists upon and to which it attaches severe and sure sanctions.

Change as a Factor in Innovation

Change begets change, and therefore change itself can be regarded as a factor in innovation. A newly-invented or a newly borrowed element in a culture may render associated elements awkward and may call for additional changes (see pp. 217–220). In fact, a single innovation may inaugurate a whole series of novelties (see pp. 201, 218). The introduction of literacy, for instance, may demand a whole chain of adjustments in the culture, including such correlates as a school system, teachers, teacher-training centers and programs, textbooks, libraries, newspapers, printers, publishers, higher standards of living, higher employment requirements, higher wages, etc. Apartment houses encourage the limitation of children, the development of diminutive furniture, new patterns of cooking, washing clothes, and pet-keeping — to borrow Barnett's apt examples (1953:92).

Compatibility as a Factor in Culture Change

Among the most important variants in culture change and persistence is cultural compatibility, especially compatibility with the existing basic assumptions, attitudes, and goals — in a word, with the "soul" or "psychology" of the people (Chapter Seven). According to the imperative of selection, a society tends to select those novelties from among the many possibilities which are in harmony with its configurational system. The configuration, the "soul" or "psychology" of the people has, therefore, rightly been called the "watchdog" of cultures: nothing dare enter a culture that the "watchdog" does not allow. A novelty will be accepted by the society only if the configurational system remain unimpaired or if the innovation can somehow be fitted into the system through reinterpretation. For instance, since foreign words generally do not affect the value-system, they usually enter the language without too much difficulty. Pennsylvania Dutch is known for its large collection of amusing loanwords. On the other hand, sometimes loanwords are fully in conformity with the "mentality" of the times and are actually required. Thus, according to estimates of lexicographers, the English vocabulary may be as high as 90 percent Latin, thanks especially to the borrowings that entered the language as a result of the Norman Conquest, the spirit of the Renaissance, and the demands of modern times for a suitable scientific and technical nomenclature. Ideological incompatibility makes the introduction of birth control devices among Catholics a difficult "problem," as it does also among the Moslems, who regard children as a gift from Allah. Similarly, if the innovation means that the rich and politically powerful of today are going to be the poor and powerless of tomorrow, the resistance of the rich and politically powerful is understandably going to be vehement. One of the fears of the Southern whites is that if the Negro should ever become the white man's equal, the white man will not remain the Negro's equal for very long: political and economic power of the South would pass over to the Negro, and discrimination would be reversed. Much of the prejudice against the Church in the United States and much of the suspicion of well-meaning non-Catholics regarding the intentions of the Church in this country is based on a similar fear. Unfounded as such fears may be, the acceptance of new ideas that threaten the existing value-system will always be a very slow process indeed. Competitive civil service until recent times was unthinkable in Japan, because in the Japanese configurational system hereditary rank alone made sense whenever there was a question of priority (Honigmann, 1959:230). Similarly, the idea of democracy does not quite fit into the mentality of a people whose loyalties are limited almost entirely to family, village, or the locality. What is commonly called "Chinese corruption" in politics is usually kinship loyalty, and it would require considerable adjustment in the Chinese value-system before important changes in loyalty patterns could be introduced. Financial co-operation among non-kin is said to be unthinkable in Pakistan, since according to Pakistani values one should have sense enough not to trust anyone except one's own kin (Honigmann, 1959:230). The Japanese accepted many of the Chinese ways but refused such elements as foot-binding, since this custom was incompatible with the Japanese abhorrence of mutilation. The Japanese also rejected Chinese rhymed tonal poetry:

in Chinese, rhyme and tone were necessary to distinguish poetry from prose, but since Japanese is not tonal, this practice was incompatible and therefore unacceptable (Kroeber, 1948:416). The Navaho did not accept the Ghost dance (see pp. 250–251), for any association with disembodied spirits was unthinkable and abhorred (Hill, 1944:523–527).

The principle of selectivity is active even in societies in which Westernization seems to be progressing at an incredible rate. Despite the general impression one may get, Ghana, Japan, Indonesia, and other rapidly developing nations are "going Western" only in a limited way — as far as technology is concerned and only as much as is compatible with the traditional configurational system and as much as the cultural "watchdog" will allow.

Watchdogs are not equally-good watchdogs, and none are really thiefproof. Not seldom are incompatible elements linked to desirable novelties, so that if the novelty is accepted, the undesirable elements linked to it are also accepted, for you cannot have your cake and eat it too. At times the cultural "watchdog" dozes off and hidden incompatible elements enter into the way of life, the incompatibility coming to the open only after it is too late. Then, too, the configurations themselves can change so as to allow incompatible elements to enter.

Factionalism

Within a society one finds distinct interest-groups, each with its own grievances and ambitions. If an innovation seem to advance the interests of the group, the segment in question will tend toward accepting and developing the innovation; if the novelty appear detrimental to the interests of the particular segment of the society, that segment will resist the innovation. Among the important variables in culture change, therefore, is factionalism or group loyalties and group interests. One of the main obstacles to social and economic change in Latin America is factionalism, the wealthy class insisting on a status quo favorable to itself. Federal aid to education, racial justice, and other legislation brought before the U. S. Congress meet with opposition chiefly on account of factionalism. In a word, *the relative force of opposing factions constitutes an important factor in culture change and persistence.*

Although the individuals of a society tend to be stanch defenders of the traditional ideology, societies, especially the more complex ones, often include factions that are dissatisfied with their traditional worldview — the discontented "revolutionaries" or "Utopians" who would not only not oppose but would welcome the undermining of existing ways and values. "Utopians" may not be a factor as important as Karl Mannheim claims in his *Ideology and Utopia* (New York, 1936); nevertheless, the existence and relative importance of the two opposing groups ("Utopians" versus the "ideologists") must be reckoned among the variables affecting culture change (Wallace, 1961:130–133).

CONDITIONS FAVORING ORIGINATION[1]

Proper Motivations

1. Conscious Desire for Reward

The consciousness that a certain invention or discovery will bring the originator a material reward or honor may sometimes be responsible for special effort and ultimately for the innovation. However, reward, whatever its nature, is not to be regarded as the chief incentive in origination. Joseph Rossman in his study *The Psychology of the Inventor* (Washington, 1931, cited by Barnett, 1953:42) points out how, among the 710 inventors questioned, the most frequently mentioned motivations were "love of inventing," and "desire to improve" rather than any reward. In fact, not seldom must the originator labor in an unsympathetic atmosphere with little if any hope of recognition. Many years had elapsed before the Mendelian laws and the so-called "Pap smear" cancer test were recognized and applauded.

2. Subliminal Wants

The incentive just mentioned was a *conscious* desire for reward. As Barnett rightly emphasizes, in human behavior there is actually a "fluid interplay" of motives, only some of them being conscious. Responsible for origination may be, first of all, an *unconscious peripheral goal*, as in the case of an inventor who stumbles on the solution of a particular problem "accidentally." Actually, the inventor has been pondering over the problem for many days, months, and even years, and now the problem rests in his subconscious

---

[1] After Barnett, 1953:39–181 and Honigmann, 1959:200–205.

mind. Then, through some random activity, the solution "comes to him from nowhere." Examples offered by Barnett to illustrate a case of unconscious peripheral motivation include Edison's remarkable discovery that carbon could be used as an incandescent lamp filament and the back-folding airplane wings invented by an engineer while absent-mindedly doodling with two paper clips and a pencil. Another unconscious goal frequently responsible for origination is central rather than peripheral. The origination is a response to a deep-seated drive, a kind of self-realization or ego-need, e.g., a mania for power, a guilt complex, deep jealousy.

3. The Reconciliation of Conflicting Ideas

Not seldom the basic motive behind an origination is the desire to reconcile conflicting ideas. The originator is faced with a dilemma and seeks "a way out." The novel interpretations of the Bible employed by some Southern Christians to defend their segregationist views exemplify such attempts to reconcile conflicting ideas. The "equal but separate" opportunities for all citizens regardless of race or creed is a novel interpretation of the United States Constitution, resulting from an attempt to reconcile prejudice with democracy.

4. Obstacles and Handicaps

The attempt to overcome obstacles and handicaps frequently serves as a forceful motivation for origination, e.g., eyeglasses, hearing aids, false teeth, artificial limbs, toupees, and the various beauty aids.

5. Creativity

An artist frequently works for no other reason than "for art's sake." A scholar spends many hours in deep thought and study out of pure love for truth and knowledge. A musician plays his instrument because he loves music. Creativity, more than anything else, is responsible for new art techniques and styles and scientific concepts and theories.

6. Relief From Non-Physical Discomfort

Attempts to avoid boredom may lead to important inventions and discoveries. Many an important and useful invention has been made by a hobbyist.

7. Desire for Efficiency and Effectiveness

The desire for efficiency and effectiveness, as is often the case in business, medicine, and the armed forces, gives rise to numerous inventions and discoveries.

The Size and Complexity of the Cultural Inventory

Innovators, although frequently true geniuses, are never omniscient or omnipotent: they must operate at all times within a given framework — that of their cultural inventory. Inventions are built upon the past, and discoveries are, as a rule, gradual rather than radical. The history of music is a clear example of progressive development. Even if all Neanderthals had had the musical ability of a Beethoven they would scarcely have produced anything more complicated than a kindergarten ditty. A Beethoven symphony with its complicated orchestration was unthinkable at that particular period of human development. Similarly, even if every Pithecanthropos had had the mind of our present-day Nobel Prize winners, with the cultural inventory available at the time the Pithecanthropos geniuses could have scarcely developed anything more dangerous than a slingshot — never a hydrogen bomb. Originators are individuals who somehow manage to climb over the wall of traditional behavior; but to do so they must use a ladder obtained from *their* side of the wall. The richer the inventory the greater the possibility of new combinations.

Channeling of the Inventory

A rich cultural inventory divided among many individuals rather than funneled into the same individual is not necessarily conducive to origination. The wealth of ideas must be channeled into the same individual. Culture change is essentially a change of *ideas* (see pp. 196–197), and ideas can exist only in the mind of the individual. If there is to be a new combination of ideas it must occur in one and the same mind. In other words, the greater the opportunity for a concentration of ideas in one and the same mind, the greater the opportunity for origination; hence the importance of unrestricted sharing of knowledge through a school system, learned societies, public libraries, etc.

Collaboration of Effort

If several minds work on the same problem, there is a better chance of arriving at a solution than if a solitary individual must solve it. Collaboration accelerates inventions and discoveries especially because it is mutually stimulating and enlightening. Such collaboration is made possible in some cultures more than in others, e.g., through publications, research centers, symposia, professional associations.

Meeting of Divergent Ideas

A clash of ideas provokes critical discussion and frees the individual from grooved thinking. Some cultures provide greater opportunity for a conjunction of differences of ideas than others and therefore are disposed for origination, e.g., through contact with traders from different cultures, by a favorable attitude toward marriages with individuals having different cultural backgrounds, a pioneering, crusading, or warlike spirit, love of travel, etc.

Competition

Very few factors encourage origination to the extent that competition does. The competition may be between rival products, television programs, political parties, religious groups, warring nations, and numberless other opposing groups. One of the most basic reasons for the high standard of living in the United States and for its rapid industrial growth — and both facts presuppose numberless originations — is the highly competitive spirit of American business. Today Russia and the United States are in a fierce economic, social, and ideological struggle, a fact greatly responsible for the rapid changes taking place. During World War II, when competition was a matter of life and death, numberless inventions and discoveries were made at a rate unparalleled in history.

In a way, competition is an ideal atmosphere for origination, for it activates many other conditions favoring invention and discovery. Thus, for instance, competition presupposes not only a very favorable attitude toward change but also an intense desire for it. Then, too, almost a constant meeting and comparing of rival ideas takes place. In competition there is also a deliberate funneling of ideas into the same individuals. Then, too, in competition organized programs of experimentation are set up, a fact that favors origination.

Competition tends to create symbols, slogans, and rituals, which, in turn, tend to intensify the existing rivalry. Thus, some Protestant groups intensify their existing opposition to the Catholic Church through such negative symbols as the Inquisition, Index, and "popery." An analysis of these symbols would show the Protestant that the Inquisition he fears has long been dead and buried; the Index that arouses feelings of indignation in the freedom-loving Protestant heart in practice deprives one of little freedom; and the "popery" that makes some Protestants shudder at the very thought objectively happens to be the most important spiritual leadership in the world today. Nevertheless, the Inquisition, the Index, and the Papacy remain basic negative symbols for some Protestant groups, intensifying their opposition to the Church. Anything that intensifies competition, by that very fact, intensifies the tendency toward origination; such symbols, whether positive or merely negative, stimulate the members of an organization to work more effectively and efficiently toward the goals of the organization by abandoning out-of-date techniques and introducing entirely new approaches.

Competition is frequently intensified by rumors and lies. The Bible Belt hatred for things Catholic, as is only too well known, has given rise to many a myth about the Church, her priests, monasteries, and convents. It should be noted that at times competitors do not exactly *lie* but propose the ideals of their rivals as something inferior or bad. "Have a *real* cigarette! Have a Camel!" implies that the other brands are not real cigarettes. Or, as another advertiser of cigarettes puts it, "It's what's up front that counts!" as if other filter cigarettes did not use proper tobacco "up front." The competition between Catholic and Protestant missionaries has encouraged a considerable amount of new ideas about missionary methods. It took North American Protestants to wake up Latin American Catholics, as it took Communist agitation to arouse U. S. interest in the deplorable socio-economic conditions in Latin countries. Competition, at times, may become extremely intense and develop into a kind of fight to the finish, aiming to put the rival completely "out of business."

Some societies look more favorably upon competition than others. Some may curtail competition through socially approved discrimination and monopolies, as did the Incas by reserving science for the nobility. In the United States much talent (and therefore also much capability for invention and discovery) is being wasted through discrimination against the Negro in schools and industry. Some cultures curtail competition by associating it with the "danger of losing face" or by means of a "gentleman's agreement" not to compete. Some societies may discourage competition within a limited segment of the social group, considering competition within the extended family, lineage, or clan as "wrong," very much the same way as we are inclined to consider it "wrong" to compete with our own brothers and sisters.

Competition, no doubt, is an important factor in origination. However, it should be noted, since competition is a form of stress, it tends to stimulate invention and discovery in the direction of the stress alone, and therefore the originations resulting from competition tend to be limited in scope.

Deprivation

Although the dictum "Necessity is the mother of invention" is generally overemphasized, the fact remains that whenever an individual is deprived of a desirable or necessary object he will tend to improvise and seek a substitute. Nativism (see pp. 248–258) is to a large extent a response to deprivation. The Hitler era was an era of *Ersatz* products ranging from food to fuel and building materials. The Nazis were able to win the support of the German people by constantly emphasizing the deprivations they were suffering on account of the injustice of the Versailles Treaty and the existing world situation of "have" and "have-not" nations. Communism finds much of its strength in the undeniable misery and injustice that prevails throughout the world today and in the past deprivations associated with colonialism.

Deprivation encourages origination. However, it should be noted, since, as in the case of competition, deprivation implies stress, the resulting innovations tend to be limited in scope and to be in the direction of the stress concerned.

Leisure and Peace of Mind

Social and political stability, leisure, and peace of mind are favorable conditions for origination. When there is sufficient leisure and quiet, when the mind is free and relaxed, and when, consequently, the interests are varied, the innovations tend to become likewise more diversified than in a crisis or under stress. A peaceful mind is open to many directions of change rather than only in the direction of the stress.

Barnett speaks also of a "simulated leisure" as being conducive to origination. By the term he means encouragement and support

which contribute to leisure, quiet, and peace of mind, e.g., sub-
sidies, collaboration in research, recognition.

CONDITIONS FAVORING DIFFUSION[2]

Anthropologists have succeeded in isolating a rather large number of regularities favoring or obstructing diffusion; they have also
pointed out that some conditions can actually work both ways, in
favor as well as against diffusion. In order to borrow something
(and that is the basic notion of diffusion) there must be: (1) a
lender and a borrower, (2) contact of some kind between the two,
(3) some reason or motive for borrowing, and (4) something that
is "borrowable." The variables affecting diffusion will, therefore,
fall under one of the following heads, depending on whether they
refer to (1) the type of community in contact, (2) the type of
contact, (3) the type of motive for borrowing, and (4) the type
of element borrowed.

Community Factors

Borrowing cannot take place unless there is someone to borrow
and someone to lend, unless there is a donor and a recipient culture.
The societies in question may be large or they may be small; they
may be homogeneous or they may be heterogeneous; they may be
aggressive, indifferent, or passive; they may form a dominant or a
minority group; their ways of life may be simple or complex. Such
variants may have an important bearing on cultural borrowing and
therefore will now be examined.

1. THE SIZE OF THE COMMUNITY

There is too much evidence against the supposition that a larger
group necessarily becomes the donor while the smaller group necessarily becomes the recipient. The fact is that the size of the communities in a potential borrowing-lending position is too easily
outweighed by other factors. The pygmies of the Ituri forest are
a classic example of how a numerically weaker society can remain
uninfluenced by a numerically stronger neighbor. On the other
hand, there are many examples of a numerically smaller group

[2] After Honigmann, 1959: 217–232; Herskovits, 1950: 523–541; Keesing,
1958:384–417.

influencing a larger community. The white planters, government and business people, and missionaries throughout Africa and the Pacific are outnumbered by far by the indigenous population; nevertheless, they, the smaller group, generally influence the larger group rather than vice versa. The active Communists are a relatively small minority, but in 35 years have deeply influenced the life of a third of the world.

The fact is that the size of a community can work either way, for or against borrowing. In a smaller community the members generally interact with one another much more closely than in a large community, and close interaction favors change. On the other hand, a small community is usually more homogeneous than a large community, and homogeneity, allowing little latitude of behavior, favors persistence.

2. The Particular Segment Involved

In diffusion, the actual borrowers and lenders may be either the entire community or only a portion of it. Although at first sight it may seem that contact with an entire society would be more favorable to diffusion than contact with only a segment of the community, there are a number of counterbalancing factors that come into play.

First of all, the segment involved may be composed of very active and aggressive individuals. The World Health Organization, the Peace Corps, and missionaries are such active and aggressive agents of diffusion. What matters is not so much how many individuals are working but how much is being done. The Communists are usually a relatively small segment of the population in any country, but they make up for their small numbers by organization, dedication, and action. The small Communist segment consists mainly of teen-agers and young adults between the ages of 15 and 25. This age group is precisely the one that is most idealistic, just beginning adult life with its responsibilities, and overflowing with energy and hope for a better world, ready to make any sacrifice demanded of them. As an outstanding authority on Communism expressed it: "More Communists have died in our generation for Communism than Christians have died for Christianity." Group enthusiasm, a sense of leadership and mission, and belief in the cause give power and momentum to the aggressiveness of Communism. "Every Communist a leader! Every factory a fortress!"

The size of the active segment is not the all-important factor. Christ compared His Kingdom on earth to the "least" of all seeds:

> The kingdom of heaven is like to a grain of mustard seed, which a man took and sowed in his field. Which is the least indeed of all seeds; but when it is grown up, it is greater than all herbs, and becometh a tree, so that the birds of the air come, and dwell in the branches thereof (Matt. 13:31-32).

Not the size but the hidden potential counts — the zeal, dedication, sense of mission, leadership, and willingness to sacrifice. The early Church certainly had all these characteristics, so much so that even the enemies of Christianity had to admit that the blood of martyrs was but the seed of Christians.

The second important consideration refers to the borrowing segment and its relative position in the social structure. *Some segments may constitute the main centers of power in the society and be the chief currents of communication.* Once an influential segment has accepted a change, the borrowed novelty will be readily accepted by the other members of society as well. Sometimes, in fact, the segment involves only a very few individuals, whose social position, however, enables them to determine the policy of the entire group. History of Christianization in Europe and of the Reformation provides not a few examples of the principle *Qualis rex talis grex.*

3. Dominant Versus Minority Position in Diffusion

A dominant group tends to accept less from the minority than vice versa, a fact that may very well be due not so much to the status itself as to the motivation for borrowing or not borrowing (see pp. 287-292). The dominant group's avoidance of the ways peculiar to the minority may be a matter of self-respect, while the minority group's acceptance of the ways peculiar to the majority may be a matter of prestige. At times and in certain aspects of culture the dominant group tries to force the minority to adopt the "superior" ways; at times the minority group may actually be assimilated by the dominant group. On the other hand, a proud majority may insist on "pure blood" and on a "live-and-let-live" policy, while the no-less-proud minority may not only resent the superior position of the opposition but actually despise its ways and positively resist any attempt to introduce elements from the dominant culture. Just what the result of a dominant-minority relationship will be in regard to diffusion will depend not so much on the relationship as on the cumulative effect of the various factors that may come into play in such a situation.

4. MIGRATION AND DIFFUSION

A group or a segment of a group away from its home territory is more likely to borrow foreign culture elements than a group or segment at home (Luzbetak, 1958b:52–53). More Irish have given up their faith in England and America than in Ireland. On the other hand, Japanese migrant groups in Brazil enter the Church more readily than their brethren in the homeland. Migrant laborers leaving their tribal areas and settling down in the slum districts of African cities quickly give up their moral standards and other patterns of behavior, which they have rigorously observed while at home.

Contact Factors in Diffusion

No borrowing is possible unless the potential borrower and lender somehow come in contact with one another. This contact may be close and immediate (as in acculturation) or it may be remote and indirect (as often happens when individual culture elements diffuse). The contact may be of long duration or it may be short-lived. The contact may be friendly or hostile. What bearing do such variables have on culture borrowing?

1. THE INTENSITY OF CONTACT

Other things being equal, the more intense the contact, the more suitable it is for diffusing cultural elements. On the one extreme is total isolation (the society is geographically separated from other cultures and has no communication with the outside world); on the other extreme is the situation of two or more very closely interacting communities following different ways of life but economically interdependent and on very friendly terms.

Total isolation is usually more hypothetical than real, for even the most remote tribes are generally in contact with other cultures at least to some degree. Thus, even the most remote tribes of the Pacific may be in contact with Hong Kong industries, indirectly and remotely, but in contact nonetheless. The contact may consist of a single European, a gold-prospector perhaps, or a scientist collecting geological or biological specimens, or a solitary missionary. The European pays his native employees with bits of colorful cloth or some cheap jewelry obtained from coastal stores supplied by

Chinese merchants or by an occasional Japanese ship that stops en route at a Chinese port. In such indirect contact situations, usually artifacts rather than beliefs or values will enter the culture, although there is sufficient evidence that beliefs and values can also "migrate" over large expanses of land and sea.

Although geographic isolation does not necessarily exclude diffusion, it greatly limits the opportunities for borrowing. In fact, as indicated above (see p. 213), isolated cultures tend to stagnate, while the richest cultures have always been those fortunately situated on the crossroads of culture contact. The cultural persistence associated with such geographic isolation is known as *tarriance*.

Geographic isolation, however, is not the only form of isolation that makes diffusion difficult. "Blocked communication" (Honigmann, 1959:230), such as illiteracy and linguistic barriers, may be obstacles to diffusion as serious as geographic isolation itself. On the other hand, despite geographic difficulties, literacy and the knowledge of the language of a distant culture may open vast possibilities for borrowing through such media as books, newspapers, radio, and movies.

2. Friendly Versus Hostile Contact

Inasmuch as friendship encourages close interaction, friendship is conducive to diffusion. A television commercial, for instance, emphasizes the fact that the viewer should immediately go to his "friendly" Ford dealer, and a basic principle of salesmanship is friendliness and the admission that "the customer is always right." Hostility encourages prejudice and avoidance, both of which militate against close interaction, while friendship encourages close interpersonal relationship, admiration, and even intermarriage. Intermarriage, in particular, links one community to another; and, especially if the woman belongs to a dominant group, intermarriage may become an important channel of diffusion.

Hostility, however, does not make contact ineffective and diffusion impossible. The borrowing may take place because the novelty is associated with prestige, utility, or some other value. The Japanese have perhaps never imitated the Americans more than during World War II when the superior engineering techniques of the Americans were considered desirable, regardless of the dislike of the Japanese for Americans.

3. The Duration of the Contact

Culture contact may be of long or of short duration. Normally, one would expect a perfect correspondence between the duration of contact and its effects. Nevertheless, on account of the interplay of factors, the time element often recedes in importance. Margaret Mead in her *New Lives for Old* has shown how in a matter of a few decades the Manus people changed their way of life completely while the neighboring peoples have undergone no such radical or rapid change.

Motivational Factors and Diffusion

1. Reasons for Borrowing, Felt-Needs

An element will most easily diffuse if it be rewarding or if it at least promise to solve a problem or ease a tension. One of the basic techniques used in diffusing Communism is the emphasis placed on the rewarding nature of the system.

However, only *felt*-needs move individuals to borrow new ways, and a need that is felt is necessarily relevant to the culture. What some societies consider to be a need, others do not; what some societies regard as rewarding, others do not; what some societies consider useful, desirable, or necessary, others do not. What may be a "matter of life and death" in one case may be "not worth bothering about" in another.

At times the reward is self-evident and the felt-need only too obvious, in which case the innovation tends to be accepted without questioning. The white man's weapons (the rifle) and his steel implements have everywhere been looked upon by primitive tribes as rewarding, and the acceptance of such cultural elements was almost spontaneous. Communism has a special attraction because it promises what a suffering population hungers for most — bread and justice. Missionary success in Africa was to no small measure due to the timely arrival of missionaries — timely because the African *felt* the inadequacy of his own way of life. The history of the Christianization of Europe shows how the social climate was providentially prepared for the acceptance of Christianity. On the other hand, rewards that are not felt are no rewards at all. One does not, as a rule, buy something one does not feel he needs, especially if the object involves a great expense or risk, or calls for a great sacrifice. Ancestor worship, witchcraft, syncretistic beliefs and practices, so common throughout the missionworld today, will not be given up until the society in question feels the inadequacy of ancestor worship, witchcraft, and syncretism on the one hand and the adequacy of Christian ways on the other.

One of the rewards most frequently associated with diffusion is prestige. A foreign element is quickly integrated in the local way of life if the acceptance bring prestige to the borrowers. The steel axe readily diffused among the Yir Yoront aborigines of Australia, not only because of its superior cutting qualities but because the new steel implement was reinterpreted as a kind of Stone Age Cadillac. Cigars, expensive cars, and fancy clothes are valued highly by the American Negro subculture largely on account of the prestige value of cigars, large automobiles, and expensive clothes. The German immigrant of the low artisan class in Brazil took to horseback riding because in his country of origin the practice, as Honigmann points out (1959:219), was the privilege of the nobles, while in his country of adoption the practice was a status symbol among the upper-class gauchos. American advertisers, as is well known, make a special effort to attach prestige to their products by associating the particular product with "people of distinction." Thus, the advertisements for whiskey frequently show the interior of an elegant colonial home, with people dressed in expensive formal gowns and tuxedos, standing around a liquor table and being served by a dignified butler holding a bottle of the particular potion "of distinction." Advertisements of automobiles show them parked in front of a fancy hotel or night club, with a young wealthy couple (again dressed in formal gown, mink stole, and wearing a corsage, or, as the case may be, in tuxedo) ready to be driven home by a chauffeur after a most pleasant but expensive evening. American products are advertised as products used by popular heroes, such as movie stars and baseball players, in the hope that the prestige of such individuals would rub off on the product advertised. A brand of cigarettes is advertised as the choice of smokers who are not just ordinary American citizens, but "he-men," one and all, doing unusual and dangerous jobs. Through some magic the sponsor of an action is supposed to pass his prestige on to whatever he touches, approves, or is associated with. In political campaigns the President generally supports lesser candidates of his party, appearing with them at special rallies or arranging to be photographed shaking hands with them. The prestige and popularity of the President is somehow supposed to rub off on the hopeful senator or governor. Father Ricci found this very same approach useful in China; his sponsor was the Emperor himself, whose approval and backing were greatly responsible for the prestige the missionary enjoyed among all who knew or heard of him.

2. INTEREST

It is not sufficient that the need for borrowing be felt; an *interest* in the felt-need is required also. The Chukchee, as Ruth Benedict (1956:185–186) observed, have never adopted the Eskimo igloo, while the Eskimo never adopted the Chukchee reindeer breeding, not because they did not feel the need for igloos or reindeer, as the case may be, but because interest in igloos and reindeer was lacking.

Felt-needs might be best looked upon as a *theoretical* appreciation, while interest implies a *practical* appreciation of the particular need that might be filled by means of diffusion. Theoretically, two birds are worth twice as much as one, but we still claim that "a bird in the hand is worth two in the bush." Similarly, although the New Guinea highlander found coffee growing as a cash crop theoretically rewarding, he showed little interest in the idea some years ago when a serious attempt was made to encourage coffee growing among the local people. The promised reward (cash) was indeed theoretically appreciated, but it was too distant, requiring four years of waiting before the coffee would be "practically" rewarding. For much the same reason health programs in underdeveloped areas of the world do not readily take root when *preventive* medicine is emphasized. People readily accept aspirin, quinine, sulfa drugs, and penicillin because the reward is immediate and "practical"; they are, however, slow in accepting ideas about swamp draining, improving the native diet, and sanitation, for the rewards of preventive medicine appear too distant to be real, and therefore are too "theoretical." Even some sophisticated individuals of highly civilized countries are relatively slow in accepting preventives against influenza and polio, not because they do not theoretically acknowledge the value of these innovations but because they lack the necessary practical interest. The lack of interest in civil defense is likewise due, to no small measure, to the fact that the rewards of the program, although theoretically appreciated, are too distant to get excited about. The spiritual activities of the missionary are difficult because the rewards offered are necessarily distant and even "not of this world" (John 18:36).

A further reason for the lack of practical interest is the fact that at times the advantages associated with a novelty are neutralized or even outweighed by the disadvantages. A change in English orthography would indeed be rewarding, but the changeover appears too difficult to those who would have to make the change. Adults would once again have to go to school; entire libraries would have to be reprinted, or, as an alternative, anyone wishing to read a book published prior to the spelling reform would have to know as much about the old orthography as if no orthographic changes had taken place. Of course, the changes in spelling would not have to be so radical as these objections suppose; but, then, the benefits from the minor changes would also be minor and therefore not worthwhile — at least such is the reasoning of some opponents of English spelling reform.

A theoretical reward that is regarded as *impossible* will likewise fail to arouse the necessary practical interest. Theoretical appreciation of a novelty, and even an eagerness to adopt it, will not move the individual to action if he feel helpless and if the goal seem unreal. As much as we may dislike the American custom of expensive funerals, there is little we, as individuals, can do about the custom. If someone of the family should die, we would most likely have a relatively expensive funeral for him. Similarly, despite our personal appreciation of the metric system, in our daily lives we still continue to measure distances in miles, length in yards, feet, and inches, weights in pounds and ounces, and capacity in gallons, quarts, and pints. A country may be very eager to improve its social and economic state, but since it lacks the necessary means and personnel, the situation remains unaltered. A feeling of helplessness is indeed greatly responsible for the lack of practical interest.

Finally, it should be noted, there are also *negative rewards* that serve as incentives. Briefly, they consist in relief from pressure of an aggressive innovator or an overenthusiastic agent of culture change. It is very much like buying a cheap brush or book from a persistent salesman, merely to get rid of him. Freedom from pressure is freedom from vexation. For the same reason it happens quite frequently in democratic countries that a small pressure-group succeeds in imposing its views and preferences on the entire nation. Sometimes a nation may submit to a foreign government and unfair military rule, accept heavy burdens, and obey unjust and tyrannical laws merely to get momentary relief from the pressure exerted. In fact, tyranny itself may sometimes be regarded as the lesser evil.

3. EMOTIONS

Emotions, no less than rewards and practical interest, can move individuals to borrow foreign traits. Among the chief emotions involved are bias and prejudice, fear, and discontent.[1]

Prejudice, often associated with hate and fear, renders individuals blind to potential rewards that might have otherwise served as incentives for borrowing. Sometimes the prejudice is so strong that even the most rewarding elements in a foreign culture are despised and avoided. During World Wars I and II there was little chance of Americans borrowing German patterns, that is, other than those that appeared militarily advantageous. During both World Wars the American mind was too prone to regard "German" and "bad" as synonymous. A joke that fell flat was sometimes referred to as a "German" joke, and even innocent sauerkraut was called "liberty cabbage."

On the other hand, bias inclines one to exaggerate the rewarding nature of a novelty and therefore it also inclines one to accept the novelty. Usually bias is limited in scope, and the resulting diffusion will likewise tend to be limited. American machinery is respected and accepted almost everywhere as "superior," but other aspects of American culture may not be so acceptable. Americans consider French cooking as "superior" and do not hesitate to borrow French recipes and even to label purely American discoveries with such unauthentic titles as "French Dressing" and "Franco-American Spaghetti." Immigrants to the United States seem to be predisposed toward anglicisms but are very intolerant in regard to ideology. It was no problem at all for the immigrant from Slovakia to introduce certain English loanwords into their language, e.g.,

lakopa = "jail" (English "lock up" + Slovak feminine singular nominative suffix –a)
šarap = "keep quiet" (English "shut up!")
barbiršapa = "barber shop" (English "barber shop" + Slovak feminine singular nominative suffix –a)
dipo = "railroad station" (English "depot")

[1] Discontent has been sufficiently treated under Factionalism, pp. 275–276.

There are numberless such parallels in Italian, German, and other languages spoken in the United States by European immigrants.

Prejudice has always been a serious obstacle to diffusion. It was opposition to the Catholic Church that kept England from accepting the Gregorian calendar until 1752 and Russia until 1918 (Kroeber, 1948:410). And there is a story told of how the American practice of gum-chewing achieved considerable acceptance in England. What blue-blooded English gentleman would stoop so low as to imitate the cow in the pasture and the uncouth Yankee? The problem of popularizing such a disgusting item on the British market was great indeed. However, so the story goes, the Wrigley advertising staff discovered a secret passageway to the British mouth. It was all a matter of proper advertising: "Chew Wrigley's Gum! It's British-made!" The word "British" somehow gave the gum a different flavor, and it sold — an apt illustration indeed of the role of prejudice in resistance to change.

Prejudice and fear are frequently the result of some past experience. A Navaho chanter once tried to introduce a new fertility dance, a dance that was to produce a superabundance of food. He painted potatoes on the backs of the dancers, who were instructed to cough and vomit in the dance as from overeating. However, soon after the performance a serious epidemic of whooping cough broke out and many of the Navaho Indians died. The deaths were blamed on the dance, in which coughing was an essential part. Others died of diarrhea, which, in turn, was blamed on the vomiting act. Others died of measles, sores, and small pox, which looked very much like the eyes of the potatoes painted on the backs of the dancers (Herskovits, 1950:486). This experience was handed down from generation to generation, so that today there is little hope of ever introducing a dance with the elements of coughing, vomiting, and potatoes.

Diffusability

The last group of factors, now to be described, includes certain characteristics of the culture element itself which render it suitable or unsuitable for borrowing. The culture element must be "borrowable," and one element may be more "borrowable" or "diffusable" than another.

1. SIMPLE VERSUS COMPLEX CULTURE ELEMENTS

Simple customs are more easily borrowed than complex ones. Thus, for instance, primitives can without too much difficulty borrow such traits as pots, pans, tin cans, bottles, beads, matches, a certain amount of clothing, and the like, but not the complicated technology involved in manufacturing such items. Nonsymbolic elements will be more "borrowable" than symbolic ones; ritual and ideology are much more difficult to accept than purely utilitarian elements like bush knives and blankets.

2. USEFULNESS AND ATTRACTIVENESS

A naturally useful and attractive element tends to diffuse more rapidly than something that is indifferent, useless, or perhaps even unattractive (Keesing, 1958:400). The natural usefulness of a steel implement and the inherent superiority of a rifle, as already pointed out, make such culture traits highly diffusable. Similarly, some foreign words seem to be pithier and seem to hit the nail on the head even more than the choicest Anglo-Saxon expressions, e.g., de luxe, en route, vice versa, milieu, in cognito, vis-à-vis, and such prefixes as "super-," "anti-," and "trans-." Instrumentalities, such as tools, etiquette, military tactics, and the like are among the most mobile of customs.

3. FORM, USAGE, MEANING, FUNCTION

As explained above (see pp. 215–217), form is more readily accepted than usage, meaning, or function.

4. EARLY LEARNING

Early learning favors persistence (Keesing, 1958:410). The most resistant to change are habits of thought, sentiment, and action acquired in early personality formation. Fear of black magic and vengeful spirits, certain sex behavior, habits of speech, gestures and facial expression, and love for certain foods, all associated with earlier stages of enculturation, are among the most difficult patterns to change. Early learning is least critical and early emotional experiences are usually the deepest. Missionaries will generally find it difficult to introduce religious or scientific ideas that contradict beliefs based on early learning and childhood experiences. One of the most difficult problems in a health program, for instance, will be that of changing the dietary habits of a people — habits acquired quite early in life and linked with many childhood experiences.

5. Basic Survival

Any custom believed to be essential for survival will be among the most difficult to displace (Keesing, 1958:410–412). The Catholics of Poland regard their faith as basic for survival, and every effort made by the Communists to wipe out religion in Poland has ended in vehement opposition and failure. In many parts of the world ancestor worship is regarded as absolutely necessary for survival, and, as a consequence, ancestor worship becomes one of the missionary's most difficult problems.

6. Alternatives

Customs allowing a relatively large range of alternatives, leaving much to personal taste, self-expression, and competition, are among the most mobile elements in a culture (Keesing, 1958:411–412).

7. Cultural Focus

The most mobile of all culture elements are the ones that fall within the cultural focus, provided that the change supports and advances the center of interest. Herskovits (1950:542–560) was the first to emphasize the rate of change that occurs within the cultural focus. By the term he meant "the tendency of every culture to exhibit greater complexity, greater variation in the institutions of some of its aspects than in others." Focus might be considered as a kind of summary of the whole culture, a way of characterizing the whole way of life and putting it in a nutshell. Thus, Mediaeval Europe might be characterized by its supernaturalism, Renaissance by its love for art and secular learning, and present-day Western civilization by its emphasis on technology (Herskovits, 1950:542). It is, therefore, rightly called the *Zeitgeist*, the concept being closely related to what has been said above about the "soul," "philosophy," "mentality," "psychology," and "basic values" of a society (see Chapter Seven). As Ruth Benedict explained the process: "Because all peoples defend their own way of life, it is easy to understand that one way in which cultures have grown richer and more complex has been by elaborating and multiplying their own most cherished customs. They carry further and further their favorite customs" (1956:189). Thought and discussion naturally center around the most "cherished" and "favorite" interests. "Where your treasure is, there will your heart be also" (Matt. 6:21). Thought and discussion give rise to new ideas; new ideas encourage experimentation and acceptance if the corresponding novelties promise to advance and benefit the center of interest. The greatest variation, complexity, and growth will consequently be found within the cultural focus.

On the other hand, if the innovation threatens the center of interest, the focus of culture becomes the area of strongest resistance; a society will always be least inclined to abandon its central interest and will vehemently resist innovations that appear detrimental to its most basic values and emotionally charged attitudes.

SUMMARY AND SELECTED MISSIOLOGICAL APPLICATIONS

Summary

1) Many factors are involved in culture change, and there is a constant interplay of factors, the cumulative effect determining change or persistence.

2) Variants involved in culture change in general are the following. Other things being equal: (1) the presence of suitable innovators favors change; (2) anticipation of change favors change; (3) the greater the freedom of inquiry and action, the greater the chance for innovation; (4) the more forceful and effective the social controls, the more persistent the culture; (5) change begets change; (6) compatibility favors change, incompatibility favors persistence; (7) the relative force of opposing factions constitutes an important factor in culture change and persistence.

3) Conditions favoring origination are the following: (1) proper motivation (e.g., conscious and subconscious wants, desire to reconcile conflicting ideas or to overcome obstacles and handicaps, creativity, relief from discomfort, desire for efficiency and effectiveness); (2) the size and complexity of the cultural inventory; (3) the channeling of the inventory into the same individual; (4) such factors as collaboration of effort, meeting of divergent ideas, competition, deprivation, and leisure and peace of mind.

4) Conditions favoring diffusion are the following: (1) the rela-

tive size of the borrowing and lending society can work either way, for or against diffusion; (2) the relative strength and aggressiveness of the particular segment actually diffusing the foreign element and the ability of the receiving segment to communicate with the rest of society favor change; (3) a dominant and minority status can work for as well as against diffusion; (4) migrations favor diffusion; (5) intense contact favors diffusion; (6) contact over a longer period favors diffusion but is not a requirement for it; (7) diffusion requires both a theoretical as well as a practical appreciation (felt-needs and interest) of the foreign element; (8) emotions can work for as well as against diffusion (bias and prejudice); (9) one foreign element may be more diffusable than another inasmuch as it may be simple or complex, useful and attractive or useless and unattractive, associated with early enculturation, allowing a relatively large range of alternatives, affecting the form, usage, meaning, or function, connected with basic survival, or belonging to the center of interest. The most mobile of all culture elements are the ones that fall within the cultural focus, provided that the change supports and advances the center of interest.

Selected Missiological Applications

1. THE GENERAL PURPOSE OF THE STUDY OF FACTORS INVOLVED IN CHANGE

The two basic reasons for the missionary's interest in anthropological theory regarding conditions favoring culture change are (1) to understand more fully the difficulties connected with missionary work and (2) to direct desired change more effectively.

1) It does not take much imagination to appreciate the advantages of studying any resistance to the Gospel or socio-economic betterment in the light of the various factors mentioned in the present chapter. Much of the resistance experienced by a missionary may very well be due to a lack of freedom of inquiry and action and a socially transmitted unfavorable attitude toward any change. Opposition to the missionary message may be due to a basic and wide incompatibility of the Gospel with the existing life-way. Or, perhaps, the particular doctrine threatens the people's center of interest or tends to undermine a traditional pattern regarded as important as survival itself. The lack of co-operation which the missionary experiences may be due to factionalism, social control,

conflicting currents of communication, or some other factor discussed in the present chapter.

2) In directing culture change — whether introducing new socio-economic or religious ideas, or attempting to guide secondary processes, or, perhaps, attempting to maintain or restore cultural and social equilibrium — the missionary would do well to select policies and employ techniques that reflect modern anthropological thought regarding factors favoring or discouraging culture change. For instance, in the theory discussed above, the suitability of innovators has been emphasized (see pp. 269–270). Keeping this particular factor in mind, the missionary would realize that not everyone in his parish, school, or hospital is an ideal innovator. He would also realize that missionary effectiveness depends to a large measure on the ability of the agent of change to recognize personalities who make the best innovators and to win their support — innovators who possess the necessary stability, leadership, and other characteristics of an ideal innovator discussed above. Then, too, as we have seen, innovations are most easily introduced if they be presented as highly rewarding, as supplying a felt-need, as being consistent with the life-way of the people — all important guidelines for a sound missionary approach.

The factors enumerated in the present chapter, although not intended to exhaust the subject, have been many, and the possible practical missionary applications that might be drawn from them are equally as many. The following considerations are chosen because of their special missiological import.

2. The Social Structure and Culture Change

A number of sociological considerations already mentioned might at this point once again be profitably brought together and re-examined from the viewpoint of culture change and missionary work. It has, for instance, been emphasized that the mission personnel, as much as possible and without deliberately neglecting any particular segment of society, should be placed in strategic positions, that is, in positions that can influence roles and institutions rather than isolated, socially insignificant individuals (see pp. 118–120). Also emphasized were the facts of uneven social change (see pp. 219, 261) and that some individuals and segments of society have a greater potential for changing culture than others, for they are the "powerhouses" in the particular social structure and constitute the main currents of communication (see pp. 283–284).

The head of the family has certainly more to say about culture change than a small child; the elders and rulers of a village have more to say than the ordinary villagers. Certain individuals, such as chieftains, governors, presidents, emperors, and popes have with one stroke of the pen changed the course of history and the character of cultures. The male segment of a society usually has more capacity for change than the female, the educated more than the uneducated, the rich more than the poor. The existence of such centers of power, however, are not to be assumed just because they exist in the missionary's society; rather, in each society they must be discovered through careful research. The shanty town dwellers of Latin America have greater potential for change today than the conservative aristocrats; the poor, not the rich, are the "powerhouses" of change that will before long decide the future of the Latin American life-way.

Such "powerhouses" of change in more complex societies include especially: (1) the government and military or police force with their power to legislate and enforce; (2) political parties with their ability to control the state; (3) the various social classes with their esprit de corps and ambitions; (4) the numberless interest-groups with their ambitions, grievances, energetic leaders, clever techniques, e.g., labor unions, business, the professions, farmers, factory workers, merchants, landowners, the press, radio, and other mass media, parents of school children, teachers, university administrators and professors, university students, etc. (cf. *C.I.F. Reports*, 1962: 316).

Although the missionary, like the Church he represents, must at all times avoid meddling in purely secular matters, especially politics, he cannot afford to be indifferent to "powerhouses" of change and the existing currents of communication within the society. The Communists are definitely *not* indifferent: they infiltrate the "powerhouses" and direct the power of each toward Communistic goals. The Church must not align herself with political parties, particular labor unions, the rich or the educated, but she must not remain indifferent to their views, activities, and goals. "To the learned and unlearned alike I am debtor" (Romans 1:14). The teaching of the Gospel must penetrate the minds of these important individuals and groups of individuals, whether they be politicians, labor leaders, university professors, students, factory workers, or whoever may constitute the chief potentials for culture change. As Father Charles Couturier, S.J., puts it:

> If then it is no part of the Church's business to determine what economic and juridical arrangements are most suitable to a given temporal situation, it does fall to her to draw the attention of the various societies to the moral principles that should govern their whole activity and to urge their detailed application, while leaving to each society the responsibility of working out the best practical arrangement (1960:56).

Nida speaks of a "Roman Catholic principle of concentrating on the ruling elite" (1961d:95). The fact is that the Church, despite abuses at certain times of her history and in some countries today, has no such "principle." Pius XI in his *Rerum Ecclesiae* admonishes the missionaries "not to neglect" the elite (no. 37). "Not to neglect" is by no means synonymous with "to concentrate on." The official and wise teaching of the Church is rather to appreciate the special power and communication potential in whatever segment of society it may be found. The fact is that often the elite does constitute the chief "powerhouse" of change and is the chief current of communication; where this is the case, there the policy of the Church is to make good use of its potential in carrying out her divine mission.

> As we know from history and experience, the common people are quick to follow in the footsteps of their leaders, once these have been converted to Christianity (*Rerum Ecclesiae*:38).

Or, in the words of John XXIII:

> Native priests [should] . . . be able to give life to movements of penetration among the cultured classes, especially in the countries that have an ancient and high culture. In this respect it will suffice to cite, for all, the example of Father Matteo Ricci. It is also the native clergy that must "bring every mind into captivity to the obedience of Christ" as that incomparable missionary St. Paul said. Thus they will enjoy "the esteem of the elite and the learned in their own countries." Following their own judgment, Bishops will, at the opportune time, establish centers of culture . . . (*Princeps Pastorum*:17).

After a careful analysis of the social structure of a people has been made, the missionaries should be able to recognize the corresponding centers of power and the direction and relative force of the various currents of communication. The greatest communication potential is not always from up to down, from the upper class to the lower, from the elite to the ordinary citizen. It is wrong to imagine that once the social and intellectual elite accepts an innovation the rest of society will *infallibly* follow. We have already seen how, for instance, the Guatemalan indigena considers it a sin to imitate the ladinos.

The *possible* communication potential of the ruling classes and the elite should always be considered by the missionary when deciding upon a concrete apostolic approach. However, such a potential should not be exaggerated or taken as some kind of dogma. The potential was present in China during Father Ricci's time, but such a potential does not exist everywhere and at all times. Today, for instance, the current of communication in Latin America is not vertical but horizontal: the few rich families communicate among themselves, while the poor form closed inter-communicating groups among themselves. The face of Latin America will be changed not by the isolated, snobbish, status-quo-loving aristocrats nor the tradition-upholding villagers or peons but the rapidly growing Latin shanty town dwellers, the main "powerhouse" of change and the potentially strongest current of communication in that part of the world.

In a society no segment is really unimportant and therefore should not be neglected. However, one segment may be relatively more important, and this relative importance should not be overlooked when deciding upon a missionary policy or technique. The male segment of a community, for example, may, as is usually the case, be more important than the female segment as far as culture change is concerned. In an effort to Christianize the non-Christian world the missionaries cannot afford to project an image of the Church as being feminine, for women only, as the German saying puts it, "Kinder, Küche, Kirche" — the woman's realm being "children, the kitchen, and the church." Once such an image is created, an extremely important "powerhouse" of Christianization is destroyed. Such an image can easily be created or perpetuated by the missionary by catering, so to speak, for the co-operative children and women. The fact is that the unco-operative men are too important to neglect. Moreover, every culture assigns certain behavior, objects, emotions, and language to women and certain behavior to men. If liturgy and instruction in religion acquire a feminine image, the men, the important centers of power and communication, will regard Christianity as "not for us." The motivations suggested in sermons and in catechism class must not be those that in the given culture make sense to women alone. Even in Western countries religion is sometimes presented exclusively as something "sweet" and "soft" and "angelic." A Christianity that is limited to "sweet Infant Jesus" or "my poor suffering Savior" is not the full Gospel; and, despite the fact that both the Incarnation and the Passion of Our Lord are essential aspects of Christianity, over-emphasis of the "sweet" and "suffering" may alienate an important potential from the young Church in mission areas by giving the more important half of the community the impression that Christianity is indeed only for women. Unless the missionaries constantly keep the present practical application in mind they may, without even realizing it, be creating among an important segment of the community a "not-for-me" image of the Church.

3. Social Control and Missionary Effort

It has been pointed out that, other things being equal, the more forceful and effective the social controls, the more persistent the culture. Aspects of culture to which the society applies little or no pressure will tend to change more readily than those which the society insists upon and to which it attaches severe and inevitable sanctions (see pp. 272–273). The missionary would do well to study the social controls that exist among his people: what these controls are, how severe the pressure, how inevitable the sanction, and which sanctions are attached to which traditional patterns. The system of social control in question may differ essentially from that found in the missioner's culture. To understand the lack of co-operation on the part of his flock, the instability of converts, and the out-right rejection of the Gospel, the missioner must study the local social controls and evaluate them in accord with local norms.

Among the main negative controls which ought to be investigated by the missionary are the following. (1) *Physical punishment* would include such pressures as duels, ordeals, corporal punishment, imprisonment, exile, mutilation, and execution. (2) *Fines* are a very common negative control, the severity of which must be judged in accord with native (not the missionary's) values. They are payable to the state, community, chief, or the offended party, or someone else, depending on the particular written or customary law. Bloodwite is a fine paid as compensation for homicide, often as a substitute for the vendetta. (3) *Gossip*, especially where face-saving is an important value, may serve as a very forceful social control. Human beings, no matter who they may be, are sensitive to group comment. Individuals may drop out of the catechumenate or stop coming to school because it is being whispered that they are attending classes merely to avoid work at home. (4) *Commands* are among the most common controls. Just who may give a valid order and what the force of the command will be will vary from culture to culture. The command may come, for example, from the head of the family, from an elder of the tribe, from a teacher, from a priest, or from a policeman. A maternal uncle's command may be far more effective than that of a parent, and a sorcerer's wish may have the force of a very strict order that no one would dare disobey. (5) *Ridicule* is not only one of the most common forms of social control but also among the most effective. A child learns many a skill, including the use of language, among other reasons, so as not to be laughed at by its playmates. Very effective anywhere and at any age are offensive nicknames. Socialistically inclined politicians will avoid going too far to the left for fear of being called "Communists" or "un-American." (6) *Threats* of physical punishment or sorcery, the anger of secret societies, or any other threat, the seriousness and force depending especially on the particular value-system, keep many an individual within approved bounds. A reluctant bride in the South Seas finally submits to the coaxing of her family and marries a man she positively dislikes, because she fears a threatened illness or death through sorcery if she does not submit. Similar threats may be responsible for a Christian girl's agreeing to be the second wife of a polygamist or to marry a divorced man. (8) *Taboos* are traditional prohibitions to which are annexed such sanctions as revenge on the part of a spirit or ancestor, disease, or death. An action is avoided for fear of the threatened calamity to follow if the taboo should be disregarded. Especially in more primitive societies, such fears, stemming from past convictions and experience, may occasion many a relapse into former pagan ways. Even after Baptism, many of the old superstitious fears persist; the convert may not be able to explain his feelings in so many words, but, despite his repeated renunciation of former beliefs, succumbs to the deeply-ingrained subconscious fears. The impression made on the Melanesian mind from earliest childhood by the oft-repeated ghost stories, "proving beyond the least shadow of doubt" that the departed are vengeful beings unless placated by pig-sacrifices, are *deep* impressions and may take generations before they are completely obliterated. The Christian has personally known tribesmen who have "seen" ghosts; in fact, he himself may have "seen and spoken" with the ancestors, or remembers how seriously ill he became after transgressing a traditional taboo. (8) *Scolding*, especially if persistent, may influence the behavior of the individual. Many things are done contrary to one's own likes and dislikes simply "to keep peace in the family." The excuse given by a pupil for running away from a boarding school may be: "My father is always hollering at me for not being at home to help him with the firewood." Many a tradition is kept alive, thanks to the scolding of the older generation.

The following are the main positive social pressures. (1) *Education*, the positive effort on the part of the society to ensure the individuals mastery of the approved ways is undoubtedly the most pervasive and effective form of social control (see pp. 78–79). An important part of this training deals with the inner logic or the configurational system, which gives direction to practically the whole life-way (see pp. 157–161). For example, the reason for not selling land among some tribes of Central Africa is the learned assumption that the only thing you can sell is what you yourself have made. Since God made the land He alone can sell it. Such underlying basic assumptions serve to control a wide range of behavior. (2) *Rewards* as factors encouraging culture change have already been described (see pp. 276–278, 287–291). Very often the resistance to the Gospel or to a new socio-economic idea is not due to any particular attachment to un-Christian or unscientific traditional patterns but on account of the reward (e.g., prestige) that would otherwise have to be sacrificed. To change such customs, substitute rewards must be found. A missionary who preaches only sacrifice and an endless list of do's and don'ts makes Christianity look very unattractive indeed. (3) A special form of reward useful for introducing new ideas and maintaining traditional patterns is *praise and admiration*. A child that is not accepted by good companions will seek acceptance and admiration in a gang of juvenile delinquents. The new ideas brought by missionaries must offer the local people sufficient occasions for praise and admiration, for otherwise these rewards will be sought in former un-Christian practices. Prestige and praise have long been used by the Church in the past and are still being used today. A layman may be declared a Knight

of St. Gregory, or an outstanding scholar may become a member
of the Papal Academy of Sciences. A Chinaman, an Indian, an
African, a Filipino, and a Japanese have become cardinals, Princes
of the Church. Distinguished Catholic laymen in mission territories
should be singled out and honored by the local Bishop and even
proposed for papal honors. Catechists and teachers should be shown
respect by the missionaries, and every effort should be made to
attach prestige to their particular roles. (4) In some societies *security*
constitutes the chief form of social control: since the individual
feels utterly dependent on his fellows for his food, for the required
bridewealth, for protection against enemies, and for survival in
general, to act contrary to the approved ways would endanger this
security. (5) By perpetuating and developing a religious or magical
art, the society perpetuates and spreads its religious and magical beliefs and values. As a result of art, Buddhism was able to spread
more rapidly throughout the East. Religious art can very profitably
be used by the missionary too. (6) *Ceremonies* may function as a
form of social control, as they usually do. Communists are fond
of parades and demonstrations because they appreciate the power of
symbol and ceremony in moving individuals to action. One of the
chief functions of Liturgy is Christian *living* (Hofinger, ed., 1958:
21–28; Gonzaga, 1960:191–201). (7) Also to be numbered among
the positive social controls are *propaganda, slogans, advertising,* and
public opinion (cf. Murray, 1946:525–567; Ewing, ed., 1958).

Considerable space has been devoted to social pressure and culture change because the subject has a very important bearing on
everyday missionary techniques. A knowledge of the traditional system of control should enable the missionary (1) better to understand the difficulties facing any agent of change and (2) it should
suggest some effective controls which the missioner himself may
be able to use in introducing change and in maintaining the changes
which have been successfully introduced.

4. THE APOSTOLATE AS A SPECIALIZATION

To what extent should apostolic work be a specialized form of
activity in the Church? Like some of the other factors involved in
culture change, specialization can work for as well as against innovation. Consequently, in spreading Christianity, the Church should
encourage specialization where it should be encouraged and discourage specialization where it should be discouraged.

1) Specialization as an Obstacle to Effective Apostolic Work.
Throughout the Catholic world today there is a healthy trend back
to the pristine total involvement in apostolic work of all members
of the Church and away from considering the apostolate as the exclusive concern of "specialists" called "missionaries." In fact, the
word "missionary" may, before long, disappear. Not only "specialists"
but every true Christian must be totally involved in the religious
and social mission of the Church.

> The missionary spirit and the Catholic spirit, We have said before,
> are one and the same thing. Catholicity is an essential note of the
> true Church. This is so to such an extent that a Christian is not truly
> faithful and devoted to the Church if he is not equally attached and
> devoted to her universality, desiring that she take root and flourish in
> all parts of the earth (Pius XII, *Fidei Donum*:62).

"Every Christian a missionary!" is once again becoming a principle and a reality. Religious congregations and orders not primarily
missionary in character are now sending their members to the
farthest corners of the earth as never before; diocesan clergy are
volunteering for spiritually indigent areas of Latin America and elsewhere; various lay movements are rapidly expanding their activities.
Above all, the bishops of Europe and America are beginning to
consider the world as their common concern, fully in accord with
the teaching of Pius XI:

> If none of the faithful can claim exemption from this missionary duty,
> is any exemption conceivable for the clergy who, through the unutter-
> able generosity of Christ Our Lord participate in His priestly aposto-
> late? Is any exemption possible for you, Venerable Brothers, who are
> adorned with the fullness of the priesthood and divinely constituted
> the rulers of your clergy and Christian people? We read that Jesus
> Christ ordered not only Peter, whose See We govern, but all the
> Apostles, of whom you are the successors, to "go into the whole world
> and preach the Gospel to every creature" (Mark 16:35). From this
> it is evident that Ours is the primary responsibility for the spread
> of the faith, whereas each of you should unhesitatingly share this
> burden with Us . . . (*Rerum Ecclesiae*:9).

Pius XII was no less emphatic when he admonished his bishops:

> Without doubt, Jesus has entrusted His entire flock to the Apostle
> Peter alone and to his successors, the Roman Pontiffs: "Pasce agnos
> meos, pasce oves meas — Feed my lambs, feed my sheep" (John
> 21:16–18). But, if every Bishop is the proper pastor only of that
> portion of the flock entrusted to his care, his quality as a legitimate

successor of the Apostles by Divine institution renders him jointly responsible for the apostolic mission of the Church. . . . This mission, which must embrace all nations and all times did not cease with the death of the Apostles. It continues in the person of all the Bishops in communion with the Vicar of Jesus Christ . . . (*Fidei Donum*:59–60).

In the early Church missionary activities were not regarded as a form of specialization: to be a Christian was to be a missionary, a spirit that prevailed during the first five centuries of the Christian era. The subsequent channelization of apostolic interests into a specialized group tended to make apostolic interests accidental to Christianity (cf. Hoffman, 1962b). Bishops began to regard missionary activities as a work of supererogation rather than a duty. The early missiologists, e.g., Thomas a Jesu, regarded apostolic work as the special task of kings. Later, apostolic work was regarded as the task of the Roman Pontiffs alone and of no special concern to the bishops of older churches, who had their own dioceses to worry about. In fact, the Codex of Canon Law fails to include the missionary apostolate among the various duties annexed to the episcopacy. Until very recent times, bishops of Europe and America generally regarded missionary work as something laudable indeed and worthy of support but "someone else's worry." Parish priests felt that they satisfied their missionary obligations by having an annual collection for the Society of the Propagation of the Faith and for an occasional visiting missionary. To see that this is no longer the case, one need but observe the deeply apostolic spirit of the Second Vatican Council and the general trend in the Church toward a total involvement in apostolic activities.

Specialization works against the spread of Christianity by restricting the flow of ideas and action. Nothing could be more detrimental to the apostolic cause than to regard mission activities as a kind of appendage to the Church, the more or less exclusive concern of specialists called "missionaries."

2) **Specialization as a Distinct Need in the Modern Apostolate.** We are not contradicting ourselves when we now say that a considerable amount of specialization is nevertheless called for. Since specialization can work *for* as well as *against* culture change, the Church should discourage specialization only where it obstructs apostolic work, and encourage specialization where specialization promotes missionary progress. The strides made in Medicine and Physics,

for example, have been possible mainly through specialization. The Church will, therefore, be wise to encourage (besides an involvement of her total membership in apostolic work) also a total involvement *in depth through specialization.*

For this reason there will always be a need for organizations specifically designed for apostolic activities. Specifically-missionary societies, such as the White Fathers, Maryknollers, and the Divine Word Missionaries, and such lay groups as the Grail and the Association for International Development will always be an asset to the Church in her apostolic work, precisely because they are groups of specialists. Societies with prime focus on the Missions have not only a useful missionary tradition, spirit, and interest but also a structure specifically geared to mission needs. They are also in an ideal position to provide specifically-missionary training for their members. The missionary vocation calls for specialized training that the regular program of a diocesan seminary and the ordinary monastery or convent are usually not equipped to provide. Just as a diocesan seminary must train its seminarians for the special problems of the *local* diocese, so there will always be need for specialized mission organizations with their training centers, the prime concern of which would be the preparation of the modern apostle for the needs peculiar to spiritually or socio-economically indigent areas. As Pius XII expressed this need:

> . . . it is not enough to have those dedicated to this apostolate educated and formed, while yet in their homeland, in every kind of virtue and ecclesiastical study. Let them learn besides those specialized disciplines and sciences which are calculated to be highly useful for them later on when they will be heralds of the gospel among foreign peoples (*Evangelii Praecones*:31).

But besides special knowledge and skill, the missionary apostolate calls for special character formation which fits the religious worker to operate in a strange cultural milieu and other conditions peculiar to mission areas. No concentrated course or crash-program is possible when character formation is in question. So-called "missionary virtues," especially empathy and adaptability, require guidance and years of development. Even careful selection of mission personnel, however useful and necessary, will not serve as a satisfactory substitute.

Despite the fact that organizations not specifically-missionary lack a structure primarily geared to mission needs and despite the fact that the Missions are not their primary interest, such groups have nevertheless vital roles to play in missionary progress and methods. They have specialties of their own, such as parish missions, social work, education, publications, youth work, and other aspects of the apostolate, which would be a great asset to the Church in any mission country. Not seldom such groups are even outstanding in their field of specialization, a field which the strictly-missionary societies might not be in a position to develop as efficiently as these non-specifically-missionary groups.

Despite the practical difficulties involved, such groups must provide special training for those members of their organization who will be assigned to the Missions. On-the-job training will be helpful and, in fact, necessary, but such training will hardly be enough. There will always be need for a pre-mission training fitted in somehow with the regular program and primary requirements of the organization.

But why insist on a special missionary training? Are not basic principles as valid in Africa as in Europe or America? The answer is, of course, as obvious as the fact that a soldier intended for jungle warfare or the Arctic must be given *special* training. It would hardly be enough to give such a soldier the basic principles of discipline and combat and leave the rest to his own imagination and ingenuity. The essential difference between a missionary and a non-missionary is the fact that their battlefields are different: in the one case the battlefield is strange, totally unfamiliar, and even unnatural, while in the other case the battlefield is as familiar as one's own home and neighborhood. A missionary needs more than a general training in Theology, Education, Medicine, Agronomy, or Engineering; for, an individual can be a great success at home but an utter failure abroad. As J. W. Masland so aptly put it in his contribution in *The Art of Overseamanship* (1960:97), "You can send an Einstein to an Iraqi village, but if he cannot get over what he knows to the villagers, he will be a failure."

A missionary needs a *missionary* training. Such a training will differ in various ways from that of a non-missionary. (1) There will be a difference as to *content-matter and emphasis* in the curriculum. Cultural Anthropology and Descriptive Linguistics, for example, are vital in any missionary curriculum worthy of the name; but this would hardly be true of a curriculum of a diocesan seminary. Or again, a professor of Moral Theology in an American or

European seminary, preparing young men for the home diocese, might justifiably skip over the First Commandment rather rapidly, but in a training center geared to mission needs the First Commandment would call for nothing less than a very thorough treatment. Moreover, since the missioner will have to stand on his own feet perhaps more often than his counterpart at home, he will need a better grounding in certain basic principles, and special emphasis will have to be placed on such principles. On the Missions there is less opportunity to consult the chancery (if there happens to be such a thing as a chancery); there is, therefore, less reliance on the opinions and decisions of others. Moreover, in mission areas the religious worker is generally called upon not merely to continue a well-established and tested educational, medical, or religious program but to pioneer in these fields — a situation requiring a good foundation in certain basic concepts, principles, and methods that might not be necessary in a situation where pioneering is not called for. (2) There will be a difference also in *methods and practical applications.* A missionary educator or nurse will need techniques that make sense not only in the sophisticated environments of a large American city but, as much as possible, cross-culturally. For this reason some missionary-Sisters have their own teacher-training colleges; they rightly feel the need for a mission-oriented course in Education. The "tricks of the trade" learned in Pastoral Theology, Homiletics, Catechetics, and Liturgy intended for "home use" will always be an asset on the Missions, but such knowledge does not guarantee effectiveness in a strange culture. The professor of Homiletics in a diocesan seminary, for instance, may very well emphasize the necessity of a "logical" buildup of a sermon, "graceful" and "meaningful" gestures, and a "natural" modulation of the voice, but the professor of Homiletics in a *missionary* training center would have to do more: he would not, of course, describe the oratorical practices of all countries of the world, but he would be aware of those oratorical practices and recommendations which may make sense *only* in the home-country. He would have to re-examine Homiletic theory cross-culturally and call the attention of his budding orators to the fact that, once they leave their culture or subculture, logic may somehow cease to be logic (Chapter Seven); the monotonous delivery, which the budding orators had such a difficult time to overcome, may be the preferred and more dignified form of delivery on the Missions; and the "graceful" gestures, which they seem finally to have mastered, may actually turn out to be those of a local maniac. The professor of Homiletics would have to remind the budding orator also that as he speaks, his "strange" listeners will be reinterpreting his message in accord with *their* cultural context (not his), and that, unlike the orator at home, the missionary-orator will have to *direct* this reinterpretation (see pp. 214–220). The same, of course, holds for the missionary educator and catechist, who will have to do far more listening and less talking than the orator, educator, and catechist in the home-country, never forgetting the wise observation of Epictetus that Nature has given us only one tongue but two ears so that we might hear from others twice as much as we say. Directing cultural reinterpretation will be a major task of any orator, educator, or any other worker in a strange cultural environment, a task that is almost non-existent in the home-country, where the culture of the speaker and the listeners is one and the same. Similarly, to teach seminarians the beauties of Liturgy with little reference to its variability may be allowable in a diocesan seminary or a monastery in Europe or America, but it would be a very imperfect way of teaching Liturgy to future missionaries. To teach Catechetics to future missionaries in a way other than cross-culturally would be just as wrong.[4]

Moreover, the Missions need not only workers trained specifically for mission conditions but also a large number of experts in the truest sense of the word. Modern apostolic approaches should be truly representative of the twentieth century and the jet-age, not the horse-and-buggy days. The Missions need specialists in every possible modern scientific field that might enable the Church to carry out her worldwide religious and social mission more effectively. The Church needs agronomists, dieticians, social workers, educators, sociologists, credit union specialists, urbanization experts, and anthropologists. There is indeed plenty of room for specialization in apostolic work.

Mission specialists must be given every opportunity to channel their ideas into the same minds, for only in this way will new, progressive ideas arise (see p. 278); there must be a collaboration

---

[4] Among the more valuable contributions to cross-cultural communication as far as the missionary is concerned are: E. T. Hall, *The Silent Language*; E. A. Nida, *Message and Mission*; L. W. Doob, *Communication in Africa*. See General Bibliography for facts of publication.

of effort among mission specialists, a meeting of divergent ideas, mutual stimulation, even competition and challenge (see pp. 278 281), and, above all, sufficient leisure, peace of mind and opportunity (see pp. 281–282). All this can be made possible through such well-known means as publications, symposia, workshops, and research and co-ordinating centers. Specialization comes to life through such professional and semi-professional missiological periodicals as the *Christ to the World*, *C.I.F. Reports*, the Hong Kong and the Japanese *Mission Bulletins*, the India *Clergy Monthly*, and the excellent non-English missiological journals now available. Specialization comes to life through such meetings as the liturgical conference held at Nijmegen, Holland, in September, 1959, the International Study Week on Mission Catechetics held at Eichstatt, Germany, in July, 1960, and the Fordham University annual meeting of mission-specialists. Above all, specialization becomes fruitful if a "home" is provided for the mission-specialist — a research and co-ordinating center, such as that suggested by Richard Cardinal Cushing of Boston in September, 1961. Such a center would be a "powerhouse" of missionary activity (Cushing, 1961; Shaw, 1961). It would ensure army-like co-ordination among the various missionary groups in their various undertakings. Such a center would aim to promote research in any and every specialized field that would contribute to the efficiency, effectiveness, and success of the Church's spiritual and social mission; it would co-ordinate such research; it would itself undertake research as much as possible. The center could promote research in various ways: it could provide professional guidance for missionaries doing research work; it could serve as a liaison between a qualified research worker and a foundation; it could serve as a catalyst in university, seminary, and professional circles, and among missionaries themselves. It would serve as a clearing house of information. Very much valuable research is already being done by various government and private agencies; in fact, there are a number of Catholic missiological research groups in existence already (cf. *C.I.F. Reports*, I [1962], 176). Unfortunately, however, missionaries do not know what is being done and what is not, and this valuable research is not being made use of; a co-ordinating center and clearing house would indeed bring such research to life and action. A research center would need a good library, well-kept-up archives and a complete file of sources of information. Such a center would also contribute toward a constant improvement in missionary training. Finally, since the battle front must rely to a large extent on the home front, the center would be deeply interested in research and dissemination of information regarding the best methods of obtaining the necessary support from the home-country, especially as far as public relations, finances, and recruitment are concerned. Particularly suited for mission research are the Catholic universities in spiritually and socio-economically indigent areas of the world.

Specialization is by no means a missionary luxury; on the contrary, modern specialization in the various scientific and practical fields is as necessary as apostolic efficiency, effectiveness, and success. (1) No business or government can successfully operate exclusively on tradition, common-sense, and on a kind of hit-or-miss policy. Mission work is a multi-million-dollar "business" — not to say anything about the infinite value of souls and the untold suffering and injustice in the modern world that must be alleviated. Such a "business" calls for modern research by fully-qualified scientists and specialists, regardless of the cost. (2) Apostolic methods need specialists because the modern apostle lives in a revolutionary period. The leisurely pace of the past has become suicidal. Specialists in the various fields of knowledge and skill must help gear apostolic methods to the speed of our times. (3) The problems and needs of today are to a large extent new. New needs call for new approaches. To discover such new approaches calls for specialists. It is their task to re-think, re-shape, and to bring the apostolic aproach up to date.

To sum up — specialization, whatever its nature, can work both ways, for as well as against a desired change, a fact which the Church cannot afford to overlook. The Church must encourage specialization where specialization should be encouraged, and discourage it where it should be discouraged.

SELECTED READINGS

1. **General Theory Regarding Conditions Favoring or Discouraging Change**
    * 1) H. G. Barnett, *Innovation: The Basis of Cultural Change*, pp. 39–180.
    * 2) J. J. Honigmann, *The World of Man*, pp. 200–232.
      3) F. M. Keesing, *Cultural Anthropology*, pp. 384–417.
    * 4) M. J. Herskovits, *Man and His Works*, pp. 523–560.

2. Examples Illustrating Variants in Culture Change

    1) M. Mead, *New Lives for Old.*
    * 2) J. Gillin, *The Ways of Men: An Introduction to Anthropology,* pp. 209–220.
    3) W. W. Hill, "The Navaho Indians and the Ghost Dance of 1890," *American Anthropologist,* XLVI (1944), 523–527, reprinted in *Reader in Comparative Religion* (Lessa and Vogt, eds.), pp. 478–482.

3. The Missionary and Conditions Favoring or Discouraging Change

    1) J. Franklin Ewing, ed., *Communication Arts in Mission Work: 1956 Conference of Mission Specialists at Fordham University.*
    * 2) J. Hofinger, et al., *Worship: The Life of the Missions,* pp. 21–30.
    3) Most Rev. Lino Gonzaga y Rasdesales, "Missionary Importance of the Revision of the Ritual," in *Liturgy and the Missions: The Nijmegen Papers* (J. Hofinger, ed.), pp. 191–201.
    * 4) E. A. Nida, *Message and Mission: The Communication of the Christian Faith,* pp. 94–136.
    5) M. Mead, ed., *Cultural Patterns and Technical Change.*
    6) E. H. Spicer, ed., *Human Problems in Technological Change.*
    7) G. M. Foster, *Traditional Cultures: And the Impact of Technological Change.*

REVIEW QUESTIONS

1. What is meant by "an interplay of factors"? (p. 269)
2. Who is a "suitable" innovator? (pp. 269–270)
3. How does the attitude of a society toward change encourage or discourage modifications in the life-way? (pp. 270–273)
4. How can change itself be regarded as a factor in change and persistence? (p. 273)
5. How does cultural compatibility enter into change? (pp. 273–275)
6. How does factionalism affect change and persistence? (pp. 275–276)
7. What are the chief motivations for origination? (pp. 276–278)
8. Does the size and complexity of the cultural inventory favor or discourage origination? (p. 278)
9. Briefly describe the other factors involved in origination. (pp. 278–282)
10. Does the size of the community affect diffusion? (pp. 282–286)
11. Does a dominant position encourage or discourage borrowing from a minority group? (pp. 284–285)
12. Do migrations encourage diffusion? (p. 285)
13. Does the intensity of contact affect diffusion? (pp. 285–286) What about friendly versus inimical contact? (p. 286)

14. Does the duration of contact have anything to do with diffusion? (p. 287)
15. What is the difference between a felt-need and interest? Are they to be considered as important factors in diffusion? (pp. 287–291)
16. Do emotions affect cultural borrowing? How? (pp. 291–292)
17. Are some culture elements by their very nature more diffusable than others? (pp. 292–294) What is the relation between the rate of change and the cultural focus? (pp. 294–295)
18. Why should the missionary be interested in studies pertaining to factors involved in culture change? (pp. 296–297)
19. How is social structure involved in culture change? (pp. 283–284, 297–301)
20. What is meant by "social control"? How does it affect culture change? What bearing does it have on missionary work? (pp. 272–273, 301–304)
21. To what extent should missionary work be a specialization in the Church? Give your reasons. (pp. 304–312)

TOPICS FOR CLASSROOM DISCUSSION AND PAPERS

1. Write a critical review of E. A. Nida's article "The Roman Catholic, Communist, and Protestant Approach to Social Structure," *Practical Anthropology*, Supplement (1960), 21–26.
2. What factors discussed in the present chapter are exemplified in M. Mead's *New Lives for Old?*
3. What factors discussed in the present chapter are exemplified in Wm. J. Coleman's *Latin-American Catholicism: A Self-Evaluation*, World Horizon Reports, No. 23, Maryknoll Publications?
4. What factors discussed in the present chapter seem to be involved in Islamic resistance to Christianity? Some useful ideas will be found in V. Courtois, "How to Present the Christian Message to the Muslims," *Christ to the World*, I (1956), No. 6, 63–73; Father Charles de Foucauld, "The Apostolate in Mohammedan Circles," *Christ to the World*, V (1960), 65–74; see also the special section on Islam in the back numbers of Hong Kong *Mission Bulletin*.
5. What factors discussed in the present chapter seem to be involved in Amish resistance to change? For ethnographic material see W. M. Kollmorgen, *The Old Order Amish of Lancaster County*, Pennsylvania, U. S. Dept. of Agriculture, Washington, 1942; W. J. Schreiber, *Our Amish Neighbors*, University of Chicago Press and University of Toronto Press, 1962.
6. How can Liturgy, religious art, music, dance, etc., serve as a social control in a Christian community? (See, for instance, Paul Brunner, "Teaching Power of the Liturgy," Hong Kong *Mission Bulletin*, X [1958], 997–1000; J. Hofinger, et al., *Worship: The Life of the Missions*, Notre Dame Press, 1958.)

7. Study the history of a flourishing Christian community in Asia, Africa, or Oceania, or of a particular period of European Church History and indicate the factors discussed in the present chapter that seem to have been important contributing factors in the missionary effort concerned.

8. Prejudice is an important factor involved in culture change. Show that this is a fact in the Orient. (Read, for instance, Thomas Ohm, *Asia Looks at Western Christianity*, Herder and Herder, New York, 1959.)

9. How might you influence the elite of India? (For preliminary ideas see Most Rev. Wm. Bouter, "To Bring Christ to the Intellectuals of India," *Christ to the World*, I [1956], No. 6, 56–62.)

10. Compare what the author has said about specialization (see pp. 304–312) with:

    1) G. M. Korb, "The Scientific Scrutiny of Mission Methods," *The American Ecclesiastical Review*, February, 1961;

    2) John McCreanor, S.M.A., "Rethinking Our Missionary Approach," *Worldmission*, XIII (1962), 40–46;

    3) Russel Shaw, "The Church — Comfortable or Suffering," *Ave Maria*, October 14, 1961;

    4) Richard Cardinal Cushing, *The Modern Challenge of the Missions*, pamphlet reprint, Sullivan Bros., Lowell Mass., 1961;

    5) R. Hoffman, "Bishops and the Worldwide Apostolate," *The Jurist*, XXII (1962);

    6) Very Rev. Maurice Quéguiner, "Theology of Missionary Cooperation," *Christ to the World*, VII (1962), 491–504;

    7) Canon Auguste Croegaert, "The Responsibility of the Bishops for the Propagation of the Faith all over the World," *Christ to the World*, V (1960), 331–334.

11. Catherine Berndt speaks of some differences in missionary methods as followed by various denominations in New Guinea in her "Socio-cultural Change in the Eastern Central Highlands of New Guinea," *Southwestern Journal of Anthropology*, IX (1953), 112–138. Comment on her views.

12. Describe and evaluate William Duncan's missionary approach in British Columbia. See Homer G. Barnett, "Applied Anthropology in 1860," *Applied Anthropology* (now *Human Organization*), I (1942).

13. Describe the difficulties arising from the incompatibility of Christian moral standards and non-Christian marriage customs. See, for instance, J. Davidson, "Protestant Missions and Marriage in the Belgian Congo," *Africa*, XVIII (1948), 120–128.

14. State in clear hypotheses or principles the policies or recommendations expressed in one or more of the following:

    1) Cyril Daryll Forde, et al., *Missionary Statesmanship in Africa: A Present Day Demand upon the Christian Movement*, Hartford Seminary Foundation, 1953;

316 DYNAMICS OF CULTURE

2) J. Merle Davis, *New Buildings on Old Foundations: A Handbook on Stabilizing the Younger Churches in Their Environment,* New York and London, International Missionary Council, 1945;
3) Robert N. Rapoport, "Changing Navaho Religious Values: A Study of Christian Missions to the Rimrock Navahos," Peabody Museum, Cambridge, Mass., 1954.

CHAPTER TWELVE

WHY CULTURES ARE WHAT THEY ARE

THE present chapter discusses an important paradox: on the one hand, cultures are unique; on the other hand, all cultures are basically the same. Cultures differ in their content, structure, and configuration; at the same time they share a common framework. Why so similar and yet so different?

THE COMMON FRAMEWORK OF ALL CULTURES

The basic similarity of cultures is called "the common framework of cultures," "the aspects of culture," "the common denominator of culture," and "the culture scheme." Murdock in his "The Common Denominator of Cultures" (1945:124) presents what he calls a

partial list of items, arranged in alphabetical order to emphasize their variety, which occur, so far as the author's knowledge goes, in every culture known to history or ethnography: age-grading, athletic sports, bodily adornment, calendar, cleanliness training, community organization, cooking, co-operative labor, cosmology, courtship, dancing, decorative art, divination, division of labor, dream interpretation, education, eschatology, ethics, ethnobotany, etiquette, faith healing, family, feasting, fire making, folklore, food taboos, funeral rites, games, gestures, gift giving, government, greetings, hair styles, hospitality, housing, hygiene, incest taboos, inheritance rules, joking, kin-groups, kinship nomenclature, language, law, luck superstitions, magic, marriage, mealtimes, medicine, modesty concerning natural functions, mourning, music, mythology, numerals, obstetrics, penal sanctions, personal names, population policy, postnatal care, pregnancy usages, property rights, propitiation of supernatural beings, puberty customs, religious ritual, residence rules, sexual restrictions, soul concepts, status differentiation, surgery, tool making, trade, visiting, weaning, and weather control.

This "partial list" includes no less than seventy-three categories of human ways that seem to find expression in every culture and which might easily be reduced to six or seven major units — the "aspects

317

of culture" or "universals" — that constitute the framework of any and all life-ways.

Tylor hinted at a scheme in his definition of culture: "Culture or civilization is that complex whole which includes knowledge, belief, art, morals, law, customs, and any other capabilities and habits acquired by man as a member of society" (1874:1).

Seven years later, Wissler suggested that culture is composed of (1) language; (2) arts of life, *i.e.*, economic life; (3) arts of pleasure, *i.e.*, music, dancing, poetry, etc.; (4) science, *i.e.*, religion, magic, knowledge; and (5) society. He later proposed another scheme (1923:74), which, although suffering from important omissions, was very well received and for some time regarded as *the* classic framework for ethnographies. Wissler's scheme was as follows:

1. *Speech*
   a. Language
   b. Writing Systems
   c. Other Means of Communication
2. *Material Traits*
   a. Food Habits
   b. Shelter
   c. Transportation and Travel
   d. Dress
   e. Utensils
   f. Weapons
   g. Occupations and Industries
3. *Art*
   a. Carving
   b. Painting
   c. Music
   d. Drawing, etc.
4. *Mythology and Scientific Knowledge*
5. *Religious Practices*
   a. Ritualistic Forms
   b. Treatment of the Sick
   c. Treatment of the Dead
6. *Family and Social Systems*
   a. The Forms of Marriage
   b. Methods of Reckoning Relationship
   c. Inheritance
   d. Social Control
   e. Sports and Games
7. *Property*
   a. Real and Personal Property
   b. Standards of Value and Exchange
   c. Trade

8. *Government*
   a. Political Forms
   b. Judicial and Legal Procedures
9. *War*

The suggested outlines of Linton, Herskovits, and the *Notes and Queries* are here reproduced since they can serve as useful models for arranging one's field notes and for presenting one's data in the form of a complete monograph. It should be noted, however, that in filing and presenting ethnographic materials, adjustments to the specific culture will have to be made, and there will always be sufficient room for personal taste.

Linton suggested:

1. *Material Culture* (e.g., housing, clothing, settlements, handicrafts, pottery, metallurgy, trade, transportation, food, hunting, fishing, gathering, farming, animal husbandry, marketing, etc.)
2. *Social Organization* (e.g., marriage, family, kinship, courtship, war, amusement, rank, etiquette, property rights, government, law, etc.)
3. *Art* (e.g., songs, dances, painting, carving, etc.)
4. *Religion* (e.g., magic, divination, ancestor worship, divine kingship, priesthood, sacred places, times, persons, taboos, the hereafter, etc.)
5. *Language.*

Herskovits suggests a similar scheme in his *Man and His Works* (1950:634):

1. *Material Culture and Its Sanctions* (e.g., technology and economics)
2. *Social Institutions* (e.g., organization, education, politics)
3. *Man and the Universe* (e.g., belief systems, control of power)
4. *Aesthetics* (e.g., graphic and plastic arts, folklore, music, drama, etc.)
5. *Language.*

The outline of the *Notes and Queries* distinguishes between "Social Anthropology" and "Material Culture," dividing the former as follows:

1. *Social Structure* (e.g., territorial arrangement, sex and age, family, kinship, lineage and class, social stratification, etc.)
2. *Social Life of the Individual* (e.g., daily routine, training and education, life cycle from conception to marriage, sexual development, marriage, old age, death and disposal of the dead, etc.)
3. *Political Organization* (political systems, law, justice, property, etc.)
4. *Economics* (production, distribution, exchange, consumption)

5. *Ritual and Belief* (religious beliefs and practices concerning man, concerning supernatural beings and agencies, forms of ritual, magical beliefs and practices, witchcraft and sorcery, ritual medicine and therapy, ritual beliefs concerned with physical phenomena, with economic activities, with social structure)

6. *Knowledge and Tradition* (recording and communication, reckoning and measurement, cosmology, seasons, weather, calendar, geography and topography, vegetation, man and the animal kingdom, medicine and therapy, history and myths, stories, sayings and songs)

7. *Language* (gesture, sign-language and signals, phonology, grammar, semantics).

Many other schemes, of course, have been proposed. The functionalists base their schemes on basic needs and corresponding responses. E. T. Hall presents an interesting outline in table form in *The Silent Language* (1959:222–223). The most comprehensive outline devised so far is that of the Human Relations Area Files (*Outline of Cultural Materials*, G. P. Murdock, et al., New Haven, 1961, fourth edition). The latter system may very well be adopted with some modifications by the missionary for his own collection of data. The following is a small sample of the 2000 titles, broken down to 88 categories. The Files make no attempt to unite the major units into more comprehensive categories that would more closely correspond to the general notion of "aspects" or "universals."

19 Language
  191 Speech
  192 Vocabulary
  193 Grammar
  194 Phonology
  195 Stylistics
  196 Semantics
  197 Linguistic Relationships
  198 Special Languages
20 Communication
  201 Gestures and Signs
  202 Transmission of Messages
  etc.
22 Food Quest
  221 Annual Cycle
  222 Collecting
  223 Fowling
  224 Hunting and Trapping
  etc.

23 Animal Husbandry
  231 Domesticated Animals
  232 Applied Animal Science
  233 Pastoral Activities
  234 Dairying
  235 Poultry Raising
  etc.
24 Agriculture
  241 Tillage
  242 Agricultural Science
  243 Cereal Agriculture
  244 Vegetable Production
  etc.
77 Religious Beliefs
  771 General Character
  772 Cosmology
  773 Mythology
  etc.

DETERMINANTS OF CULTURE

To return to our original problem — why should all cultures on the one hand have the same over-all framework and on the other be unique, each with its infinitude of differences? Although anthropologists have not been able to give us a fully satisfactory answer, they have successfully isolated a number of factors that cast considerable light on the problem. Kluckhohn has summed up the solution by saying that all cultures constitute so many somewhat different answers to essentially the same questions posed by human situations (1953:520).

To most anthropologists of the nineteenth century, Darwin's theory of evolution was a "universal law," a very handy form of magic, a kind of hocuspocus that could explain almost any scientific problem, including the present one concerning the paradoxical variability of cultures on the one hand and their uniformity on the other. Another early, oversimplified solution was Adolf Bastian's theory of "elementary ideas" (Elementargedanken): since all men have the same inborn "ideas," their behavior has to be fundamentally the same. The differences in the ways of man were attributed to external stimuli of the particular "geographic provinces." Thus inventiveness of man was overemphasized while historical contacts and consequent borrowings (except in higher stages of cultural development) were discounted as relatively unimportant. Some anthropologists, on the other hand, well into the twentieth century and the present time, overemphasized historical contacts, underestimating human inventiveness and other factors — the so-called "diffusionists." Others, again, overemphasized the influences of physical environment on human behavior (Ratzel and the environmental determinists). Others were blind to everything except "universal social laws" (the Durkheimians). Simplicity of hypothesis is desirable whenever possible, but simplicity is not in itself a valid criterion for judging scientific fact. The common framework of cultures and their uniqueness — their paradoxical uniformity and variability — should not be attributed to any single a priori dogma; for, not one but many factors are responsible for the paradoxical situation under discussion.

The Biological Basis of Human Ways

Whatever man thinks, feels, says, or does is somehow based on or at least modified by his biological and instinctive makeup. How-ever, biological determinism, which attributes every aspect of hu-man behavior to instinct, is naïve. It is quite true that there is a very close connection between the instinct of hunger and human subsistence patterns, between sex drives and family life, but instinct by itself can never explain culture. I eat because I am hungry, but the fact that I eat at or about 7:00 a.m. or that I eat corn flakes and milk, bacon and eggs, toast, coffee and a roll at this particular time does not depend on any instinct or genes but on my American training.

That man's biological makeup is one of the bases of human ways is self-evident. All societies without exception, for example, need food, drink, and rest; all normal human beings must urinate and defecate. In response to such needs all societies have developed nutritional and other corresponding adaptations. There is also the universal instinct in man to play, to learn, and to defend himself. Sex, too, is a biological necessity for the continuation of the human species. Sex calls for approved ways of behavior and corresponding sanctions. Such approved ways and sanctions are as common as sex itself. All men go through the same phases of life: infancy, child-hood, puberty, youth, adulthood, and old age. Consequently, all societies, regardless of their otherwise distinct ways, have modes of behavior that are similar inasmuch as they are associated with the same problems, e.g., nourishment, infant care, child training, court-ship, marriage, and care for the aged. All mankind must cope with time, place, and quantity because all human beings are biological entities. All men, too, are subject to accidents, disease, injury, and death, calling for ways of healing bruises, curing diseases, avoiding danger, and of disposing of corpses. In short, *man's biological consti-tution gives rise to problems that are common to all societies; such common problems are a partial reason for the common framework of cultures.*

Biological similarities, therefore, do explain to some extent the similarities in the over-all design of cultures. But does it follow that biological differences are responsible for cultural differences? What influence, if any, does race have on cultural patterns and the uniqueness of cultures?

Culture is a societal, not racial possession. Racial traits or genes as such are not culture determinants, or, at least, there is no posi-tive evidence that they are. A society as well as a culture may include a variety of distinct races. In Germany, for example, we find so-called Alpine and Nordic types, distinct Caucasoid races; however, culturally a Nordic is undistinguishable from his Alpine compatriot. Moreover, within a given race one will find a relatively wide variety of physical types, since "race" is only a classification of biological traits based on averages. Despite such individual differences within the same race, individuals learn the way of life with more or less equal ease or difficulty. The fact is that any normal human being, regardless of race, is able to master the way of life of any society whatsoever, provided he is given an equal opportunity. A Korean child in an American orphanage from infancy will be culturally indistinguishable from his American playmates, speaking with a perfect American accent, using the same forceful slang, hitting as many home runs, and consuming as many lollipops per hour as any normal American youngster; in a word, the Korean orphan will speak, think, feel, act, have the same interests, and master the same skills as any normal American orphan. African languages have "exotic" speech sounds not on account of the large lips characteristic of Africans but on account of the particular cultural conditioning. An Oriental with his diminutive nose might with just as much right and logic conclude that Frenchmen and Americans tend to speak through their noses "because French and American noses are so large." The African has "rhythm in his bones" only because rhythm was put into his bones after he was born.

Although racism is one of Man's oldest and most widespread myths, racist philosophy as such is of relatively recent origin. Not Adolf Hitler but the nineteenth-century Frenchmen Arthur Gobineau and the English-German Houston Stewart Chamberlain are the inventors of the "superman." Their followers were many, and the volumes for which they are ultimately responsible have also been many. The chief topic discussed in such works centered around slave-trade in America, the authors, at first, justifying and encouraging slavery and then, after the Emancipation Proclamation, apologizing for the abolished practices. Such racist philosophers and apologists were to be found on both sides of the Atlantic: Hunt in England, for instance, and Knox and Nott in America. Racism broke out again after World War I, this time with the "classic" publications of Lothrop Stoddard and Madison Grant. The climax, of course, was reached under the Nazis with their "Aryan superrace," a form of racism that reached pathological proportions.

Racism seems to have received its most severe defeats soon after World War II, thanks especially to the program and policies of the United Nations, the almost complete disappearance of colonialism, the trend of underdeveloped nations toward complete independence and full equality with former colonial powers, the agitation of Communistic groups, the rise of nativistic movements and revolts, the activities of interracial organizations, the National Association for the Advancement of Colored People, and other Negro groups. Although the Negro in the United States has more than sufficient reason to be impatient, still he cannot deny the great strides made, evidenced, for instance, by the non-discriminatory policies of the U. S. armed forces, the effort made by many labor unions against discrimination, the assigning of capable Negroes to diplomatic and other important government posts, and civil rights legislation. Encouraging also are the statements and actions of not a few church leaders. The official pronouncement of the Catholic Bishops of the United States made at their annual meeting in November, 1958, for instance, is an excellent example of a realistic and balanced view of the complicated, two-sided problem, taking into full account the deep historical, political, economic, and social implications. There is also the fact that today the Negro has acquired a political significance, very seriously considered by the politicians of the North. One should also not leave out of the picture the fact that the average income of the American Negro could be rightly envied by some people of Europe, an income that is anything but that of a slave. The Negroes of the United States have a purchasing power which can be effectively used to threaten stores across the nation that discriminate against Negro employees. Finally, as the Secretary of State pointed out to a British audience decrying the unfortunate incident of 1962 in which the University of Mississippi tried to bar a Negro from becoming its first non-white student: "Do you realize that there are more Negroes attending American universities than there are Englishmen attending British universities?" The Negro has indeed traveled a long way since the days of slavery.

However, anyone acquainted with the actual conditions will hardly be satisfied with the progress made: there is still much to be done. The Council of Economic Advisors reported to the U. S. Congress on September 25, 1962, that America's gross material product could rise 2.5 percent "if the educational achievements of non-whites were fully utilized by removal of discrimination in employment" (*U. S. News and World Report*, October 8, 1962, p. 14). Naïve rationalization is still acceptable in some parts of America, as if "equal but separate" civil rights were possible. Racism is being justified even by extravagant interpretations of the Bible and from pulpits. Some Latter-Day Saints, for example, adhering closely to the teaching of the *Book of Mormon* and their traditional views, still believe that the Negroes are the cursed descendants of Laman and Lemuel, a wicked people of the Old Testament who dared to wage war against the children of Nephi, the favorites of God. God became very angry with Laman and Lemuel and marked them for all times with a darkly pigmented skin. In April, 1959, the Utah State Advisory Committee to the U. S. Commission of Civil Rights reported that:

> The Mormon interpretation of the curse of Canaan . . . together with unauthorized, but widely accepted statements by Mormon leaders in years past, has led to the view among many Mormon adherents that birth into any race other than white is a result of inferior performance in pre-earth life, and that by righteous living dark-skinned races may again become "white and delightsome" (*Time*, April 13, 1959, p. 96).

In recent years attempts have been made to prove "scientifically" that the Negro was inferior to the white man, and that he should become reconciled to the "fact," for there is no way of changing a person's genes. So much of this "scientific" nonsense has been published that at its annual convention in November, 1961, the American Anthropological Association took an official stand against such views.

It is, of course, biologically *possible* for one race to be superior to another and therefore physically more disposed for higher intelligence and special aptitudes. *De facto*, however, so far tests have not been able to substantiate any such suppositions, the report of the Governor of Alabama's scientific commission notwithstanding (W. C. George, *The Biology of the Race Problem*, 1962). Occasionally one may hear extravagant claims about Jewish mental superiority attributable to Jewish competitive spirit and inbreeding. Scientific testing so far has indicated that differences in learning powers and intelligence, whether we speak of the Negro or the Jew or the "Aryan," are more due to nurture than nature, more due to social environment and education than heredity.

Similarly, unprejudiced studies show that lack of cultural opportunities rather than race are responsible for the higher crime rate
for certain groups. Such character traits as laziness, unreliableness,
cruelty, lack of cleanliness, and other undesirable qualities are not
to be attributed to genes, even when such traits commonly occur
among one race more than another, but to economic, social, and
educational opportunities. Blue eyes, blond hair, long narrow head-
form, and other "Aryan" characteristics are as much a sign of
nobility, self-discipline, intelligence, bravery, or any other desirable
human quality as a heavy beard is a sign of literary genius.

Rather, all evidence points to the equality of races in intelligence, aptitude, and desirable qualities of character. Given an
equal opportunity, all races, despite the diversity of genes, could
attain the same level of culture, learning, morality, or technical
achievement. The following is a summary of the arguments and
tests used in studying the relationship between mental abilities
and race.

1) *Comparative Studies of the Brain.* So far no valid relationship between brain size, weight, and structure on the one hand and
mental capacity on the other has been established. It has been
discovered that some African groups have smaller and lighter brains
than Europeans and that the African brain has a less specialized
structure; however, we still have no evidence that would prove
beyond doubt that the African brain size and form actually lower
the mental capacity of the African below that of the European.
Dr. W. C. George's Alabama report also shows that the average
brain weight of whites is 100 grams, or 8 percent, greater than that
of the Negroes, that the frontal lobes of American white are larger
and more sulcified, more regular, and that the supragranular layer
of the cortex is 14 percent larger in whites than in Negroes. The
report, like other attempts in "scientific" racism, fails to show that
it is really the brain, not nurture, that is responsible for the lower
IQ of the American Negro and for the relatively greater incidence
of criminality among the colored.

2) *Sense Perception Tests.* Hearing, smelling, feeling, and color-
matching tests have shown that sense perception is practically the
same irrespective of race. The differences are attributable to training
rather than to the senses themselves. Thus, for example, the American Indians were keen observers of human and animal footprints.
The New Guinea highlanders seem to hear the sound of an airplane

long before the Europeans do, not because the white planter, government official, or missionary has poorer hearing but because the sound of a motor is "interesting" to the native, and everyone tends to pay attention to "interesting" sounds.

The following story illustrates this fact quite well. A farmer was once walking with his sophisticated, city-bred friend through a busy, noisy street. "Listen to the chirp of the cricket!" remarked the farmer. The "city-slicker" was dumfounded: how could anyone hear the feeble chirp of a cricket in the midst of such a racket? The farmer, however, insisted that he could hear the chirp quite distinctly, and to prove that he was not imagining things, he led his city-friend to a crack in the wall of a brick building — and there he was, the little chirper chirping just as the farmer had said. "But how can you hear a cricket in such noise? You farmers must have better ears," said the astonished urbanite. "I'll show you," replied the farmer, as he flipped a coin that bounced on the sidewalk. Suddenly a dozen people turned to the tinkle of the coin. "How can *they* hear the faint click of a dime in all that noise?" observed the farmer, and then answering the question himself he said, "You see, it all depends on what you were taught to be interested in" (Hoebel, 1956:175–176).

3) *Intelligence Tests.* Although one cannot deny the validity of modern intelligence tests, if properly conducted and evaluated, such tests become very inadequate when applied across cultures or subcultures. The results are greatly suspect because the difference in cultural background may be partly responsible for the type of answers given, and, at times, it is not an easy matter to prepare tests suited to the particular culture or subculture. The *word tests* of the Binet-Simon type have shown that the whites in America are able to score the highest marks, the Orientals come out second best, the Mexicans third, Indians fourth, and the Negroes last. Such results, however, may not be due to difference in intelligence but rather to difference in mastery of English and to differences in social background and educational opportunities. Language in particular is absorbed from one's cultural environment. If the results of such tests were to be attributed to genes, it would be difficult to understand why many individuals with Negro blood should score as high or even above the average white and why a considerable number of whites should have lower scores than the average Negroes. *Performance tests,* not requiring the use of words, are definitely

more suitable for cross-cultural testing. The Goddard-Silvester Board (consisting of different shaped pieces of wood that must be placed in appropriate holes), the Porteus Maze Test, and similar tests have given whites higher scores than the Bantu and Hopi. The results, however, can be rightly suspected on the grounds that the non-white children tested were considerably less familiar with pencils, toys, blocks, jigsaw puzzles, and other equipment called for in the tests. Even the idea of tests and the required haste were totally unfamiliar to the non-white children. The most promising tests for cross-cultural research are perhaps the *Projective Tests*, such as the Rohrschach and the T.A.T. These tests, however, are still only in the experimental stage, especially when applied across cultures and subcultures (cf. Lindzey, 1961; Kaplan, 1961; Firth, 1958:13–37).

We might best conclude the present discussion with the words of R. Firth:

> To say that the savage is inferior in mentality to ourselves, or that he has the mind of a child, indicates the ignorance and prejudice of the speaker. It is absurd at this stage of our knowledge to assert that we have proof that any particular group of people such as the Australian aborigines or South African Bantu, are by the nature of their minds for ever precluded from taking advantage of education, and from reaching that cultural level which we have attained (1958:37).

Physical Environment as a Culture Determinant

The study of the influences of habitat on biological organisms is known as Ecology. Human Ecology is interested in the influence of habitat on man's way of life — on his culture rather than his physical form. By "habitat" is meant especially the climate, altitude, physical features of the region, the flora, fauna, and natural resources. Human Ecology is also known as "Human Geography" or "Anthropogeography."

From ancient times — in fact, as far back as Hippocrates (460–357 B.C.) — the theory has been suggested again and again that the physical qualities of a region are primarily, if not exclusively, responsible for a people's culture and achievements. Like most extreme views, environmental determinism has a grain of truth too. That grain of truth is the fact that, although environment does not play the whole or even chief role in culture development, it does have a role to play.

The evidence against environmental determinism is threefold. (1) Similar cultures are often found in different physical environments. Polynesia is a classic example of such a situation: the cultures are very much alike, although the environments, owing to the vastness of the Polynesian area, are sometimes quite different. (2) On the other hand, different cultures may be found in identical or very similar environments. One need but compare the cultures in such geographically similar regions as the Central Australian desert and the Sahara; the Himalayas, the Swiss Alps, and the Caucasus; Alaska and Northern Siberia; European settlements on a South Sea Island and native villages only a few miles from these centers; or, finally, the southwest U. S. A., where we find the Navaho shepherds and the Pueblo farmers. (3) A culture can change while the geographic conditions remain the same. Food-gatherers have become food-producers in the same environment, as was the case with the American Indians of the Plains. A little over a century ago the culture along the Mississippi River and the Great Lakes was quite different from what it is today. Rapidly industrializing India, China, Indonesia, and Japan have taken on a new cultural appearance with no change in natural setting.

Environment, therefore, is not the paramount factor in molding cultures. Physical environment may *affect* cultures but does not *effect* them. (1) Physical environment sets certain material and technological limits to the particular mode of adaptation. The climate may, for instance, greatly limit the type of food produced; hunting and herding practices may be set in accord with the rhythm of the various seasons; the materials used in manufacturing artifacts will depend on the available resources; the techniques and materials for housing, gardening, hunting, clothing, art, and religion will be kept within the bounds of the particular environment. The Eskimo adapts himself to his environmental poverty by making very good use of every possible raw material, such as blubber, bones, walrus tusks, skins, scarce pieces of wood, and even snow. The influence of environment is limited mainly, but, as we shall see, not exclusively, to materials and techniques. (2) Environment may, moreover, set a certain limit to experience, knowledge, contact, and interaction with other groups, and therefore may affect also the philosophy, religion, art, and social forms. Ideas expressed in art are frequently based on the natural characteristics of the area. The Sepik River artist of New Guinea finds his motifs in the fauna of the region, the alligators, birds, and fish, but somehow he never thinks of carving an elephant or polar bear. The South Sea Islanders and Africans get many of their ideas for their dances from the animal life that surrounds them. The Supreme Being of the Asiatic pastoralists is the Sky God. In the vast, open steppeland nothing seems so mighty and all-embracing as the heavenly vault stretching on all sides from horizon to horizon. Harsh living conditions may encourage certain religious rites, giving them a special form and function corresponding to the physical environment: in arid regions, for example, prayers and sacrifices may be offered especially for rain. Natural barriers, such as mountains, rivers, and oceans may isolate a people, allowing very little contact with the outside world, greatly limiting the amount of diffusion that might take place.

No matter to what degree culture may be dependent on environment, man is never a submissive slave of his habitat; rather, man tends to become the master of Nature. As Malinowski expressed it in his article "Culture" in the *Encyclopedia of the Social Sciences*, there is no such being as a true *Naturmensch*, a human being that freely submits to Nature. Man, no matter how primitive and no matter how harsh the physical world about him, is a maker of tools and implements, the weapons which he as a rational being uses in his struggle with Nature. His mastery over Nature is proportional to his technological advancement. Thanks to our present-day technological knowledge and skill, explorers and scientists are able to live in the Antarctic in relative comfort, despite the subzero weather and the icy blasts sweeping across the world's most lifeless continent. European settlers and officials in tropical Africa and the Pacific may enjoy the comforts of electric appliances, such as refrigerators and air conditioners. Immense dams have been constructed and the most arid lands are now artificially watered by means of great feats of irrigational engineering. Sterile soils are made fertile, exhausted farmlands enriched; new plants are being developed and propagated, plants that are far more nourishing and far more suitable for the particular climate. It may be quite true that environment helps mold man's ways (his culture), but it is also true that man molds the physical world in which he lives. Perhaps the most important publication on this facet of culture is the result of a symposium held in 1955 on human utilization of habitat, a publication with the appropriate title of *Man's Role in Changing the Face of the Earth* (W. L. Thomas, ed., Chicago, 1956;

see also the December 28, 1960, symposium of the American Association for the Advancement of Science held in New York and published in *American Anthropologist*, LXIV [1962], 15–59). Whether man has at his disposal advanced applied science or only simple implements, he is somehow able to answer with confidence even the challenges of the severe physical environments of the frozen North and the arid deserts of Africa and Australia. The losses may indeed be great and the battle difficult, but somehow man, not the environment, turns out to be the victor.

Human Psychology as a Culture Determinant

The sensitive and rational equipment of man are the same irrespective of race, physical environment, or culture. All human beings have the same inherited instincts, the same senses, the same emotions of fear, joy, love, hate, pride, shame; all human beings have memories and reasoning powers; all human beings have symbolic behavior and are able to learn and to form habits. The operation of this psychological mechanism is the same for all; psychological "laws" are transcultural and transracial, as true of the Stone Age primitive as of the most civilized and intellectual societies of Europe and America. This universal agreement in psychological equipment and operation is, without doubt, greatly responsible for the common structure of cultures, while the uniqueness of cultures is partly explained by the uniqueness of the psychological "starting-points" (see pp. 157–161). The responses to the so-called integrative needs, as explained by the functionalists (see pp. 178–179), throw still further light on the paradox.

Social Needs as a Culture Determinant

To what extent the social or derived needs explain the variability and uniqueness of cultures has been sufficiently shown above (see pp. 176–177).

Historical Accidents as Determinants

Responsible more than anything else for the great variety of cultures throughout the world are the numberless historical events of each society — the extraordinary personalities, factions, wars, pestilences, and especially the culture contacts and the resulting diffusion. Such historical events have differed from society to society, and the consequent modifications of cultures have likewise differed from society to society. Moreover, modifications do not depend only on the particular experience but also on the interplay of all former experiences that have been handed down from generation to generation. The variability of cultures, therefore, is quite understandable in the light of historical facts.

The more we know about the history of culture, the better will we be able to understand why cultures are what they are. Archaeology has successfully unveiled many a mystery of man's cultural past. Modern Ethnohistory is also making satisfactory headway. Perhaps the greatest proponent of the historical approach to the understanding of cultures was Father Wilhelm Schmidt (see pp. 47–49, 52, 208). Whether the anthropologists of today accept his culture-historical method and conclusions or not, they must share his concern about culture-historical goals. A knowledge of culture without a knowledge of its history will always be a very imperfect knowledge indeed.

In concluding the discussion on the determinants of culture it might be well to point out that: (1) anthropologists do not as yet know or claim to know *all* the determinants of culture; (2) as intimated above, additional cultural uniqueness arises from the fact that the various culture determinants are interrelated and cross over generations; (3) some universal similarities may be due to the so-called principle of limited possibilities. The classical example of the principle is that of the oar. Oars, wherever they may be found, are fundamentally similar in material and construction, because they can hardly be otherwise. In order to be a good, practical oar, it must be of the right size, that is, neither too long nor too short, neither unwieldy nor too small to provide the necessary leverage; nor should it be too heavy and unable to float; moreover, the oar must be of a handy thickness on one end and have a blade on the other.

SUMMARY AND SELECTED MISSIOLOGICAL APPLICATIONS

Summary

Cultures are what they are — similar in basic framework and unique in detail — not on account of any single determinant. There are many determinants involved, an interplay of determinants that continues from generation to generation, each generation contributing its share to the development of the culture. The chief determinants are man's common biological, social, and psychological needs and makeup, his physical environment, and especially the numberless unique historical accidents. Cultures are "so many somewhat distinct answers to essentially the same questions posed by human biology and by the generalities of the human situation" (Kluckhohn, 1953:520).

Selected Missiological Applications

1. THE MISSIONARY AND THE PHYSICAL ENVIRONMENT

The prime concern of the Church will always be the spiritual needs of Man. However, the Church cannot be indifferent to the difficult and often bitter struggle of a people with its unsympathetic physical environment. Through educational programs, co-operation, and expert guidance the religious worker must be in the forefront in Man's attempt to cope with the problems of climate, food, and health. In the words of Pope John XXIII:

> We have today an undeniable duty towards men, in justice and charity, to do everything possible to ensure the subsistence of undernourished peoples, to develop everywhere a more reasonable exploitation of the riches of the soil and underground for the benefit of a rapidly-growing world population . . . (Message to the Semaine Sociale of Angers, July, 1959).

It was for this reason that Pius XII urged future missionaries not to be satisfied with purely ecclesiastical disciplines, however important such a training may be:

> Let them learn besides those specialized disciplines and sciences which are calculated to be highly useful for them later on when they will be heralds of the gospel among foreign peoples. . . . Let them be sufficiently instructed in the facts and methods of medicine, of agriculture . . . and other similar sciences (Evangelii Praecones:31).

2. THE MISSIONARY AND RACIAL PREJUDICE

Although missionaries are usually the ones that are least prone to be anti-racial — or, at least, they so imagine — they nevertheless cannot escape the influence of the prejudiced views of others and that of their own ethnocentrism. This hidden influence is betrayed in various ways. (1) Sometimes one hears even so-called experienced missionaries claim that their people have "the mentality of a child," a belief that is rooted in racial prejudice rather than based on objective inquiry. A few personal reflections might best illustrate what is meant. I have no doubt that the illiterate Stone Age primitives of New Guinea have more than once said the very same thing of me and perhaps of all the sophisticated whites they have met: "He has the mentality of a child!" When walking through unfamiliar territory and suddenly caught in a rainstorm I invariably did not know where to seek shelter; I had to ask someone or follow the crowd — very much like a New Guinea child. When I was thirsty I had to ask my carriers whether the unfamiliar stream we happened to be crossing was polluted or whether the water was used for drinking — a question even a small child would be ashamed to ask. When I had to cross treacherous mountain streams I had to hold on to someone who was used to crossing rapids and who found no difficulty in leaping from one slippery stone to another — again like a helpless New Guinea child. When I was tempted by a fruit along the trail I had to ask if it was edible or not — a fact any small child of walking age should know. I once had Stone Age adults laugh to my face when I made the "childish" suggestion that the builders of a house high up in the mountains use a certain type of grass for thatching which I had found useful when building my house, some 2000 feet lower. The fact was that such grass — as every New Guinea child knows — just does not grow at such an altitude. In a word, anyone has "the mentality of a child" in matters foreign to his culture. Children of primitives could put most American scout masters to shame in such basic boy-scout arts as tying knots, starting a fire, and tracking. Simple peoples may have "the mentality of a child" only as far as Western technology is concerned, but what about their survival techniques? their art? their religious and ceremonial life? What about their mastery of the social order and their complicated social organization? (2) Another way in which the religious worker betrays his racial prejudice is through his paternalistic attitude and behavior. Paternalism is an attitude of pity driving the missioner to do everything for his people rather than to teach them how to help themselves. Endless hours spent bandaging wounds and distributing medicines cease to be charity if no effort is made to teach the people how to avoid the wounds and sicknesses they come to have healed. Paternalism is not charity; rather, it is a disguised form of racial superiority and is usually recognized as such by the local people. They accept your gift but hate you for it. (3) Native leadership and partnership with the local people have not always been fostered with the enthusiasm that they merit (see pp. 104–108, 230–239). a fact that again betrays the missioner's racial prejudice. Undesirable traits of character making the local people unsuitable for partnership and leadership are consciously or unconsciously attributed to genes rather than to a lack of educational opportunities — to nature rather than nurture — resulting at best in a half-hearted attempt to develop a native leadership and to share responsibility.

SELECTED READINGS

1. **The Common Framework of Cultures**

    * 1) G. P. Murdock, "The Common Denominator of Cultures," in *The Science of Man in the World Crisis* (Linton, ed.), pp. 123–142.
      2) M. J. Herskovits, *Man and His Works*, pp. 229–240.
    * 3) C. Kluckhohn, "Universal Categories of Culture," in *Anthropology Today* (Kroeber, ed.), pp. 507–523.
      4) E. T. Hall, *The Silent Language.*

2. **Determinants of Culture**

      1) R. Firth, *Human Types*, pp. 13–37.
      2) W. M. Krogman, "The Concept of Race," in *The Science of Man in the World Crisis* (Linton, ed.), pp. 38–62.
      3) O. Klineberg, "Racial Psychology," in *The Science of Man in the World Crisis* (Linton, ed.), pp. 63–77.
      4) H. L. Shapiro, "Society and Biological Man," in *The Science of Man in the World Crisis* (Linton, ed.), pp. 19–37.
      5) M. F. Ashley Montagu, *Man's Most Dangerous Myth: The Fallacy of Race.*
    * 6) R. Benedict, *Race: Science and Politics.*
    * 7) C. Kluckhohn, *Mirror for Man*, pp. 102–144.
      8) J. Barzun, *Race: A Study in Modern Superstition.*
      9) O. C. Cox, *Caste, Class and Race.*
    * 10) K. Little, *Race and Society.*
      11) A. L. Kroeber, *Anthropology*, pp. 124–205, 572–582.
      12) A. Rose, *The Roots of Prejudice.*
      13) S. Patterson, *Colour and Culture in South Africa: A Study of the Cape Coloured People Within the Social Structure of South Africa.*
      14) G. Myrdal, *An American Dilemma.*
      15) W. L. Thomas, ed., *Man's Role in Changing the Face of the Earth.*

336 DYNAMICS OF CULTURE

16) R. Piddington, *An Introduction to Social Anthropology*, Vol. 2, pp. 443–482.
17) M. Bates, "Human Ecology," in *Anthropology Today* (Kroeber, ed.), pp. 700–713.

3. "Scientific" Racism

1) J. Comas, " 'Scientific' Racism Again?" *Current Anthropology*, II (1961), 303–340.
2) J. Comas, "More 'Scientific' Racism," *Current Anthropology*, III (1962), 284, 289–302.
3) M. Nash, "Race and Ideology," *Current Anthropology*, II (1962), 285–302.
4) C. Putnam, *The Road to Reversal*.
5) C. Putnam, *Race and Reason: A Yankee View*.
6) W. C. George, *The Biology of the Race Problem*.

REVIEW QUESTIONS

1. What does the "basic similarity" of cultures consist in? What terms are used to express this "similarity"? (p. 317)
2. To what extent is man's biological makeup responsible for the basic similarity and the uniqueness of cultures? (pp. 321–328)
3. Which of the following statements do you believe to be true? Give your reasons.
    1) Africans are naturally lazy.
    2) Gypsies are born-musicians.
    3) The American Negro has rhythm in his bones.
    4) The Zulu have unpronounceable speech sounds because their vocal organs are quite different from ours.
4. Give a short history of racism. (pp. 323–324)
5. What is the status of racism today? (pp. 324–326)
6. What are some of the tests used in studying the relationship between mental abilities and race? What have the results of such tests so far revealed? (pp. 326–328)
7. What is Human Ecology? (p. 328) To what extent does the physical environment determine culture? (pp. 329–331) Why is environmental determinism untenable? (p. 329)
8. How does human psychology affect culture? (p. 331) Social needs? (p. 331)
9. What are historical accidents? Are they important determinants of culture? Why? (pp. 331–332)
10. Are missionaries sometimes racially prejudiced? How is the prejudice shown? (pp. 333–335)
11. What is the principle of limited possibilities? (p. 332)

TOPICS FOR CLASSROOM DISCUSSION AND PAPERS

1. Debate: It is possible for a highly motivated, zealous, charitable, sympathetic missionary to be racially prejudiced.
2. Man is not a slave but master of his physical environment. Read a monograph about the Eskimos, the pygmies of Central Africa, or the Australian aborigines and show how the people adjust themselves to a very adverse physical environment.
3. Describe the efforts of the modern missionary apostolate in regard to helping simple peoples to adjust themselves to difficult physical environments.
4. Will an American Negro missionary in Africa or Melanesia be more acceptable to the Africans and Melanesians than his white counterpart? Is his race an asset as far as identification with the people is concerned? Debate. Read, for instance, Harold R. Isaacs, "Back to Africa," *New Yorker Magazine*, May 13, 1961, reprinted in *Practical Anthropology*, X (1963), 71–88.

V.

EPILOGUE

CHAPTER THIRTEEN

THE CHURCH AND CULTURES

ONE of the chief problems facing the Second Vatican Council is to spell out in unmistakable terms the proper relationship between the Church and the local cultures. It is the same problem missionaries have been discussing from the time of the Apostles — the problem of accommodation. Although accommodation is perhaps the most frequently discussed subject in missionary circles, the concept needs considerably more clarification. Even missiologists treating the subject as experts in the field have, until now, been basing their descriptions and recommendations almost exclusively on Sacred Scriptures, papal documents, decisions and directives of the Sacred Congregation for the Propagation of the Faith, and Mission History (past experience and "common-sense"), with relatively little regard for anthropological concepts and principles. Although the sources just mentioned must at all times be held in high esteem when treating the subject of the relation between the Church and the local cultures, the problem is as much anthropological as it is theological. Accommodation, after all, is an accommodation between the Church (Theology) and the particular culture (Anthropology).

"Accommodation" may be defined as "the respectful, prudent, scientifically and theologically sound adjustment of the Church to the native culture in attitude, outward behavior, and practical apostolic approach." By "Church" is meant primarily the religious worker in the Missions and the authorities to which apostolic work is entrusted. This definition will now be analyzed and explained by bringing together the various concepts and principles treated in the preceding chapters — by a kind of synopsis of the present course. In so doing we shall recall: (1) the aims of accommodation, (2) its psycho-cultural and socio-cultural background, (3) its subject, (4) its object, (5) its limits, (6) the manner of accommodating, and (7) the difficulties involved.

THE AIMS OF MISSIONARY ACCOMMODATION

Justice

One of the most basic natural rights of a society is its right to its own culture, its right to its own national distinctiveness, its own character. As Pius XII so clearly expressed it:

> The right to existence, the right to the respect from others, the right to one's own good name, the right to one's own culture and national character . . . (these) are exigencies of the law of nations dictated by nature itself (Allocution, December 6, 1953, in *Acta Apostolicae Sedis*, XLX [1953], 794–803).

In other words, Pius XII places the right to one's own culture and national character on the same level with the right to one's own good name and existence itself. To deprive a people of this right would be a flagrant violation of justice, whether it be done by a selfish capitalist, a fanatical Communist, or a well-meaning missionary.

However, this premise of justice leads to a paradox; for, as we have seen again and again, the missionary is by his very vocation an agent of culture change (pp. 5–6, 183–186, 229–230). The saying that "a missionary is sent to pagan lands not to *change* cultures but to *preserve* them" must be taken with a rather large grain of salt, otherwise the saying becomes a nonsensical cliché. The greatest cultural transformation in the history of mankind was, after all, brought about by the First Missionary, Christ Himself, Who was sent precisely to be an Agent of Culture Change — to be "the Light of man" (John 1:4), "the Way, and the Truth, and the Life" (John 14:6), and to set the world on "fire" (Luke 12:49). The divine mission of the Church is none other than to continue the work of the First Missionary, to "make disciples of all nations" (Matt. 28:19), and to transform the world in accord with the Gospel without compromising the least "iota" of it (Matt. 5:13–19). The divine mission of the Church is to be an uncompromising agent of culture change, like Christ Himself.

Although the prime concern of the Church is a Kingdom that is "not of this world" (John 18:36), religion and morality remain essential aspects of any cultural inventory (see pp. 60–63, 73–74, 178). The Church cannot change the religion and moral life of a people without changing the particular culture; for, if a part is modified, the whole becomes thereby something different. The missionary, therefore, *is* an agent of culture change.

We have seen also that, although the Church's prime concern was the salvation of souls, the socio-economic betterment of peoples was also of special interest to Her, in fact, a "duty" (see pp. 9–11). Thus, the Church becomes an agent of change even in things of this world, not as a matter of choice but of obligation. Moreover, when describing the organization and dynamics of culture (Chapters Six to Eleven) we have seen how closely intermeshed the various aspects of a life-way actually are. It is, therefore, impossible to bring about changes in religion and morality without in some way affecting the entire organism, the entire culture. Sometimes, in order to bring about a change in religion and morality it may be necessary to bring about changes in other aspects of culture first (see pp. 148–154). Finally, as emphasized above, the most effective and least disorganizing approach to any culture change, religious or otherwise, is to work with the whole culture and with culture as a whole. In a word, whether missionaries like the label of "agent of culture change" or not, that is their vocation.

Missionary work, therefore, is a paradox: on the one hand, the missionary is required by natural law to respect the right of a people to its own culture and national character; on the other hand, he is commanded to transform the world. There is only one answer to this paradox — missionary accommodation. The first aim of accommodation between the Church and the local cultures, therefore, is not merely to be "obliging" or "accommodating," as the term might imply, but to be *just*.

Consistency With the Nature of the Church

Christ founded a visible society that was to have catholicity as one of its major and unmistakable marks.

> The Catholic Church is supranational by her very nature. . . . She cannot belong exclusively to any particular people, nor can she belong more to one than to another. . . . She cannot be a stranger anywhere (Pius XII, Christmas Message, 1945).

Or in the eloquent words of John XXIII: the Church

> . . . does not identify herself with any particular culture not even with the occidental culture to which her history is so closely bound. Her mission belongs to another order, to the order of the religious salvation of man. Rich in her youthfulness which is constantly renewed by the

breath of the Holy Spirit, the Church is ever ready to recognize, to welcome and indeed to encourage all things that honor the human mind and heart even if they have their origin in places of the world that lie outside this Mediterranean basin which was the providential cradle of Christianity (*Princeps Pastorum*:16).

The task of the Church, therefore, is to make Africans into *African* Christians, Indians into *Indian* Christians, Japanese into *Japanese* Christians — not into American or European Christians. The only way to accomplish this task is through accommodation.

Missionary Effectiveness

The third aim of accommodation is no less important than the first two mentioned — apostolic effectiveness. In fact, the most basic assumption of a course in Applied Missionary Anthropology is that the cross-cultural approach to the apostolate constitutes not only the least disorganizing approach but also the most effective (Chapter One). In fact, any approach that is not culturally relevant and actually geared into the particular life-way of the people is both theologically as well as scientifically suspect (see pp. 39–46). Communists and other would-be reformers may have other techniques at their disposal, especially politics and force, but the missionary has only one basic tool — effective communication. Throughout the present course (almost on every page of it) the necessity of communicating on the *native* wavelength has been stressed. Accommodation is the tuning of our missionary approach, attitude, and outward behavior to the proper frequency. No matter what art or science a religious worker might wish to apply, whether he have the spiritual or the temporal advancement of the people in mind, whether the art or science be sacred or profane, he must apply that art or science in cultural perspective, that is, with the way of life of the particular society ever before his eyes (Luzbetak, 1962:64).

THE PSYCHO-CULTURAL AND SOCIO-CULTURAL BACKGROUND OF ACCOMMODATION

It was with purpose that much time and space were devoted to the description of the process of learning a culture, known as "enculturation" (see pp. 73–79, 82–103). We have all been born into a particular system of thought, attitude, and action. Enculturation has been so successful that, as a rule, the individual's thoughts, feelings, and actions seldom conflict with those of his society. The lessons learned during the process of enculturation have been mastered so well that they become a kind of "second nature." To part from this "second nature" calls for considerable violence to self. To make matters even more difficult, the constant presence of social controls, such as rewards, praise, ridicule (see pp. 301–304) come into play. Then there is also the fact that culture is structured (see Chapter Six) and based on an inner logic that pervades the entire life-way, with one socially acquired habit of thought, attitude, and behavior intermeshed with and mutually fortified by others. Accommodation, which takes all these culturological facts into consideration, is, therefore, not a matter of choice but of necessity.

THE SUBJECT OF ACCOMMODATION

Who is to accommodate to whom? Our definition of accommodation (see p. 341) uses the Church as point of reference, but by no means does the definition imply that accommodation is one-sided, for there are certain limits beyond which the Church will not and may not go (see pp. 95–103, 183–186, 347–351). Accommodation is mutual: it is not a one-sided condescension, for the Church goes as far as possible while expecting the new Christian community to come the rest of the way. The Church accommodates to the local culture; the new Christian community accommodates to the Church, and that at a great price. The Kingdom of God demands of the new Christian that he sell all that he has so as to be able to buy the "pearl of great price" (Matt. 13:44–46). In fact, entrance into the Kingdom of God may require of the community that its members "cut off limbs" and "pluck out eyes" (cf. Matt. 5:29–30).

THE OBJECT OF ACCOMMODATION

The object of accommodation is as broad as culture itself — but "culture" as understood in Anthropology. "Culture," the object of accommodation, means much more than most missionaries and even some missiologists imagine. To describe the object of accommodation as "the garb of the Church," the pure externals that are "not essential" to Christian living, is too vague and too limited and seems to imply that accommodation is one-sided. Or again, according to the notion of some, the object of accommodation is "culture" indeed, but only in the sense of "the lofty things of human life," such as art, music, science, philosophy, and religion. Culture does include "the lofty things of human life," but the object of accommodation is much broader, in fact, as broad as human life itself. This fact explains why so much emphasis has been placed on the nature of culture (Chapters Three to Five), the organization of culture (Chapters Six to Eight), and the dynamics of culture (Chapters Nine to Eleven); for, *all that has been said about the nature, organization, and dynamics of culture falls under the object of accommodation.* Any other type of accommodation is superficial and sometimes hardly worthy of the name.

First of all, culture has an inventory. The *total* inventory must be regarded as the object of accommodation — the entire physical, social, and ideational adaptation of a society and all that the total life-way embraces — literally, "all things to all men" (1 Cor. 9:19–22).

But, as we have seen, culture is more than just the manifest or overt inventory of a life-way: it is more than such manifest forms as food getting, housing, clothing, ornamentation, eating habits, etiquette, gardening techniques, family, ownership, trade, government, war, law, philosophy, magic, mythology, science, music, language, and ritual. All these items have meanings, usages, and functions besides form; and meanings, usages, and functions are objects of missionary accommodation too (see pp. 139–140, 215–217). In other words, culture, as we have seen, is anything but a heap of unrelated parts; culture is an "organism," a system (see pp. 135–190). Accommodation, therefore, calls for an adjustment in attitude, outward behavior, and approach also in regard to the peculiar structuring of the local life-way; the Church must accommodate to the local culture also insofar as it is a *system* of interconnected subsystems and these in turn made up of interwebbed functionally organized elements. The Church must, therefore, adjust herself not only to distinct, random items, but to functioning and integrated parts. Dwellings, gardens, weddings, funerals, magico-religious patterns, and everything else in the cultural inventory must at all times be viewed in all their details and with all their meanings, usages, and functions, as they are structured or peculiarly interlocked with one another. The local culture, in turn, when adjusting itself to the requirements of the Gospel must likewise make the adjustment not in terms of isolated items but as parts of a living organism. Accommodation would be the simplest thing in the world if its object were not to include the structure of cultures and if it would involve only isolated culture elements. It would be only then that one would blindly follow the missiological rule of thumb "Retain whatever is neutral or good in the native culture!" On account of cultural linkages, even innocent and so-called "good" or "neutral" elements may have to be removed, substituted, or in some way modified.

Underlying the culture is the "configuration," "philosophy," "psychology," or "soul" of the people (Chapter Seven). In other words, accommodation refers also to the relationship between the Church and the local underlying assumptions, values, and goals.

Finally, the object of accommodation includes not only the whole culture and culture as a whole but also the *actual* and *living* culture — the ever-changing life-way (Chapters Nine to Eleven). Accommodation is not opposed to acculturation or culture change as such. On the contrary, the object of accommodation is the culture as it actually is, today and now, and it supposes due appreciation of future foreseeable trends and needs. Since some decades ago the Chinese preferred European architecture of the time, the missionaries would indeed have acted foolishly if they had insisted on the ancient non-functional design of the Imperial Court buildings as did the Apostolic Delegate (McGuire, 1962:33). If everything else would make sense, and if a tribe in a Central African jungle were to ask me to erect a Gothic cathedral for them, I would build a Gothic cathedral if that were what the actual culture appreciated and demanded. Modern Japan wants ultra-modern architecture, and accommodation would in this case seriously consider ultra-modern construction and design. In a word, the object of accommodation is not an ancient, obsolete way of life but the actual, living, changing culture.

THE LIMITS OF ACCOMMODATION

Accommodation does not, of course, require the Church or her missionaries to "go native" (see pp. 97, 99, 189–190). The policy does not imply that everything Western or non-native is to be tabooed from the African or Asian churches. The Kingdom that *Christ* founded and the Gospel that was *His* must be preached by the Church. Since He did not establish His Kingdom on earth in a vacuum but among the Chosen People and in given historical circumstances, His doctrine, although universally valid, was clothed in a Judaic and Hellenic garb. If Christianity, when introduced among a people, were to be stripped of all that was foreign, the Bible itself would have to be outlawed, bread and wine could not be used for Mass, and the Church could not have a visible head residing in a foreign country. Accommodation calls merely for *nativization*. It requires of the Church and her missioners perfect understanding or "empathy" (see pp. 95–97, 100–103) and, as far as possible, identification with the local cultures. Just as Christ "emptied himself" (Phil. 2:6–7) of the ways most natural to Him (the Son of God became the Son of Man), so the missioner must be willing to sacrifice his ways and values in favor of those of his people. The Church must go *as far as possible* in adjusting her demands and expectations to the ways and values of the new Christian community, for that is the meaning of "identification." The important words here are "as far as possible." *The limits set by Christ — Faith (which includes the nature of the Church), prudence, reason, and the goals of the apostolate — are the limits of accommodation.* Whatever is imprudent or unreasonable can never be the object of accommodation. To go against the dictates of prudence and reason would militate against the missionary policy of adaptation. To restrict one's medication to folk medicine when more sophisticated medicines are available would not be prudent; never to wash simply because the local people never care to wash would likewise be unreasonable. Nor would it be prudent for a missionary to adopt native ways or to insist on traditional practices if the people themselves would object. The local culture will generally tell the American missionary how American or un-American he should be in his external adoption of native ways and values as far as his own behavior is concerned (see pp. 99–100). Missionaries in the South Seas do not run around in a gee-string, among other reasons because the people do not want them to. They do not chew betel nut for the same reason. The expectations of the people are an important norm of prudence to be considered in judging the limits of accommodation.

Prudence also requires proper timing of whatever is done, the introduction of novelties not excluded. The only sound pedagogical procedure is from the known to the unknown, from the felt-needs to the still-unfelt needs, from the appreciated to the still-unappreciated (see pp. 65–68, 287–291). This is particularly true of the indirect apostolate: education, health programs, and agricultural improvements call for the prudent accommodation of proper timing (see pp. 148–154). Although in regard to the essentials of faith and morals there is no room for only a partial introduction of Christianity (through compromise or by hiding the disagreeable doctrines from the prospective convert), nevertheless, instruction in Christian Doctrine must progress along sound pedagogical lines, which presupposes, above all, proper sequence or timing. Such proper timing enables the new Christian to grasp the otherwise-confusing doctrines and helps prevent the formation of the only-too-frequent hodgepodge of Christianity and paganism.

Another important limitation to actual adoption and approval of native ways and values that needs further clarification is Faith. As a general rule (and only as a general rule, for all the other limitations must be considered too), customs that are ethically good or neutral, i.e., do not go contrary to the teaching of the Church or her discipline, are to be upheld, regardless of what the feelings of the missionary may be. This rule of thumb, considerably oversimplified, might be more accurately stated by making use of the missiologist's triple distinction of (1) the essentials of Faith, (2) the externals of the Church, and (3) the garb of the Church (Couturier, 1960:xii–xiii, 131–132; Voss, 1946:22). Since the last two categories mentioned belong to the so-called "accidentals" and are of purely human origin, they should not be blindly insisted upon by the missionary or Church authorities but introduced with due consideration for native needs.

The Church has the strict obligation of preserving the deposit of Faith in its entirety and purity. No jot or tittle may be compromised, even if by so doing one could win over a whole nation to the Church or prevent a serious persecution or schism. The Church may not tolerate any beliefs or practices that are contrary to revealed truth; nor may she tolerate a double standard, one for mission lands and another for "mature" Christian countries. Thus, accommodation is never justified in regard to the worship of nature-spirits, promiscuity, or polygamy.

By "externals" or "exterior form" of the Church we mean the purely human aspects of the constitution of the Church and Canon Law. Such external unity does not per se enjoy precedence over the principle of accommodation in the sense that unity of Faith does. Factors contributing to external unity do not have an absolute value, e.g., the ritual, seminary curriculum, Latin, or celibacy; they do, however, have a *distinct* value, which Church authorities must weigh against the arguments favoring nativization. Just as nativization is not to be followed blindly, so the various factors contributing to external unity should not become a kind of fetish. Nevertheless, as far as the individual missionary is concerned, he has no choice but to carry out the official policy and law of the Church rather than his personal ideas. These purely human laws, after all, come from the legitimate authority of the Church, an authority that by reason of its universality is obliged to keep in mind not only local needs and advantages but also those of the whole Church. If this authority finds that such "externals" are vital to the universal Church, the missionary has no choice but to operate within the given framework. The authority that has given the missionary jurisdiction to carry on apostolic work has the right to set the limits within which the missioner (and the missionary-anthropologist) must operate (see p. 40). For this reason, recourse must be had to the Sacred Congregation for the Propagation of the Faith or the local Bishop or some other competent authority whénever, for the good of the apostolic cause or the welfare of the local people, the missionary feels it advisable to go beyond these official limits. These limits, although deserving the highest respect, are, however, not beyond questioning. In fact, if missionary activities are to make progress and if the particular needs of the time and place are to be duly respected, such purely human laws (however important they may seem) will be constantly re-examined by the Church, carefully re-evaluated, and wisely brought up to date rather than clung to blindly and uncompromisingly as to a dogma of faith.

The garb of the Church, as Father G. Voss, S.J., describes it, comprises "all the other features that make up the external appearance of the Church — for example, the means and methods of Christian instruction, various institutions of social work and Christian charity, non-liturgical religious celebrations and popular devotions, ecclesiastical art and architecture, and certain popular customs and civil institutions that make up part and parcel of the life of the individual in his concrete circumstances" (1946:22). As far as the garb of the Church is concerned accommodation has a free rein.

The final limitation to internal approval and external adoption of native ways is set by the aims of the apostolate. Even though a traditional pattern be regarded as good in itself, and not contrary to Faith or one of the other limitations mentioned above, accommodations may nevertheless be out of place if they lead to dangerous cultural or social disorganization, seriously delay Christianization or hinder its integration into the native life-way, or if they prove to be a serious drag on the missionary effort. For the same reason, whatever gives rise to syncretistic beliefs and practices is to be regarded as outside the area of accommodation.

MANNER OF ACCOMMODATING

On account of the extensiveness of the subject it is well-nigh impossible to summarize all that has thus far been said about the proper manner of accommodating. In fact, such a summary would be tantamount to a summary of the entire course. Accommodation, according to our definition, is an adjustment "in attitude, outward behavior, and practical apostolic approach" (see p. 341). By "attitude" is meant "empathy" and, whenever possible, internal acceptance or approval; by "outward behavior" is meant "actual adoption" of native ways. The "apostolic approach" referred to consists essentially in *directing* change, the direction being in the realm of ideas and by means of effective communication.

OBSTACLES TO ACCOMMODATION

Personal Structuring

At the root of most difficulties associated with accommodation is the difference in the enculturation of the missionary and the older churches on the one hand and the new Christian communities on the other (see Chapter Four).

Missionary Negativism

If the Church would have only a negative goal in the non-Christian world, the basic policy of accommodation would indeed be out of place. The fact is that the Church sends out her missionaries with a positive goal, rather than with a purely negative one. The modern apostle, true to his vocation, will see his task in the same light as Christ saw His, Who came "not to destroy but to fulfill" (Matt.

5:17). A missionary whose mind is completely occupied with the "pagan" culture's "falsehood," "immorality," "darkness," "depravation," and "blindness," who sees among his adopted people nothing but "spiritual misery," "sin," and "the night of heathenism" — such a missionary ought to have his spiritual eyes examined. His vocation and the task for which he was commissioned by the Church is something quite positive: to make the beautiful in the so-called "pagan" heart even more beautiful, to seek out the naturally good in order to make it supernaturally perfect, to present Christianity not as an enemy of the existing way of life but as a friend possessing the secret that will enable the non-Christian culture reach its God-intended perfection.

To see nothing but a depraved nature in a non-Christian heart may have been consistent with the teaching of the Reformation but is definitely not in accord with the teaching of the Catholic Church. As Pius XII put it in his 1945 Christmas message, the Church

> is placed in the center of history of the whole human race. . . . As Christ was in the midst of men, so, too, His Church, in which He continues to live, is placed in the midst of the peoples. As Christ assumed a real human nature, so too the Church takes to herself the fullness of all that is genuinely human, wherever and however she finds it, and transforms it into a source of supernatural energy.[1]

Timidity

It takes courage to be original, and accommodation calls for a considerable amount of originality. It also takes a considerable amount of humility to accept new ways. It is much easier to stay in a groove than to get out of it. Fear of making a mistake by accommodating to native ways and values is one of the most common obstacles to accommodation. The only one who will not make a mistake in carrying out the policy of missionary accommodation will be the missionary who never accommodates — but that is precisely the biggest mistake. Prudence and caution ever, timidity never! Msgr. J. Malenfant, O.F.M.Cap., speaking at a special conference on accommodation in India, expressed this thought as follows:

---

[1] Quoted from E. J. Murphy, S.J., "The Concept of Mission," in *The Global Mission of the Church*, Fordham University, 1962, p. II–4.

Let us repeat it often: to effect adaptation in a prudent manner, to avoid grave mistakes and false steps, one needs a deep Catholic sense, a good knowledge of Catholic history and tradition, especially of the first introduction of the faith in various countries. One needs also more than a minimum of theological and liturgical knowledge. One needs also a sense of discipline, detachment from personal views, and a knowledge of what the Holy See can and is willing to permit or not. But the fact that the task is difficult, and even perilous, is no reason why it should not be undertaken . . . (Rocha, 1957:48).

Timidity is, of course, often due to ignorance of native ways and values, and of matters cultural in general; in a word, timidity is often due to ignorance of basic concepts, principles, and techniques of Cultural Anthropology. It is an understandable fear but not a justifiable ignorance.

SELECTED READINGS

   * 1) J. J. Considine, M.M., *Fundamental Catholic Teaching on the Human Race*, pp. 59–75.
     2) C. Couturier, S.J., *The Mission of the Church.*
   * 3) G. Voss, S.J., "Missionary Accommodation," *Mission Academia Studies,* October, 1946.
     4) E. J. Murphy, S.J., *Teach Ye All Nations.*
     5) E. J. Murphy, S.J., "The Concept of Mission: Popes and Theologians," in *The Global Mission of the Church:* Proceedings of Fordham University Conference of Mission Specialists, January 19–20, 1962, pp. II, 1–5.
     6) P. C. Scharper, "Mission and Culture," in *The Global Mission of the Church,* pp. IV, 1–5.
     7) R. Duignan, "Early Jesuit Missionaries: A Suggestion for Further Studies," *American Anthropologist,* LX (1958), No. 4, pp. 725–732.
   * 8) M. D. W. Jeffreys, "Some Rules of Directed Culture Change under Roman Catholicism," *American Anthropologist,* LVIII (1956), 721–731.

∖ REVIEW QUESTIONS

1. Define "accommodation." (p. 341)
2. What are the chief aims of accommodation? (pp. 342–344)
3. Describe the triple (psychological, sociological, and culturological) background of accommodation? What makes accommodation necessary? (pp. 344–345)
4. Who is to accommodate to whom? (p. 345)
5. Describe the full object of accommodation. (pp. 345–347)

EPILOGUE

6. What are the limits of accommodation? (pp. 347–351)
7. What is meant by "the manner of accommodating"? (p. 351)
8. What are the chief obstacles to accommodation? (pp. 351–353)

TOPICS FOR CLASSROOM DISCUSSION AND PAPERS

1. Write a critical review of R. Duignan's article.
2. Write a critical review of M. D. W. Jeffrey's article.
3. Read one of the following biographies and write an article on the style of Jeffrey's:
   1) J. Broderick, S.J., St. Francis Xavier, New York, 1952;
   2) V. Cronin, A Pearl to India, New York, 1959;
   3) V. Cronin, The Wise Man from the West, New York, 1957;
   4) C. F. King, S.V.D., A Man of God: Joseph Freinademetz: Pioneer Divine Missionary, Techny, Ill., 1959.
4. Describe, analyze, and comment on a case study of accommodation, e.g., J. A. Loewen's "Good News for the Waunana," Practical Anthropology, VIII (1961), 275–278; A. F. Schaefer, S.V.D., "A Post Turns into the Cross," Worldmission, XI (1960–1961), No. 4, 41–47; H. Aufenanger, S.V.D., "Primitivity along the Sepik," Worldmission, XI (1960–1961), 58–68. Go through Mission Bulletin, Christ to the World, C.I.F. Reports for additional possibilities.
5. To what extent do you think we should encourage conservatism or a return to traditional patterns in a rapidly Westernizing society? Are you not inviting conflicts and disequilibrium in the culture and society? Do you agree with M. Berndt and Wm. A. Smalley in their "Modern Asians and Western Churches," Practical Anthropology, IX (1962), 134–136?
6. To what extent can St. Paul's methods be the modern apostle's? Times, after all, have changed, and some of his methods cannot be relevant today. Which ones? See, for instance, L. L. Noble, "Can St. Paul's Methods be Ours?" in Practical Anthropology, VIII (1961), 180–185. We are interested in anthropological arguments only.
7. Discuss the possibilities of accommodation in one or several of the following items, bringing in as many of the principles discussed in the present course as possible.
   1) The missionary's garb
   2) The nakedness of the local people
   3) Body ornamentation, tatooing, scarification, hair-do
   4) Habitation
   5) Use of fire as a religious symbol
   6) Food taboos; other taboos
   7) The caste system
   8) Local marriage impediments, wedding ceremonies, trial marriages, child marriages, polygamy
   9) Initiation rites; circumcision

10) Local prayer forms, style of language in prayer, posture in prayer, shoes and dress in prayer
11) Native architecture, art, music
12) Native philosophy
13) Leadership

8. Evaluate and compare the following studies, using as much as possible the terminology and theory of the present course:
   1) Jacques Maritain, "The Church and the Earth's Cultures," *Mission Studies*, I (1950), No. 1, 41–48;
   2) Christopher Dawson, *The Historic Reality of Christian Culture*, Harper and Brothers, New York, 1960;
   3) Adrian Hastings, ed., *The Church and the Nations*, Sheed and Ward, New York, 1959.

9. Evaluate and compare the following articles and papers:
   1) Most Reverend P. Carretto, "Missionary Adaptation to Local Conditions," *Asia* (formerly Hong Kong *Mission Bulletin*), XII (1960), 236–240;
   2) Bishop James E. Walsh, "Missionary Accommodation of Popular Cultures," Hong Kong *Mission Bulletin*, IX (1957), 215–221;
   3) Diarmuid O'Laoghaire, S.J., "The Church and National Culture," *Worldmission*, X (1959), No. 3, 40–45.
   N.B. see also the various articles in *Mission et cultures non-chretiennes: Rapports et compte rendu de la XXIXe semaine missiologie*, Louvain: Desclée de Brouwer, 1959.

10. What adaptations might be made regarding the Sacrament of Baptism? For ideas read:
    1) R. Sprinkle, M.M., "Post Baptism Practice," Hong Kong *Mission Bulletin*, VIII (1956), 563–567, 631–637;
    2) Paul Brunner, "The Liturgy of Baptism in the Missions," Hong Kong *Mission Bulletin*, XI (1959), 237–255;
    3) Boniface Luykx, "Adaptation of Liturgy in the Missions," Hong Kong *Mission Bulletin*, XI (1959), 786–794.

11. Enumerate a list of principles that might be useful in regard to adaptation in liturgical art. For some useful reading and examples see, e.g.:
    1) Carlito De Souza, "Christian Art in India," Hong Kong *Mission Bulletin*, X (1958), 651–657;
    2) J. Hofinger, "Liturgical Arts in the Missions," Hong Kong *Mission Bulletin*, X (1958), 1001–1010;
    3) *Liturgical Arts: A Quarterly Devoted to the Arts of the Catholic Church*, e.g., XXVI (1958).

12. Summarize and analyze culturologically (using terminology and concepts of the present course) William J. Coleman, M.M., *Latin-American Catholicism: A Self-Evaluation*, World Horizon Reports, No. 23, Maryknoll Publications or James (1959), Rycroft (1958), MacEoin (1962).

13. With what statements would you agree or disagree and which would

you modify in Rev. Isidore P. Umana's article "An African Priest Speaks Out His Mind," *Worldmission*, XI (1960), No. 2, 62–70? We are interested only in anthropological problems and arguments.

14. What general liturgical reforms do you think ought to be made for the new churches of Africa, Asia, and other mission areas? Give culturological reasons for any suggestion made. (Consult: J. Hofinger, ed., *Liturgy and the Missions: The Nijmegen Papers*, Kenedy and Sons, New York, 1960.)

15. As an applied anthropologist, evaluate the mission methods of Father Lebbe or Bartolomé de las Casas. See Rippy Nelson (1936); Hanke (1952); de Jaegher (1954). In what way do their methods agree or disagree with those of Father Charles de Foucauld? See, for instance, Voillaume (1955).

16. What anthropological concepts and principles treated in the present course have been applied in Pope John XXIII's *Pacem in Terris?*

TOPICAL BIBLIOGRAPHY AND ADDITIONAL READINGS*

Accommodation (missionary action in cultural context, the principle of cultural relevancy, missionary adaptation): Aufenanger (1960–1961); St. Augustine, *De doctrina christiana*; Berndt, Smalley (1962); Breda (1933); Bresillac (1956); Burke, T. (1957); Carretto (1960); Considine (1961); Cronin, V. (1955), (1959); Davis, J. (1945); Dooley (1960); Duignan (1958); Hastings (1959); Jeffreys (1956); King (1959); Kittler (1957); Maritain (1950); Murphy (1958); Nida (1954), (1960a), (1960b), (1960e); Noble (1962); Smalley (1956), (1958); Talbot (1956), (1961); Umana (1960); Walsh, J. (1957); Wonderly (1961); *Mission et cultures,* etc. (1959); Couturier (1960); Van Bekkum (1958); Amaladasan (1960); de Souza (1958); Bühlmann (1960), (1961). For more on accommodation, see following heads: Adjustment to Strange Culture, Administration, Applied Anthropology, Art and Music, Catechetics, Church Law, Communication, Education, Health, Industry, Liturgy, Mission Methods, Missiology, Missionary and Anthropology, Technical Assistance, Agronomy, Community Development. See also required or recommended readings in text, especially pp. 19–20, 353.

Acculturation: Beals, R. (1953); Berndt, R. (1951), (1954); Hogbin (1939), (1958); Hutchinson (1957); Kroeber, ed. (1953); Linton, ed. (1940); Redfield, Linton, Herskovits (1936); Segundo (1962); Siegel (1955); Spicer (1954); Spindler (1955); Tax, ed. (1952b); Thurnwald (1932), (1938); Thomas, W. L., ed. (1955); Useem, Useem (1955); Wagner (1936); Westermann (1949). See also under Culture Change.

Adjustment to a Strange Culture (difficulties experienced outside one's own cultural environment): Adams, D. (1959); Buckwalter, *et al.* (1960); Cleveland, Mangone, Adams (1960); McCoy (1962); Hall, E. T. (1959); Hall, Trager (1953); Hardy (1958); Hart (1962); Lederer, Burdick (1958); Mangone (1960); Masland (1960); Nida (1954), (1960e); Oberg (1960); Ong (1958); Reyburn (1960a); Rosengrant (1960); Spector, Preston (1961); Spector, *et al.* (1961); Smalley (1963). See also under Accommodation, Enculturation. See also Selected Readings pp. 20, 108–109, no. 2.

Administration (Anthropology in administration, government policies in cultural context): Barnett (1956); Brown, Hatt (1935); Buswell (1961); Drake (1960); Dubin (1951); Keesing (1953b); Leighton (1945), (1949); Mair (1957); Nadel (1947); Wagner (1936); Westermann (1949). See also under Applied Anthropology.

Agronomy (Anthropology and Agronomy, land reform problems, new dietary habits, etc.): Brossard (1961); Felton (1960); Food and Agriculture Or-

---

* See General Bibliography for complete titles and facts of publication.

ganization (1949a), (1949b); Howard (1947); *Land Reform, etc.* (1951); Sasaki, Adair (1952); Singh (1952); Spicer, E. H. (1952). See also under Health.

Applied Anthropology: Barnett (1942a), (1958); Brown, Hutt (1935); Caudill (1953); Foster (1952); Hackenberg (1962–1963); Lang (1961–1962); Mead, ed. (1953); Nash (1959); Paul (1953); Peattie (1958); Smith, E. W. (1934); Anthropological Society of Washington (1956). See also under Accommodation, Adjustment to Strange Culture, Agronomy, Art and Music, Communication, Community Development, Culture Change, Disorganization, Education, Group Relations, Health, Industry, Leadership, Linguistics, Migration, Nativism, Rapport, Social Structure, Specialization, Technical Assistance, Urbanization. See text, pp. 3–4, notes 2 and 3.

Archaeology (elementary notions and techniques): Braidwood (1948); Oakley (1949); Zeuner (1952). See also text, p. 53, Selected Readings, No. 8.

Art and Music (basic notions regarding primitive art and ethnomusicology, missionary adjustment and adaptation): Adam (1940); Boas (1927); Haselberger (1961); Nettl (1956); "Sacred Music, etc." (1957); de Souza (1958). See also the special issue of *Practical Anthropology*, "Developing Hymnology in New Churches," IX (1962), No. 6.

Bibliographies (some useful bibliographies dealing with subjects treated in present volume): Keesing (1953a); Leeson (1952); Siegel (1955); Smalley (1960a); Considine (1960); Macklin (1957); Vriens (1960); Polgar (1962). See also bibliographies after articles in Kroeber, ed. (1953) and below, p. 365.

Catechetics and Homiletics (geared to missionary needs): Grasso (1961); Hofinger (1957b), (1958a), (1959), (1961) (1962); Hofinger, ed. (1961); Hymes (1962); Bühlmann (1961); Ramsauer (1960). See also under Communication.

Church Law (adjustment of Canon Law to mission needs): de Reeper (1952), (1957).

Communication (intercultural communication, difficulties and principles): Bühlmann (1961); Capell (1959); Courtois (1956); Ewing, ed. (1958); de Foucauld (1960); Hall, E. T. (1959), (1960); Hymes (1962); Hofinger, *et al.* (1958); Nida (1947), (1952), (1954), (1960a), (1961c); Powdermaker (1955); Smith, B. (1957); Walsh, E. (1958); Pike (1954–1955). See also under Catechetics, Reinterpretation, Configuration.

Communism (psychological and socio-cultural approaches, what the missionary might learn from the communist): Hyde (1956), (1960), (1961), (1962); Djilas (1957); McFadden (1939); Schwarz (1960).

Community Development (the role of the missionary and Anthropology in community development): Batten (1954), (1957); Bauer (1957); Burke, McCreanor, O'Grady (1960); Drew (1947); Dube (1955), (1956); Ewing (1961); Foster (1955); Gilbert (1962–1963); Goodfriend (1958); Little (1953); Mason (1959); *Ministry, etc.* (1957); Myrdal (1957); Paul (1953); Randhwa (1951); Ruopp (1953); Shannon (1957); *Study Kit, etc.* (1957); Taylor, C. (1956); *Technical Assistance, etc.* (1958); de Sautoy (1958). See all references under Applied Anthropology.

Configuration (concepts, theories, applications): Benedict (1934), (1946); Coleman (1958); Dubois (1955); Gorer (1943); Kaschmitter (1955); Kluckhohn (1949b); Kluckhohn, C., Kluckhohn, F. (1948); Nakamura (1960); Northrop (1946); Northrop, ed. (1949); Nida (1961a), (1961b),

(1961c), (1960c); Opler (1945), (1946); Scharmach (1953); Tempels (1949); Wang (1946); Warner (1953); Webb (1962). See also under Culture Personality and Society. See also text, Selected Readings, p. 169.

Culture, Notion (the nature of culture as understood in Anthropology): Bidney (1944), (1953a); Blumenthal (1940); Goldstein (1957); Hall, E. T. (1959); Hoebel (1956); Kluckhohn, Kelly (1945); Kroeber (1952); Kroeber, Kluckhohn (1952); Malinowski (1938), (1944); Nadel (1955); Warner (1953); Warner, et al. (1949); White (1959). See text, Selected Readings, p. 70–71.

Culture, Personality, and Society (the role of culture in the behavior of the individual, in personality formation, national character): Bateson (1942); Bateson, Mead (1942); Caudill (1952); Dubois (1944); Gorer (1948), (1955); Gorer, Rickman (1949); Honigmann (1954); Hsu (1948), (1953); Kaplan (1961); Klingeberg, ed. (1944); Kluckhohn, C., Kluckhohn, F. (1948); Kluckhohn, Murray (1948); Linton (1945); Mead (1942), (1953); Métraux, Mead (1954); Parrinder (1951); Rodnick (1955); Wallace (1961); Whiting, Child (1953). See text, Selected Readings, p. 169; see also under Enculturation.

Culture Change — Directing Change: Kietzman (1958); Kietzman, Smalley (1960); Barnett (1942); Pike, K. (1961); Powdermaker (1955); Rapoport (1954); Sharp (1952); Sibley (1960–1961); Wagner (1936); Holmberg (1960). See under Accommodation, Applied Anthropology, Missionary and Anthropology, Mission Methods.

Culture Change — Factors: Adams, Preiss, eds. (1960); Barnett (1942a), (1942b), (1953); Bascom, Herskovits (1959); Barney (1957); Beals, A. (1955); Berndt, C. (1953); Brunner (1958); Coleman (1958); Colson (1953); Cooper (1941); Courtois (1956); Beaglehole (1957); Doob (1935); Dube (1955); Forde (1953); Geertz (1957); Gillin (1948); Herskovits (1945), (1950); Kollmorgen (1942); Kroeber, ed. (1953); Luzbetak (1958b); Mead (1956); Mead, ed. (1937); Ohm (1959); Packard (1957); Pieper (1952); Reay (1959); Steward (1949); Thompson (1948); Thurnwald (1932); Wallace (1961); Wiener (1950); Wilson, G., and Wilson, M. (1945); Schreiber (1962); Francis, E. K. (1955). See Selected Readings, p. 207, Nos. 2–3, pp. 312–313, Nos. 1–3. See also under Innovators, Social Structure, Specialties.

Culture Change — Processes Involved: Belshaw (1954); Benedict (1956); Bruner (1956); Gillin (1948); Hall, R. (1943); Harrison (1954); Herskovits (1945), (1950); Kroeber (1944), (1948), (1957); Mandelbaum (1941); Murdock (1956); Retif (1962); Wilson (1945); Thompson (1950). See under Reinterpretation, Syncretism, Nativism, Disorganization. See also text, Selected Readings, pp. 261–264.

Culture Change — Theories Regarding: Anthropological Society of Washington (1959); Barnett (1942b), (1953); Childe (1936), (1951), (1953), (1956); Clough (1951); Dawson (1960); Foster (1960); Haeckel (1959); Heine-Geldern (1960); Hodgen (1952); Holmberg (1958); Koppers (1955); Macklin (1957); Malinowski (1945); Redfield (1950), (1953b), (1955b); Steward (1949), (1955), (1956); Watson (1952), (1953); White (1943); Gluckman (1949); Murdock (1949). See text, Selected Readings, pp. 207–209.

Culture Shock: see under Adjustment to a Strange Culture, Enculturation, Rapport.

Determinants of Culture: see under Ecology, Functionalism, Culture Change — Theories, Race and Culture. See text, Selected Readings, pp. 335–336.

Disorganization (cultural and social "pathology," disequilibrium, disintergration): Thomas, Znaniecki (1927); Bühler (1957); Coninx, Langenfeld (1958); Fady (1955); Hutchinson (1957); Gluckman (1955); Redfield (1939); Sharp (1952); Smith, E. W. (1927); Synnott (1961); *Social Implications, etc.* (1956); Walsh, Furfey (1958). See under Migrations, Urbanization. See text, Selected Readings, pp. 263–264, No. 6.

Ecology (the influence of the physical environment on culture): Baker (1962); Bates (1953); Forde (1949); Frake (1962); Spencer, Gillen (1927); Theodorson (1961). See Selected Readings, pp. 335–336, No. 2.

Education (Anthropology in Education): Adams, D. (1959); Henry (1960); Mead (1957); National Society for the Study of Education (1959); Spindler, ed. (1955); Williams, F. (1951). See also under Catechetics, Communication, Configuration, Values.

Enculturation (the process of learning a culture): Whiting (1941); Whiting and Child (1953); Mead (1928), (1930). See text, Selected Readings, p. 108, No. 1. See also under Adjustment to a Strange Culture.

Ethnography (aspects of Ethnography of particular interest to the missionary-anthropologist): Goodenough (1962); Gilbert (1962–1963); Piddington (1950), (1957); Hilger (1960); Junker (1960); Spencer, ed. (1954); Malinowski (1922). See also under Applied Anthropology, Field Work and Methods.

Field Work and Methods of Research: Bennett (1948); Garrett (1942); Goode and Hatt (1952); Nadel (1951); Lang (1959); Murdock, *et al.* (1961); Royal Anthropological Institute (1951); Mead, Metraux (1953); Herskovits (1950). See under Applied Anthropology, Ethnography. See also text, Selected Readings, p. 52, No. 6.

Function: Bennett, Tumin (1948); Firth (1955); Firth, ed. (1957); Gluckman (1949); Malinowski (1922), (1945); Nadel (1955); Newell (1947); Piddington (1950), (1957); Radcliffe-Brown (1922), (1948a), (1948b), (1952); Schneider, D. (1953); Sharp (1952). See under Integration. See also text, Selected Readings, pp. 154–155.

Group Relations (group dynamism, tensions, and conflicts): "Evangelization and Teamwork" (1958); Hendry (1952); Khare (1962); Lafarge (1951); Sherif (1962); Trecker (1952); Utterback (1950); Williams, R. (1947).

Health (the missionary and Anthropology in health and illness): Ackerknecht (1947), (1949); Canova (1958); Caudill (1953); Foster (1958); Kluckhohn, C. (1949a); Krogman (1951); Leiman (1956); Luzbetak (1958a); Lewis (1955); MacGreggor (1960); Marriott (1955); Murdock (1952); National Research Council (1943); Paul, ed. (1955); Polgar (1962); Ritchie (1950); Rivers, ed. (1922); Schneider (1955); Simmons, Wolff (1954); Wellin (1955). See under Applied Anthropology, Community Development. See also text, p. 3, note 2.

Industry (the missionary and Anthropology in industry): Chapple (1953); Richardson (1955), (1961); Shimkin (1952). See also Technical Assistance.

Innovators (the role of the innovators in directing culture change): Smalley (1956); Brown (1944); Powdermaker (1955). See under Culture Change — Factors, Rapport, Leadership.

Integration: Hoyt (1961); Goode (1951); Marwick (1952); Neumeyer (1958); Reyburn (1959); Steward (1953). See under Function, Configuration.

Lay-Apostolate (the role of the layman in the social and religious mission of the Church): Gilligan (1954); Grenot (1956); How to Be a Leader, etc. (1962); Lay Apostolate, etc. (1957); Philips (1956); Schaefer (1956); Suenens (1956), (1953); Thorman (1962). See under Leadership, Innovators, Rapport.

Leadership (directing change through local leadership): Cardijn (1955); Cartwright, (1953); Dimcock, Trecker, (1949); Dugal (1959–1960); Ewing, ed. (1954); Gidwani, Valunjkar, Chowdry (1962); Hemphill (1947); Hendry, (1952); Homes-Siedle (1954); How to Be a Leader, etc. (1962); Klein (1956); Lawlor (1954); Meek (1937); Meyer (1955); Nida, Wonderly (1963); papal encyclicals; Ross, Hendry (1957); Sherif (1962); Tead (1935); Trecker (1952); Schmidlin, (1931); Useem (1952); Utterback (1950); Hyde (1960), (1961), (1962). See under Lay-Apostolate, Innovators, Rapport.

Linguistics, Applied: Brooks (1960); Francis, W. N. (1958); Fries (1945), (1952); Gudshinsky (1951); Knox (1949); Nida (1947), (1952), (1957); Lado (1957), (1962); Stevick (1955); Gleason (1960).

Linguistics, Descriptive: Bloch, Trager (1942); Bloomfield (1933); Elson, Pickett (1962); Gleason (1961); Hall, R. (1950); Hockett (1958); Joos (1957); Hoijer, ed. (1954); Merrifield (1962); Pike, E., et al. (1954); Pike, K. (1945), (1947), (1948); Sapir (1921), (1960); Smalley (1961); Whorf (1941).

Liturgy (missionary accommodation in worship): Amaladasan (1960); Blomjous (1960); Bühlmann (1960); Brunner (1957), (1958), (1959); Conolly (1957); Gonzaga (1960); Griffiths (1960); Hofinger (1958c); Hofinger, et al. (1958), (1960), (1961); Luykx (1959), (1960); Pretorius (1950); Schaefer (1960–1961); van Bekkum (1958); van Cawelaert (1960); van Melckebeke (1960).

Medical Missions: see Health.

Mentality: see Configuration, Culture Personality and Society.

Migrations (disorganization associated with migrations): Coninx, Langenfeld (1958); Fady (1955); Moore (1957); Thomas, Znaniecki (1927).

Missiology (nature of missiology): Clarkson (1952); Couturier (1960); Hoffman (1960), (1962a), (1962b); Jetté (1950); Murphy (1958), (1962); Schmidlin (1931), (1933); Vriens (1960).

Missionary and Anthropology (the role of Anthropology in apostolic methods): Amyot (1955), (1956); Buswell (1961); Ewing (1951), (1957); Fehderau (1961); Gusinde (1958); Hickmann (1961); Junod (1935); Kietzman (1958); Luzbetak (1961), (1962); Meert (1956); Newell (1947); Reyburn (1953); Rosenstiel (1959); Smith, E. W. (1924); Smith, G. H. (1945).

Missionary Methods (missionary methods in the light of cultural integration): Korb (1961); Luzbetak (1961), (1962); McGuire (1962); Moyersoen (1962); Proceedings of the Lima, etc. See also under Administration, Agronomy, Art and Music, Catechetics and Homiletics, Communication, Community Development, Disorganization, Education, Health, Integration, Social Mission of Church, Social Structure. See pp. 261–264.

National Character: see Culture Personality and Society, Configuration.

Nativism (Revivalism, Messianism, Prophetism, excessive nationalism, etc.): Burridge (1960); Farquhar (1929); Guiart (1951); Hill, W. (1944);

Inglis (1957), (1959); Ishida (1963); Koppers (1959); Krader (1956); Lesser (1933); Linton (1943); Mooney (1896); Mühlmann, ed. (1961); Stanner (1958); Sundkler (1960); Thrupp, ed. (1962); Wallace (1956a), (1956b); Wallis (1943). See text, Selected Readings, pp. 262–263, No. 3.

Personality and Culture: see Culture Personality and Society, Configuration.

Psychology: see Culture Personality and Society, Configuration.

Race and Culture (biological determinants of culture): Barzun (1937); Benedict (1940); Dahlberg (1942); Dunn (1951); Hallowell (1945); Haring (1956); Havighurst (1955); Klineberg (1935), (1945); Kaplan (1961); Nash (1962); Lindzey (1961); Little (1952); Myrdal (1944). See text, Selected Readings, pp. 335–336, Nos. 2–3.

Rapport (proper relationship between an agent of culture change and the recipient society): Cartwright (1953); Dooley (1960); Dunning (1962); Keller (1956); Michonneau (1949), (1957); Spector, Preston (1961). See under Innovators, Adjustment to Strange Environment. See Selected Readings, p. 263, No. 4.

Readers in Anthropology (selections pertinent to present course): Coon, ed. (1948); Evans-Pritchard, ed. (1954); Fried, ed. (1955), (1956); Gillin, J., ed. (1954); Hoebel, Jennings, Smith, eds. (1955); Kroeber, ed. (1953); Mead, Callas (1953); Goldschmidt, ed. (1954); Lessa, Vogt (1958); Linton, ed. (1945); Shapiro, ed. (1956); Thomas, W. L., ed. (1955), (1956).

Reinterpretation: Nida (1960c); Messenger (1959). See under Culture Change — Process, Nativism, Syncretism. See also text, Selected Readings, pp. 262–263, Nos. 2–3.

Religion (non-Christian religions, patterns, and functions): Goode (1951); Koppers (1952); Lessa, Vogt (1958); Luzbetak (1954), (1956); Schmidt (1926–1955); Wallis (1939). See under Textbooks.

Social Mission of the Church: Abrecht (1961); Bruehl (1939); Chinigo (1957); Considine (1958), (1960), (1961); Crane (1959); de Montcheuil (1954); Donavan (1950); Drummond (1955); Ewing (1955); Ewing, ed. (1955); Feree (1951); Felton (1960); Giordano (1943); Hall, C. (1947); Harte (1956); Hatton (1961); Kerby (1944); Landis (1947); Lewis (1959), (1960); Messner (1949); Mihanovich (1950); Morris (1957); Murphy (1961); Nuesse, Harte (1951); O'Connor (1952); Pollock (1955); Putz (1957); Reyburn (1960b); Saliege (1949); Suhard (1953). See the various missionary and social encyclicals. See also under Community Development, Disorganization, Education, Health, Industry, Migrations, Technical Assistance, Urbanization.

Social Organization (cross-cultural analysis and description): Lowie (1920), (1948); Evans-Pritchard, ed. (1954); Firth (1951); Fortes (1949); Honigmann (1959); Murdock (1949); Nadel (1957); Redfield (1956a); Ross (1959). See the section on social organization in the various recommended textbooks.

Social Structure and Culture Change: Blau (1959–1960); Bouter (1956); Coleman (1958); Cox (1948); Drake (1960); Dugal (1959–60); Eisenstadt (1956); Ghurye (1952); Nida (1960d); Sibley (1960–1961). See under Culture Change — Factors, Subsocieties.

Socialization: see Enculturation.

Specialization (specialization as a factor in culture change and as a missionary policy): Barnett (1953); Croegaert (1960); Cushing (1961); Korb (1961); Luzbetak (1961); *Planning Agencies, etc.* (1962); Shaw (1961).

Spiritual Nature of Mission Work (not denied by the missionary-anthropologist): Chautard (1943); "Christ the Soul of Our Apostolate" (1959); "Efficiency in the Apostolate" (1959); "Holiness and Techniques, *etc.*" (1956); *Mystici Corporis* (1943); McCoy (1962); Scumois (1961); Schütte (1960).

Subsocieties and Subcultures: Cohen (1955); Davis, A. (1941); Dollard (1949); Fichter (1951), (1954); Gillin, Murphy (1950–1951); Kenny (1961), (1962); Redfield (1930), (1941), (1947), (1955a), (1956b). See text, Selected Readings, pp. 129–130, No. 2.

Syncretism (Christo-Paganism): Anathil (1961); Andersson (1958); Barber (1941); Barnett (1957); Bastide (1960); Berndt, R. (1952–1953); Belshaw (1950); Bushnell (1958); Cannon (1942); Herskovits (1937), (1941); Ishida (1963); LaBarre (1938), (1960); Laternari (1960); Lawrence (1954); Metraux, A. (1959); Nida (1960c), (1961a); Oakes (1951); Simpson (1962); Slotkin (1952), (1955), (1955–1956), (1956); Sundkler (1960); Wallace (1956b); Wonderly (1958); Worsley (1957). See also under Nativism. See text, Selected Readings, pp. 262–263, Nos. 2–3.

Technical Assistance (the role of Anthropology and the missionary in technical assistance): Erasmus (1957); Foster (1962); Green (1962); Hoselitz (1957); Hunt (1957); Hunter, Knowles (1957); "I saw Technical Assistance, *etc.*" (1957); Lang (1961–1962); Leighton (1945); Mosher (1957); Mead, ed. (1953); Owen (1957); Spicer (1952); Spicer, ed. (1952); Tannous (1957); Theodorson (1953). See under Agronomy, Community Development, Disorganization, Education, Health, Industry, Urbanization.

Textbooks (recommended manuals to accompany present course): Beals, Hoijer (1953); Boas (1938); Broom, Selznick (1958); Chapple, Coon (1942); Evans-Pritchard (1951), (1954); Firth (1938), (1951); Gillin (1948); Goldschmidt (1959); Herskovits* (1950); Hoebel (1958); Honigmann (1959); Jacobs, Stern (1947); Keesing (1958); Kroeber (1948); Linton (1936), (1955); Lowie (1934); Piddington (1950), (1957).

Urbanization (urban societies, growth of cities, industrialization, urban problems): Beals, R. (1951); Bergel (1955); Comhaire (1952); Comhaire, Cahnman (1959); Davis, Golden (1954); Gist (1956); Gutkind (1960); Hatt, Reiss (1957); Marris (1960); Mayo (1945); *Urbanization, etc.* (1957); Redfield (1953b); Wonderly (1960). See under Disorganization. See also text, Selected Readings, pp. 263–264, No. 6.

Values: Bidney (1935b); Kenny (1962–1963); Kluckhohn, C. (1951); Kluckhohn, F. (1961); *Value in Action, etc.* (1958); Holmberg (1960); Redfield (1953b). See cultural relativism under Accommodation, Adjustment to a Strange Cultural Environment, Configuration, Enculturation, Culture Personality and Society, Rapport; for extreme relativism, see Herskovits.

Variation: Flannery (1960); Kluckhohn, F. (1961).

* Recommended except for his extreme cultural relativism.

APPENDIX TWO

USEFUL PERIODICALS AND OTHER STUDY AIDS

I. ANTHROPOLOGICAL JOURNALS:

American Anthropologist. The American Anthropological Association, 1530 P Street, N.W., Washington 5, D. C.

Anthropological Quarterly. Catholic University of America, Washington 17, D. C.

Anthropos. St. Augustin ü, Siegburg, Rhld., W. Germany. (Formerly Fribourg, Switzerland.)

Current Anthropology. University of Chicago, 1126 East 59th St., Chicago 37, Illinois.

Human Organization. The Society for Applied Anthropology, Rand Hall, Cornell University, Ithaca, N. Y.

Man: A Monthly Record of Anthropological Science. Royal Anthropological Institute, 21 Bedford Square, London, W.C.1.

Southwestern Journal of Anthropology. University of New Mexico, Albuquerque.

II. PERIODICALS WITH FOCUS ON MISSIONARY PROBLEMS:

C.I.F. Reports. The Center of Intercultural Formation, Cuernavaca, Mexico.

Christ to the World. Rome, Italy. (U. S. agent: Maryknoll Bookshelf, Maryknoll, N. Y.)

Good Tidings. East Asian Pastoral Institute, P.O. Box 1815, Manila, Philippines. (U. S. agent: Sadlier, New York.)

Lumen Vitae. International Centre for Studies in Religious Education, 184, Rue Washington, Brussels 5, Belgium.

Mission Bulletin. Hong Kong. (No longer published.)

Occasional Bulletin. Missionary Research Library, 3041 Broadway, New York 27, N. Y.

Practical Anthropology. Tarrytown, N. Y.

Worldmission. Society for the Propagation of the Faith, 366 Fifth Ave., New York.

(Periodicals with focus on particular areas available, e.g., Oceania, University of Sydney, or Africa, Oxford University. Excellent missiological journals available in non-English languages, e.g., *Zeitschrift für Missionswissenschaft und Religionswissenschaft,* Aschendorf, Münster, Germany: *Neue Zeitschrift für Missionswissenschaft: Nouvelle Revue de science missionaire,* Seminar Schöneck, Beckenried, Switzerland. Other, non-strictly missiological periodicals, e.g., the *Mensaje,* Casilla 10445, Santiago, Chile, carry many articles of practical missiological interest.

364

III. READERS IN ANTHROPOLOGY:

C. S. Coon (ed.), *A Reader in General Anthropology*. New York, Henry Holt, 1948.

E. E. Evans-Pritchard (*et al.*), *The Institutions of Primitive Society*. Glencoe, Ill., Free Press, 1954.

M. H. Fried (ed.), *Readings in Anthropology*. New York, Thomas Y. Crowell, 1959. (2 vols.)

J. P. Gillin (ed.), *For a Science of Social Man*. New York, Macmillan, 1954.

Hoebel, Jennings, Smith (eds.), *Readings in Anthropology*. New York, McGraw-Hill, 1955.

A. L. Kroeber (ed.), *Anthropology Today: An Encyclopedic Inventory*. University of Chicago, 1953.

R. Linton (ed.), *The Science of Man in the World Crisis*. New York, Columbia University Press, 1945.

M. Mead and N. Calas (ed.), *Primitive Heritage: An Anthropological Anthology*. New York, Random House, 1953.

H. L. Shapiro (ed.), *Man, Culture, and Society*. New York, Oxford University Press, 1956.

W. L. Thomas, Jr. (ed.), *Current Anthropology: A Supplement to Anthropology Today*. University of Chicago, 1956.

IV. ENCYCLOPEDIAS:

Encyclopaedia of the Social Sciences. Editor-in-Chief, Edwin R. A. Seligman; Associate Editor, Alvin Johnson. Popular edition in 8 volumes. New York, Macmillan Company, 1937.

V. BIBLIOGRAPHIES:

Bibliografia Missionaria. Roma, Pontificia Università de Propaganda Fide. (Current missiological literature. 25 volumes. Last volume published, 1962.)

International Bibliography of Social and Cultural Anthropology. Paris, UNESCO. (For current literature.)

Human Relations Area Files Behavior Science Bibliographies. New Haven, Yale University. (Bibliographies for specific areas available, e.g., Philippines, Southeast Asia, Indonesia, Burma.)

D. G. Mandelbaum, G. W. Lasker, and E. M. Albert, eds., *Resources for the Teaching of Anthropology*. (Including "A Basic List of Books and Periodicals for College Libraries," compiled by R. and M. Beckham.) American Anthropological Association, Memoir 95, 1963.

For other bibliographies, see under "Bibliographies," p. 358.

VI. TEXTBOOKS (Introductory courses in Cultural Anthropology):

See under "Textbooks," p. 363.

VII. AUDIO-VISUAL AIDS:

W. Goldschmidt (ed.), *Ways of Mankind: Thirteen Dramas of Peoples of the World and How They Live*. L.P. Records. National Association of Educational Broadcasters, Urbana, Ill.

For available anthropological films, see J. J. Honigmann, *The World of Man*, New York, Harper, 1959. The films are indicated at the end of the various chapters.

VIII. ETHNOGRAPHIC COLLECTIONS (short surveys):

G. P. Murdock, *Africa: Its Peoples and Their Culture History.* New York, Toronto, London, McGraw-Hill, 1959.

S. and Ph. Ottenberg (eds.), *Cultures and Societies of Africa.* New York, Random House, 1960.

D. Oliver, *The Pacific Islands.* Cambridge, Mass., Harvard University Press, 1951.

J. H. Steward and L. Faron, *Native Peoples of South America.* New York, Toronto, London, McGraw-Hill, 1959.

E. R. Service, *A Profile of Primitive Culture.* New York, Harper, 1958.

W. Goldschmidt, *Exploring the Ways of Mankind.* New York, Holt, Rinehart, Winston, Inc., 1960.

GENERAL BIBLIOGRAPHY

ABRECHT, Paul
1961   The Churches and Rapid Social Change. Garden City, N. Y., Doubleday.
ACKERKNECHT, Erwin H.
1947   "Primitive Surgery," American Anthropologist, 49:25–45.
1949   Medical Practices. Bureau of American Ethnology, Bulletin 143.
ADAM, Leonhard
1940   Primitive Art. Harmondsworth, Penguin Books Ltd. (Rev. ed. 1949.)
ADAMS, Don
1959   "Cultural Pitfalls of a Foreign Educational Adviser," Peabody Journal of Education, No. 36. (Reprinted, Practical Anthropology, 9:179–184).
ADAMS, R. N., et al.
1960   Social Change in Latin America Today. Council on Foreign Relations. New York, Harper.
ADAMS, R. N., and PREISS, J. J., eds.
1960   Human Organization Research: Field Relations and Techniques. Homewood, Ill., Dorsey.
AMALADASAN, Swami
1960   "Sacred Music in the Service of Mission Liturgy," in Hofinger (ed.), Liturgy and the Missions, pp. 221–235.
AMYOT, J. (S.J.)
1955–56 "The Mission Apostolate in Its Cultural Context," Mission Bulletin, Hong Kong, VII (1955), 736–739; VIII (1956), 8–13.
ANATHIL, George M. (S.V.D.)
1961   "Are Hindu renascent movements a help or an obstacle for the spreading of Chtristianity in India," Neue Zeitschrift für Missionswissenschaft, 17:224–233.
ANDERSSON, Efraim
1958   Messianic Popular Movements in the Lower Congo. Studia Ethnographica Upsaliensia XIV. Upsala, Sweden, Almqvist and Wiksells Boktryckeri AB.
ANTHROPOLOGICAL SOCIETY OF WASHINGTON
1956   Some Uses of Anthropology: Theoretical and Applied.
1959   Evolution and Anthropology: A Centennial Appraisal.
1962   Anthropology and Human Behavior.
ARGYRIS, Chris
1962   Interpersonal Competence and Organizational Effectiveness. Homewood, Dorsey, Ill.
AUFENANGER, Henry (S.V.D.)
1960–61 "Primitivity along the Sepik," Worldmission, 11, 4:58–68.
AUGUSTINE, St.
De Doctrina Christiana.

BAILEY, Frederick G.
1958   Caste and the Economic Frontier: A Village in Highland Orissa. New York, The Humanities Press.
BAKER, Paul T.
1962   "The Application of Ecological Theory to Anthropology," American Anthropologist, 64:15–21.
BARBER, Bernard
1941   "Acculturation and Messianic Movements," American Sociological Review, 6:663–669. (Reprinted in Lessa and Vogt, eds., Reader in Comparative Religion, pp. 474–478.)
BARNETT, Homer G.
1940   "Culture Processes," American Anthropologist, 42:21–48.
1942a   "Applied Anthropology in 1860," Applied Anthropology (now Human Organization), 1, 3:19.
1942b   "Invention and Culture Change," American Anthropologist, 44:14–30.
1953   Innovation: The Basis of Cultural Change. New York, Toronto, London, McGraw-Hill Book Company, Inc.
1956   Anthropology in Administration. Evanston, Ill., Row, Peterson and Co.
1957   Indian Shakers: A Messianic Cult of the Pacific Northwest. Carbondale, Ill., Southern Illinois University Press.
1958   "Anthropology as an Applied Science," Human Organization, 17:9–11.
BARNEY, G. Linwood
1957   "The Meo — An Incipient Church," Practical Anthropology, 4:31–50.
BARZUN, Jacques
1937   Race: A Study in Modern Superstition. New York, Harcourt, Brace and Company.
BASCOM, William R., and HERSKOVITS, Melville J.
1959   Continuity and Change in African Cultures. Chicago, Chicago University Press.
BASTIDE, Roger
1960   Les Religiones Africaines au Brésil: Vers une Sociologie des Interpénétrations de Civilisations. Bibliothèque de Sociologie Contemporaine. Paris, Universitaires de France.
BATES, Marston
1953   "Human Ecology," in A. L. Kroeber (ed.), Anthropology Today, pp. 700–713.
BATESON, Gregory
1942   "Morale and National Character," in G. Watson (ed.), Civilian Morale, Boston, pp. 71–91.
BATESON, Gregory, and MEAD, Margaret
1942   Balinese Character. New York, New York Academy of Sciences.
BATTEN, T. R.
1954   Problem of African Development. London, Oxford University Press. (Two vols. Second ed.)
1957   Communities and Their Development. London, Oxford University Press.
BAUER, P. T.
1957   Economic Analysis and Policy in Underdeveloped Countries. Durham, N. C., Duke University Press.

BEAGLEHOLE, Ernest
1957   "Cultural Factors in Economic and Social Change," in Shannon
        (ed.), Underdeveloped Areas, pp. 417–423.
BEALS, Allan R.
1955   "Interplay among Factors of Change in a Mysore Village," in
        M. Marriott (ed.), Village India: Studies in the Little Com-
        munity, The American Anthropological Association Memoir 83.
BEALS, Ralph L.
1951   "Urbanism, Urbanization, and Acculturation," American Anthro-
        pologist, 53:1–10.
1953   "Acculturation," in A. L. Kroeber (ed.), Anthropology Today,
        pp. 621–641.
BEALS, Ralph L., and HOIJER, Harry
1953   An Introduction to Anthropology. New York, Macmillan Co.
        (Seventh Printing, 1952.)
BEARDSLEY, Richard K., HALL, John W., and WARD, Robert E.
1959   Village Japan. Chicago, Chicago University Press.
BEEKMAN, John
1959   "Minimizing Religious Syncretism among the Chols," Practical
        Anthropology, 6:241–250.
BELSHAW, Cyril S.
1950   "The Significance of Modern Cults in Melanesian Development,"
        The Australian Outlook, 4:116–125. (Reprinted in abridged
        form in Lessa and Vogt, eds., Reader in Comparative Religion,
        pp. 486–492.)
1954   Changing Melanesia. Melbourne, Oxford University Press.
BENEDICT XV
1919   Maximum Illud. Translated by William Connolly, S.J. Printed
        in Thomas J. M. Burke, S.J. (ed.), Catholic Missions: Four
        Great Encyclicals, New York, Fordham University Press.
BENEDICT, Ruth
1934   Patterns of Culture. Boston, London, Houghton Mifflin Co.
        (Reprinted in paperback Mentor Book, The New American
        Library, New York.)
1940   Race: Science and Politics. (Reprinted 1959, New York, Viking
        Press.)
1946   The Chrysanthemum and the Sword. Boston, Houghton Mifflin
        Co.
1948   "Anthropology and the Humanities," American Anthropologist,
        50:583–593.
1956   "The Growth of Culture," in Harry L. Shapiro (ed.), Man,
        Culture, Society, pp. 182–195. (Written 1948.)
BENNETT, John W.
1948   "The Study of Cultures: A Survey of Technique and Methodology
        in Field Work," American Sociological Review, 13:672–689.
BENNETT, John W., and TUMIN, Melvin M.
1948   Social Life: Structure and Function. New York, Alfred A. Knopf.
BERGEL, E. C.
1955   Urban Sociology. New York, McGraw-Hill.
BERNDT, Catherine H.
1953   "Socio-cultural Change in the Eastern Central Highlands of New
        Guinea," Southwestern Journal of Anthropology, 9:112–138.

BERNDT, Manfred, and SMALLEY, William A.
    1962   "Modern Asians and Western Churches," Practical Anthropology,
            9:134-136.
BERNDT, Ronald M.
    1951   "Influence of European Culture on Australian Aborigines,"
            Oceania, 21:229-235.
    1952-53 "A Cargo Movement in the Eastern Central Highlands of New
            Guinea," Oceania, 23:40-65, 137-158, 202-234.
    1954   "Reaction to Contact in the Eastern Highlands of New Guinea,"
            Oceania, 24:191-228, 255-274.
BIDNEY, David
    1944   "On the Concept of Culture and Some Cultural Fallacies,"
            American Anthropologist, 46:30-44.
    1953a   Theoretical Anthropology. New York, Columbia University Press.
    1953b   "The Concept of Value in Modern Anthropology," in A. L.
            Kroeber (ed.), Anthropology Today, pp. 682-699.
BLAU, Peter M.
    1959-60 "Social Integration, Social Rank, and Processes of Interaction,"
            Human Organization, 18:152-157.
BLOCH, Bernard, and TRAGER, George L.
    1942   Outline of Linguistic Analysis. Baltimore, Linguistic Society of
            America.
BLOMJOUS, Bishop Joseph J.
    1960   "Mission and Liturgy," in Hofinger (ed.), Liturgy and the Mis-
            sions, pp. 39-46.
BLOOMFIELD, Leonard
    1933   Language. New York, Henry Holt and Co.
BLUMENTHAL, A.
    1940   "A New Definition of Culture," American Anthropologist, 42:571-
            586.
BOAS, Franz
    1927   Primitive Art. Paperback reprint, New York, Dover Publications,
            Inc., 1955.
BOAS, Franz, et al.
    1938   General Anthropology. Boston, New York, London, etc., D. C.
            Heath and Company.
BORNEMANN, Fritz (S.V.D.)
    1954   "Verzeichnis der Schriften von P. W. Schmidt," Anthropos,
            49:385-432.
BOUTER, Most Reverend William
    1956   "To Bring Christ to the Intellectuals of India," Christ to the
            World, 1, 6:56-62.
BRAIDWOOD, Robert J.
    1948   Prehistoric Men. Chicago Natural History Museum Popular Series,
            Anthropology, No. 37.
BREDA, Gregorius von (O.F.M.Cap.)
    1933   Die Muttersprache: Eine Missions- und Religionswissenschaftliche
            Studie über die Sprachenfrage in den Missionsgebieten. Münster,
            Westfälische Vereindruckerei Akt. Ges.; Hertogenbosch, Holland,
            Tenlings' Uitgevers-MaatschappijsHertogenbosch.
BRESILLAC, Bishop Melchior De Marion-
    1956   The Missioner. Washington, Queen of Apostles Seminary.

BROOKS, Nelson
1960   *Language and Language Learning: Theory and Practice.* New York and Burlingame, Harcourt, Brace and Company.
BROOM, Leonard, and SELZNICK, Philip
1958   *Sociology: A Text with Adapted Readings.* Evanston, Ill. and White Plains, N. Y., Row, Peterson and Company. (Second edition.)
BRASSARD, S. (O.M.I.)
1961   "Improving the Diet of the African by Better Agricultural Methods," in D. J. Hatton (ed.), *Missiology in Africa Today,* pp. 42–46.
BROWN, G. Gordon
1944   "Missions and Cultural Diffusion," *American Journal of Sociology,* 50:214–219.
BROWN, G. Gordon, and HUTT, A.
1935   *Anthropology in Action.* London, Oxford University Press.
BROWN, L. C. (S.J.), et al.
1954   *Social Orientations.* Chicago, Loyola University Press.
BRUEHL, C.
1939   *The Pope's Plan for Social Reconstruction.* New York, Devin-Adair.
BRUNER, Edward M.
1956   "Cultural Transmission and Cultural Change," *Southwestern Journal of Anthropology,* 12:191–199.
BRUNNER, Paul
1957   "Liturgical Adaptation of Indigenous Music," *Mission Bulletin,* Hong Kong, 9:668–669.
1958   "Teaching Power of the Liturgy," *Mission Bulletin,* Hong Kong, 10:997–1000.
1959   "The Liturgy of Baptism on the Missions," *Mission Bulletin,* Hong Kong, 11:237–255.
BUCKWALTER, Albert, GRIMES, Joseph E., and REYBURN, William D.
1960   "How Do I Adjust to Giving?" *Practical Anthropology,* Supplement, pp. 100–109.
BÜHLER, Alfred
1957   "Kulturkontakt und Kulturzerfall: Eindrücke von einer Neuguineareise," *Acta Tropica,* 14:1–35.
BÜHLMANN, Walbert (O.F.M.Cap.)
1960   "The Necessity for Liturgical Renewal in Africa Today," in Hofinger, *Liturgy and the Missions,* pp. 103–111.
1961   "Adapting Catechesis to Missionary Conditions," in John Hofinger, S.J. (ed.), *Teaching All Nations,* pp. 59–72.
BURKE, L. (S.M.A.), McCREANOR, J., and O'GRADY, John (Msgr.)
1960   *Training Missionaries for Community Development: A Report on Experiences in Ghana.* Princeton, N. J., National Conference of Catholic Charities.
BURKE, Thomas J. M. (S.J.), ed.
1957   *Catholic Missions: Four Great Missionary Encyclicals.* Incidental Papers of the Institute of Mission Studies, No. 1. New York, Fordham University Press.
BURRIDGE, K. O. L.
1960   *Mambu: A Melanesian Millenium.* London, Meuthen.

372   GENERAL BIBLIOGRAPHY

BUSHNELL, John
  1958   "La Virgen de Guadalupe as Surrogate Mother in San Juan Atzingo," *American Anthropologist*, 60:261–265.
BUSWELL, James O., III
  1961   "Anthropologist and Administrator," *Practical Anthropologist*, 8:157–167.

CANNON, W. B.
  1942   " 'Voodoo' Death," *American Anthropologist*, 44:169–181.
CANOVA, Francesco
  1958   "To Heal and to Teach," *Worldmission*, 9, 3:72–80.
CAPELL, A.
  1959   "Interpreting Christianity to Australian Aborigines," *International Review of Missions*, 48(No.190):145–156.
CARDIJN, Joseph
  1955   *Challenge to Action*. Chicago, Fides Press.
CARRETTO, Most Rev. Peter
  1960   "Missionary Adaptation to Local Conditions," *Mission Bulletin*, Hong Kong, 12:236–240.
CARTWRIGHT, Dorwin, and ZANDER, Alvin, eds.
  1953   *Group Dynamics: Research and Theory*. Evanston, Ill., Row, Peterson and Company.
CAUDILL, William
  1952   *Japanese-American Personality and Acculturation*. Genetic Psychology Monographs No. 15.
  1953   "Applied Anthropology in Medicine," in A. L. Kroeber (ed.), *Anthropology Today*, pp. 771–806.
CHAPPLE, Eliot D.
  1953   "Applied Anthropology in Industry," in A. L. Kroeber (ed.), *Anthropology Today*, pp. 819–831.
CHAPPLE, Eliot D., and COON, Carleton Stevens
  1942   *Principles of Anthropology*. New York, Henry Holt and Co.
CHAUTARD, Dom J. B.
  1943   *The Soul of the Apostolate*. Authorized translation by Rev. J. A. Moran, S.M. Techny, Ill., Mission Press.
CHILDE, V. Gordon
  1936   *Man Makes Himself*. London, Watts and Company.
  1951   *Social Evolution*. London, Watts and Company.
  1953   *What is History?* New York, Henry Schuman.
  1956   *Piecing Together the Past*. New York, Praeger.
CHINIGO, M.
  1957   *The Pope Speaks: The Teaching of Pope Pius XII*. New York, Pantheon.
"Christ, the Soul of Our Apostolate," *Christ to the World*, 4:124–132.
CLARK, Grahame
  1939   *Archaeology and Society*. London, Methuen and Co. (Second revised edition, 1947.)
CLARKSON, John F. (S.J.)
  1952   "The ABC's of Missiology," *Worldmission*, 3:337.
CLEVELAND, Harlan, and MANGONE, Gerard J.
  1957   *The Art of Overseamanship*. Syracuse University Press.
CLEVELAND, Harlan, MANGONE, Gerard J., and ADAMS, John Clarke
  1960   *The Overseas Americans*. New York, Toronto, and London, McGraw-Hill.

CLOUGH, Shephard B.
1951   *The Rise and Fall of Civilization: An Inquiry into the Relation-ship between Economic Development and Civilization.* New York, McGraw-Hill.
CODRINGTON, Bishop R. H.
1891   *The Melanesians.* Oxford. Reprinted by Human Relations Area Files, Inc., New Haven, 1957.
COHEN, Albert K.
1955   *Delinquent Boys: The Culture of the Gang.* Glencoe, Ill., Free Press.
COLEMAN, William J. (M.M.)
1958   *Latin-American Catholicism: A Self-Evaluation.* World Horizon Reports No. 23. Maryknoll, N. Y., Maryknoll Publications.
COLLIER, John, Jr., and BUITRON, Anmbal
1949   *The Awakening Valley.* Chicago University Press.
COLSON, Elizabeth
1953   "Social Control and Vengeance in Plateau Tonga," *Human Problems in British Central Africa*, 11:10–47.
COMAS, Juan
1961   " 'Scientific' Racism Again?" *Current Anthropology*, 2:303–340.
1962   "More Scientific Racism," *Current Anthropology*, 3:284, 289–302.
COMHAIRE, Jean
1952   *Urban Conditions in Africa.* London, Oxford University Press. (Second edition.)
COMHAIRE, Jean, and CAHNMAN, Werner J.
1959   *How Cities Grew.* Madison, N. J., Florham Park Press.
CONINX, L., and LANGENFELD, A.
1958   "To Bring Christ to Gold Mine Workers in Equatorial Africa: A Social Movement of Africans for Africans, The Excelsior Union," *Christ to the World*, 3:309–321.
CONOLLY, J. (Rev.)
1957   "The Challenge of the Assisi Conference," *Mission Bulletin*, Hong Kong, 9:436–440.
CONSIDINE, John J. (M.M.)
1958   *New Horizons in Latin America.* New York, Dodd, Mead and Co.
1960   *The Missionary's Role in Socio-Economic Betterment.* West-minster, Md., Newman Press. (Considine, ed.)
1961   *Fundamental Catholic Teaching on the Human Race.* World Horizon Reports No. 27. Maryknoll, N. Y., Maryknoll Pub-lications.
COON, Carleton Stevens
1948   *A Reader in General Anthropology.* New York, Henry Holt and Co.
COOPER, John Montgomery (Msgr.)
1941   *Temporal Sequence and the Marginal Cultures.* Washington, Catholic University of America, Anthropology Series No. 10.
COURTOIS, V.
1956   "How to Present the Christian Message to the Muslims," *Christ to the World*, 1, 6:63–73.
COUTURIER, Charles (S.J.)
1960   *The Mission of the Church.* Baltimore, Helicon Press. (Translated by A. V. Littledale from the French original.)

COX, Oliver Cromwell
    1948   *Caste, Class, and Race.* Garden City, Doubleday and Company.
CRANE, Paul (S.J.)
    1959   "A Look at the Problems of Mission Work," *America,* October 17,
             1959.
CROEGAERT, Canon Auguste
    1960   "The Responsibility of the Bishops for the Propagation of the
             Faith all over the World," *Christ to the World,* 5:331–334.
CRONIN, John F. (S.S.)
    1959   *Social Principles and Economic Life.* Milwaukee, Bruce.
CRONIN, Vincent
    1955   *The Wise Man from the West.* New York, Dutton Company.
    1959   *A Pearl to India.* New York, Dutton.
CUSHING, Richard Cardinal
    1961   *The Modern Challenge of the Missions.* Sullivan Bros., Lowell,
             Mass. (Pamphlet, reprint from the Boston *Pilot.*)

DAHLBERG, Gunnar
    1942   *Race, Reason, and Rubbish.* New York, Columbia University
             Press.
DAVIDSON, J.
    1948   "Protestant Missions and Marriage in the Belgian Congo,"
             Africa, 18:120–128.
DAVIS, Allison, GARDNER, B. B., and GARDNER, Mary
    1941   *Deep South.* Chicago, University of Chicago Press.
DAVIS, J. Merle
    1945   *New Buildings on Old Foundations: A Handbook on Stabilizing
             the Younger Churches in their Environment.* New York and
             London, International Missionary Council.
DAVIS, Kinsley, and GOLDEN, Hilda Hertz
    1954   "Urbanization and the Development of Pre-Industrial Areas,"
             Economic Development and Cultural Change, 3:6–24.
DAWSON, Christopher
    1960   *The Historic Reality of Christian Culture.* New York, Harper.
DE FOUCAULD, Father Charles
    1960   "The Apostolate in Mohammedan Circles," *Christ to the World,*
             5:65–74.
DE JAEGHER, Raymond J.
    1954   *The Apostle of China Father Lebbe.* Translated by M. G. Carroll.
             London, Catholic Truth Society.
DE LA BEDOYERE
    1943   *Christianity in the Market Place.* London, Dakers.
DE MONTCHEUIL, Y.
    1954   *A Guide for Social Action.* Chicago, Fides.
DE REEPER, John
    1952   *A Missionary Companion: A Commentary on the Apostolic
             Faculties.* Westminster, Md., Newman.
    1957   *The Sacraments on the Missions: A Pastoral Theological Supple-
             ment for the Missionary.* Dublin, Browne and Nolan Ltd.
DE SOUZA, Carlito
    1958   "Christian Art in India," *Mission Bulletin,* Hong Kong, 10:651–
             657.

DE VAULX, Bernard
1961   History of the Missions. Vol. 99 of the Twentieth Century
        Encyclopedia of Catholicism. New York, Hawthorn Books, Inc.
DIMCOCK, Hedley S., and TRECKER, H. B.
1949   Supervision of Group Work and Recreation. New York, Associa-
        tion Press.
DJILAS, Milovan
1957   The New Class: An Analysis of the Communist System. New
        York, Praeger.
DOLLARD, John
1949   Caste and Class in a Southern Town. New York, Harper. (Second
        edition.)
DONAVAN, J. D.
1950   "The Sociologist Looks at the Parish," American Catholic
        Sociological Review, June, 1950.
DOOB, Leonard W.
1935   Propaganda, Its Psychology and Technique. New York, Henry
        Holt and Co.
1961   Communication in Africa: A Search for Boundaries. New Haven
        and London, Yale University Press.
DOOLEY, Thomas A.
1960   Dr. Tom Dooley's Three Great Books. New York, Farrar, Straus,
        and Cudahy.
DRAKE, St. Clair
1960   "Traditional Authority and Social Action in Former British
        West Africa," Human Organization, 19:150–158.
DREW, Fry and Ford
1947   Village Housing in the Tropics. London, Lund Humphries.
DRUMMOND, W. F. (S.J.)
1955   Social Justice. Milwaukee, Bruce.
DU SAUTOY, Peter
1958   Community Development in Ghana. London, Oxford University
        Press.
DUBE, Shyama Charan
1955   Indian Village. London, Rutledge & Kegan, Paul.
1956   Some Problems of Communication in Rural Community De-
        velopment. Ithaca, N. Y., Cornell University India Program.
        (Mimeographed.)
DUBIN, Robert
1951   Human Problems in Administration. New York, Prentice-Hall.
DUBOIS, Cora A.
1944   The People of Alor: A Socio-psychological Study of an East
        Indian Island. Minneapolis, University of Minnesota Press.
1949   Social Forces in Southeast Asia. Minneapolis, University of Min-
        nesota Press.
1955   "The Dominant Value Profile of American Culture," American
        Anthropologist, 57:1232–1239.
DUGAL, Brijinder Singh
1959–60 "The Village Chief in the Indian Construction Industry,"
        Human Organization, 18:174–176.
DUIGNAN, Peter
1958   "Early Jesuit Missionaries: A Suggestion for Further Study,"
        American Anthropologist, 60:725–732.

DUNN, Leslie C.
    1951   Race and Biology. Paris, UNESCO.
DUNNING, R. W.
    1962   "Interpersonal Relations: The Peasant's View," Human Or-
            ganization, 21:21–24.

EATON, Joseph W.
    1952   "Controlled Acculturation: A Survival Technique of the Hutter-
            ites," American Sociological Review, 17:331–340.
"Efficiency in the Apostolate," Christ to the World, 4(1959):533–546.
EISENSTADT, S. N.
    1956   From Generation to Generation: Age Groups and Social Structure.
            London, Routledge and Kegan Paul.
ELKIN, A. P.
    1953   Social Anthropology in Melanesia. Issued under the auspices of the
            South Pacific Commission. London, Melbourne, and New York,
            Oxford University Press.
ELSON, Benjamin, and PICKETT, Velma
    1962   An Introduction to Morphology and Syntax. Santa Ana, Calif.,
            Summer Institute of Linguistics.
ERASMUS, Charles J.
    1957   "An Anthropologist Views Technical Assistance," in Shannon
            (ed.), Underdeveloped Areas, pp. 295–308.
    1961   Man Takes Control. Minneapolis, University of Minnesota Press.
"Evangelization and Team Spirit," Christ to the World, 3(1958):283–294.
EVANS-PRITCHARD, E. E.
    1951   Social Anthropology. London, Cohen and West.
EVANS-PRITCHARD, E. E., ed.
    1954   The Institutions of Primitive Society. Glencoe, Ill., Free Press.
EWING, J. Franklin (S.J.)
    1951   "Applied Anthropology for the Missionary," Worldmission, 2,
            1:105–107.
    1955   "Local Social Custom and Christian Social Action," in J. Franklin
            Ewing (ed.), Social Action in Mission Lands, pp. 25–55.
    1957   "Anthropology and the Training of Missionaries," The Catholic
            Educational Review, 55:300–311.
    1961   "Community Development and the Missionary," in D. J. Hatton
            (ed.), Missiology in Africa Today, pp. 25–41.
EWING, J. Franklin (S.J.), ed.
    1953   The Training of Converts. Proceedings of the Fordham Uni-
            versity Conference of Mission Specialists, First Annual Meeting,
            January 24–25, 1953. New York, Fordham University Press.
    1954   Local Leadership in Mission Lands. Proceedings of the Fordham
            University Conference of Mission Specialists, Second Annual
            Meeting, January 23–24, 1954. New York, Fordham Uni-
            versity Press.
    1955   Social Action in Mission Lands. Proceedings of the Fordham Uni-
            versity Conference of Mission Specialists, Third Annual Meeting,
            January 22–23, 1955.
    1958   The Role of Communication Arts in Mission Work. Proceedings
            of the Fordham University Conference of Mission Specialists,
            Fourth Annual Meeting, January 21–22, 1956. New York,
            Fordham University Press.

1962   *The Global Mission of the Church.* Proceedings of the Fordham University Conference of Mission Specialists, Tenth Annual Meeting, January 19–20, 1962. New York, Fordham University Press.

FADY, Most Reverend Joseph (W.F.)
1955   "Migrant Labor in Nyasaland," *Worldmission,* 6:417–422.

FARQUHAR, John Nicol
1929   *Modern Religious Movements in India.* London, Macmillan and Co.

FEHDERAU, Harold W.
1961   "Missionary Endeavor and Anthropology," *Practical Anthropology,* 8:221–223.

FELTON, R. A.
1960   *The Pulpit and the Plow.* New York, Friendship Press.

FEREE, William (S.M.)
1951   *The Act of Social Justice.* Dayton, Ohio, Marianist Publications.
1956   "Social Justice and Social Order," *Social Order,* May, 1956.

FICHTER, Joseph H.
1951   *Southern Parish: Volume One, The Dynamics of a City Church.* University of Chicago Press.
1954   *Social Relations in the Urban Parish.* University of Chicago Press.

FIRTH, Raymond
1938   *Human Types: An Introduction to Social Anthropology.*
(1958)   London, Thomas Nelson and Sons. (Paperback reprint, Mentor Books, New York, The New American Library of World Literature, Inc., 1958.)
1951   *Elements of Social Organization.* London, Watts and Company.
1955   "Function," in W. L. Thomas, Jr. (ed.), *Current Anthropology,* pp. 237–258.

FIRTH, Raymond, ed.
1957   *Man and Culture: An Evaluation of the Work of Malinowski.* London, Routledge and Kegan Paul.

FLANNERY, Regina
1960   "Individual Variation in Culture," in A. Wallace (ed.), *Selected Papers of the Fifth International Congress of Anthropological and Ethnological Sciences, Philadelphia, September 1–9, 1956.* Philadelphia, University of Pennsylvania Press, pp. 87–92.

FOOD AND AGRICULTURE ORGANIZATION (U.N.O.)
1949a   *Essentials of Rural Welfare.* U.N.O. Publications.
1949b   *Educational Approaches to Rural Welfare.* U.N.O. Publications.

FORDE, Cyril Daryll
1949   *Habitat, Economy and Society.* New York, E. P. Dutton and Co., Inc. (Seventh edition.)
1953   "The Conditions of Social Development in West Africa: Retrospect and Prospect," in *Missionary Statemanship in Africa: A Present-Day Demand upon the Christian Movement.* Proceedings of the Study Conference May, 28–31, 1953, of the Kennedy School of Missions. Proceedings published in *Civilisations, Quarterly Review* of the International Institute of Differing Civilizations, Brussels, Belgium, 3:471–489.

FORTES, Meyer, ed.
1949   *Social Structure: Studies Presented to A. R. Radcliffe-Brown.* London, Oxford University Press.

FOSTER, George M.
1952   "Relationship between Theoretical and Applied Anthropology: A Public Health Program Analysis," Human Organization, 11:5–16.
1955   "Guidelines to Community Development Programs," Public Health Reports, Vol. 70.
1957   "Some Social Factors Related to the Success of a Public Health Program," in Shannon (ed.), Underdeveloped Areas, pp. 371–385.
1958   Problems in Intercultural Health Programs. Social Science Research Council Pamphlet No. 12. New York, Social Science Research Council.
1960   Culture and Conquest: America's Spanish Heritage. New York, Viking Fund, Wenner-Gren Foundation.
1962   Traditional Cultures: And the Impact of Technological Change. New York, Harper and Row Publishers.
FRAKE, Charles O.
1962   "Cultural Ecology and Ethnography," American Anthropologist, 64:53–59.
FRANCIS, E. K.
1955   In Search of Utopia — The Mennonites in Manitoba. Glencoe, Ill., The Free Press.
FRANCIS, W. N.
1958   Structure of American English. New York, Ronald Press.
FRANKEL, Sally Herbert
1953   The Economic Impact on Under-Developed Societies. Oxford, Basil Blackwell.
FRIED, Morton H., ed.
1959   Readings in Anthropology (2 vols.). New York, Crowell.
FRIES, Charles C.
1945   Teaching and Learning English as a Foreign Language. Publications of the English Language Institute, University of Michigan, No. 1. Ann Arbor, University of Michigan Press.
1952   The Structure of English. New York, Harcourt, Brace and Company.

GANTIN, Archbishop Bernardin
1960   "Will Africa Be Christian?" Christ to the World, 5:495–500.
GARRETT, Annette
1942   Interviewing: Its Principles and Methods. New York, Family Service Association of America.
GEERTZ, C.
1957   "Ritual and Social Change: A Javanese Example," American Anthropologist, 59:32–54.
GEORGE, W. C.
1962   The Biology of the Race Problem. New York, National Putnam Letters Committee.
GHURYE, G. S.
1952   Caste and Class in India. New York, Philosophical Library.
GIDWANI, K. A., VALUNJKAR, T. N., and CHOWDRY, Kamla
1962   "Leader Behavior in Elected and Non-Elected Groups," Human Organization, 21:36–42.
GILBERT, Scott
1962–63 "Tanganyika and the Peace Corps: Unanswered Questions," Human Organization, 21:286–289.

GILLIGAN, M. T.
  1954   "Preparing the Local Laity for Leadership," in J. Franklin Ewing
          (ed.), *Local Leadership in Mission Lands*, pp. 117–137.
GILLIN, John
  1942   "Acquired Drives in Culture Contact," *American Anthropologist*,
          44:545–554.
  1944   "Cultural Adjustment," *American Anthoropologist*, 46:429–447.
  1945   "Parallel Culture and Inhibitions to Acculturation in a Guatemalan
          Community," *Social Forces*, 24:1–14.
  1948   *The Ways of Men: An Introduction to Anthropology*. New York,
          Appleton-Century-Crofts, Inc.
GILLIN, John, ed.
  1954   *For a Science of Social Man*. New York, Macmillan.
GILLIN, John, and MURPHY, E. J.
  1950–51 "Notes on Southern Culture Patterns," *Social Forces*, 29:422–432.
GIORDANO, Igino
  1943   *The Social Message of Jesus*. Paterson, St. Anthony's Guild.
GIST, N. P., and HALBERT, L. A.
  1956   *Urban Society*. New York, Crowell.
GLEASON, H. A., Jr.
  1955   *An Introduction to Descriptive Linguistics*. New York, Henry
  (1961) Holt and Company. (Revised edition, 1961.)
  1960   "Linguistics in the Service of the Church," *Hartford Quarterly*,
          1:7–27. (Reprinted, *Practical Anthropology*, 9:205–219.)
GLUCKMAN, Max
  1949   "An Analysis of the Sociological Theories of Bronislaw Malinow-
          ski," in *Rhodes-Livingstone Papers*. Capetown.
  1955   *Custom and Conflict in Africa*. Oxford, Basil Blackwell.
GOLDSCHMIDT, Walter
  1959   *Man's Way: A Preface to the Understanding of Human Society*.
          Cleveland and New York, The World Publishing Company.
GOLDSCHMIDT, Walter, ed.
  1954   *Ways of Mankind: Thirteen Dramas of Peoples of the World and
          How They Live*. Boston, Beacon Press. (Recorded broadcasts
          on L.P. records available: *The Ways of Mankind*, Urbana, Ill.,
          National Association of Educational Broadcasters.)
  1960   *Exploring the Ways of Mankind*. New York, Holt, Rinehart and
          Winston, Inc.
GOLDSTEIN, L. J.
  1957   "On Defining Culture," *American Anthropologist*, 59:1075–1079.
GONZAGA y RASDESALES, Most Reverend Lino
  1960   "Missionary Importance of the Revision of the Ritual," in J.
          Hofinger (ed.), *Liturgy and the Missions*, pp. 191–201.
GOODE, William J.
  1951   *Religion among the Primitives*. Glencoe, Ill., Free Press.
GOODE, William J., and HATT, Paul K.
  1952   *Methods in Social Research*. New York, Toronto, and London,
          McGraw-Hill.
GOODENOUGH, Ward H.
  1962   "The Growing Demand for Behavioral Science in Government,"
          Human Organization, 21:172–176.
GOODFRIEND, A.
  1958   *Rice Roots*. New York, Simon and Schuster.

GORER, Geoffrey
1943   "Themes in Japanese Culture," *Transactions of the New York Academy of Sciences* (second series), 5:106–124.
1948   *The American People.* New York, W. W. Norton and Co., Inc.
1955   *Exploring English Character.* London, The Cresset Press.
GORER, Geoffrey, and RICKMAN, J.
1949   *The People of Great Russia.* London, Cresset Press.
(1950)   New York, Chanticleer Press (1950).
GRASSO, Domenico (S.J.)
1961   "The Core of Missionary Preaching," in Hofinger (ed.), *Teaching All Nations,* pp. 39–58.
GREEN, James W.
1962   "Success and Failure in Technical Assistance," *Human Organization,* 20:2–10.
GRENOT, Father
1956   "Lay Missionary Apostolate in Dahomey," *Christ to the World,* 1, 4:50–52.
GRIFFITHS, Bede (Rev.)
1960   "Liturgy and the Missions," *Mission Bulletin,* Hong Kong, 12:148–154.
GUDSCHINSKY, Sarah
1951   *Handbook of Literacy.* (Revised, 1953.) Santa Ana, Calif., Summer Institute of Linguistics.
GUIART, J.
1951   "Cargo Cults and Political Evolution in Melanesia," *Mankind,* May, 1951.
GUITTON, Jean
1953   *Make Your Mind Work for You.* New York, Macmillan.
GUSINDE, Martin (S.V.D.)
1954   "Wilhelm Schmidt, S.V.D., 1868–1954," *American Anthropologist,* 56:858–870.
1958   *Die völkerkundliche Ausrüstung des Missionars.* Steyler Missionsschriftenreihe. Steyl, Holland, Steyler Verlagsbuchhandlung.
GUTKIND, Peter C. W.
1960   "Congestion and Overcrowding: An African Urban Problem," *Human Organization,* 19:129–134.

HAAR, Ter
1948   *Adat Law in Indonesia.* Translated from the Dutch and edited by E. Adamson Hoebel and A. Arthur Schiller. New York, Institute of Pacific Relations.
HACKENBERG, Robert A.
1962–63   "Process Formation in Applied Anthropology," *Human Organization,* 21:235–238.
HAECKEL, Joseph
1959   "Zur gegenwärtigen Forschungensituation der Wiener Schule der Ethnologie," *Beiträge, Symposium* 1958, Wenner-Gren Foundation.
HALL, Cameron P.
1947   *Economic Life: A Christian Responsibility.* New York, Federal Council of Churches of Christ in America.
HALL, Edward T.
1959   *The Silent Language.* Garden City, N. Y., Doubleday and Co., Inc.

HALL, Edward T., and TRAGER, George L.
1953   Human Nature at Home and Abroad. Washington, Foreign Service Institute, Department of State.
HALL, Edward T., and WHYTE, William Foote
1960   "Intercultural Communication: A Guide to Men of Action," Human Organization, 19:5–12.
HALL, Robert A., Jr.
1943   Melanesian Pidgin English: Grammar, Texts, Vocabulary. Baltimore, Linguistic Society of America.
1950   Leave Your Language Alone! Ithaca, N. Y., Linguistica.
1955   Hands Off Pidgin English. Sydney, Pacific Publications.
(1960) Second revised edition, paperback, Doubleday Anchor Book, with new title of Linguistics and Your Language. Garden City, N. Y., Doubleday and Company, Inc., 1960.
HALLOWELL, A. Irving
1945   "The Rorschach Technique in the Study of Personality and Culture," American Anthropologist, 47:195–210.
1955   Culture and Experience. Philadelphia, Univ. of Pennsylvania Press.
HANKE, Lewis
1952   Bartolomé de las Casas — Historian. Gainesville, University of Florida Press.
HARDY, R.
1958   Kampong. Garden City, N. Y., Doubleday and Co.
HARING, D. G., ed.
1956   Personal Character and Cultural Milieu: A Collection of Readings. Syracuse, N. Y., Syracuse University Press. (Third edition.)
HARRISON, H. S.
1954   "Discovery, Invention, and Diffusion," in Singer, Holmyard, Hall (eds.), A History of Technology, Vol. I. Oxford, Clarendon Press.
HART, Donn V.
1962   "Overseas Americans in Southeast Asia: Fact in Fiction," Practical Anthropology, 9:60–84.
HARTE, Thomas J. (C.Ss.R.)
1956   Papal Social Principles: A Guide and Digest. Milwaukee, Bruce.
HASELBERGER, Herta
1961   "Method of Studying Ethnological Art," Current Anthropology, 2:341–384.
HASTINGS, Adrian, ed.
1959   The Church and the Nations. New York, Sheed and Ward.
HATT, P. K., and REISS, A. J.
1957   Cities and Society: The Revised Reader in Urban Sociology. Glencoe, Ill., Free Press.
HATTON, Desmond J. (Msgr.)
1961   Missiology in Africa Today. Dublin, Gill.
HAVIGHURST, Robert J., and NEUGARTEN, Bernice L.
1955   American Indian and White Children. Chicago, University of Chicago Press.
HEINE-GELDERN, Robert
1960   "Recent Developments in Ethnological Theory in Europe," in A. Wallace (ed.), Selected Papers of the Fifth International Congress of Anthropological and Ethnological Sciences, pp. 49–53.

HEMPHILL, John Knox
  1947   Situation Factors in Leadership. College Park, Md., University
          of Maryland Press.
HENDRY, Charles E.
  1952   The Role of Groups in World Reconstruction. New York,
          Woman's Press.
HENNINGER, Joseph (S.V.D.)
  1956   "P. Wilhelm Schmidt SVD 1868–1954: Eine biographische
          Skizze," Anthropos, 51:19–60.
HENRY, Jules
  1960   "A Cross-cultural Outline of Education," Current Anthropology,
          1:267–305.
HENRY, Jules, et al.
  1955   "Symposium on Projective Testing in Ethnography," American
          Anthropologist, 57:245–270.
HERSKOVITS, Melville J.
  1937   "African Gods and Catholic Saints in New World Religious
          Belief," American Anthropologist, 39:635–643.
  1941   The Myth of the Negro Past. New York, Harper.
  1945   "The Process of Cultural Change," in R. Linton (ed.), The
          Science of Man in the World Crisis, pp. 143–170.
  1950   Man and His Works. New York, Alfred A. Knopf. (Fourth print-
          ing. First published 1948.)
  1952   Economic Anthropology: A Study of Comparative Economics.
          New York, Alfred A. Knopf.
HICKMAN, John M.
  1961   "Understanding the Juggler," Practical Anthropology, 8:217–220.
HILGER, Sister M. Inez
  1960   Field Guide to the Ethnological Study of Child Life. Behavior
          Science Field Guide, Vol. I. New Haven, Conn., Human
          Relations Area Files Press.
HILL, Reuben
  1949   Families under Stress. New York, Harper.
HILL, W. W.
  1944   "The Navaho Indians and the Ghost Dance of 1890," American
          Anthropologist, 46:523–527. (Reprinted in Lessa and Vogt, eds.,
          Reader in Comparative Religion, pp. 478–482.)
HOCKETT, Charles F.
  1958   A Course in Modern Linguistics. New York, Macmillan.
HODGEN, Margaret T.
  1952   Change and History. Viking Fund Publications, XVIII. New
          York.
HOEBEL, E. Adamson
  1954   The Law of Primitive Man: A Study in Comparative Legal
          Dynamics. Cambridge, Mass., Harvard University Press.
  1956   "The Nature of Culture," in Shapiro (ed.), Man, Culture, and
          Society, pp. 168–181.
  1958   Man in the Primitive World: An Introduction to Anthropology.
          New York, Toronto, and London, McGraw-Hill.
HOEBEL, E. Adamson, JENNINGS, Jesse D., and SMITH, Elmer R.
  1955   Readings in Anthropology. New York, Toronto, and London,
          McGraw-Hill.
HOFFMAN, Ronan (O.F.M.Conv.)

1960   *Pioneer Theories of Missiology*. Washington, D. C., Catholic University of America Press.

1962a   "The Development of Mission Theology in the Twentieth Century," *Theological Studies*, 23:419–441.

1962b   "Bishops and the Worldwide Apostolate," *The Jurist* (Washington, D. C.), 22, 1:1–26.

HOFINGER, Johannes (S.J.)

1957a   "Ist in der Mission ein eigener Stand der Diakone anzustreben?" *Zeitschrift für Missionswissenschaft und Religionswissenschaft*, 41:201–213.

1957b   "Missionary Catechesis in Mission Lands," *Mission Bulletin*, Hong Kong, 9:506–510.

1958a   "Missionary Approach to Catechetics," *Mission Bulletin*, Hong Kong, 10:20–33.

1958b   "A Christocentric Survey of Doctrine," *Mission Bulletin*, Hong Kong, 10:447–459.

1958c   "Liturgical Arts in the Missions," *Mission Bulletin*, Hong Kong, 10:1001–1010.

1959   "Catechetical Approach to Mission Liturgy," *Mission Bulletin*, Hong Kong, 11:28–35.

1961   *Imparting the Christian Message*. Notre Dame, Ind., University of Notre Dame Press.

1962   *The ABC's of Modern Catechetics*. New York and Chicago, William H. Sadlier, Inc. (In collaboration with William J. Reedy.)

HOFINGER, Johannes (S.J.), ed.

1958   *Worship: The Life of the Missions*. (Translated by Mary Perkins Ryan.) Notre Dame, Ind., University of Notre Dame Press.

1960   *Liturgy and the Missions: The Nijmegen Papers*. New York, Kenedy.

1961   *Teaching All Nations: A Symposium on Modern Catechetics*. Herder and Herder. (English version revised and partly translated by Clifford Howell, S.J.)

HOGBIN, Herbert Ian

1934   *Law and Order in Polynesia: A Study of Primitive Institutions*. New York, Harcourt, Brace and Company.

1939   *Experiments in Civilization*. London, Routledge and Sons.

1958   *Social Change*. Josiah Mason Lectures Delivered at the University of Birmingham. London, C. A, Watts.

HOIJER, Harry, ed.

1954   *Language in Culture*. Proceedings of a Conference on the Interrelations of Language and Other Aspects of Culture. The American Anthropological Association Memoir No. 79.

"Holiness and Technique: Natural and Supernatural Means of Apostolate," *Christ to the World*, 1, 4:132–141.

HOLMBERG, Allan R.

1958   "The Research and Development Approach to the Study of Change," *Human Organization*, 17:12–16.

1960   "Changing Community Attitudes and Values in Peru: A Case Study in Guided Change," in Adams (*et al.*), *Social Change in Latin America*, pp. 63–107.

HOMES-SIEDLE, Most Rev. J. (W. F.)

1954   "The New Outlook for the Foreign Missionary in Developing

Local Leadership," in Ewing (ed.), Local Leadership in Mission Lands, pp. 138–146.

HONIGMANN, John J.
1954 Culture and Personality. New York, Harper.
1959 The World of Man. New York, Harper.

HOSELITZ, Bert
1957 "Problems of Adapting and Communicating Modern Techniques to Less Developed Areas," in Shannon (ed.), Underdeveloped Areas, pp. 400–417.

Housing in Ghana. UN Publications, No.57.II.H.3.

Housing in the Tropics. UN Publications, Housing and Town and Country Planning Bulletin, No.52.IV.2.

How to Be a Leader by Communicating Your Ideas. New York, The Christophers (1962).

HOWARD, T. E.
1947 Agricultural Handbook for Rural Pastors and Laymen: Religious, Economic, Social, and Cultural Implications of Rural Life. Des Moines, Iowa, National Catholic Rural Life Conference.

HOYT, Elizabeth E.
1961 "Integration of Culture: A Review of Concepts," Current Anthropology, 2:407–426.

HSU, Francis L. K.
1948 Under the Ancestors' Shadow: Chinese Culture and Personality. New York, Columbia University Press.
1953 Americans and Chinese: Two Ways of Life. New York, Henry Schuman.
1961 Psychological Anthropology: Approaches to Culture and Personality. Homewood, Ill., Dorsey.

HUNT, Chester L.
1957 "Cultural Barriers to Point Four," in Shannon (ed.), Underdeveloped Areas, pp. 316–321.

HUNTER, John M., and KNOWLES, William H.
1957 "The Problems of Point Four," in Shannon (ed.), Underdeveloped Areas. pp. 309–316.

HÜRTGEN, B.
1957 "Sakraler Tanz," Zeitschrift für Missionswissenschaft, 41:193–200.

HUTCHINSON, Bertram
1957 "Some Social Consequences of Missionary Activity among South African Bantu," Africa, Journal of the International African Institute, 27:160–177. (Reprinted in Practical Anthropology, 6:67–76.)

HYDE, Douglas
1956 One Front Across the World. Westminster, Md., Newman.
1960 "Lessons to be Drawn from the Communist Experience: A Stimulant for Our Zeal," Christ to the World, 5:371–389.
1961 "Training for Leadership: What Communists Are Doing," Christ to the World, 6:395–409.
1962 "Training Catholics for Leadership," Christ to the World, 7:87–108.

HYMES, Dell H.
1962 "The Ethnography of Speaking," in Anthropology in Human Behavior, Anthrop. Society of Washington.

ILLICH, Ivan D. (Msgr.)
    1958   "Missionary Poverty: Basic Policies for Courses of Missionary Formation," *Horizontes*, Faculty Review of the Catholic University of Puerto Rico, Fall, 1958.

INGLIS, Judy
    1957   "Cargo Cults: The Problem of Explanation," *Oceania*, 27:250–263.
    1959   "Interpretation of Cargo Cults — Comments," *Oceania*, 30:155–159.

"Intellectual Apostolate," *Christ to the World*, III (1958), 42–59.

I Saw Technical Assistance Change Lives. UN Publications No.57.I.10. New York, 1957.

ISHIDA, Yoshiro
    1963   "Mukyokai: Indigenous Movement in Japan," *Practical Anthropology*, 10:21–26, 43.

JACOBS, Melville, and STERN, B. J.
    1947   *Outline of Anthropology*. New York, Barnes and Noble, Inc.

JAMES, Preston
    1959   *Latin America*. New York, Odyssey.

JASPAN, M. A.
    1953   "A Sociological Case Study: Communal Hostility to Imposed Social Change in South Africa," in Ruopp (ed.), *Approaches to Community Development*, pp. 97–120.

JEFFREYS, M. D. W.
    1956   "Some Rules of Directed Culture Change under Roman Catholicism," *American Anthropologist*, 58:721–731.

JETTÉ, F. (O.M.I.)
    1950   *Qu'est-ce que la missiologie*. Ottawa, Editions de l'Université.

JOHN XXIII
    1959a   Message to the *Semaine Sociale* of Angers, July, 1959.
    1959b   *Princeps Pastorum*. (November 28, 1959. Official translation released by the International Fides Service, Rome.)
    1962   *Mater et Magistra*. English transl. New York, Paulist Press.
    1963   *Pacem in Terris*, English transl. New York, Paulist Press.

JOHNSON, Harry M.
    1960   *Sociology: A Systematic Introduction*. New York and Burlingame, Harcourt, Brace and Company.

JOOS, Martin
    1957   *Readings in Linguistics: The Development of Descriptive Linguistics in America since 1925*. Washington, American Council of Learned Societies.

JUNKER, Buford H.
    1960   *Field Work: An Introduction to the Social Sciences*. University of Chicago Press.

JUNOD, Henri Philippe
    1935   "Anthropology and Missionary Education," *International Review of Missions*, 24 (No. 94):213–228.

KAPLAN, Bert
    1961   *Studying Personality Cross-Culturally*. Evanston, Ill., Row, Peterson.

KARDINER, Abram
    1945   *The Psychological Frontiers of Society.* New York, Columbia University Press.
KASCHMITTER, William A. (M.M.)
    1955   "How Different Is the Oriental," *Worldmission,* 6, 1:29–69.
KEESING, Felix M.
    1941   *The South Seas in the Modern World.* New York, John Day Co.
    1953a   *Culture Change: An Analysis and Bibliography of Anthropological Sources to 1952.* Stanford, Calif., Stanford University Press; London, Geoffrey Cumberledge, Oxford University Press.
    1953b   *Cultural Dynamics and Administration.* Pacific Science Congress, Proceedings No. 7. Auckland, New Zealand.
    1958   *Cultural Anthropology: The Science of Custom.* New York, Rinehart.
KELLER, James (M.M.)
    1956   "To Make the Lay and Missionary Apostolate More Efficient," *Christ to the World,* 1, 6:88–96.
KELLOGG, W. N. and L. A.
    1933   *The Ape and the Child.* New York, McGraw-Hill.
KELSO, Jack, and EWING, George
    1962   *Introduction to Physical Anthropology Laboratory Manual.* Boulder, Colo., Pruett Press.
KENNY, Michael
    1961   "Twentieth Century Spanish Expatriates in Cuba: A Sub-Culture?" *Anthropological Quarterly,* 34:85–93.
    1962   "Twentieth Century Spanish Expatriates in Mexico: An Urban Sub-Culture," *Anthropological Quarterly,* 35:169–180.
    1962–63 "Social Values and Health in Spain," *Human Organization,* 21:280–285.
KERBY, William J.
    1944   *The Social Mission of the Church.* Washington, Catholic University of America Press.
KHARE, R. S.
    1962   "Group Dynamics in a North Indian Village," *Human Organization,* 21:201–213.
KIETZMAN, Dale W.
    1958   "Conversion and Culture Change," *Practical Anthropology,* 5:203–210.
KIETZMAN, Dale W., and SMALLEY, William A.
    1960   "The Missionary's Role in Culture Change," *Practical Anthropology,* Supplement (1960), 85–90.
KING, Clifford J. (S.V.D.)
    1959   *A Man of God: Joseph Freinademetz Pioneer Divine Word Missionary.* Techny, Ill., Divine Word Publications.
KITTLER, Glenn D.
    1957   *The White Fathers.* Doubleday Image Book (1961). Garden City,
    (1961)   N. Y., Doubleday.
KLEIN, Alan F.
    1956   *Role Playing in Leadership Training.* New York, Association Press.
KLINEBERG, Otto
    1935   *Race Differences.* New York, Harper.
    1945   "Racial Psychology," in R. Linton (ed.), *The Science of Man in the World Crisis,* pp. 63–77.

KLINEBERG, Otto, ed.
1944   Characteristics of the American Negro. New York, Harper.
KLUCKHOHN, Clyde
1949a   Mirror for Man: The Relation of Anthropology to Modern Life.
        New York and Toronto, McGraw-Hill (Whittlesey House).
1949b   "The Philosophy of the Navaho Indians," in F. S. Northrop (ed.),
        Ideological Difference and World Order.
1951   "Values and Value Orientations in a Theory of Action," in T.
        Parsons and E. A. Shils (eds.), Toward a General Theory of
        Action. Cambridge, Mass., Harvard Press.
1953   "Universal Categories of Culture," in A. L. Kroeber (ed.),
        Anthropology Today, pp. 507-523.
KLUCKHOHN, Clyde and Florence
1948   "American Culture: Generalized and Class Patterns," in Conflicts
        of Power in Modern Society: 1947 Symposium of the Con-
        ference on Science, Philosophy, and Religion, New York, 1948,
        pp. 106-182.
KLUCKHOHN, Clyde, and KELLY, William H.
1945   "The Concept of Culture," in R. Linton (ed.), The Science of
        Man in the World Crisis, pp. 78-106.
KLUCKHOHN, Clyde, and MURRAY, Henry A.
1948   Personality in Nature, Society, and Culture. (With the collabora-
        tion of David M. Schneider.) New York, Alfred A. Knopf.
KLUCKHOHN, Florence Rockwood
1961   Variation in Value Orientation. Evanston, Ill., and Elmsford,
        N. Y., Row, Peterson.
KNOX, Ronald A. (Msgr.)
1949   The Trials of a Translator. New York, Sheed and Ward.
KOHLER, W.
1925   The Mentality of Apes. New York, Harcourt, Brace.
KOLLMORGEN, W. M.
1942   The Old Order Amish of Lancaster County, Pennsylvania. U. S.
        Department of Agriculture, Washington, D. C.
KOPPERS, Wilhelm (S.V.D.)
1950   "Levy-Bruhl und das Ende des 'prälogischen Denkens' der Primi-
        tiven," in Corrado Gini (ed.), Abhandlungen des 14. Inter-
        nationalen Soziologenkongresses (Band IV), Rom, 30. August–
        3. September 1950, Roma, Società Italiana di Sociologia, pp.
        1–7.
1952   Primitive Man and His World Picture. (Translated by Edith
        Raybould.) London and New York, Sheed and Ward.
1955   "Diffusion: Transmission and Acceptance," in William L. Thomas
        (ed.), Current Anthropology, pp. 169–184.
1959   "Prophetismus und Messianismus als völkerkundliches und uni-
        versalgeschichtliches Problem," Saeculum, 10:38–47.
KORB, G. M.
1961   "The Scientific Scrutiny of Mission Methods," The American
        Ecclesiastical Review, 144:114–121.
KRADER, Lawrence
1956   "An Atavistic Movement in Western Siberia," American An-
        thropologist, 58:282–292.
KROEBER, Alfred Louis

1944   *Configurations of Culture Growth.* Berkeley, Calif., University of California Press.
1948   *Anthropology: Race, Language, Culture, Psychology, Prehistory.* New York, Harcourt, Brace. (Revised edition, 1948; originally published, 1923.)
1950   "Anthropology," *Scientific American,* 183:87–94.
1952   *The Nature of Culture.* Chicago, University of Chicago Press.
1955   "History of Anthropological Thought," in William L. Thomas (ed.), *Current Anthropology,* pp. 293–311.
1957   *Style and Civilization.* Ithaca, N. Y., Cornell University Press.

KROEBER, Alfred Louis, ed.
1953   *Anthropology Today.* Chicago, University of Chicago Press. (Selections re-edited by Sol Tax, Phoenix paperbound edition, University of Chicago Press.)

KROEBER, Alfred Louis, and KLUCKHOHN, Clyde
1952   *Culture: A Critical Review of Concepts and Definitions.* (With the assistance of Wayne Untereiner and appendices by Alfred G. Meyer.) Papers of the Peabody Museum of American Archaeology and Ethnology, Vol. XLVII, No. 1. Cambridge, Mass., Harvard University Press.

KROGMAN, Wilton Marion
1945   "The Concept of Race," in R. Linton (ed.), *The Science of Man in the World Crisis,* pp. 38–62.
1951   "The Role of Physical Anthropology in Dental and Medical Research," *American Journal of Physical Anthropology,* n.s., 9:211–218.

LA BARRE, Weston
1938   *The Peyote Cult.* Yale University Publications in Anthropology No. 19. New Haven, Conn., Yale University Press.
1960   "Twenty Years of Peyote Studies," *Current Anthropology,* 1:45–60.

LADO, Robert
1957   *Linguistics across Cultures: Applied Linguistics for Language Teachers.* Ann Arbor, Mich., The University of Michigan Press.
1962   *Language Teaching: A Scientific Approach.* (Prepublication MS.) New York, McGraw-Hill.

LAFARGE, John (S.J.)
1951   "Psychologists Study Group Relations," *Social Order,* March, 1951.

LAFITAU, Joseph François (S.J.)
1724   *Moeurs des sauvages américains comparées aux moeurs des premiers temps.* Paris. (4 vols.)

Land Reform: Defects in Agrarian Structure as Obstacles to Economic Develop-
1951   ment. UN Publication No.51.II.B.3. New York.

LANDIS, Benson Y.
1947   *Manual on the Church and Cooperatives.* New York, Federal Council of Churches of Christ in America.

LANG, Gottfried O.
1959   "Theoretical Methods and Approaches," *Anthropological Quarterly,* 32:41–66.
1961–62 "Economic Development and Self-Determination," *Human Organization,* 20:164–171.

GENERAL BIBLIOGRAPHY 389

LATERNARI, Vittorio
1960 *Movimenti Religiosi di Libertá e di Salvezza dei Popoli Oppressi.* Milano, Feltrinelli Editore.
LAWLOR, Richard V. (S.J.)
1954 "Church Tradition and Current Policy on Local Leadership in Mission Lands," in J. F. Ewing (ed.), *Local Leadership in Mission Lands,* pp. 4–26.
LAWRENCE, P.
1954 "Cargo Cult and Religious Beliefs among the Garia," *International Archives of Ethnography,* No. 1.
"Lay Apostolate by the Legion of Mary in Places Deprived of Priests: A Consultation," *Christ to the World,* II (1957), 94–101.
LEDERER, William, and BURDICK, Eugene
1958 *The Ugly American.* New York, W. W. Norton.
LE GROS CLARK, Wilfrid E.
1949 *History of the Primates: An Introduction to the Study of Fossil Man.* London, British Museum. (Fifth edition, 1956.)
LEESON, Ida
1952 *Bibliography of Cargo Cults and Other Nativistic Movements in the South Pacific.* Noumea, New Caledonia, South Pacific Commission. (South Pacific Commission Technical Papers No. 30.)
LEIGHTON, Alex, H.
1945 *The Governing of Men.* Princeton University Press.
1949 *Human Relations in a Changing World.* New York, Dutton.
LEIMANA, J.
1956 *Public Health in Indonesia: Problems and Planning.* The Hague, Van Dorp.
LESSA, William A., and VOGT, Evan Z., eds.
1958 *Reader in Comparative Religion: An Anthropological Approach.* Evanston, Ill., and White Plains, N. Y., Row, Peterson.
LESSER, Alexander
1933 "Cultural Significance of the Ghost Dance," *American Anthropologist,* 35:108–115. (Reprinted in J. M. Yinger [ed.], *Religion, Society, and the Individual,* pp. 490–496.)
1952 "Evolution in Social Anthropology," *Southwestern Journal of Anthropology,* 8:134–146.
LEVY-BRUHL, Lucien
1923 *Primitive Mentality.* Translated from the French by Lilian A. Clare. New York, Macmillan.
LEWIS, Oscar
1951 *Life in a Mexican Village: Tepoztlán Restudied.* Urbana, Ill., University of Illinois Press.
1955 "Medicine and Politics in a Mexican Village," in Paul and Miller (eds.), *Health, Culture, and Community,* pp. 403–434.
1959 *Five Families: Mexican Case Studies in the Culture of Poverty.* New York, Basic Books, Inc.
1960 *Tepoztlan: Village in Mexico.* New York, Henry Holt.
LINDZEY, Gardener
1961 *Projective Technique and Cross-Cultural Research.* The Century Psychology Series. New York, Appleton-Century-Crofts.

LINTON, Ralph
    1936   *The Study of Man: An Introduction.* New York, Appleton-Century-Crofts.
    1939   "The Social Consequence of a Change in Subsistence Economy," in A. Kardiner (ed.), *The Individual and His Society,* New York, Columbia University Press, pp. 282–290. (Reprinted in Hoebel, Jennings, and Smith [eds.], *Readings in Anthropology,* pp. 350–356.)
    1940   "Acculturation," in Linton (ed.), *Acculturation in Seven American Indian Tribes,* Chapters VIII–X.
    1943   "Nativistic Movements," *American Anthropologist,* 45:230–240. (Reprinted in Lessa and Vogt [eds.], *Reader in Comparative Religion,* pp. 466–474.)
    1945   *The Cultural Background of Personality.* New York, Appleton-Century-Crofts.
    1955   *The Tree of Culture.* New York, Alfred A. Knopf.
LINTON, Ralph, ed.
    1940   *Acculturation in Seven American Indian Tribes.* New York, Appleton-Century-Crofts.
    1945   *The Science of Man in the World Crisis.* New York, Columbia University Press.
    1949   *Most of the World.* New York, Columbia University Press.
LITTLE, Kenneth
    1952   *Race and Society.* Paris, UNESCO.
    1953   "Social Change in a Non-literate Community," in Ruopp (ed.), *Approaches to Community Development,* pp. 80–86.
LOEWEN, Jacob A.
    1961   "Good News for Waunana," *Practical Anthropology,* 8:275–278.
LOMBARDI, Riccardo (S.J.)
    1958   *Towards a Better World.* New York, Philosophical Library.
LOWIE, Robert H.
    1920   *Primitive Society.* New York, Liveright Publishing Co.
    1934   *An Introduction to Cultural Anthropology.* New York, Rinehart.
    (1940)   (Enlarged and revised 1940.)
    1937   *The History of Ethnological Theory.* New York, Rinehart.
    1948   *Social Organization.* New York, Rinehart.
LUYKX, Boniface (O.Praem.)
    1959   "Adaptation of Liturgy in the Missions," *Mission Bulletin,* Hong Kong, 11:786–794.
    1960   "Adaptation of Liturgy in the Missions," in J. Hofinger (ed.), *Liturgy and the Missions,* pp. 76–88.
LUZBETAK, Louis J. (S.V.D.)
    1951   *Marriage and the Family in Caucasia: A Contribution to the Study of North Caucasian Ethnology and Customary Law* Vienna-Mödling, St. Gabriel.
    1954   "The Socio-Religious Significance of a New Guinea Pig Festival," *Anthropological Quarterly,* 27:59–80, 102–128.
    1956   "Worship of the Dead in the Middle Wahgi (New Guinea)," *Anthropos,* 51:81–96.
    1958a   "Treatment of Disease in the New Guinea Highlands," *Anthropological Quarterly,* 31:42–55.
    1958b   "The Middle Wahgi Culture: A Study of First Contacts and Initial Selectivity," *Anthropos,* 53:51–87.

1961 "Toward an Applied Missionary Anthropology," *Anthropological Quarterly*, 34:165–176.
1962 "An Applied Anthropology for Catholic Missions," in K. Müller (ed.), *Missionsstudien*, pp. 68–83.

LYND, Robert Staughton and Helen Merrel
1929 *Middletown*, New York, Harcourt, Brace.

MAC EOIN, Gary
1962 *Latin America: The Eleventh Hour.* New York, P. J. Kenedy and Sons.

MAC GREGGOR, Francis
1960 *Social Sciences in Nursing.* New York, Russel Sage Foundation.

MACKLIN, June
1957 "Culture Change," in J. B. Gittler (ed.), *Review of Sociology: Analysis of a Decade*, pp. 531–545.

MADSEN, William
1957 *Christo-Paganism: A Study of Mexican Religious Syncretism.* New Orleans, Middle American Research Institute.

MAIR, Lucy Philip
1957 *Studies in Applied Anthropology.* London, University of London — Athlone Press.

MALINOWSKI, Bronislaw
1922 *Argonauts of the Western Pacific.* London.
(1932) New York, Dutton (1932).
1938 "Culture," in *Encyclopedia of the Social Sciences.*
1944 *A Scientific Theory of Culture and Other Essays.* Chapel Hill, University of North Carolina Press.
1945 *The Dynamics of Culture Change: An Inquiry into Race Relations in Africa.* New Haven, London, Yale University Press.

MANDELBAUM, David G.
1941 "Culture Change among the Nilgiri Tribes," *American Anthropologist*, 43:19–26.

MANGONE, Gerard J.
1960 "Cultural Empathy," in J. Rosengrant, et al., *Assignment Overseas*, pp. 38–50.

MANNHEIM, Karl
1936 *Ideology and Utopia.* New York, Harcourt, Brace.

Manuale Pastorale pro territoriis Societatis Verbi Divini in Indonesia con creditis. Editum tamquam manuscriptum in usum exclusivim Sacerdotum nostrorum. Datum Atambuae (Indonesia), in festo S. Joseph Opificis, 1 Maii, 1957.

MARITAIN, Jacques
1950 "The Church and the Earth's Cultures," *Mission Studies*, 1, 1:41–48.

MARRIOTT, McKim
1955 "Western Medicine in a Village of Northern India," in Paul and Miller (eds.), *Health, Culture, and Community*, pp. 239–268.

MARRIS, Peter
1960 "Slum Clearance and Family Life in Lagos," *Human Organization*, 19:123–128.

MARWICK, Max G.
1952   "The Social Context of Cewa Witch Beliefs," Africa, 22:120–135, 215–233.
MASLAND, John W.
1960   "Factor X: What is Different about Being Abroad," in Cleveland and Mangone (eds.), The Art of Overseamanship, pp. 95–102.
MASON, E. S.
1959   Economic Planning in Underdeveloped Areas. New York, Fordham University Press.
MAYO, E.
1945   The Social Problems of an Industrial Civilization. Boston, Harvard Graduate School of Business Administration.
MC COY, Joseph A. (S.M.)
1962   Advice from the Field: Towards a New Missiology. Baltimore and Dublin, Helicon Press.
MC CREANOR, John (S.M.A.)
1962   "Rethinking Our Missionary Approach," Worldmission, 13, 3:40–46.
MC FADDEN, Charles J. (O.S.A.)
1939   The Philosophy of Communism. Boston, Cincinnati, Chicago, and San Francisco, Benziger.
MC GUIRE, Frederick (C.M.)
1962   "Mission and Actuality," in Ewing (ed.), The Global Mission of the Church, pp. vii, 1–4. (Also appeared as "The Church and the 'revolution of rising expectations,'" Shield, XLI [1962], No. 5, 26–27, 33.)
MC KEVITT, Peter
1944   The Plan of Society. Dublin, Catholic Truth Society.
MEAD, Margaret
1928   Coming of Age in Samoa. New York, Wm. Morrow. (Mentor Paperback, 1949.)
1930   Growing up in New Guinea. New York, Morrow. (Mentor Paperback, 1953.)
1942   And Keep Your Powder Dry. New York, William Morrow.
(1944)   (British edition entitled The American Character, London, 1944.)
1953   "National Character," in A. L. Kroeber (ed.), Anthropology Today, pp. 642–667.
1956   New Lives for Old: Cultural Transformation — Manus, 1928–1953. New York, William Morrow.
1957   "Professional Problems of Education in Dependent Countries," in Shannon (ed.), Underdeveloped Areas, pp. 340–350.
MEAD, Margaret, ed.
1937   Cooperation and Competition among Primitive Peoples. New York, McGraw Hill.
1953   Cultural Patterns and Technical Change. UNESCO.
MEAD, Margaret, and CALAS, Nicolas, eds.
1953   Primitive Heritage: An Anthropological Anthology. New York, Random House.
MEAD, Margaret, and MÉTRAUX, Rhoda
1953   The Study of Culture at a Distance. Chicago, University of Chicago Press.
MEEK, Charles Kingsley
1937   Law and Authority in a Nigerian Tribe: A Study in Indirect Rule. London, Oxford University Press.

MEERT, Jacques
    1956   "Outstanding Missionary Problems in the Congo and Black Africa," Christ to the World, 1, 6:74–87.
MEGGERS, Betty J.
    1954   "Environmental Limitation on the Development of Culture," in American Anthropologist, 56:801–824.
MERRIFIELD, William R., et al.
    1962   Laboratory Manual for Morphology and Syntax. Santa Ana, Calif., Summer Institute of Linguistics.
MESSENGER, JOHN C.
    1959   "The Christian Concept of Forgiveness and Anang Morality," Practical Anthropology, 6:97–103.
MESSNER, J.
    1949   Social Ethics: Natural Law in the Modern World. St. Louis, Herder.
MÉTRAUX, Alfred
    1959   Voodoo in Haiti. London (and Commonwealth Countries), Andre Deutsch, Esq. Publishers; New York, Oxford University Press. (Selections of the book reprinted in Charles Leslie [ed.], Anthropology of Folk Religion, a paperback Vintage Book, Alfred A. Knopf and Random House.)
MÉTRAUX, R., and MEAD, M.
    1954   Themes in French Culture: A Preface to a Study of the French Community. Stanford, Calif., Stanford University Press.
MEYER, B. F. (M.M.)
    1955   Lend Me Your Hands. Chicago, Fides.
MICHONNEAU, Abbé
    1949   Revolution in a City Parish. Westminster, Md., Newman.
    1957   "Visits to Families and Contact with Militants," Christ to the World, 2:354–362.
MIHALIC, Francis (S.V.D.)
    1957   Grammar and Dictionary of Neo-Melanesian. Techny, Ill., The Mission Press.
MIHANOVICH, Clement S.
    1950   Current Social Problems. Milwaukee, Bruce.
MILLOT, René-P.
    1961   Mission in the World Today. Vol. 100 of the Twentieth Century Encyclopedia of Catholicism. New York, Hawthorn Books.
MINISTRY OF COMMUNITY DEVELOPMENT, Government of India
    1957   A Guide to Community Development.
Mission et cultures non-chretiennes: Rapports et compte rendu de la XXIXe
    1959   semaine de missiologie. Louvain, Desclée.
MONGTAGU, M. F. Ashley
    1945   Man's Most Dangerous Myth: The Fallacy of Race. New York, Columbia University Press.
    1951   An Introduction to Physical Anthropology. Second edition. Springfield, Ill., Thomas. (First edition, 1945; third edition, 1960.)
    1960   A Handbook of Anthropometry. Springfield, Ill., Thomas.
MOOMAW, I. W.
    1957   Deep Furrows. New York, Agricultural Missions.
MOONEY, James
    1896   The Ghost-Dance Religion and the Sioux Outbreak of 1890. Annual Reports of the Bureau of American Ethnology No. 14.

MOORE, Wilbert E.
1957   "The Migration of Native Laborers in South Africa," in Shannon
        (ed.), Underdeveloped Areas, pp. 79–87.
MORGAN, M.
1958   Doctors to the World. New York, Viking.
MORRIS, John J. (S.J.)
1957   "Bishops, Priests, and Credit Unions," Social Order, November,
        1957.
MOSHER, Arthur T.
1957   Technical Cooperation in Latin American Agriculture. Chicago,
        University of Chicago Press.
MOYERSOEN, Jean (S.J.)
1962   "Rethinking Our Priestly Apostolate," Christ to the World,
        7:505–516.
MÜHLMANN, W. E., ed.
1961   Chiliasmus und Nativismus: Studien zur Psychologie, Soziologie,
        und historiachen Kasuistik der Umsturzbewegungen. Berlin,
        Dietrich Reimer Verlag.
MÜLLER, Karl (S.V.D.), ed.
1962   Missionsstudien, Nr. 1. Studia Instituti Missiologici Societatis
        Verbi Divini, St. Augustin/Siegburg (Germany), Washington,
        and Buenos Aires.
MURDOCK, George P.
1945   "The Common Denominator of Cultures," in R. Linton (ed.),
(1957) The Science of Man in the World Crisis, pp. 123–142. (Eighth
        printing, 1957.)
1949   Social Structure. New York, Macmillan.
1952   "Anthropology and Its Contribution to Public Health," American
        Journal of Public Health, January, 1952.
1956   "How Culture Changes," in Shapiro (ed.), Man, Culture, and
(1957) Society, pp. 247–260. (Second printing, 1957.)
MURDOCK, George P., et al.
1961   Outline of Cultural Materials, New Haven, Human Relations
        Area Files.
MURPHY, Edward L. (S.J.)
1958   Teach Ye All Nations. New York, Benziger.
1961   "The Function of the Missionary in the Socio-Economic Status in
        a People," in Hatton (ed.), Missiology in Africa Today, pp.
        47–57.
1962   "The Concept of Mission: Popes and Theologians," in Ewing
        (ed.), The Global Mission of the Church, pp. II, 1–5. (Printed
        also in Shield, XLI [1962], No. 5, pp. 2–3, 22 under the title
        of "The Concept of Mission and Its Development.")
MURRAY, Raymond W. (C.S.C.)
1935   Introductory Sociology. New York, Crofts.
(1947) (Thirteenth printing, 1947.)
1950   Sociology for a Democratic Society. New York, Appleton-Cen-
        tury-Croft.
MYRDAL, Gunnar
1944   An American Dilemma. New York, Harper. (2 vols.)
1957   Rich Lands and Poor: The Road to World Prosperity. Vol. XVI
        of "World Perspectives" Series, planned and edited by Ruth
        Nanda Anshen. New York, Harper.

Mystici Corporis (Pius XII, June 29, 1943.)
1943   Introduction and notes by Joseph Bluett, S.J., "The Mystical Body of Christ," New York, America Press.

NADEL, S. F.
1947   *The Nuba: An Anthropological Study of the Tribes of Kordofan.* London, Oxford University Press.
1951   *The Foundations of Social Anthropology.* London, Cohen and West.
1955-56   "Understanding Primitive Peoples," *Oceania*, 26:157–173.
1957   *The Theory of Social Structure.* Glencoe, Ill., Free Press.

NAKAMURA, Hajime
1960   *The Ways of Thinking of Eastern Peoples.* Tokyo, Japanese National Commission for UNESCO.

NASH, Manning
1959   "Applied and Action Anthropology in the Understanding of Man." *Anthropological Quarterly*, 32:67–81.
1962   "Race and the Ideology of Race," *Current Anthropology*, 3:285–302.

NATIONAL RESEARCH COUNCIL
1943   *The Problem of Changing Food Habits.* Bulletin 108. Washington, D. C.

NATIONAL SOCIETY FOR THE STUDY OF EDUCATION
1959   *Community Education, Principle and Practices from World-Wide Experience.* Fifty-eighth Yearbook. University of Chicago.

NETTL, Bruno
1956   *Music in Primitive Culture.* Cambridge, Mass., Harvard University Press.

NEUMEYER, Martin H. and Esther S.
1958   *Leisure and Recreation: A Study of Leisure and Recreation in Their Sociological Aspects.* New York, Ronald.

NEWELL, W. H.
1947   " 'Functional' Social Anthropology and the Christian Missionary Method," *International Review of Missions*, XXXVI (1947), No. 142, pp. 253–257.

NIDA, Eugene A.
1947   *Bible Translating.* New York, American Bible Society.
1952   *God's Word in Man's Language.* New York, Harper.
1954   *Customs and Cultures: Anthropology for Christian Missions.* New York, Harper.
1957   *Learning a Foreign Language: A Handbook Prepared Especially for Missionaries.* New York, Friendship Press. (Revised ed.)
1960a   *Message and Mission: The Communication of the Christian Faith.* New York, Harper.
1960b   "Many Cultures as Our Own Witness," in Rosengrant, *et al.*, *Assignment Overseas*, pp. 51–65.
1960c   "Mariology in Latin America," *Practical Anthropology*, Supplement (1960), 7–15.
1960d   "The Roman Catholic, Communist, and Protestant Approach to Social Structure," *Practical Anthropology*, Supplement (1960), 21–26.
1960e   "The Ugly Missionary," *Practical Anthropology*, 7:74–78.
1961a   "Christo-Paganism," *Practical Anthropology*, 8:1–14.

1961b   "The Indigenous Churches in Latin America," *Practical Anthropology*, 8:99–105.
1961c   "Communication of the Gospel to Latin Americans," *Practical Anthropology*, 8:145–156.
1961d   Review of C. Couturier, *The Mission of the Church. Practical Anthropology*, 8:93–96.
NIDA, Eugene A., and WONDERLY, William L.
1963   "Selection, Preparation, and Function of Leaders in Indian Fields," *Practical Anthropology*, 10:6–16.
NOBLE, Lowell L.
1961   "Can St. Paul's Methods Be Ours?" 8:180–185.
1962   "A Culturally Relevant Witness to Animists," *Practical Anthropology*, 9:220–222.
NORTHROP, F. S. C.
1946   *The Meeting of East and West: An Inquiry Concerning World Understanding.* New York, Macmillan.
NORTHROP, F. S. C., ed.
1949   *Ideological Difference and World Order.* New Haven, Yale University Press.
NUESSE, C. J., and HARTE, T. J. (C.Ss.R.)
1951   *The Sociology of the Parish.* Milwaukee, Bruce.

OAKES, Maud
1951   *The Two Crosses of Todos Santos: Survival of Mayan Religious Ritual.* New York, Pantheon Books.
OAKLEY, Kenneth P.
1949   *Man the Tool-Maker.* London, British Museum (Natural History).
(1956)   (Third edition, 1956.) (Also available in America as a Pantheon paperback, Chicago, University of Chicago Press.)
OBERG, Kalervo
1960   "Cultural Shock: Adjustment to New Cultural Environments," *Technical Assistance Quarterly Bulletin*, New York, Technical Information Clearing House. Reprinted in *Practical Anthropology*, 7:177–182.
O'CONNOR, John J.
1952   "Industrial-Age Apostles," *Social Order*, November, 1952.
OHM, Thomas
1959   *Asia Looks at Western Christianity.* New York, Herder and Herder.
O'LAOGHAIRE, Diarmuid (S.J.)
1959   "The Church and National Culture," *Worldmission*, 10, 3:40–45.
OLIVER, Douglas L.
1951   *The Pacific Islands.* Cambridge, Mass., Harvard Univesity Press.
ONG, Walter J.
1958   "That American Way," *America*, November 22, 1958.
OPLER, Morris Edward
1945   "Themes as Dynamic Forces in Culture," *American Journal of Sociology*, 51:198–206.
1946   "An Application of the Theory of Themes in Culture," *Journal of the Washington Academy of Sciences*, 36:137–165.
OWEN, David
1957   "Technical Assistance for Economic Development," in Shannon (ed.), *Underdeveloped Areas*, pp. 321–330.

PACKARD, Vance
　　1957　　The Hidden Persuaders. New York, David McKay.
PARRINDER, Geoffrey
　　1951　　West African Psychology: A Comparative Study of Psychological and Religious Thought. London, Lutterworth Press.
PATTERSON, Sheila
　　1953　　Colour and Culture in South Africa: A Study of the Cape Coloured People Within the Social Structure of South Africa. London.
PAUL, Benjamin D.
　　1953　　"Respect for Cultural Differences," Community Development Bulletin, 4:42–47.
PAUL, Benjamin D., ed.
　　1955　　Health, Culture, and Community: Case Studies of Public Reactions to Health Programs. New York, Russell Sage.
PEATTIE, Lisa R.
　　1958　　"Interventionism and Applied Science in Anthropology," Human Organization, 17:4–8.
PENNIMAN, Thomas K.
　　1936　　One Hundred Years of Anthropology. Cambridge, University Press.
　　(1952)　　Revised edition (1952), London, Gerold Duckworth.
PHILIPS, G.
　　1956　　The Role of the Laity in the Church. Chicago, Fides.
PIDDINGTON, Ralph
　　1950　　An Introduction to Social Anthropology. Vol. I. Edinburgh and London, Oliver and Boyd Publishers.
　　1957　　An Introduction to Social Anthropology. Vol. II. Edinburgh and London, Oliver and Boyd Publishers.
PIEPER, J.
　　1952　　Leisure: The Basis of Culture. New York, Pantheon.
PIKE, Eunice V., and COWAN, Florence
　　1959　　"Mushroom Ritual versus Christianity," Practical Anthropology, 6:145–150.
PIKE, Evelyn G., and Staff
　　1954　　Laboratory Manual for Pike's Phonemics. Glendale, Calif., Summer Institute of Linguistics.
PIKE, Kenneth L.
　　1945　　The Intonation of American English. Ann Arbor, University of Michigan Press.
　　1947　　Phonemics: A Technique for Reducing Languages to Writing. Ann Arbor, University of Michigan Press.
　　1948　　Tone Languages: A Technique for Determinining the Number and Type of Pitch Contrasts in a Language, with Studies in Tonemic Substitution and Fusion. Ann Arbor, University of Michigan Press.
　　1954–55　Language in Relation to a Unified Theory of the Structure of Human Behavior. Glendale, Calif., Summer Institute of Linguistics. (Part I, 1954; Part II, 1955.)
　　1961　　"Stimulating and Resisting Culture Change," Practical Anthropology, 8:267–274.
PIKE, Kenneth L. and Eunice V.
　　1955　　Live Issues in Descriptive Linguistic Analysis. Glendale, Calif., Summer Institute of Linguistics.

398 GENERAL BIBLIOGRAPHY

PIUS XI
   1926   *Rerum Ecclesiae.* English translation by Glenn F. Williams, S.J.,
           in Burke (ed.), *Catholic Missions: Four Great Encyclicals.*
PIUS XII
   1943   *Mystici Corporis.* Acta Apostolicae Sedis, XXXV (1943).
   1945   *Christmas Message.* Acta Apostolicae Sedis, XXXVIII (1946).
   1947   *Mediator Dei.* Acta Apostolicae Sedis, XXXIX (1947).
   1950   *Humani Generis.* Acta Apostolicae Sedis, XLII (1950).
   1951   *Evangelii Praecones.* Acta Apostolicae Sedis, XLIII (1951). Eng-
           lish translation by Clarence McAuliffe, S.J., in Burke (ed.),
           Catholic Missions: Four Great Encyclicals.
   1953   Allocution, December 6, 1953. Acta Apostolicae Sedis, XLX
           (1953), 794–803.
   1957a   Second Congress of Lay Apostles, October 6, 1957.
   1957b   *Fidei Donum.* English Translation in Burke (ed.), *Catholic
           Missions: Four Great Encyclicals.*
           NOTE: Official English translations of papal encyclicals available
           at National Catholic Welfare Conference, Washington, D. C.
"Planning Agencies for Latin America," *C.I.F. Reports,* I (1926), 176.
POLGAR, Steven
   1962   "Health and Human Behavior: Areas of Interest Common to the
           Social and Medical Sciences," *Current Anthropology,* 3:159–
           205.
POLLOCK, Robert, C.
   1955   *The Mind of Pius XII.* New York, Crown.
POWDERMAKER, Hortense
   1955   "Communication and Social Change: Based on a Field Study in
           Northern Rhodesia," *Transactions of the New York Academy
           of Sciences,* series 2, XVIII (1955), No. 5, pp. 430–440
"Preservation of Tradition, Material Progress Furthered by Catholic Church in
           Japan," *Mission Bulletin,* Hong Kong, IX (1957), 708–709.
PRETORIUS, Pauline
   1950   "An Attempt at Christian Initiation in Nyasaland," *International
           Review of Missions,* XXXIX (1950), No. 155, pp. 284–291.
Proceedings of the Lima Methods Conference of the Maryknoll Fathers. Mary-
           knoll, N. Y., Maryknoll Publications, 1954.
PUTNAM, Carleton
   1961   *Race and Reason: A Yankee View.* Washington, Public Affairs
           Press.
   1962   *The Road to Reversal.* New York, National Putnam Letters Com-
           mittee.
PUTZ, L. J. (C.S.C.)
   1957   *The Modern Apostle.* Chicago, Fides.

QUÉGUINER, Maurice (Very Rev.)
   1962   "Theology of Missionary Cooperation," *Christ to the World,*
           7:491–504.

RADCLIFFE-BROWN, Alfred R.
   1922   *The Andaman Islanders.* London. (Cambridge, Cambridge Uni-
   (1948) versity Press, 1933; 1948, new edition, Glencoe, Ill., Free
           Press.)

1948a   A Natural Science of Society. A transcript of the famous faculty
(1957)   seminar presented by Radcliffe-Brown at the University of
         Chicago. Chicago, University of Chicago Press, 1948; Glencoe,
         Ill., Free Press, 1957.
1948b   "On the Concept of Function in Social Science," American An-
         thropologist, 37:394-395.
1952   Structure and Function in Primitive Society: Essays and Address.
         London, Cohen and West; Glencoe, Ill., Free Press.
RADIN, Paul
1927   Primitive Man as Philosopher, New York, D. Appleton.
(1957)   (Dover paper back edition, 1957.)
RAHMANN, Rudolf (S.V.D.)
1956   "Fünfzig Jahre 'Anthropos,'" Anthropos, 51:1-18.
1957   "Vier Pioniere der Völkerkunde, den Patres Paul Arndt, Martin
         Gusinde, Wilhelm Koppers und Paul Schebesta zum siebzigsten
         Geburtstag," Anthropos, 52: 263-276.
RAMSAUER, Martin (S.J.)
1960   "The Demands for a Mission Catechism," Asia (formerly Mission
         Bulletin, Hong Kong), 12:370-376.
1961   "A Good Mission Catechism," in Hofinger (ed.), Teaching All
         Nations, pp. 174-191.
RANDHWA, M. S., ed.
1951   Developing Village India. Bombay, Longmanns.
RAPOPORT, Robert N.
1954   Changing Navaho Religious Values: A Study of Christian Mis-
         sions to the Rimrock Navahos. Cambridge, Mass., Peabody
         Museum.
REAY, Marie
1959   The Kuma: Freedom and Conformity in the New Guinea High-
         lands. Melbourne, Melbourne University Press.
REDFIELD, Robert
1930   Tepoztlán, A Mexican Village: A Study of Folk Life. Chicago,
         University of Chicago Press.
1939   "Culture Contact without Conflict," American Anthropologist,
         41:514-517.
1941   Folk Culture of the Yucatan. Chicago University Press.
1947   "The Folk Society," American Journal of Sociology, 52:293-308.
1950   A Village That Chose Progress: Chan Kom Revisited. Chicago,
         University of Chicago Press.
1953a   "Relation of Anthropology to the Social Sciences and to the
         Humanities," in Kroeber (ed.), Anthropology Today, pp. 728-
         730.
1953b   The Primitive World and Its Transformation. Ithaca, N. Y.
         Cornell University Press.
1955a   The Little Community: Viewpoints for the Study of a Human
         Whole. Chicago, University of Chicago Press.
1955b   From Primitive Life to Civilization. Chicago, University of Chicago
         Press.
1956a   "How Human Society Operates," in Shapiro (ed.), Man, Culture,
         and Society, pp. 345-368.
1956b   Peasant Society and Culture. Chicago, University of Chicago Press.
1959   "Anthropology's Contribution to the Understanding of Man,"
         Anthropological Quarterly, 32:3-21.

REDFIELD, Robert, LINTON, Ralph, and HERSKOVITS, Melville J.
  1936   "Memorandum on the Study of Acculturation," *American Anthropologist*, 38:149–152.
Report on the World Social Situation. UN Publications No. 57.IV.3., New York, 1957.
RETIF, Louis and André
  1962   *The Mission of the Church in the World.* London, Burns and Oates. (Also, *The Church's Mission in the World*, Vol. 102 of the Twentieth Century Encyclopedia of Catholicism, New York, Hawthorn Books.)
REYBURN, Marie Fetzer
  1953   "Applied Anthropology among the Sierra Quechua of Ecuador," *Practical Anthropology*, 1:15–22.
REYBURN, William D.
  1959   "Polygamy, Economy, and Christianity in the Eastern Cameroun," *Practical Anthropology*, 6:1–19.
  1960a   "Identification in the Missionary Task," *Practical Anthropology*, 7:1–15.
  1960b   "Christian Responsibility toward Social Change," *Practical Anthropology*, 7:124–131.
  1962   "Africanization and African Studies," *Practical Anthropology*, 9:97–110.
RICHARDS, A. I.
  1944   "Practical Anthropology in the Lifetime of the International African Institute," *Africa*, 14:289–301.
RICHARDSON, F. L. M.
  1955   "Anthropology and Human Relations in Business and Industry," in *Yearbook of Anthropology — 1955*. New York, Wenner-Gren.
  1961   *Talk, Work, and Action.* Monograph No. 3. Society for Applied Anthropology.
RIPPY, J. F., and Nelson, J. T.
  1936   *Crusaders of the Jungle.* Chapel Hill, N. C., University of North Carolina Press.
RITCHIE, Jean A. S.
  1950   *Teaching Better Nutrition.* FAO, UN Publications.
RIVERS, W. H. R., ed.
  1922   *Essays on the Depopulation of Melanesia.* Cambridge University Press.
ROBERTS, P.
  1962   *English Sentences.* New York, Harcourt, Brace.
ROCHA, Victor, ed.
  1957   *Apostolic Approach.* Second Inter-Diocesan Conference of Priests, May, 1957. Pachmarhi, M.P., India.
RODNICK, David
  1955   *The Norwegians: A Study in National Culture.* Washington, Public Affairs Press.
ROSE, Arnold
  1944   *The Negro in America.* New York. (A condensation of G. Myrdal's *The American Dilemma*.)
  1951   *The Roots of Prejudice*, UNESCO.
ROSE, Edward
  1947–48 "Innovations in American Culture," *Social Forces*, 26:255–276.

ROSENGRANT, John, et al.
1960   Assignment Overseas: How to Be a Welcome Resident and a
        Worthy Christian Abroad. New York, Crowell.
ROSENSTIEL, Annette
1959   "Anthropology and the Missionary," Journal of the Royal Anthro-
(1961) pological Institute, 89:107–115. (Reprinted in Practical An-
        thropology, 8:15–24.)
ROSNER, J. (S.A.C.)
1961   "Misssionary Adaptation in Theory and Practice," in Hatton
        (ed.), Missiology in Africa Today, pp. 96–108.
ROSS, Murray G.
1959   Community Organization: Theory and Principles. New York,
        Harper.
ROSS, Murray G., and HENDRY, C. E.
1957   New Understanding of Leadership. New York, Association Press.
ROSSMAN, Joseph
1931   The Psychology of the Inventor. Washington, Inventor's Pub-
        lishing Co.
ROUSE, Irving
1953   "The Strategy of Culture History," in Kroeber (ed.), Anthro-
        pology Today, pp. 57–76.
ROWE, J. W.
1946   The Inca Culture at the Time of the Conquest. In Vol. 2 of
        J. H. Steward, ed., Handbook of South American Indians.
        Washington, Smithsonian Institution.
ROYAL ANTHROPOLOGICAL INSTITUTE OF GREAT BRITAIN
AND IRELAND
1929   Notes and Queries on Anthropology. London, Routledge and
(1951) Kegan Paul. (Sixth edition, 1951.)
RUOPP, Phillips, ed.
1953   Approaches to Community Development. A symposium intro-
        ductory to problems and methods of village welfare in under-
        developed areas. The Hague, van Hoeve Ltd.
RYCROFT, W. Stanley
1958   Religion and Faith in Latin America. Philadelphia, Westminster.
"Sacred Music in the Missions," Mission Bulletin, Hong Kong, IX (1957),
        533–535.

SALIEGE, Jules Cardinal
1949   Who Shall Bear the Flame, Chicago, Fides.
SAPIR, Edward
1921   Language: An Introduction to the Study of Speech. New York,
        Harcourt, Brace. (Paperback reprint, Harvest Books, Harcourt,
        Brace.)
1960   Culture, Language and Personality: Selected Essays. (Selected
        essays edited by David G. Mandelbaum.) Berkley and Los
        Angeles, University of California Press.
SASAKI, Tom, and ADAIR, John
1952   "New Land to Farm: Agricultural Practices Among the Navaho
        Indians of New Mexico," in Spicer (ed.), Human Problems in
        Technological Change, pp. 97–112.
SAUNDERS, Lyle
1954   Cultural Difference and Medical Care. New York, Russell Sage.

SCHAEFFER, Alphonse (S.V.D.)
1956   "How Laymen Successfully Struggled Against Superstition in New
        Guinea," *Christ to the World,* 1, 5:42–44.
1960–61 "A Post Turns into the Cross," *Worldmission,* 11, 4:41–47.
SCHARMACH, Bishop Leo (M.S.C.)
1953   *Manuale Missionariorum.* Kokopo, New Britain, Catholic Mission
        Vunapope.
SCHARPER, P. C.
1962   "Mission and Culture," in Ewing (ed.), *Global Mission of the
        Church,* pp. IV, 1–5.
SCHEBESTA, Paul (S.V.D.)
1954   "Pater Wilhelm Schmidt, S.V.D., 1868–1954," *Man,* LIV (1954),
        No. 128, pp. 89–90.
SCHMIDLIN, Joseph
1931   *Catholic Mission Theory.* (A translation of *Katolische Missions-
        lehre im Grundriss.*) Techny, Ill., Mission Press.
1933   *Catholic Mission History.* (Edited by Matthias Braun, S.V.D. A
        translation.) Techny, Ill., Mission Press.
SCHMIDT, Wilhelm (S.V.D.)
1939   *The Culture Historical Method of Ethnology: The Scientific Ap-
        proach to the Racial Question.* Translated by S. A. Sieber. New
        York, Fortuny.
1926–55 *Der Ursprung der Gottesidee.* 12 vols. Münster, Aschendorf.
SCHNEIDER, David M.
1955   "Abortion and Depopulation on a Pacific Island," in Paul (ed.),
        Health, Culture, and Community, pp. 211–235.
1953   "A Note on Bridewealth and the Stability of Marriage," *Man,*
        53:55–57.
SCHREIBER, William J.
1962   *Our Amish Neighbors.* University of Chicago Press and University
        of Toronto Press.
SCHUETTE, John (S.V.D.)
1960   "The Primacy of Religious and Spiritual Endeavors in the Mis-
        sions," in Hofinger (ed.), *Liturgy and the Missions,* pp. 47–58.
SCHWARZ, Fred
1960   *You Can Trust the Communists (to be Communists).* Engle-
        wood Cliffs, N. J., Prentice-Hall.
SEGUNDO, Juan Luis (S.J.)
1962   "The Passage to Pluralism in Latin America," *C.I.F. Reports,*
        1:313–322.
SERVICE, Elman Rogers
1958   *A Profile of Primitive Culture.* New York, Harper.
SEUMOIS, André (O.M.I.)
1961   *L'Anima dell'Apostolato Missionario.* Parma, Editrice Missionaria
        Italiana.
SHANNON, Lyle W., ed.
1957   *Underdeveloped Areas: A Book of Readings and Research.* New
        York, Harper.
SHAPIRO, Harry L.
1945   "Society and Biological Man," in Linton (ed.), *The Science of
        Man in the World Crisis,* pp. 19–37.
SHAPIRO, Harry L., ed.
1956   *Man, Culture, and Society.* New York, Oxford University Press.

SHARP, J. Lauriston
  1952   "Steel Axes for Stone Age Australians," *Human Organization*,
  (1952)   XI (1952), No. 2. (Reprinted in Spicer [ed.], *Human Prob-*
  (1960)   *lems in Technological Change*, pp. 69–90; also in *Practical
          Anthropology* 7:62–73.)
SHAW, Russel
  1961   "The Church — Comfortable or Suffering," *Ave Maria*, October
          14, 1961.
SHERIF, Muzafer, ed.
  1962   *Intergroup Relations and Leadership: Approaches and Research
          in Industrial, Ethnic, Cultural, and Political Areas.* New York,
          John Wiley.
SHIMKIN, Dimitri B.
  1952   "Industrialization, A Challenging Problem for Cultural Anthro-
          pology," *Southwestern Journal of Anthropology*, 8:84–91.
SIBLEY, Willis E.
  1960–61 "Social Structures and Planned Change: A Case Study from the
          Philippines," *Human Organization*, 19:209–211.
SIEGEL, Bernard J., ed.
  1955   *Acculturation: Critical Abstracts, North America.* Stanford An-
          thropological Series, No. 2. Stanford, Calif., Stanford University
          Press; London, Geoffrey Cumberlege, Oxford University Press.
SIMMONS, Leo W., and WOLFF, Harold G.
  1954   *Social Science in Medicine.* New York, Russell Sage.
SIMPSON, George E.
  1962   "The Shango Cult in Nigeria and in Trinidad," *American An-
          thropologist*, 64:1204–1219.
SINGH, Rudra Datt
  1952   "An Introduction of Green Manuring in Rural India," in Spicer
          (ed.), *Human Problems in Technological Change*, pp. 55–68.
SLOTKIN, J. S.
  1952   "Menomini Peyotism," in *Transactions of the American Philo-
          sophical Society*, XLII (1952), Part 4.
  1955   "Peyotism, 1521–1891," *American Anthropologist*, 57:202–230.
  1955–56 "The Peyote Way," *Tomorrow*, 4:64–70. (Reprinted in Lessa and
  (1958)   Vogt [eds.], *Reader in Comparative Religion*, pp. 482–486.)
  1956   *The Peynote Religion: A Study in Indian-White Relations.* Glen-
          coe, Ill., Free Press.
SMALLEY, William A.
  1956   "The Gospel and the Cultures of Laos," *Practical Anthropology*,
          3:47–57.
  1958   "Cultural Implications of an Indigenous Church," *Practical An-
          thropology*, 5:61–65.
  1959a   "The Moral Implications of Social Structure," *Practical Anthro-
          pology*, 6:140–144.
  1959b   "Some Questions about Missionary Medicine," *Practical An-
          thropology*, 6:90–95.
  1960a   *Selected and Annotated Bibliography of Anthropology for Mis-
          sionaries.* Occasional Bulletin, XI (1960), No. 1. New York,
          Missionary Research Library.
  1960b   "Anthropological Study and Missionary Scholarship," *Practical An-
          thropology*, 7:113–123.
  1960c   "Religious Systems and Allegiance to Christ," *Practical Anthro-
          pology*, 7:223–226.

1961   Manual of Articulatory Phonetics. 2 vols. Tarrytown, N. Y.,
        Practical Anthropology.
1963   "Culture Shock, Language Shock, and the Shock of Self-Dis-
        covery," Practical Anthropology, 10:49–56.
SMITH, Bruce L.
1957   "Communications Research on Non-Industrial Countries," in
        Shannon (ed.), Underdeveloped Areas, pp. 360–368.
SMITH, Edwin W.
1924   "Social Anthropology and Missionary Work," The International
        Review of Missions, 13:518–531.
1927   The Golden Stool: Some Aspects of the Conflict of Cultures in
        Modern Africa. London, The Society for the Propagation of the
        Gospel in Foreign Parts.
1934   "Anthropology and the Practical Man," Journal of the Royal
        Anthropological Institute, 64:xiii–xxxvii.
SMITH, Gordon Hedderly
1945   The Missionary and Anthropology: An Introduction to the Study
        of Primitive Man for Missionaries. Chicago, Moody Press.
Social Implications of Industrialization and Urbanization in Africa South of the
        Sahara. Prepared by the International African Institute, London.
        Paris, UNESCO, 1956.
SPECTOR, Paul, and PRESTON, Harley O.
1961   Working Effectively Overseas. Prepared for the Peace Corps by
        the Institute for International Services of the American Institute
        of Research. Washington, American Institute for Research.
SPECTOR, Paul, et al.
1961   Instructional Situations. A supplement to Spector and Preston,
        Working Effectively Overseas.
SPENCER, Baldwin, and GILLEN, F. J.
1927   The Arunta. London, Macmillan.
SPENCER, Robert F., ed.
1954   Method and Perspective in Anthropology: Papers in Honor of
        Wilson D. Wallis. Minneapolis, University of Minnesota Press.
SPICER, Edward H.
1952   "Sheepman and Technicians: A Program of Soil Conservation on
        the Navajo Indian Reservation," in Spicer (ed.), Human Prob-
        lems in Technological Change, pp. 185–208.
1954   "Spanish-Indian Acculturation in the South-West," American An-
        thropologist, 56:663–684.
SPICER, Edward H., ed.
1952   Human Problems in Technological Change: A Casebook. New
        York, Russell Sage.
SPINDLER, George D.
1955   Sociocultural and Psychological Processes in Menomini Accultura-
        tion, University of California Publications in Culture and
        Society, Vol. V.
SPINDLER, George D., ed.
1955   Education and Anthropology. Stanford, Calif., Stanford University
        Press.
SPINDLER, George D., and GOLDSCHMIDT, Walter
1952   "Experimental Design in the Study of Culture Change," South-
        western Journal of Anthropology, 8:68–83.

SPINDLER, Louise D.
1962 *Menomini Women and Culture Change.* American Anthropological Association Memoir 91.
SPRINKLE, R. (M.M.)
1956 "Post Baptism Practice," *Mission Bulletin,* Hong Kong, 8:536–567.
STANNER, W. E. H.
1958 "On the interpretation of Cargo Cults" *Oceania,* 29:1–25.
STEVICK, Earl W.
1955 *Helping People Learn English: A Manual for Teachers of English as a Second Language.* New York and Nashville, Abingdon Press.
STEWARD, Julian H.
1949 "Cultural Causality and Law: A Trial Formulation of the Development of Early Civilizations," *American Anthropologist,* 51:1–27.
1951 "Levels of Sociocultural Integration: An Operational Concept," *Southwestern Journal of Anthropology,* 7:374–390.
1953 "Evolution and Process," in Kroeber (ed.), *Anthropology Today,* pp. 313–327.
1956 *The Theory of Culture Change: The Methodology of Multilinear Evolution.* Urbana, Ill., University of Illinois Press.
STEWARD, Julian H., ed.
1946–50 *Handbook of South American Indians.* 6 vols. Smithsonian Institution. Bureau of American Ethnology, Washington, Government Printing Office.
STEWARD, Julian H., and FARON, Louis C.
1959 *Native Peoples of South America.* New York, Toronto, and London, McGraw-Hill.
Study Kit on Training for Community Development. UN Publication No. 57.IV.6.
STURZO, Luigi
1944 *Inner Laws of Society: A New Sociology.* New York, Kenedy.
SUENENS, Leon-Joseph Cardinal
1956 *The Gospel to Every Creature.* London, Burns, and Oates. (Transl. from French by Louise Gavan Duffy.)
1963 *The Nun in the World.* Westminster, Md., Newman.
SUHARD, E.
1953 *The Church Today.* Chicago, Fides.
SUNDKLER, Bengt
1960 "Bantu Messiah and White Christ," *Practical Anthropology,* 7:170–176.
SYNNOTT, F. (O.P.)
1961 "The Apostolate to the Migratory Workers," in Hatton (ed.), *Missiology in Africa Today,* pp. 115–125.

TALBOT, Francis X. (S.J.)
1956 *Saint Among the Hurons.* Garden City, N. Y., Doubleday. (Doubleday Image Book.)
1961 *Saint Among Savages.* Garden City, N. Y. Doubleday. (Doubleday Image Book; originally, Harper, 1935.)
TANNOUS, Afif I.
1957 "Positive Role of the Social Scientist in the Point Four Program," in Shannon (ed.), *Underdeveloped Areas,* pp. 287–295.

406   GENERAL BIBLIOGRAPHY

TAX, Sol
  1955a   "The Integration of Anthropology," in Thomas (ed.), *Current Anthropology*, pp. 313–328.
  1955b   "From Lafitau to Radcliffe-Brown," in Eggan (ed.), *Social Anthropology of North American Indians*, pp. 445–481.
TAX, Sol, ed.
  1952a   *Heritage and Conquest: The Ethnology of Middle America.* Glencoe, Ill., Free Press.
  1952b   *Acculturation in the Americas: Proceedings and Selected Papers of the XXIXth International Congress of Americanists.* Chicago, University of Chicago Press.
TAYLOR, Carl C.
  1956   *A Critical Analysis of India's Community Development Programme.* The Community Projects Administration, Government of India.
TAYLOR, John V.
  1950   "The Development of African Drama for Education and Evangelism," *International Review of Missions*, XXXIX (1950), No. 155, pp. 292–301.
TEAD, O.
  1935   *The Art of Leadership.* New York, McGraw-Hill.
Technical Assistance: What? How? Why? UN Office of Information, No. 58.I.9 (1958).
TEMPELS, Placide
  1949   *La Philosophie Bantoue.* Paris, Editions Africaines.
THEODORSON, George A.
  1953   "Acceptance of Industrialization and Its Attendant Consequence for the Social Patterns of Non-Western Societies," *American Sociological Review*, 18:477–484.
  1961   *Studies in Human Ecology.* Evanston, Ill. and Elmsford, N. Y., Row, Peterson.
THOMAS, William I., and ZNANIECKI, Florian
  1927   *The Polish Peasant in Europe and America.* (2 vols., second edition.) New York, Alfred A. Knopf.
THOMAS, William L., ed.
  1955   *Current Anthropology.* University of Chicago Press. (Parts I–III
  (1956)   of *Yearbook of Anthropology — 1955*, Wenner-Gren Foundation, republished by University of Chicago Press under title of *Current Anthropology*, 1956.)
  1956   *Man's Role in Changing the Face of the Earth.* Chicago, University of Chicago Press.
THOMPSON, Laura
  1948   "Attitudes and Acculturation," *American Anthropologist*, 50:200–215.
  1950   *Culture in Crisis: A Study of the Hopi Indians.* New York, Harper.
THORMAN, Donald J.
  1962   *The Emerging Layman: The Role of the Catholic Layman in America.* Garden City, N. Y., Doubleday.
THRUPP, S. L., ed.
  1962   *Millennial Dreams in Action: Essays in Comparative Study.* Supplement No. 2 to *Comparative Studies in Society and History.* Hague, Mouton and Co.

THURNWALD, Richard
    1932   "The Psychology of Acculturation," *American Anthropologist*, 34:557–569.
    1938   "The African in Transition: Some Comparisons with Melanesia," *Africa*, 11:174–186.

TITIEV, Mischa
    1959   *Introduction to Cultural Anthropology: On the Role of Cultural Forces in Man's Behavior.* New York, Henry Holt.

TRECKER, Audrey and Harleigh
    1952   *How to Work with Groups.* New York, Woman's Press.

TYLOR, Edward B.
    1874   *Primitive Culture: Researches into the Development of Mythology, Philosophy, Religion, Language, Art, and Custom.* 2 Vols. London, John Murray. (Third edition, 1891.)

UMANA, Isidore P.
    1960   "An African Priest Speaks out His Mind," *Worldmission*, 11, 2:62–70.

Urbanization of Asia and the Far East. UNESCO, 1957.

USEEM, Andrew, and USEEM, Ruth Hill
    1955   *The Western-Educated Man in India.* New York, Dryden.

USEEM, John
    1952   "Democracy in Process: The Development of Democratic Leadership in the Micronesian Islands," in Spicer (ed.), *Human Problems in Technological Change*, pp. 261–280.

UTTERBACK, William E.
    1950   *Group Thinking and Conference Leadership.* New York, Rinehart.

"Value in Action" Symposium, Human Organization, XVII (1958), 2–26.

VAN BEKKUM, Bishop Wilhelm (S.V.D.)
    1958   "The Liturgical Revival in the Service of the Missions," *Liturgical Arts*, 26:76–82.

VAN CAUWELAERT, Bishop Jean (C.I.C.M.)
    1960   "Local Customs and the Liturgy," in Hofinger (ed.), *Liturgy and the Missions*, pp. 202–220.

VAN MELCKEBEKE, Bishop Carlo (C.I.C.M.)
    1960   "The Urgency of Liturgical Renewal in the Far East," in Hofinger (ed.), *Liturgy and the Missions*, pp. 96–102.

VICEDOM, C. F.
    1962   "An Example of Group Conversion," *Practical Anthropology*, 9:123–128.

VOSS, G. (S.J.)
    1946   "Missionary Accommodation," *Mission Academia Studies*, October, 1946.

VRIENS, Livinius (O.F.M.Cap.)
    1960   *Critical Bibliography of Missiology.* Nijmegen, Bestelcentrale de V.S.K.B.Publ.

WAGNER, Gunter
    1936   "The Study of Culture Contact and the Determination of Policy," *Africa*, 9:317–333.

WALLACE, Anthony F. C.
    1956a   "Revitalization Movements," *American Anthropologist*, 58:264–281.

1956b   "New Religions Among the Delaware Indians 1600–1900," *Southwestern Journal of Anthropology*, 12:1–21.
1961   *Culture and Personality*. New York and Toronto, Random House.

WALLACE, Anthony F. C., ed.
1960   *Selected Papers of the Fifth International Congress of Anthropological and Ethnological Sciences, Philadelphia, September 1–9 1956: Men and Cultures*. Philadelphia, University of Pennsylvania Press.

WALLIS, Wilson D.
1939   *Religion in Primitive Society*. New York, Crofts.
1943   *Messiahs: Their Role in Civilization*. Washington, American Council on Public Affairs.

WALSH, Edward A.
1958   "Communications and the Missionary," in Ewing (ed.), *Communication Arts in Mission Work*, pp. 5–24.

WALSH, Bishop James E. (M.M.)
1957   "Missionary Accommodation of Popular Cultures," *Mission Bulletin*, Hong Kong, 9:215–221.

WALSH, M. E., and FURFEY, P. H.
1958   *Social Problems and Social Action*. Englewood Cliffs, N. J., Prentice-Hall.

WANG, Kung-hsing
1946   *The Chinese Mind*. New York, John Day.

WARNER, W. Lloyd
1953   *American Life: Dream and Reality*. Chicago, University of Chicago Press.

WARNER, W. Lloyd, and associates
1949   *Democracy in Jonesville*. New York, Harper.

Water and the World Today. UN Publications No. 57.1.9.E (1957). New York, UN.

WATSON, James Bennet
1952   *Cayuá Culture Change: A Study in Acculturation and Methodolgy*. American Anthropological Association Memoir 73.
1953   "Four Approaches to Culture Change," in Spencer (ed.), *Method and Perspective in Anthropology,* pp. 103–116. From *Social Forces*, 32:137–145.)

WEBB, Herschel
1962   *An Introduction to Japan*. New York, Columbia University Press.

WELLIN, Edward
1955   "Water Boiling in a Peruvian Town," in Paul (ed.), *Health, Culture, and Community*, pp. 71–103.

WEST, James
1945   *Plainville, U.S.A.* New York, Columbia University Press.

WESTERMANN, Diedrich
1949   *The African Today and Tomorrow*. (Rev. ed) London, Oxford University Press.

WHITE, Leslie A.
1943   "Energy and the Evolution of Culture," *American Anthropologist*, 45:335–356.
1949   *The Science of Culture: A Study of Man and Civilization*. New York, Farrar, Straus and Co. (Paperback reprint, Grove Press, New York.)

1959   "The Concept of Culture," *American Anthropologist*, 61:227–251.
WHITING, John W. M.
    1941   *Becoming a Kwoma: Teaching and Learning in a New Guinea Tribe.* New Haven, Yale University Press.
WHITING, John W. M., and CHILD, I. L.
    1953   *Child Training and Personality: A Cross-Cultural Study.* New Haven, Yale University Press.
WHORF, B. L.
    1941   "The Relation of Habitual Thought and Behavior to Language," in L. Spicer et alii, *Language, Culture, and Personality*, Menasha, Sapir Memorial Publications Fund.
WIENER, Norbert
    1950   *The Human Use of Human Beings: Cybernetics and Society.*
    (1956)   New York, Houghton Mifflin. (Paperback reprint, Doubleday Anchor Books, 1956. Doubleday and Co., Garden City, N. Y.)
WILLEMS, Emilio
    1955   "Protestantism as a Factor of Culture Change in Brazil," *Economic Development and Cultural Change*, 3:321–333.
WILLIAMS, F. E.
    1951   *The Blending of Cultures: An Essay on the Aims of Native Education.* Official Research Publication No. 1. (A republication of Territory of Papua Anthropology Report No. 16.) Port Moresby, Government Printer.
WILLIAMS, Robin M.
    1947   *The Reduction of Intergroup Tensions.* Social Research Council Bulletin 57.
WILSON, Godfrey and Monica
    1945   *The Analysis of Social Change: Based on Observations in Central Africa.* Cambridge, Cambridge University Press.
WISSLER, Clark
    1923   *Man and Culture.* New York, Crowell.
WONDERLY, William L.
    1958   "Pagan and Christian Concepts in a Mexican Indian Culture," *Practical Anthropology*, 5:197–202.
    1960   "Urbanization: The Challenge of Latin America in Transition," *Practical Anthropology*, 7:205–209.
    1961   "Indian Work and Church-Mission Integration," *Practical Anthropology*, 8:193–199.
WORSLEY, Peter
    1957   *The Trumpet Shall Sound: A Study of "Cargo" Cults in Melanesia.* London, Macgibbon and Kee.

YERKES, R. M. and A. W.
    1929   *The Great Apes.* New Haven, Yale University Press.

ZBOROWSKI, Mark, and HERZOG, Elizabeth
    1952   *Life Is with People: The Jewish Little-Town of Eastern Europe.* New York, International Universities Press.
ZEUNER, Frederick E.
    1952   *Dating the Past.* (Third rev. edition.) London, Methuen.
ZUCKERMAN, S.
    1932   *The Social Life of Monkeys and Apes.* London, Kegan Paul, Trench, and Trubner.

BIBLIOGRAPHICAL SUPPLEMENT: 1964-1969

I. THEORY

A. BASIC ANTHROPOLOGICAL READING AND REFERENCE

Beals, Ralph L. and Hoijer, Harry. *An Introduction to Anthropology.* 3rd rev. ed. New York: Macmillan Co., 1965. xxiii, 788 pp.

> An excellent integrated introduction to Anthropology, covering the major anthropological fields of Physical Anthropology, Archaeology, Linguistics, and Cultural Anthropology.

Beattie, John. *Other Cultures: Aims, Methods and Achievements in Social Anthropology.* New York: The Free Press, 1964. 295 pp. paperback.

> A complete, undergraduate presentation of the scope, method, and content of British social anthropology.

Holmes, Lowell D. *Anthropology: An Introduction.* New York: The Ronald Press, 1965. 384 pp.

> An introductory course, general in character. Helps the beginning student appreciate cultural relativism and gives him insights into actual problems and the American "philosophy of life."

Hammond, Peter B., ed. *Cultural and Social Anthropology: Selected Readings.* New York: Macmillan Co., 1964. 498 pp. paperback.

> A useful collection of basic readings for college-level students.

Spiro, Melford E., ed. *Context and Meaning in Cultural Anthropology.* New York: The Free Press, 1965. 464 pp.

> Twenty-five leading social scientists discuss the recent developments in Anthropology: the concept of culture, structure, change, and methods of studying culture.

Taylor, Robert B. *A Compact Introduction to Cultural Anthropology.* Boston: Allyn and Bacon, Inc., 1969. 208 pp. paperback.

> A succinct treatment of culture, structure, change, and methodology. Includes useful bibliography.

International Encyclopedia of the Social Sciences. New York: Collier-Macmillan Library Services, Dept. AS6.

> 1600 leading social scientists contributed to this two-million dollar successor of the original 1937 classic.

411

B. HISTORY OF ANTHROPOLOGY

Harris, Marvin. *The Rise of Anthropological Theory*. New York: Thomas Y. Crowell Co., 1968. 652 pp.
A comprehensive and critical treatment of cultural anthropology from the beginning to the present.

C. FIELD METHODS

Richardson, Stephen A., Dohrenwend, Barbara Snell, and Klein, David. *Interviewing: Its Forms and Functions*. London: Basic Books, Inc., 1965. viii, 380 pp.
A summary of the traditional interviewing procedures in Sociology, Psychology, and Anthropology. The focus is on interaction between the interviewer and respondent rather than on the content of the interview. Topics treated include, e.g., participant-observer techniques, question formulation, dangers and problems.

Beals, Alan R. *Culture in Process*. New York: Holt, Rinehart and Winston, Inc., 1967. 304 pp. paperback.
Essentially a textbook in introductory anthropology; however, can serve as an excellent guide to fieldwork methods.

Collier, John, Jr. *Visual Anthropology: Photography as a Research Method*. New York: Holt, Rinehart and Winston, Inc., 1967.

Epstein, A. L., ed. *The Craft of Social Anthropology*. New York: Barnes and Noble, Inc., U.S. Distributors for Tavistock Publications of London, 1967. paperback.
Nine essays designed to teach field research methods and to serve as guide for anthropologists in the field. All contributors are experienced researchers. Emphasis on accuracy and on nature of problem to be investigated. Bibliography.

Jongmans, D. G. and Gutkind, P. C., eds. *Anthropologists in the Field*. Van Gorcum and Co., N. V., 1967. 277 pp.
Emphasis is on the participant-observer technique. Includes annotated bibliography.

Mead, Margaret. *Anthropolgists and What They Do*. New York: Franklin Watts, Inc., 1965. 209 pp.
An interesting, lively description of museum and field methods by means of a "visit" to eighteen anthropologists who describe their approach to field research and anthropological study.

Powdermaker, Hortense. *Stranger and Friend: The Way of an Anthropologist*. New York: W. W. Norton and Co., 1966. 315 pp.
An autobiography describing own field techniques. With selected bibliography.

Shusky, Ernest, L. *Manual for Kinship Analysis*. (Studies in Anthropological Method.) New York: Holt, Rinehart and Winston, 1965. viii, 84 pp.

A manual for studying kinship designed specifically for the beginning student. Bibliography.

Williams, Thomas Rhys. Field Methods in the Study of Culture. (Studies in Anthropological Method.) New York: Holt, Rinehart and Winston, 1967. xii, 76 pp.

Subjects covered include such basic considerations as: the type of preparation needed, initial contact, research step-by-step procedures, and termination of research. Includes bibliography and recommended readings.

D. AREA STUDIES: GENERAL AREA-ORIENTATION, AREA REFERENCE WORKS, AREA BIBLIOGRAPHIES

1. AFRICA

African Systems of Thought: Studies Presented and Discussed at the Third International African Seminar in Salisbury, December, 1960. New York: Oxford University Press, 1965. viii, 392 pp. (Published for the International African Institute.)

Twenty-one papers, mostly by anthropologists, on the religion of a variety of culture areas in Africa.

Gibbs, James L., ed. *Peoples of Africa.* New York: Holt, Rinehart and Winston, Inc., 1965. 594 pp.

A pleasant "tour" through 15 societies south of the Sahara, pointing out along the way the similarities and diversities. Bibliographies and maps. English-speaking African societies are somewhat over-represented.

2. UNITED STATES

Wagley, Charles and Harris, Marvin. *Minorities in the New World: Six Case Studies.* New York: Columbia University Press.

A good anthropological study of Negro, Indian, and white minorities, illustrating situations common to countries around the world.

3. SOUTHEAST ASIA

LeBar, Frank M., Hickey, Gerald C., and Musgrave, John K., eds. *Ethnic Groups of Mainland Southeast Asia.* Human Relations Area Files Press. (Distributed by Taplinger Publishing Co. of New York), 1964. x, 288 pp.

Ethnographic, demographic, linguistic, and racial information about 151 ethnolinguistic groups. Bibliography and country-name concordance.

Kunstadter, Peter, ed. *Southeast Asian Tribes, Minorities, and Nations.* Princeton: Princeton University Press, 1967. 2 vols. 902 pp.

Twenty authorities present papers on original field work in Burma,

China, India, Laos, Malaysia, Thailand, and Vietnam. Bibliographies and maps.

4. INDIA

Hsu, Francis L. K. *Clan, Caste and Club.* Princeton: D. Van Nostrand, Inc., 1963. x, 335 pp.

An enlightening comparison of the Hindu mentality with that of the Chinese and Americans.

Mason, Philip, ed. *India and Ceylon.* (A Symposium, Institute of Race Relations.) New York: Oxford University Press, 1967. 336 pp.

Thirteen essays describing main tensions in India and Ceylon.

Singer, Milton and Cohn, Bernard. *Structure and Change in Indian Society.* Viking Fund Publications in Anthropology, 1967. 512 pp.

A review of empirical studies of India covering the last 15 years; also description of recent theoretical and methodological trends in South Asian social anthropology.

Srinivas, M. N. *Caste in Modern India and Other Essays.* New York: Asia Publishing House, 1962. 171 pp.

Six excellent essays on Indian society in general and on its structure and trends; three papers on methods and potential of Indian social anthropology; two papers on basic concepts of caste.

5. INDONESIA

Koentjaraningrat, ed. *Villages in Indonesia.* Ithaca: Cornell University Press. 428 pp.

17 full-page maps.

6. JAPAN AND KOREA

Silberman, Bernard S. *Japan and Korea: A Critical Bibliography.* Tucson: University of Arizona Press, 1962. xiv, 120 pp.

1,933 entries, mostly on Japan (1,615). English literature emphasized. Bibliography covers introductory works, bibliographies, journals, land and people, language, history, religion, philosophy, art, literature, political life, social organization, education, economic patterns, and population.

Fukutake, Tadashi. *Japanese Rural Society.* Translated by Ronald P. Dore. New York: Oxford University Press, 1967. xiv, 230 pp.

7. LATIN AMERICA

Heath, Dwight B. and Adams, Richard N., eds. *Contemporary Culture and Societies of Latin America.* New York: Random House, Inc., 1965. xi, 586 pp.

A reader in social anthropology of Middle and South America and the Caribbean. Contributions represent a variety of views. Presentation interdisciplinary. Treats of classification, agriculture and economics, social organization, worldviews.

Wagley, Charles, ed. *The Latin American Tradition: Essays on the Unity and Diversity of Latin American Culture.* New York: Columbia University Press, 1968. viii, 242 pp.

Wagley, Charles, ed. *Social Science Research in Latin America: Report and Papers of a Seminar, Stanford, California, July 8-August 23, 1963.* New York: Columbia University Press, 1964. xiv, 338 pp.

Oustanding authorities on Latin America critically evaluate the status of our knowledge (anthropology, economics, geography, history, sociology, political science, law). Bibliographies.
Wagley, Charles. *An Introduction to Brazil.* New York: Columbia University Press, 1963. xi, 322 pp.
Description and analysis of Brazil today, showing regional variety, culture, history, economics. Bibliography and map.

8. PACIFIC

Taylor, C. R., ed. *A Pacific Bibliography: Printed Matter Relating to the Native Peoples of Polynesia, Melanesia, and Micronesia.* 2nd ed. New York: Oxford University Press, 1965. xxx, 692 pp.
The best available bibliography on the Pacific area. Contains some 16,000 references, up to the year 1960. Has exhaustive index.
Vayda, Andrew P., ed. *Peoples and Cultures of the Pacific.* (A Natural History Press Book.) Garden City, New York: Doubleday Anchor Books.
Twenty-four prominent anthropologists describe the Pacific cultures of Micronesia, Melanesia, and Polynesia.

9. PHILIPPINES

Wernstedt, Frederick L. and Spencer, J. E. *The Philippine Island World: A Physical, Cultural, and Regional Geography.* Berkeley: University of California Press, 1967. xviii, 742 pp.
A comprehensive reference book on the physical environment, history, demography, agriculture, physical and cultural characteristics of five basic regions.

10. PAKISTAN

Owen, John E., ed. *Sociology in East Pakistan.* (Occasional Studies of the Asiatic Society of Pakistan, I). Dacca: Asiatic Society of Pakistan, 1962. iii, 275 pp.
A collection of data about Pakistani culture and a presentation of Pakistani social theory.

E. LINGUISTICS

Gudschinsky, Sarah C. *How to Learn an Unwritten Language.* (Studies in Anthropological Method.) New York: Holt, Rinehart and Winston, Inc., 1967. xii, 64 pp.
Concise and practical.
Hall, Robert A. *Introductory Linguistics.* Philadelphia: Chilton Co., 1964. xiii, 508 pp.
A complete introductory course in general linguistics.
Hymes, Dell. *Language in Culture and Society: A Reader in Linguistics and Anthropology.* New York: Harper and Row, 1964. xxxv, 764 pp.
Scope of Linguistic Anthropology; equality, diversity, and relativity of languages; grammar and worldview; relationship of lexicon and cultural focus; role of speech, modes of address; whistling speech

and drum signals; variations based on status of speaker and situation; language change through history. Bibliographies. Introductions to articles.

Ornstein, Jacob and Gage, William W. *The ABC's of Languages and Linguistics*. Philadelphia: Chilton Books, 1964. xiii, 205 pp.
   An interesting and useful popularization of Linguistics.

Samarin, William J. *Field Linguistics: A Guide to Linguistic Field Work*. New York: Holt, Rinehart and Winston, Inc., 1967. 256 pp.
   How to learn an unwritten language.

Nida, Eugene A. *Toward a Science of Translating, With Special Reference to Principles and Procedures Involved in Bible Translating*. Leiden: E. J. Brill, 1964. x, 331 pp.
   A pioneering, scholarly treatment of the science and art of translation, especially in relation to the Bible, in light of linguistic and communication theory, symbolic logic, psychology, and cultural anthropology.

F. CULTURAL RELATIVISM AND HUMAN ADAPTATION

Cohen, Yehudi, ed. *Man in Adaptation: The Biosocial Background and the Cultural Present*. Chicago: Aldine Publishing Co., 1967.
   A two-volume reader with a special teacher's manual by Michael Salovesh, Purdue University.

Mather, Kenneth. *Human Diversity: The Nature and Significance of Differences Among Man*. New York: Free Press, 1965.
   Human diversity is examined from the environmental, genetical, and social points of view.

G. COMMUNITY

Arensberg, Conrad M. and Kimball, Solon T. *Culture and Community*. New York: Harcourt, Brace and World, Inc., 1965. 349 pp.
   A collection of 17 papers (all but one published previously between 1942 and 1963) discussing theory of community and method for community study.

Sanders, Irwin T. *The Community: An Introduction to a Social System*. 2nd rev. ed. New York: The Ronald Press Co., 1966. viii, 549 pp.
   A beginner's introduction to the sociology of community.

H. SOCIALIZATION

Clausen, John A., ed. *Socialization and Society*. Boston: Brown and Co., 1968.

Whiting, John W., et al. *Field Guide for a Study of Socialization.* New York: John Wiley and Sons, Inc., 1966. xv, 176 pp.
   Bibliography.

I. ART AND MUSIC

Merriam, Alan P. *The Anthropology of Music.* Evanston: Northwestern University Press, 1964. xi, 358 pp.
   Theory and methodology for the study of music as human behavior. Examples from around the world.
Fraser, Douglas, ed. *The many Faces of Primitive Art: A Critical Anthology.* Englewood Cliffs, N.J.: Prentice-Hall, 1966. xi, 300 pp.
   A reader on primitive art.
Lomax, Alan. *Folk Song Style and Culture.* (With contributions by the Cantometrics Staff and with the editorial assistance of Edwin E. Erickson.) American Association for the Advancement of Science, Washington, D.C., Publication No. 88, 1968. 363 pp.
   A scholarly world-coverage.

J. WORLDVIEW, NATIONAL CHARACTER, VALUE SYSTEMS

Henry, Jules. *Culture Against Man.* New York: Random House, 1963. xiv, 495 pp.
   An analysis and critique of our American lifeway and value system: underlying values and drives, parent-child relationships, old age.
Martindale, Don, ed. *National Character in the Perspective of the Social Sciences. Annals* of the American Academy of Political and Social Sciences, March, 1967.
   This whole issue is devoted to the study of national character: theory and method; the New World, Europe, Near and Far East.
McGiffert, Michael, ed. *The Character of Americans.* Homewood, Ill.: Dorsey, 1964. paperback.
   A book of readings.
Smith, Charles Merill. *How to Become a Bishop Without Being Religious.* New York: Pocket Books, 1965. 160 pp.
   A satire on American religion-related patterns and values.

K. RELIGION FROM THE ANTHROPOLOGICAL VIEWPOINT

Evans-Pritchard, E. E. *Theories of Primitive Religion.* New York: Oxford University Press, 1965. 135 pp.

A leading anthropologist discusses various theories regarding the origin of primitive religion, why past theories are not tenable.

Fuchs, Stephen. *Rebellious Prophets: A Study of Messianic Movements.* New York: Asia Publishing House, 1965. vix, 304 pp.
   A missionary-anthropologist describes and analyzes the politico-religious movements in India.

Leach, E. R., ed. *Dialectic in Practical Religion.* (Cambridge Papers in Social Anthropology, 5.) New York: Cambridge University Press.
   Five anthropological studies examining the dialectic interplay between the concepts of practical and philosophical religion. Three of the studies are concerned with relatively civilized Buddhist villages in Ceylon and Thailand; two with more primitive peoples in Africa and New Guinea.

Schneider, Louis, ed. *Religion, Culture and Society: A Reader in the Sociology of Religion.* New York: John Wiley and Sons, Inc., 1964. xvii, 663 pp.
   A collection of seventy articles on sociology of religion: problems of research, problems of definition, function, culture, interaction, U.S. religious patterns.

Schoeps, Hans-Joachim. *The Religions of Mankind: Their Origins and Development.* Garden City, New York: Doubleday and Co., Inc.
   A concise, quite satisfactory coverage.

Turner, Victor W. *The Ritual Process: Structure and Anti-Structure.* Chicago: Aldine Publishing Co., 1968. 224 pp.
   Ritual and symbols are presented as constituting a key to the understanding of social structure and processes.

Wallace, Anthony F. C. *Religion: An Anthropological View.* New York: Random House, Inc., 1966. 300 pp.

II. PRACTICAL APPLICATION

A. DIRECTING SOCIAL CHANGE— GENERAL PRINCIPLES

Arensberg, Conrad M. and Niehoff, Arthur H. *Introducing Social Change: A Manual for Americans Overseas.* Chicago: Aldine Publishing Co., 1964. vii, 214 pp.
   A simple presentation of the concept of culture and culture borrowing. Mechanisms of "planned change" are clearly explained. A good introductory book on Applied Anthropology. Bibliography.

Foster, George M. *Applied Anthropology.* Boston: Little, Brown and Co., 1969. 256 pp. paperback.
   Primary emphasis is on role relationships of anthropologists working

in action programs rather than, as is often done, placing focus on case histories. What anthropologists do in applied situations; how they approach their task; the research required; administration involved; status considerations in an applied role.

Goodenough, Ward Hunt. *Cooperation in Change: An Anthropological Approach to Community Development.* New York: Russel Sage Foundation, 1963. 543 pp.

How to bring about desired social change by making people want change. A basically psychological approach, theory and application.

Hambidge, Gove, ed. *Dynamics of Development: An International Development Reader.* New York: Frederick A. Praeger, 1964. xxi, 401 pp.

Thirty-two articles reprinted from the *International Development Review,* dealing with population explosion, need for a middle class, problems of paying for development, administration, cultural aspects of development, agricultural programs, health and education, community development, etc.

Hollis, Peter W., ed. *Comparative Theories of Social Change.* Ann Arbor, Michigan: Foundation for Research on Human Behavior, 1966. viii, 374 pp.

Symposium papers of 20 scientists meeting with AID officials. Contains many practical suggestions for directing change. Perhaps too much jargon.

LaPiere, Richard T. *Social Change.* New York: McGraw-Hill Series in Sociology, 1965. vii, 556 pp.

A systematic analysis of how social changes come about; the conditions and functional consequences.

Niehoff, Arthur H., ed. *A Casebook of Social Change.* Chicago: Aldine Publishing Co., 1966. 312 pp.

After a brief statement of basic rules for planned social change, a series of 19 case studies are presented from Latin America, Asia, Africa, and the Middle East. Topics treated include land reform, community development, cooperatives, adult literacy programs, family planning. The cases chosen clearly illustrate the various possible techniques in introducing change, in identifying motivation and reaction. Some good analyses of successful as well as unsuccessful cases.

B. COMMUNICATION AND CULTURE CHANGE

Burke, Carl F. *God Is For Real Man.* New York: Association Press, 1966. 128 pp.

An excellent example of speaking on the wavelength of one's hearers.

Gumperz, John J. and Hymes, Dell, eds. "The Ethnography of Communication." In the *American Anthropologist*. Special issue. Part 2, vol. 66, No. 6, December, 1964.

The scope of communication; approaches for analyzing and describing; definitions; cultural limitations in communication, etc.

Rogers, Everett M. *Modernization Among Peasants: The Impact of Communication*. New York: Holt, Rinehart and Winston, 1969. 416 pp.

How peasants become modernized, mainly through communication of new ideas transferred from such external sources as government and urban centers. Treats a number of basic concepts, e.g., literacy, mass media, fatalism, cosmopoliteness, empathy, innovativeness, motivation.

Smith, Alfred G., ed. *Communication and Culture: Readings in the Codes of Human Interaction*. New York: Holt, Rinehart and Winston, Inc., 1966, xi, 626 pp.

The best essays of more than 75 well-known writers treating: (1) syntactics, i.e., relationship between symbols carrying message; (2) semantics, i.e., relationship of signs to things and events; (3) pragmatics, i.e., relationship of signs of human behavior. Includes a bibliography.

C. URBAN PROBLEMS

Luzebetak, Louis, S.V.D., ed. *The Church in the Changing City*. Techny, Illinois: Divine Word Publications, 1966. vii, 197 pp.

Outstanding U.S. social scientists discuss the role of the churches in urban situations. Bibliography.

Reissman, Leonard. *The Urban Process: Cities in Industrial Societies*. New York: The Free Press, 1964. xiv, 255 pp.

Surveys and classifies urban sociologists as "practitioners," "visionaries," "empiricists," and "theoreticians." Basic thesis: the historical process of urbanization in the West is now being repeated in underdeveloped areas of the world.

D. MISSIOLOGICAL CONSIDERATIONS— THEOLOGICAL AND PRACTICAL

Anderson, Gerald H. *Bibliography of the Theology of Missions in the Twentieth Century*. 3rd rev. ed. New York: Missionary Research Library, 1966.

Includes more than 1,500 entries. Annotated. Mainly Protestant, but chief Catholic and Orthodox writings also included.

Alexander, Calvert. *The Missionary Dimension: Vatican II and the World Apostolate*. Milwaukee: Bruce, 1967.

Missionary ideas that have come from Vatican II. Included is a translation of the Decree on the Missions.

Beaver, R. Pierce. *From Missions to Mission.* New York: Association Press, 1964.
Brief introduction to recent developments and trends.

Danielou, Jean. *The Salvation of the Nations.* Notre Dame, Indiana: University of Notre Dame Press, 1964.

Dournes, Jacques. *God Loves the Pagans.* New York: Herder and Herder, 1966.
An excellent illustration of missiology and applied anthropology in action.

Grassi, Joseph A. *A World to Win: The Missionary Methods of Paul the Apostle.* Maryknoll, New York: Maryknoll Publications, 1965. 184 pp.
A masterful portrayal of Paul's mission theology and corresponding practical approach.

Hillman, Eugene. *The Church as Mission.* New York: Herder and Herder, 1965.
There is an essential difference between the mission of the Church to Christian peoples and that to non-Christians.

Houtart, Francois and Remy, Jean. "A Survey of Sociology as Applied to Pastoral Work," in *The Pastoral Mission of the Church, Pastoral Theology.* Concilium Series, Vol. 3. Glen Rock, New Jersey: Paulist Press, 1964. pp. 89-110.

Houtart, Francois. *The Challenge to Change: The Church Confronts the Future.* New York: Sheed and Ward, 1964.

Neuner, Joseph, ed. *Christian Revelation and World Religions.* London: Burns and Oates (Compass Books), 1967.
Papers read at the 1964 Bombay Conference by Piet Fransen, Hans Kung, Joseph Masson, and Raymond Pannikar.

Quinn, Bernard. *Understanding the Small Community: Some Informational Resources for the Town and Country Apostolate.* Washington, D.C.: Center for Applied Research in the Apostolate (CARA), 1967. 58 pp.
An excellent bibliography. Fully annotated.

The Christian and the Word: Readings in Theology. Compiled at the Canisianum, Innsbruck. New York: P. J. Kenedy and Sons, 1963.

Richardson, William J., M.M., ed. *The Modern Mission Apostolate.* Maryknoll, New York: Maryknoll Publications, 1965. 308 pp.
Much practical wisdom is contained in this handbook for updating missionaries in regard to mission theology.

N.B. Included in this section of the bibliography should be the many excellent books and articles on the various documents of Vatican II now available, especially Vorgrimler, Herbert, ed. *Commentary on the Documents of Vatican II.* New York: Herder and Herder, 1967. 4 vols.

INDEX

Accommodation, aims of, 342 ff; bibliography, 19; definition of, 341; difficulties involved in, 14 f; limits, 96 ff, 103, 183, 184, 347 ff; manner of, 351; matter of justice, 342 f; and missionary effectiveness, 344; object of, 68, 345 ff; obstacles to, 351 ff; official policy of Church, 7; to Protestantism, 120 f; psychological, social, and cultural background of, 344 f; on subcultural level, 121; subject of, 345; see also Adjustment to "Strange" Culture

Acculturation, definition of, 214; terminal aspects of, 222; see also Accommodation

Adaptation, see Accommodation

Adaptive system, culture as, 60ff

Adjustment, problems of, bibliography, 20

Adjustment to "strange culture," bibliography, 108 f; see also Culture jolts, Culture shock, Empathy, Identification

Agent of culture change, aggressiveness of as factor, 283; bibliography, 313; and the individual, 229 ff; missionary's role, 20

Aggressiveness, factor in culture change, 283

Aglipayanism, form of nativism, 254

Agronomy, and cultural integration, 151 f

Alternative behavior, factor in diffusion, 294

Alternatives, definition of, 113

Anthropoid intelligence, 79 ff

Anthropological research, advantages and necessity, 50

Anthropology, bibliography, history of, 52 f; bibliography of methods of, 52; bibliography of notion of, 51; definition, 23 f; nature and scope of, 23 ff; orientations in, 27; relation to other fields, 30 f; specializations in, 53 f

Anthropos institute, 48

Anti-Nativism, form of culture shock, 98 f

Apostolic approach, in accord with the "theme theory," 163 ff; based on locus of culture, 204 ff; and cultural consistency, 182 ff; and cultural integration, 142 ff, 148 ff; and cultural

reciprocity, 188 f; and cultural relatedness, 180 ff; and culture dynamics, 203 f; directing selectivity, 245; and factors involved in culture change, 296 ff; functional, 142 ff; orientation in local psychology, 162 f; research necessary, 204; and social control, 301 ff; socio-cultural, 118 ff; specialization in, 310 f; and specialties, 300 f; see also Cultural context

Apostolic training, role of anthropology in, 18 f

Applied anthropology, aims of, 149; bibliography, 3 n; defined, 4; premises and values underlying, 33; subfields of, 3; see also Missiological anthropology

Applied research, see also Missiological research

Archaeology, defined, 28

Area studies, values of, 34

Assimilation, definition of, 222

Attitude toward change, factor in culture change, 270 f

Attractiveness, factor in diffusion, 293

Bastian, Adolph, on Elementargedanken, 321

Behavioral pattern, definition, 62

Benedict, Ruth, on configuration, 157, 159

Benedict XIV, on limits of accommodation, 186

Benedict XV, on advantages of native leadership, 105 f; on formation of native leadership, 107; on indigenous leadership, 104; on necessity of personal holiness in apostolic worker, 44

Bias, factor in diffusion, 291 f

Biological basis of culture, 321 ff

Black Muslim, form of nativism, 251

Blocked communication, factor in diffusion, 286

Boredom, factor in origination, 277

Brain, comparative studies of, 326

Canon Law, and cultural integration, 152 f

Cargo cult, causes of, 225, 257 f; forms of, 256 f

Catechetics, 41; as check on syncretism, 248; counteraction against syncretism, 248; and the cultural con-

169; definition of, 64; research in, 161
Motivations, factor in diffusion, 287 ff
factor in origination, 276
Murdock, G. P., on common framework of cultures, 317

National character, studies in, 161
Native clergy, see Indigenous clergy
Native expectations, as limit to accommodation, 99 f
Nativism, bibliography, 262; causes of, 249; in India, 254 f; in Latin America, 251 f; in North America, 250 f; notion, 248 f; in Oceania, 255 ff; typology, 249
Needs, functionalist theory of, 172 ff
Negativism, irreconcilable with apostolic goals, 36; obstacle to accommodation, 351 f
Negro, in America, 324 ff

Obstacles and handicaps, factor in origination, 277
Opler, M. E., on the "theme theory," 159 f
Organization of culture, 135 ff; see also Integration, Configuration
Origination, accidental, 211; antecedents required in, 211 f; basic, definition of, 213; difference between "invention" and "diffusion," 211; factors favoring, 276 ff; simultaneous, 212
Origination of culture change, notion of, 210

Pastoral problems, and cultural integration, 152 f
Pastoral work, see Counseling, Apostolic approach
Paternalism, a form of racism, 334 f
Peace of mind, factor in origination, 281 f
Persistence, definition of, 198; relation to change, 197
Personal conflicts, arising from change, 218 f
Personality, factor in culture change, 269 f
Philosophy of life, see Configuration
Physical anthropology, nature and scope, 24 ff
Physical environment, as culture determinant, 328 ff; culture jolts arising from, 84 f; role of Church in struggle with, 333
Pigs, function of, in New Guinea, 143 f
Pius XI, on elite, 299; on indigenous

leadership, 104; on missionary specialization, 305
Pius XII, on accommodation, 7, 36; on felt-needs, 66; on indigenous leadership, 105; on missionary accommodation, 342, 343; on missionary negativism, 36, 352; on missionary specialization, 305 f, 307; on social action, 10 f
Pluralism, stabilized, definition of, 222
Policies, see Apostolic approach
Polish migrants, Thomas and Znaniecki's study on, 227 f
Polygamy, functions of, 144, 247
Pre-catechesis, 66 f
Prediction, an aim of applied anthropology, 149, 204
Prejudice, factor in diffusion, 291 f
Premises, definition of, 158
Prestige, factor in diffusion, 288 f
Pride, factor in culture change, 270 f
Primitive cultures, reasons for anthropologist's concern for, 29 f
Processes, in culture change, 210 ff; integrative, 214 ff; terminal, in culture change, 220 ff
Prophetism, see Nativism
Protestantism, role of competition with Catholicism, 279 f; a subculture, 120 f
Psychological integration, see Configuration
Psychology, as determinant of culture, 331
"Psychology of the People," see Configuration

Race and culture, 321–328
Racism, in America, 324 ff; among missionaries, 333 ff; history of, 323 ff
Radcliffe-Brown, Alfred, 140
Ramification, definition of, 217; notion, 215
Rapport, meaning of, 230 ff
Reciprocity, notion, 172
Reconciliation of conflicting ideas, factor in origination, 277
Reduction-segregation, definition of, 221
Reformulation, see Reinterpretation
Reintegration, see Reinterpretation
Reinterpretation, notion of, 215; role of, in syncretism, 245 f; types, 215 ff
Relatedness of cultural elements, notion, 171
Relativity of culture, in asceticism, 127 f; basis for missionary empathy, 64; existence of universal values, 75; see also adjustment to "strange culture," Enculturation, Rapport

PUBLICATIONS BY THE AUTHOR

1951   *Marriage and the Family in Caucasia: A Contribution to the Study of North Caucasian Ethnology and Customary Law.* STUDIA INSTITUTI ANTHROPOS, Vol. 3, Mödling, bei Vienna, 286 pages.

1954   *Middle Wahgi Dialects: Grammar.* Catholic Mission, Banz, New Guinea, 245 pages. (Mimeographed)

1954   *Tabare Dialect: Grammar.* Catholic Mission, Alexishafen, New Guinea, 255 pages. Co-author, Rev. Paul McVinney, SVD. (Mimeographed)

1954   "The Socio-Religious Significance of a New Guinea Pig Festival," ANTHROPOLOGICAL QUARTERLY, July and October issues, pages 59-80, 102-29.

1956   "Worship of the Dead in the Middle Wahgi," ANTHROPOS, LI (1956), 81-96.

1956   *Middle Wahgi Phonology: A Standardization of Orthographies in the New Guinea Highlands.* OCEANIA LINGUISTIC MONOGRAPHS. University of Sydney, Australia. 48 pages.

1958   "The Middle Wahgi Culture: A Study of First Contacts and Initial Selectivity," ANTHROPOS, LVII (1958), 51-87.

1958   "Treatment of Disease in the New Guinea Highlands," ANTHROPOLOGICAL QUARTERLY, XXXI (1958), 42-55.

1961   "Toward an Applied Missionary Anthropology," ANTHROPOLOGICAL QUARTERLY, XXXIV (1961), 165-76.

1962   "An Applied Anthropology for Catholic Missions," MISSIONS-STUDIEN, Kaldenkirchen, Rhnld., Germany pp. 63-83.

(1963) *The Church and Cultures: An Applied Anthropology for the Religious Worker.* 3rd edition, paperback, 431 pages. William Carey Library, So. Pasadena, Calif.

1966   *The Church in the Changing City* (ed.). Divine Word Paperback. Techny, IL.

1966/67 "Anthropological Factors in Adolescent Catechesis," LIVING LIGHT, pp. 27-39.

1967   *Clergy Distribution U.S.A.: A Preliminary Survey of Priest Utilization, Availability and Demand* CARA, Washington, D.C., 143 pages.

1968   "Proper Development of Culture," MEN AND NATIONS, Catholic Action Federation, Chicago, IL.

1969   "Man Today," *The Church is Mission,* pp. 117-130. Geoffrey Chapman, Ltd., London.

1970   "Fremdheit in Primitivkulturen und Ihre Ueberwindung," *Verbum SVD,* Rome, fasciculus 1, Volume 11, 1970, pp. 18-27.

1970   "Diocesan Planning and Renewal," in *Diocesan Pastoral Council,* NCCM, Washington, D.C., pp. 43f.

to appear
1975   "Understanding 'Cross-Cultural Sensitivity': An Aid to the Identification of Objectives and Tasks of Missionary Training," VERBUM SVD.

Other Books by the William Carey Library

General

Church Growth and Group Conversion by Donald A. McGavran $2.45p

Education of Missionaries' Children by D. Bruce Lockerbie $1.95p

Everything You Need to Know to Grow a Messianic Synagogue by Phillip E. Goble $2.45p

Growth and Life in the Local Church by H. Boone Porter $2.95p

Message and Mission: the Communication of the Christian Faith by Eugene Nida $3.95p

Reaching the Unreached: A Preliminary Strategy for World Evangelization by Edward Pentecost $5.95p

Verdict Theology in Missionary Theory by A.R. Tippett $4.95p

Area and Case Studies

Aspects of Pacific Ethnohistory by Alan R. Tippett $3.95p

The Baha'i Faith: Its History and Teachings by William Miller $8.95p

A Century of Growth: the Kachin Baptist Church of Burma by Herman Tegenfeldt $9.95c

Church Growth in Japan by Tetsunao Yamamori $4.95p

Circle of Harmony: A Case Study in Popular Japanese Buddhism with Implications for Christian Mission by Kenneth J. Dale $4.95p

A New Day in Madras by Amirtharaj Nelson $7.95p

People Movements in the Punjab by Margaret and Frederick Stock $8.95p

The Protestant Movement in Italy by Roger Hedlund $3.95p

Protestants in Modern Spain: the Struggle for Religious Pluralism by Dale G. Vought $3.45p

The Religious Dimension in Hispanic Los Angeles: A Protestant Case Study by Clifton Holland $9.95p

Solomon Islands Christianity: A Study in Growth and Obstruction by A.R. Tippett $5.95p

Taiwan: Mainline Versus Independent Church Growth by Allen J. Swanson $3.95p

Understanding Latin Americans by Eugene Nida $3.95p

Theological Education by Extension

Designing a Theological Education by Extension Program by Leslie D. Hill $2.95p

An Extension Seminary Primer by Ralph Covell and Peter Wagner $2.45p

Principles of Church Growth (programmed) by Weld and McGavran $4.95xp

Theological Education by Extension (revised edition) Ralph D. Winter $9.95p

The World Directory of Theological Education by Extension by Wayne C. Weld $5.95p

Writing for Theological Education by Extension by Lois McKinney $1.45xp

Applied Anthropology

Becoming Bilingual: A Guide to Language Learning by Donald Larson and William A. Smalley $5.95xp

Christopaganism or Indigenous Christianity? by Tetsunao Yamamori and Charles Taber $5.95p

Culture and Human Values: Writings of Jacob Loewen ed. by William A. Smalley $5.95p

Customs and Cultures: Anthropology for Christian Missions by Eugene A. Nida $3.95xp

God's Word in Man's Language by Eugene Nida $2.95p

Bibliography for Cross-Cultural Workers by A.R. Tippett $3.95p, $5.95c

Manual of Articulatory Phonetics by William Smalley $4.95xp

Readings in Missionary Anthropology ed. by William Smalley $4.95xp